WILDLIFE LAW:

Conservation and Biodiversity

For Daniel, Helena and Ruben

WILDLIFE LAW:

Conservation and Biodiversity

by
Kate Cook

CAMERON
MAY
INTERNATIONAL LAW & POLICY

Published in 2004. Cameron May Ltd.
17 Queen Anne's Gate, London SW1H 9BU
Tel: +44 (0) 20 7799 3636 Fax: +44 (0) 20 7222 8517
Website: www.lexmercatoria.org
Email: enquiries@cameronmay.com

ISBN: 1 874698 01 5

Printed and bound in Great Britain
by TJ International Ltd, Padstow, Cornwall

Table of Contents

PREFACE AND ACKNOWLEDGMENTS

For many people, the conservation of wildlife is central to a concern for the environment. This is the case whether one is thinking about the Amazon rainforest or the vanishing heathlands of the West Country. The preservation of biodiversity is not only relevant to the protection of extensive and pristine habitats beyond our own borders. The UK may already have lost a large part of its natural heritage but there is much left to safeguard, some of it with a remarkable ability to adapt to semi-natural environments provided it is not completely ousted by intensive farming or urban development. From a legal point of view, the importance of biodiversity globally and locally, whether measured in economic or broader terms, and its significance for the achievement of sustainable development is now firmly recognised in international law and increasingly reflected at the regional and national levels.

The idea of writing a book on wildlife law came to me while working at the Department of the Environment, as a result of looking in vain for a book which covered domestic and European law in this area in some detail. Ten years later, having finally produced my own book on the topic, I have realised why the shelves of the DoE Legal Library were not sagging with books on conservation law. The subject is inherently interesting because of the policy issues which it seeks to address, but the multiplicity of relevant sources and the rapid pace of change in this area of law in the last 15 years make it difficult to present the topic in the orderly fashion which lawyers tend to require.

This book is intended to bring together the diverse laws directly concerned with wildlife conservation and to consider some common themes arising in the various sectors. The focus is on UK law (principally the law of England and Wales) but the intention has been to present alongside it the European Union law on which much domestic law is based, as well to outline the international framework for nature conservation. My main aim has been to produce a book that is of practical use to all those interested in the law governing wildlife conservation, whether local or international activist, civil servant, independent practitioner or student. I have sought to state the law as it was in January 2004 with indications, so far as possible, as to forthcoming changes.

I arrived at the Department of the Environment more red than green but left, some six years later, feeling that any sense of divided loyalties would be misplaced and ultimately destructive. My understanding of environmental law and policy has been shaped in large part by my experience of working in a Department alongside many colleagues whose understated personal commitment to promoting the interests of the environment in the face of inevitable professional constraints often goes unacknowledged. I had the privilege of working with many highly knowledgeable specialists in conservation issues, lawyers and non-lawyers, in particular those colleagues working in Global Wildlife Division and European Wildlife Division, as well as in English Nature, JNCC and in the European Commission and the various international bodies dealing with these issues. I would particularly like to acknowledge my debt to Patrick Szell, former head of the International and EC Division of Legal where I was fortunate enough to be placed during my time with the Department. My understanding of not only environmental law but also the process of international and European law-making is owed in large part to him and his unfailing patience in dealing with questions, whatever time zone he was in and however many meetings he was supposed to be chairing at the time. I am also indebted to my other colleagues in the Division and especially to Alistair McGlone for helpful advice and general good humour.

Since leaving the Department, I have been based at Matrix Chambers which has provided a supportive and stimulating environment in which to make the transition from government lawyer to independent practitioner. I would particularly like to thank Philippe Sands for his encouragement and support in sticking with environmental law in a new and untried habitat. Since joining Matrix, I have been able to consider issues of wildlife conservation from the other side of the fence through working with colleagues from various non-governmental organisations and have discovered the particular challenges of seeking to overturn decisions adopted by one's former colleagues.

I am very grateful indeed for the assistance provided by Anjolie Singh, Richard Summers and Rachel Taylor in helping to complete sections of the book and to Anna Edmundson at Matrix for promptly organising help with completion. I am also deeply indebted to David Morgan of JNCC (and now the CITES Secretariat) and to David Harrison of English Nature for taking the time to read through, respectively, chapters on CITES and on habitat protection and for providing helpful suggestions and comments. Any errors or omissions remain of course my responsibility.

Finally, I would like to thank Nick May, James Cameron and Christophe Landais at Cameron May for patience and forbearance above and beyond the call of duty in awaiting the completion of this book.

My own enthusiasm for wildlife dates back to happy times strolling in Verulamium with my parents and brothers, a reminder that even small areas of local biodiversity which do not contain any rare or remarkable species are invaluable in making day to day life a thing to cherish. Finally, my thanks are to Daniel for everything that matters and especially for Helena and B-W.

Kate Cook
May 2004

FOREWORD

At the start of the 21st century, an historic threshold in the long history of life on Earth has been reached. Habitat loss and degradation, the over-exploitation of wildlife and the spread of non-native species are between them leading to a decline in biodiversity may soon lead to a mass extinction event on a scale not seen on this planet for many millions of years. The causes of this alarming global trend are many and complex, and so are the remedies. One vital platform that is absolutely central for effective long-term action lies in the use of the law.

Recent decades have seen a dramatic improvement in our understanding of the declining status of many species and habitats, this in turn has helped stimulate a proliferation of legislation designed to protect particular species, habitats and important areas. Conservation law has been enacted at the national level, across the EU and internationally. And conservationists have proved time and again how a proper understanding and use of these legal codes can transform the fortunes of threatened areas and species.

Given the increasing significance of legal controls and the policies that arise from them in protecting and enhancing wildlife, it is of supreme importance that all those with the opportunity, responsibility or power to use them do so with the clearest knowledge and maximum effectiveness. Our generation may be the last that has a serious chance to save the great body of the Earth's incredible biological richness that is now at risk. The moment must be seized with the greatest vigour and best information.

Kate Cook's fantastic new overview of wildlife legislation is an important and powerful new tool for British environmentalists that I am sure will be of enormous assistance in ensuring they play their full part in the continuing process of seeking the means to conserve wildlife and habitats in our ever more crowded world.

Tony Juniper
Executive Director
Friends of the Earth

INTRODUCTION

This book looks at the law relating to the conservation of wildlife, that is, wild animals, wild plants and the ecosystems of which they form part. Traditionally, conservation law focused on larger animals and plants but, as will be seen, both general and specific protection and consideration is now extended to invertebrates and lower plants. New concepts such as biodiversity and the ecosystem approach (considered below) are also widening the focus of legal instruments to other forms of life existing in the wild such as fungi and micro-organisms as well as to genetic variability within species. Equally important is the way in which conservation law now encompasses not only traditional protective approaches: prohibiting acts harmful to specially protected sites and species, but also incorporates positive duties to take affirmative action to conserve habitats and species in the form of management schemes, recovery programmes and the maintenance of landscape features and wildlife outside designated areas.

For some time, the main threats faced by wildlife have been habitat destruction and fragmentation due to development (including the intensification of agricultural practices), over-exploitation for the purposes of trade and the effects of invasive alien species. Modern conservation law is framed largely to address these types of threats through regimes for habitat protection, for the protection of vulnerable species and through controls on trade in endangered or vulnerable species of wildlife. This book is accordingly divided into three sections dealing with each of these areas of habitat protection; species protection and trade controls. There is clearly some overlap between these regimes, controls on the introduction of alien species could arguably be classified as relating to habitat or species protection for example[1].

New threats to wildlife may not be adequately addressed within the existing framework of conservation law. The potentially devastating effects of climate change pose a distinctive new and major threat to conservation and it remains unclear whether the existing framework of conservation law will be adequate to deal with its effects on wildlife[2]. To take one example, it is likely that the geographical range of many species will change in response to changes in climate and this has implications

---

[1] The topic of alien species is considered in Part II on Species Protection (Chapter 6).
[2] For a summary of the implications see "English Nature's Position Statement on Climate Change and Nature Conservation", September 2002.

for the long term viability of the current boundaries of many protected sites. At present, habitat protection regimes are not expressly framed so as to take account of this important factor, although some general statutory duties appear to be wide enough to encompass the need to address the issue[3]. It may also be that concepts such as favourable conservation status (discussed below), which features in the European Union's Habitats Directive, will allow for some account to be taken of the implications of climate change but the rather rigid timetable for designating protecting sites under that Directive is clearly not designed with this kind of long term change in mind.

It is not easy to mark out clear boundaries in seeking to present the law relating to wildlife conservation. Whilst there now exists a core body of UK and European Union legislation (as well as international treaties) specifically concerned with the conservation and protection of wildlife, the wider range of environmental laws covering issues such as atmospheric and water quality, climate change and the release of genetically modified organisms are also of key importance in securing conservation objectives. The aim of this book however is to focus on those laws which are expressly focussed on the conservation of wildlife, and other areas of environmental law are referred to, if at all, only in outline[4]. One other important area which has not been included here is the general law relating to sea fishing and the management of fish stocks, which is a distinctive regime aimed at securing marine resources as part of EU agricultural policy but which has key conservation implications for the marine environment. Reference has of course been made to the way in which town and country planning legislation and policy pays particular regard to nature conservation. It has not been possible however to do more than highlight certain planning issues of particular relevance to nature conservation.

The Evolution of Conservation law

Although there have been important recent developments in the law relating to wildlife, this is not an entirely new area of law. Legislation

[3] See for example section 131(2) of the Environmental Protection Act 1990 which requires English Nature and the Countryside Council for Wales "in discharging their nature conservation functions to take appropriate account of actual or possible ecological changes".

[4] Among the many good titles addressing environmental law in general see "Principles of Environmental Law" Susan Wolfe & Anna White (Second Edition) Cavendish Publishing Limited and on EU law see generally Ludwig Kramer and in particular "EC Treaty and Environmental Law", Kramer, third edition, Sweet & Maxwell.

aiming to protect and conserve wildlife from threats to its survival posed by various kinds of human activity has been in place for some considerable time. In the United Kingdom, laws seeking to protect wildlife from overexploitation date back centuries, although the rationale for many of these laws was the preservation of game species from subsistence "poaching" by the rural poor. The first UK legislation aimed specifically at wildlife conservation in the sense we would understand it today was probably the 1880 Wild Birds Protection Act[5]. International treaties concerned with the protection of wildlife date back to the beginning of the twentieth century, for example a Convention for the Protection of Birds Useful to Agriculture (Paris) was adopted in 1902 and entered into force in 1908[6].

Most commentators date the beginning of modern international environmental law from the early 1970s and in particular from the 1972 United Nations Conference on the Human Environment which was held in Stockholm. Initiatives which developed as a result of that conference had an effect on the international legal framework relating to wildlife conservation as they did on other areas of environmental law, but so far as conservation law is concerned, the greatest impact probably derived from the setting of more ambitious parameters for international cooperation rather than from any specific innovation related to conservation. From a conceptual point of view it is probably the post-Rio era which is more important to an understanding of how conservation law is currently evolving (see below). However, the impetus created by Stockholm probably contributed in large part to the adoption of a number of important conservation treaties, including the 1973 Convention on International Trade in Endangered Species of Wild Fauna and Flora (CITES)[7] and the 1979 Bern Convention on the Conservation of European Wildlife and Natural Habitats[8] both of which underpin much of the UK and EU legislation discussed in this book.

Action taken at the international and European Community levels at the time of the 1992 UN Conference on Environment and Development[9], in particular the adoption of the Convention on Biological Diversity and of the European Union's Directive 92/43/EC on the conservation of natural

[5] 1880 Chapter 35, the 1880 Act was repealed by the Protection of Birds Act 1954, s 15(2), Sch 6.
[6] See Sands "Principles of International Environmental Law", Second Edition, Chapter 2 (Cambridge).
[7] Adopted at Washington on 3 March 1973 and entered into force 1 July 1975.
[8] Adopted under the auspices of the Council of Europe, Bern 19 September 1979.
[9] This conference was held in Rio de Janeiro, Brazil. For an overall assessment, see Sands, Chapter 2 page 52.

habitats and of wild fauna and flora[10], sought to bring a new coherence to a body of law which has, up until recently, existed solely in a diverse range of instruments which tackle the various threats to wildlife in many different ways. A number of the key concepts underpinning these two instruments are discussed further below.

In the UK, these international and European developments have resulted not so much in a major root and branch overhaul of the legislation, but in the buttressing of existing laws with stricter regimes for certain habitats and species "of Community interest" and with some important amendments, in particular to the regime for the protection of sites of special scientific interest (SSSIs) which underpins much of the UK law on conservation. There has also been a strengthening of the statutory framework for positive conservation measures such as the setting of targets and the drawing up of Biodiversity Action Plans (many of which derive from international and European Community obligations) which complement the protective measures found in longstanding legislation relating to wildlife.

The legislation in this area has thus evolved and continues to evolve in response to a number of interrelated factors which will be considered further in this introduction. In relation to the law-making process, the influence of international and European Union law, which has long been of great importance in this area, continues to grow. On the policy/scientific side, the development of scientific understanding of ecosystems and genetic diversity, and in particular of the rate of loss of species has acted as a catalyst for the development of the law in this area. The resultant changes in the underlying concepts upon which the legislation is based, in particular the need to focus attention on the conservation of biological diversity rather than simply on species have all had a direct effect on the international legal framework for conservation and consequently on national and regional laws dealing with wildlife. These influences are considered in turn in the next sections.

The Influence of International and European Union Law

In conservation law, as in many other areas, there is nowadays close interaction between the three levels of law-making: international[11],

[10] Council Directive 92/43/EEC of 21 May 1992, OJ No L 206, 22 July 1992, p7.
[11] In this context, I will refer to European regional agreements such as the 1979 Bern Convention (adopted under the auspices of the Council of Europe) as international to contrast them with EU legislation.

European Union and domestic. There are a number of well-established and widely supported international treaties dealing with conservation of wildlife in areas ranging from international trade in endangered species (CITES), to in-situ and ex-situ conservation of habitats and species (the CBD) as well as specific types of habitat or species (the 1971 Ramsar Convention on Wetlands of International Importance). The European Union and its member states are represented at the meetings at which these international treaties are made, supervised and revised. European integration has resulted in close coordination between the EU institutions (in practice the Commission) and its members states when participating in such international meetings. While arcane discussions as to the degree of competence (whether exclusive or shared) enjoyed by the Community in a particular field can be somewhat baffling to outsiders, for practical purposes the EU operates largely on the basis of a common position at international conservation fora. From an EU perspective, the system works best when there is a genuine effort to coordinate with full discussion and a commitment by both the Commission and the Member States to stick to what has been agreed.

From the point of view of the law-making process, there is a two-way exchange between the international and European levels. The EU will seek to promote a position internationally that is consistent either with existing EU legislation or with policy but once the international provision is finalised, whether it relates to the listing of a new species or to some other provision, the EU will adapt its rules to the new international requirements (unless in rare cases it makes a formal reservation in line with prescribed procedures). This system is most evident in relation to the regime governing trade in endangered species under the CITES Convention which is discussed in Section III but is also a feature of other regimes featured in this book. So far as domestic legislation is concerned, the UK is of course bound to implement EU law and most current conservation law derives from or is required to be consistent with, EU legislation as interpreted by the European Court of Justice. For the most part, this book focuses on the domestic and European law relating to conservation and does not elaborate in detail the international legal provisions governing a subject[12]. The exception is in

[12] For an excellent general guide to general international environmental law, including the specific rules on biodiversity, freshwater resources and the oceans and seas, see "Principles of International Environmental Law" (Second Edition) by Philippe Sands, Cambridge. See also Simon Lyster's comprehensive guide to international wildlife law, "International Wildlife Law", Grotius (1985) which, although some what out of date, provides a useful insight into the history and culture of the different wildlife treaties. All the main wildlife treaties have websites which provide easy access to details of recent meetings, decisions and so on.

Section III, dealing with the CITES regime, since there is fairly rapid and detailed adaptation of the rules at the international level and it is not really possible to understand the EU/UK regime without direct reference to decisions made under the Convention.

Attempting to present conservation law in a coherent way, whilst taking account of all three levels of decision-making is complicated by the rather piecemeal way in which it has evolved. The origins of some of the mechanisms used in modern/domestic conservation law are centuries old and stem from a time when certain wildlife was the property of the King or the elite, to be protected from the predations of common people seeking to sustain themselves with resources harvested from the wild. For example, the setting of close seasons for hunting dates back considerably further than the advent of modern environmental law. Some of the earliest international treaties dealing with what would now be termed environmental issues are those relating to wildlife, and resemble to some extent modern law seeking to guard against unsustainable use of wildlife resources. The field of conservation law is being transformed however by concepts deriving from much more modern environmental law, including the precautionary principle, biodiversity and the ecosystem approach, to name but a few (a number of these are discussed below).

From the point of view of domestic law, this piecemeal development means that older UK statutes such as the 1981 Wildlife and Countryside Act remain in place, since many of the techniques employed in that Act (listing of protected species, designation of specially protected sites) remain in common use in conservation law at all levels. Alongside these older measures, however are more recently adopted instruments such as the 1994 Conservation (Natural Habitats &c) Regulations, adopted to implement the EU Habitats Directive, which contain provisions of the traditional conservation type together with newer innovations such as a framework for assessment of the impact of development on sites, the protection of "nature corridors" and provisions governing the procedure for determining the UK's contribution to the EU's Natura 2000 network of sites. Even more recently, statutory provision for measures which used to be framed purely as policy instruments has been adopted, for example the 2000 Countryside and Rights of Way Act goes some way towards putting Biodiversity Action Plans on a statutory footing (though not as far as some had hoped). In order to understand these newer provisions it is often necessary to have regard to recommendations and other decisions adopted at the international level, for example under the auspices of the CBD much work has been done on the ecosystem approach to conservation (see below), and this is likely to affect EU and domestic conservation legislation still further in the future.

New Concepts in Conservation Law

Biodiversity: Central to current thinking about conservation and the scope of conservation law is the concept of biodiversity, or "biological diversity", which has broadened the focus of conservation law and policy. Rather than focusing exclusively on (certain) habitats and species, international conservation law calls on states to consider *variability* at a number of levels and across the full range of life forms. According to Article 2 of the Convention on Biological Diversity (the CBD), "Biological diversity" means "the variability among living organisms from all sources including, inter alia, terrestrial, marine and other aquatic ecosystems and the ecological complexes of which they are part; this includes diversity within species, between species and of ecosystems." Thus biodiversity brings the whole of the natural world into the legal arena, at both a macro and micro level.

This shift has a number of important consequences for conservation law, as can be seen from the provisions of the Convention itself: Parties are required to develop national strategies, plans or programmes for the conservation and sustainable use of biological diversity, or adapt for this purpose existing strategies, plans or programmes (Article 6)[13]. Parties to the CBD must also "as far as possible and as appropriate" identify and monitor components of biodiversity, including those "processes and categories of activities which have or are likely to have significant adverse impacts on the conservation and sustainable use of biological diversity, and monitor their effects through sampling and other techniques" (Article 7). Parties are also required to establish a system of protected areas or areas where special measures need to be taken to conserve biological diversity and to regulate or manage biological resources important for the conservation of biological diversity, whether within or outside protected areas, with a view to ensuring their conservation and sustainable use (Article 8). In carrying out environmental impact assessment under Article 14 of the Convention, each Party must introduce "appropriate procedures requiring environmental impact assessment of its proposed projects that are likely to have significant adverse effects on biological diversity with a view to avoiding or minimizing such effects" and also "introduce appropriate arrangements to ensure that the environmental consequences of its programmes and policies that are likely to have significant adverse

[13] The European Union adopted its strategy in 1998: see the Communication from the Commission to the Council and to the Parliament on a European Community Biodiversity Strategy (COM (1998) 42), followed by Council Conclusions of 21 June 1998 and the European Parliament's non-legislative resolution A4-0347/98.

impacts on biological diversity are duly taken into account". In addition, ex-situ conservation policies (Article 9) and public education and awareness programmes (Article 13) must focus on biodiversity.

Taken together, and despite the qualified language used to preface these obligations "as far as possible and as appropriate", the Convention clearly requires state parties to frame their conservation laws and policies so as to take account of biological diversity as a whole rather than merely the limited numbers of the higher order species or areas of high profile habitats which have traditionally been the focus of conservation law. As a consequence of the terms of the Convention, one would expect to see a refinement in the legal regimes for designating protected areas, monitoring environmental data and assessing environmental impacts. It is not so much that the mechanisms deployed are entirely new but that the manner of applying these mechanisms is more sophisticated. Some of the recent changes to UK and EU conservation law reflect this shift[14] but there is probably some way to go before the methodologies associated with considering biodiversity as a whole have been thoroughly integrated into conservation law and practice[15]. Lists of protected species still focus on those traditionally protected and legislation does not generally refer expressly to such issues as genetic variability. Nonetheless, the framework for designating protected areas under the habitats directive is probably broad enough to allow the member states and the Commission to have due regard to the need to protect biodiversity as a whole[16]. So far as courts are concerned, the implementation of national conservation legislation needs to be considered[17], so far as possible, against the requirements of the Convention.

The Ecosystem Approach: Another important shift in focus highlighted in the Convention is reflected in the reference to "ecosystems"

[14] Section 74 of the Countryside and Rights of Way Act 2000 imposes a duty on the part of Ministers, Government Departments and the Welsh Assembly to have regard, so far as is consistent with their functions, to the purpose of conserving biodiversity in accordance with the CBD, discussed in Chapter 7 - part II (positive action for species recovery).

[15] See the criticisms made by the House of Commons Select Committee on the Environment as to the lack of integration of biodiversity throughout other areas of national policy in its Twentieth Report, December 2000.

[16] The third recital to the Directive states that its main aim is to "promote the maintenance of biodiversity, taking account of economic, social, cultural and regional requirements". The criteria for designation of sites generally refer to "favourable conservation status" which is considered further below but the conditions for such status are apt to include those governing the maintenance of biodiversity.

[17] See the discussion of the process for designating sites for the Natura 2000 network.

in addition to habitats and species. An ecosystem is defined in Article 2 as a "dynamic complex of plant, animal and micro-organism communities and their non-living environment interacting as a functional unit". Article 8 for example calls on Parties to promote "the protection of ecosystems, natural habitats and the maintenance of viable populations of species in natural surroundings" as well as to rehabilitate and restore degraded ecosystems. Out of these references has emerged the concept of the "ecosystem approach" which has been, and continues to be, the subject of consideration by the Parties[18] . Essentially, the ecosystem approach is a strategy for the integrated management of land, water and living resources that promotes conservation and sustainable use in an equitable way. Under the ecosystem approach, management must be adaptive in order to respond to uncertainties as to the functioning of ecosystems. As indicated in CBD COP Decision V/6, the ecosystem approach does not preclude other management and conservation approaches, such as biosphere reserves, protected areas, and single-species conservation programmes, but "could, rather, integrate all these approaches and other methodologies to deal with complex situations".

Decision V/6 sets out the principles on which the ecosystem approach is based and these include: recognition that conservation of ecosystem structure and functioning should be a priority target of the ecosystem approach, and that objectives for ecosystem management should be set for the long-term. In relation to the former, the rationale for this principle is that the conservation of interactions within species, among species and between species and their abiotic environment is of "greater significance for the long-term maintenance of biological diversity than simply the protection of species".

From the point of view of existing conservation law, the ecosystem approach would again seem to require a refinement of the operation of existing mechanisms such as the protection of certain sites or the adaptation of agricultural practice in line with conservation objectives. The ecosystem approach can probably be accommodated to a large extent within the existing statutory framework provided further guidance is issued and specific account is taken of this approach in the drawing up of statutory management plans and programmes such as those required under the SSSI regime.[19] [20]

[18] See CBD COP Decisions VI/12, IV/1B and V/6 in particular.
[19] Discussed in Chapter 1 - Part I.
[20] As for example those provided for under the recent amendments to the 1981 Wildlife and Countryside Act, discussed in Chapter 1 - Part I.

Sustainable Use: Central to current debates about the operation of the international regime for regulating trade in endangered species is the question of sustainable use. The impact of this concept on conservation law principally relates to regimes governing the exploitation of wildlife resources, such as CITES. Some advocate a more protectionist approach and seek total moratoria on trade affecting particularly vulnerable species, such as elephants, whilst others seek to promote limited trade, even in products such as elephant ivory, on the basis that properly regulated, such trade can be sustainable and can provide a useful incentive to the conservation efforts of those poorer range states and communities which are usually host to such species[21]. There is a strong degree of mutual suspicion between the two camps: protectionists are suspected of being interested in securing total protection of certain species on ethical, rather than conservation, grounds, whilst some in the sustainable use camp are deemed to be cynically using the term as politically correct cover for aspirations to resume trade in lucrative products such as ivory regardless of its real sustainability. Many parties seek simply to apply the concept in ways that are genuinely achievable, but given the practical difficulties in securing compliance with controls on the ground in some range and consumer states, sustainable use remains an aspiration as much as a reality in this area.

In relation to CITES, in an attempt to reconcile protectionists with sustainable use advocates, the Parties to that Convention have recognised that "the sustainable use of wild fauna and flora, whether consumptive or non-consumptive, provides an economically competitive land-use option" but also that "there are many species for which trade would be detrimental to their survival" and accordingly have agreed that: "commercial trade may be beneficial to the conservation of species and ecosystems and/or to the development of local people when carried out at levels that are not detrimental to the survival of the species in question."[22]

The concept of sustainable use has a wider reach that the CITES regime however and is one of the three central objectives of the CBD, together with the conservation of biodiversity and the fair and equitable sharing of the benefits arising from the utilisation of genetic resources[23]. Article 2 of the CBD defines sustainable use as: "the use of components of biological diversity in a way, and at a rate, that does not lead to the long-term decline of biological diversity, thereby maintaining its potential to meet the needs and aspirations of present and future generations". The precise relationship

[21] These issues are discussed in Part III (Trade).

[22] CITES COP Resolution 8.3 adopted at Kyoto in 1992.

[23] See Article 1 of the CBD.

between sustainable use and conservation remains a matter of consideration by the Parties to the CBD[24].

"Favourable Conservation Status": The EU Habitats Directive introduced for the first time into UK law an express target for the conservation status of both habitats and species[25]. In relation to a natural habitat, "favourable conservation status" is achieved when its natural range and areas it covers within that range are "stable or increasing" and the species structure and functions which are necessary for its long term maintenance "exist and are likely to exist for the foreseeable future" and the conservation status of its typical species is favourable as defined[26]. So far as species are concerned, the conservation status of a species will be favourable when population dynamics data indicate that it is maintaining itself "on a long-term basis as a viable component of its natural habitats" and the natural range of the species is "neither being reduced nor is likely to be reduced for the foreseeable future and there is and will probably continue to be, a sufficiently large habitat to maintain its populations on a long term basis"[27] This concept provides a means by which progress in securing the directive's objectives may be measured since measures taken pursuant to the Directive are required to be designed to "maintain or restore, at a favourable conservation status, natural habitats and species of wild fauna and flora of Community interest" (Article 2(2)). Clearly once the Natura 2000 network is fully established, the conservation status of protected habitats and species will need to be kept under regular review in order to ensure that the Directive's requirements are being met and this is provided for in Articles 9 and 11 of the Directive which require the Commission to review the contribution of Natura 2000 towards the Directive's objectives and the Member States to undertake surveillance of the conservation status of the habitats and species referred to in Article 2.

The Value of Biodiversity

The aims of nature conservation law are underpinned by the value which is put upon nature or, in more current terminology, biodiversity. Nearly all the international instruments dealing with nature conservation which refer to the issue of value, refer to a range of types of value: both more

[24] See CBD COP Decision VI/13 on Sustainable Use.

[25] The general duties to secure compliance with the directive contained in regulation 3 to the 1994 Conservation (Natural Habitats etc) Regulations, SI 1994/2716 necessarily incorporate a duty to ensure that Natura 2000 has the effect of maintaining or restoring favourable conservation status in accordance with Articles 2 and 3(1) of the Directive.

[26] Article 1(e) of the Habitats Directive.

[27] Article 1(i) of the Habitats Directive.

and less anthropocentric. The objectives of the Convention on Biological Diversity (CBD), as set out in Article 1, include the conservation of biological diversity which, according to the first recital of the preamble, has "intrinsic value" as well as ecological, genetic, social, economic, scientific, educational, cultural, recreational and aesthetic values. Clearly therefore the full range of types of value to be placed on biological diversity is recognised in the Convention. All these values may also be said to underpin the other two objectives of the Convention: the sustainable use of the components of biological diversity and the equitable sharing of benefits arising from the utilisation of genetic resources. The notion of values is also relevant to the definition of "biological resources" in the Convention which include genetic resources, organisms or parts thereof, populations, or any other biotic component of ecosystems *with actual or potential use or value for humanity*"(Article 2, emphasis added).

The importance of biodiversity to humanity is not an abstract concept, it has been estimated that of 1.2 billion people living in extreme poverty worldwide, approximately 900 million live in rural areas and are therefore highly dependent on biodiversity for their livelihoods and are most severely affected by biodiversity loss, water pollution and land degradation[28]. The United Nations WEHAB Group reported that it has been estimated that the economic value of biodiversity is $2.9 trillion/year whereas that of ecosystem services is $33 trillion/year[29].

Other international Conventions on nature conservation also refer to a range of types of value to be placed on nature. The 1979 Bonn Convention on the Conservation of Migratory Species of Wild Animals states in its preamble that wild animals: "must be conserved for the good of mankind" and continues "Conscious of the ever-growing value of wild animals from environmental, ecological, genetic, scientific, aesthetic, recreational, cultural, educational, social and economic points of view". The 1979 Bern Convention on the Conservation of European Wildlife and Natural Habitats recognises that:

> "....wild flora and fauna constitute a natural heritage of aesthetic, scientific, cultural, recreational, economic and intrinsic value that needs to be preserved and handed on to future generations".

[28] See "A Framework for Action on Biodiversity and Ecosystem Management" Report of the United Nations WEHAB Working Group, August 2002 produced for WSSD.
[29] See Chairperson's Summary of the WEHAB discussions at the WSSD, report dated 31 August 2002, Doc A/Conf.199/16/Add 2.

The Bern Convention also recognizes: "....the essential role played by wild flora and fauna in maintaining biological balances." The CITES Convention states that "wild fauna and flora in their many beautiful and varied forms are an irreplaceable part of the natural systems of the earth which must be protected for this and the generations to come" and continues "Conscious of the ever-growing value of wild fauna and flora from aesthetic, scientific, cultural, recreational and economic points of view".

This international recognition of the range of values of wildlife: including those which are not readily converted into economically measurable units, whether described as intrinsic, aesthetic or cultural, is important. It means that these regimes, and the national regimes which implement them, aim to protect wildlife even in situations where a direct economic advantage is not apparent. It is of course true that provision may be made for economic interest to prevail in some circumstances but those derogations are to be interpreted narrowly. The case for nature conservation does not depend on showing that it is costless or less costly in narrow economic terms than taking no action and this should be born in mind when interpreting national and European conservation law which gives effect to those international obligations and principles. On the other hand, it is also important to revise the methodology used by economists to take account of the long term economic value of biodiversity, for example in respect of ecological services, in order to have an accurate picture of the respective costs and benefits of short term development.

United Kingdom legislation of course does not normally refer to the underlying principles which have prompted its adoption and the statutory provisions themselves rarely address the question of the value of nature in any detail. In relation to habitat protection, there is some indication of the basis for designation: SSSI's are protected as areas of "special scientific interest" by reason of their flora, fauna or geological or physiographical features but this does not do more than place a scientific value on the site[30]. Questions as to the other types of value to be placed on it are not addressed. In relation to species protection, the statutory provisions governing listing of species simply refer to the conservation status of the species concerned or the need to comply with international obligations[31].

[30] See section 28 of the Wildlife and Countryside Act 1981, discussed in Chapter 1- Part I.
[31] See for example section 22 of the Wildlife and Countryside Act 1981, discussed in Chapter 3 - Part II.

European Union legislation adopts an approach more akin to that of international treaties in that the preamble to the instrument normally sets out the reasons for which it has been adopted. It should be remembered however that the need to find an appropriate treaty basis for the measure in question governs the choice of language to a large extent and therefore reference tends to be made to objectives of the EU rather than to freestanding principles, so for example the preamble to the Habitats Directive refers to the conservation of natural habitats and of wild flora and fauna as an essential objective of general interest pursued by the Community without expounding on what types of value are attributed to wildlife under such a policy.

Institutions

The International Level: The focus of this book is largely on conservation law at the national and European levels[32] but it is important to bear in mind that at the international level, there are institutions and mechanisms overseeing the development of the international legal framework. Typically, the parties to a treaty have the power to adopt decisions or resolutions which elaborate on the interpretation of the provisions of the treaty or to set out best practice in relation to its application. These decisions are an important guide to the interpretation of the Treaty's provisions, although they may not be formally binding. There will also be prescribed procedures for the amendment of the treaty, though these will be used relatively rarely in practice, save in respect of amendments to schedules of species or habitats which are generally modified on a regular basis to take account of changes in conservation status[33]. The dispute settlement procedures which are almost always provided for in treaties are rarely used in practice but conferences or meetings of the parties provided a regular opportunity for more or less formal scrutiny of a party's compliance or non-compliance with its obligations under the treaty.

In the area of conservation, one of the most developed mechanisms for scrutinising general and specific compliance is that operated under the Bern Convention. Article 13 of the Convention provides for the establishment of a Standing Committee on which each Contracting party may be represented (by one vote). The Committee meets at least every two years and is responsible for a range of functions including: making

[32] Owing to the close interaction with the international regime, there is however a detailed discussion of institutions and decision-making at the international level in relation to the CITES regime, see Chapter 1 - Part III.

[33] See discussion of listing under the CITES regime in Chapter 1 - Part III.

recommendations to the Parties as to measures to be taken for the purposes of the Convention and making any proposal for improving the effectiveness of the Convention (Article 14). The Standing Committee operates a procedure known as the opening and closing of files by which specific complaints against Parties are considered.[34] In 1998, the Standing Committee opened a file on the UK in relation to a complaint about the about the legality, under Articles 7, 8 and 9 of the Convention, of the badger culling trial. The UK intended to carry out a controlled cull of badgers in order to investigate a suspected link with bovine TB[35] . After consideration by the Committee the file was eventually closed in 1999.

European Union Institutions: A detailed analysis of the functions and responsibilities of the various EU institutions in the area of environmental policy is beyond the scope of this book, but in considering the operation of UK conservation law it is imperative to have regard to the role of the European Union as legislator, judicial authority and enforcer. Most conservation legislation now derives from EU legislation and the latter is described in some detail in relevant chapters. The judgments of the European Court of Justice on the interpretation of EU legislation are binding on UK courts and there is extensive case law on both the wild birds directive and the habitats directive in particular[36] . These rulings may arise from references to the court by national courts of the Member States or from direct actions, often brought by the Commission against a Member State which it considers to be in violation of its obligations. Judgments of the ECJ are referred to and discussed where relevant to the area of conservation law concerned.

Finally the Commission, as "guardian of the treaties" has a key role in ensuring that Member States comply with their obligations to transpose and implement correctly EU legislation. It has been active in this role in the area of the environment and conservation law is no exception. Most recently, the Commission has been taking a number of Member States to the ECJ for failing to nominate (on time) sufficient sites for the Natura 2000 network as required by the Habitats Directive. Environmental non-governmental organisations are free to make complaints to the Commission as to the non-implementation or incorrect implementation of EU law and

[34] The purpose of the procedure is to find a satisfactory solution to problems encountered in implementation and monitor the means chosen to resolve them (Draft Recommendation T-PVS(95)12).

[35] See the discussion in Chapter 3C - Part II.

[36] Rulings on general principles such as the free movement of goods or the application of the precautionary principle may also be of direct interest.

this may result in the initiation of what is known as an infraction procedure against the Member State concerned if the Commission takes the view that the complaint is well-founded and the Member State takes no steps to remedy the matter.

UK Institutions: The specific statutory roles of Government Ministers, in particular the Secretary of State for the Environment,[37] and of the statutory conservation agencies are referred to in detail in the relevant chapters. The role of the national conservation agencies (or "Councils") is key to the operation of UK conservation law however and is worth summarising. Established under the 1990 Environmental Protection Act[38], the conservation agency for England[39] is now known as English Nature[40]. The relevant conservation agency for Wales is the Countryside Council for Wales[41], whilst in Scotland it is Scottish Natural Heritage[42].

Among the wide range of functions carried out by these bodies[43] are: notifying and overseeing the management of SSSI's[44]; advising on the environmental impact of development projects on designated sites[45]; issuing certain licences for activities which would otherwise be prohibited in relation to wildlife[46]; establishing and managing nature reserves[47] and advising the Government on a broad range of conservation issues[48]. There is a joint council of the various agencies, known as the JNCC[49] which undertakes the "special functions" of the Councils as set out in section 133 of the 1990 Act. This includes advising the Government on the development and implementation of "policies for or affecting nature conservation for Great Britain as a whole or nature conservation outside Great Britain",

[37] Currently heading the Department for the Environment, Food and Rural Affairs (DEFRA) after a number of departmental permutations from DoE to DETR.
[38] These agencies (or "Councils") replaced the Nature Conservancy Council established under the Nature Conservancy Act 1973.
[39] See section 128 of the 1990 Act.
[40] See the Countryside and Rights of Way Act 2000 section 73(4) and Schedule 8.
[41] See section 128 of the 1990 Act.
[42] SNH is established by the Natural Heritage (Scotland) Act 1991, section 1.
[43] Their general nature conservation functions are set out in sections 132-134 of the Environmental Protection Act 1990.
[44] See Part II of the 1981 Wildlife and Countryside Act as amended by the Countryside and Rights of Way Act 2000, discussed in Chapter 1 - Part I.
[45] See for example regulation 48(3) of the Conservation (Natural Habitats etc) Regulations 1994, SI 1994/1276
[46] See Chapters 2 - Part II
[47] Section 132(1)(b) of the 1990 Act and see Chapter 5 - Part I
[48] Section 132(1)(c) of the 1990 Act.
[49] See section 128(4) of the 1990 Act.

which means any nature conservation matter "of national or international importance or which otherwise affects the interests of Great Britain as a whole" or "any nature conservation matter which arises throughout Great Britain and raises issues common to England, Scotland and Wales"[50].

Following devolution, many statutory functions have been transferred to the Welsh Assembly[51] and the Scottish Parliament is now responsible for much of the conservation legislation applied in Scotland[52]. This book focuses on the law as it applies in England and Wales, although the international and EU framework is of course the same for Scotland as for the rest of the United Kingdom.

Following the publication of Lord Haskins' Rural Delivery Review in November 2003, the Secretary of State for the Environment announced that certain of English Nature's functions would be transferred to a new agency dealing with land management generally[53]. Critics have expressed concern that the independence and integrity of advice on nature conservation issues will jeopardised by this change[54]. It must be questioned why the only English statutory independent body focused exclusively on issues relating to nature conservation and biodiversity should be incorporated into a new body with a much broader focus. The effectiveness of the laws discussed in this book depends to a large extent on the Government receiving independent and robust advice from a specialist independent advisory body. It remains to be seen whether the proposed new agency will be able to fulfil that role.

Prospects for Wildlife Conservation

Emerging from the changes and influences outlined above is a refinement of the underlying rationale for conservation legislation. The most recent instruments adopted in this area, in particular the Convention on Biological Diversity, appear to draw together the varying motivations for conserving and protecting wildlife (included within the concept of biological diversity and biological resources) reflected in earlier national legislation. By firmly linking the protection of wildlife with the promotion

[50] Section 133(4) of the 1990 Act.
[51] See the Government of Wales Act 1998 and the National Assembly for Wales (Transfer of Functions) Order 1999, SI 1999/672, art 2, Sch 1.
[52] See the Scotland Act 1998, section 29 and Schedule 5.
[53] See DEFRA Press release of 27 February 2004.
[54] See Paul Brown's article "Hundreds of Jobs to Go in Rural Shake-up", Guardian 12 November 2003 and Tom Burke's article "The Nature of the Game" Guardian 12 November 2003

of sustainable development, these instruments point towards an attempt at a new accommodation between humanity and the other species with which we share this planet.

This may be both a laudable and pragmatic development but it is taking place against the backdrop of unprecedented loss in biodiversity as indicated in the recent Kuala Lumpur Ministerial Declaration adopted at the Seventh Conference of the Parties to the CBD[55]. Precise estimates of the scale and rate of loss are difficult to quantify but it has been estimated for example that current extinction rates among mammals and birds may be more than 100 times the rate expected in the absence of human activities and that for some threatened ecosystems, like coral reefs, freshwater wetlands and tropical forests the rate of species extinction may be 1,000 to 10,000 times the background rate without human interference[56]. In the light of these losses, the participants at the World Summit on Sustainable Development (WSSD) in Johannesburg in 2002 adopted the 2010 Global Biodiversity Challenge which calls for a significant reduction in the current rate of biodiversity loss by the year 2010[57] So far as Europe is concerned, the Commission reported in 2001[58] that agricultural intensification has reduced the area of wetlands by 60% in the last few decades and that 45% of butterflies, 38% of birds species and 24% of the species and subspecies of certain groups of plants are considered threatened.

Against this background, the need to ensure that existing conservation law is applied effectively and also that the changes required to meet new challenges such as climate change are introduced speedily is self-evident. Any consideration by national courts or policy makers of the fate of an individual site or species should take place against the realisation that the wider picture is at present a deeply worrying one. Piecemeal losses for the sake of short term and narrowly defined economic gains will simply exacerbate the general trend against maintaining biodiversity. Those losses jeopardise the wider economic future, whether measured in terms of the potential benefits to humanity of particular species or by the environmental services provided by biodiversity generally in maintaining the environment on which we depend. The developed world has a particular responsibility to safeguard the relatively little biodiversity remaining in its territory as

[55] The Declaration expresses the Parties alarm that biodiversity is being lost at an unprecedented rate as a result of human activities, available at www.biodiv.org .
[56] See the WEHAB Report.
[57] WSSD's Plan of Implementation adopted at Johannesburg, September 2002.
[58] Commission Communication on Biodiversity Action Plans, COM (2001) 162 final, available on the europa website.

well as to ensure that its trade, agricultural and other policies do not undermine the ability of developing countries to pursue the objective of their own sustainable development. This book focuses principally on the first of those responsibilities[59] but a critical analysis of the laws presented here should bear in mind the global picture.

[59]The regime for regulating international trade in endangered species is clearly relevant to global conservation efforts as well as regional ones.

LIST OF UK CASES AND CITATIONS

R v The Nature Conservancy Council ex parte Bolton Metropolitan Borough Council [1994] Env LR 237 QBD, CO/1453/93

Sweet v Secretary of State for the Environment and another [1989] 2 PLR 14

R v Nature Conservancy Council ex parte london Brick Company [1994] Env LR 1 QBD

R (On the application of Aggregate Industries UK Ltd) v English Nature and another [2002] EWHC 908 Admin

R v (on the application of the Hon. Patrick Fisher and others) v English Nature Case No CO/3788/2001

Southern Water Authority v NCC [1992] 3All ER 481

R v Secretary of State for the Environment ex parte Royal Society for the Protection of Birds (The Lappel Bank Case) [1997]QB 206 (Case C-44/95)

R v Secretary of State for Trade and Industry ex parte Greenpeace (No.2) (QBD) 2000 CMLR 94, CO/1336/1999 Times 19 January 2000

WWF v Secretary of State for Scotland [1991]1 CMLR 1021

R (on the application of Beevers and others) v Environment Agency CO/358/2000

ADT Actions v Secretary of State for Environment Transport and the Regions and Hart District Council CO 4040 (2000)

WWF-UK and Anor v Scottish National Heritage & Ors (Cairngorms Case) [1999] Env LR 632

R v Poole Borough Council ex parte Beebee [1991] 2 PLR 27

Sweet v Secretary of State for the Environment and NCC [1989] JPEL 927

Kirkland v Robinson [1987] Crim LR 643

Robinson v Everett [1988] Crim LR 699

RSPCA v Shilton [2003] EWHC 1696 (QBD Admin Crt)

Murphy v Rotherwick [1999] All ER (D) 1508

Bandeira and Brannigan v Royal Society for the Prevention of Cruelty to Animals 28 February 2000 164 JP 307

Director of Public Prosecution v Green and Others [2000] All ER (D) 839

West London Magistrates' Court v RSPCA CO 3431/94, 14 December 1994

Lovett v Bussey Times 24 April 1998, CO/4119/97; (1998) Env LR D1

Bandeira and Another v the RSPCA QBD, CO 2066/99, 28 February 2000 [2000] All ER (D) 258

R v Somerset CC ex parte Fewings [1995] 1 All ER 513

Greenpeace v Secretary of State for the Environment, Food and Rural Affairs [2002] EWCA 1036

The Queen on the Application of Greenpeace v (1) The Secretary of Environment, Food and Rural Affairs (2) HM Commissioners of Customs and Excise [2002] EWCA 1036

LIST OF EU CASES AND CITATIONS

Oerlemans	ECHR		
Commission v Spain (Santona Marshes Case)	C-355/90	[1993]ECR 1-04221	08/08/93
Commission v France (Basses Corbieres)	C-374/98	[2000]ECR 1-10799	07/12/00
Commission v Netherlands	C-3/96	[1998]ECR 1-1003031	19/05/98
Commission v Germany (Leybucht Dyke case)	C-57/89	[1989]ECR 2849(order of the court) 16/08/1989; [1991] 1 ECR 883 Judgment of the court)28/02/1991	
Animaux sauvages	C-435/92	[1994] ECR 1-00067	19/01/94
R v Secretary of the State for the Environment ex parte First Corporate Shipping Ltd	C-371/98	[2000] ECR 1-09235	07/11/00
Commission v France (Seine Estuary)	C-166/97	[1999] ECR 1-01719	18/03/99
Commission v Italy	C-378/01	[2003] ECR 1-02857	20/03/03
Commission v France (Marais Poitevin)	C-96/98	[1999] ECR 1-08531	25/11/99
Inter-Environment Wallonie (Need reported Name)	C-129/96	[1997] ECR 1-07411	18/12/97
Commission v France	C-220/99	[2001] ECR 1-05831	11/09/01
Commission v Germany	C-71/99	[2001] ECR 1-05811	11/09/01
Commission v Ireland	C-67/99	[2001] ECR 1-05757	11/09/01
Commission v France	C-256/98	[2000] ECR 1-02487	06/04/00
Association pour la protection des animaux	C-435/92	[1992] ECR 1-00067	19/01/04
Austria v Huber	C-336/00	[2002] ECR1-07699	19/09/02

Godefridus van der Feesten	C-202/94	[1996] ECR 1-00355	08/02/96
Godefridus van der Feesten (criminal proceedings)	C-202-94	[1996] ECR 1-00355	08/02/96
Commission v France	C-252/85	[1988] ECR 002243	27/04/88
Commission V Italy	C-159/99	[2001] ECR 1-04007	17/05/01
Commission v Germany	C-412/85	[1987] ECR 03503	17/09/87
Association pour la protection des Animaux Sauvages and Others and Prefet de Maine et Loire, Prefet de Loire-Atlantique	C-435-92	[1994] ECR 1-100067	19/01/04
Commission v Italy	C-57/89	[1994] ECR 1-000067	28/02/91
Commission v France	C-38/99	[2000] ECR 1-10941	07/12/00
Ligue pour la protection des oiseaux/Premier Ministre et Ministre de l'Amenagement du rerritoire et de l'Environment	C-182/03 (Court order only, judgment pending)	[2003] ECR 1-06887	26/06/03
Commission v Belgium	C-247/85	[1987] ECR 3029	08/07/87
Associazione Italiana per il WWF and Others	C-118/94	[1996] ECR 1-1223	07/03/96
Commission v Italy	C-262/85	[1987] ECR 3073	08/07/87
Commission v Italy	C-262/85	[1987] ECR 03073	08/07/87
Associazione Italiana per il World Wildlife Fund and Others v Regione Veneto	C-118/94	[1996] ECR 1-01223	07/03/96
Commission v France	C-252/85	[1988] ECR 2243	27/04/88
Commission v Belgium	C-247/85	[1987] ECR 3029	08/07/87
Commission v Italy	C-262/85	[1987] ECR 3073	08/07/87

Commission v Germany	C-412/85	[1987] ECR 03503	17/09/87
Commission v France	C-252/85	[1988] ECR 2243	27/04/88
Commission v Netherlands	C-236/85	[1987]ECR 03989	13/10/87
Commission v Greece	C-103/00	[2002] ECR1-01147	30/01/02
Commission v United Kingdom	C-434/01	[2003] ECR 0000	06/11/03
Anklagemyndighed v Ditlev Bluhme	C-67/97	[1998] ECR 1-08033	03/12/98
Jippes and others v Minister van Landbouw	C-189/01	[2001] ECR 1-05689	12/07/01

PART I
HABITAT PROTECTION

HABITAT PROTECTION

Loss of natural habitat is one of the major threats to the conservation of biodiversity worldwide and has also resulted in major losses to UK wildlife. Traditionally, conservation law has addressed this problem through the protection of individual sites containing natural habitats and/or rare species of special interest but recent changes have broadened the focus of legal protection to include habitats and landscape features outside designated areas. This section looks at not only the legal protection afforded to sites with statutory designation but also to legal requirements to preserve habitat and landscape features outside such sites.

There is now a well established system for the protection of designated sites which is examined in Chapters 1, 2 and 3 . The designation and protection of sites of special scientific interest (SSSI's) under the 1981 Wildlife and Countryside Act, often described as the bedrock of UK conservation law, is the longest established regime and has recently been strengthened in a number of important respects by amendments to the Act introduced by the 2000 Countryside and Rights of Way Act. The SSSI system is complemented by regimes requiring stricter protection for certain sites covered by European legislation. In practice, sites protected under the latter will also be designated as SSSIs. Both the European Wild Birds Directive (Council Directive 79/409/EEC) and the more recent Habitats Directive (Council Directive 92/43/EEC) establish systems for the designation and protection of special sites. Sites designated under both these regimes are to be included in the European network of protected areas to be known as Natura 2000. The 1994 Conservation (Natural Habitats etc) Regulations implement the Habitats Directive in the UK and provide for the designation, protection and management of "European sites". Marine sites are covered by all these regimes but their designation and protection raises particular complexities which are examined in Chapter 4.

Chapters 5 and 6 look at some other designations of importance to habitat protection. National Parks and Areas of Outstanding Natural Beauty, which are designated under the National Parks and Access to the Countryside Act 1949, are not designated solely or even primarily for their wildlife interest but they do provide some limited protection for wildlife because of the various types of restriction imposed on development in those areas. Nature Reserves are created under either the 1949 Act or the 1981 Act (in the case of National Nature Reserves) for one or both of two purposes: study and research or conservation. Limestone Pavements are a particularly vulnerable geological feature and habitat afforded specific protection under the 1981 Act by means of Limestone Pavement Orders. The protection of hedgerows under the 1997 Hedgerows Regulations is an important example of the preservation of "nature corridors" which both provide a habitat and allow species to travel between larger areas of habitat thus mitigating the effects of fragmentation of habitat.

Much of the UK's biodiversity survives in semi-natural areas which result from farming practices which predate the post-war intensification of agriculture. The way in which agriculture is practised therefore remains crucial to wildlife conservation and the legal framework for promoting environmentally friendly farming practices has been recently been strengthened. Chapter 7 looks at this framework and examines the tensions between the European Union's Common Agricultural Policy and the protection of biodiversity. Chapter 6 examines the way in which the planning system aims to take account of conservation concerns and the protection of habitat outside designated sites including in relation to buffer zones and nature corridors.

CHAPTER 1

SITES OF SPECIAL SCIENTIFIC INTEREST

Introduction

At the heart of the statutory system for protected areas of wildlife habitat in the UK is the "SSSI" designation (or "ASSI's" in Northern Ireland). The acronym "SSSI" stands for "site of special scientific interest" and the provisions governing the notification and protection of SSSIs are contained in the 1981 Wildlife and Countryside Act. Not all legally protected areas of habitat are SSSIs, for example a local nature reserve will not usually be an SSSI, but SSSIs form the basis of the UK's system of habitat protection. Their importance is indicated by the following statement in a 1998 Government Consultation paper: "The conservation of SSSIs is not sufficient on its own to deliver the protection of our wildlife but their safeguarding is an essential precondition for the success of that objective"[1]. As at 31 March 1997, there were 6,264 SSSIs covering a total of 2,084 000 ha2 in Great Britain. As at September 1998, SSSIs covered some 7% of the land in England and Wales[2].

The statutory framework governing SSSI designation and protection has recently been amended by the Countryside and Rights of Way Act 2000[3] in an attempt by the Government to address some longstanding criticisms of weaknesses in the system. In November 1999, and in the face of longstanding calls from conservationists that tighter controls were needed if sites were to be properly protected, the Government announced that it was introducing a new wildlife Bill which would provide the conservation agencies with additional powers to protect SSSI's. This followed an extensive consultation exercise carried out in 1998-99 and led to the adoption of the Countryside and Rights of Way Act 2000, Part III of which has tightened protection of SSSI's by amending the provisions of the 1981 Act[4], as well as introducing a number of other measures relating to

[1] Sites of Special Scientific Interest Better Conservation and Management: A Consultation Document for England and Wales, September 1998, DETR, Introduction, page 5.

[2] Sites of Special Scientific Interest Better Conservation and Management: A Consultation Document for England and Wales, September 1998, DETR, Introduction, page 5. As at November 2003, the figures for England were 4,112 SSSI, 1,055,390ha, 7.5% of land area (English Nature)

[3] Schedule 9 to the 2000 Act substitutes sections 28-28R for the old section 28 of the 1981 Act, repeals section 29 and makes a number of other changes to relevant provisions of the 1981 Act.

[4] The 2000 Act received Royal Assent on 30 November 2000 and most of Part III came into force on 30 January 2001, see section 103 (commencement).

the protection of wildlife which are discussed elsewhere[5]. The overall aim of Part III of the Act is to better protect and manage SSSI's, only 56% of which were in a favourable condition at the time the Bill was introduced.[6] This Chapter outlines the changes introduced by the 2000 Act and compares them with the key features of the system as it existed and was applied before the most recent amendments. Pursuant to the amendments introduced by the 2000 Act, the Government also published in May 2003 a new code of guidance on SSSI's which is also considered below[7].

The Effect of SSSI designation

SSSI designation affords a degree of protection to the special interest of the site in two ways: any development proposals which would affect the site are subjected to particular scrutiny under the planning system and in addition, the owner or occupier must notify the relevant conservation agency if he or she wishes to carry out certain potentially damaging operations of a type notified as such by the conservation agency and may not then proceed with those operations unless one of the specified conditions is met. Prior to the changes introduced by the 2000 Act, there was a power for compulsory purchase of sites if the agency was unable to negotiate a solution but, in practice, this power was little used. The 2000 Act has maintained these two aspects of the system but has introduced important changes to the latter by increasing the powers available to the agency to prevent an owner or occupier going ahead with a potentially damaging operation. The 2000 Act also places new duties to protect SSSI's on public bodies and puts a greater emphasis on securing management of the site. The evolution of the legal framework for SSSI protection is considered below in the light of the changes introduced by the 2000 Act.

Relationship with other designations

SSSI designation underpins the UK's implementation of international and European Community obligations to give special

[5] In particular section 74 of the Act places the Government under a general duty to have regard to biodiversity conservation, to list the most important species and habitat types for biodiversity conservation and introduces a specific duty to further their conservation. A key example of the way in which this duty may be implemented is in the operation of the individual biodiversity action plans drawn up under the UK's Biodiversity Action Plan, Cm2428 London HMSO January 1994 as required under the Convention on Biological Diversity, see further Part II, Chapter 7.

[6] In its 2003 Code of Guidance DEFRA states that it has set itself the target of ensuring that by 2010 95% of SSSI's are in a favourable or unfavourable but recovering position (paragraph 26)

[7] "Sites of Special Scientific Interest: Encouraging Positive Partnerships" Code of Guidance May 8 2003 available at www.defra.gov.uk . This revokes, in relation to England, the guidance issued in 1982.

protection to certain habitats. These obligations have been met in the UK by providing additional protection to sites designated as SSSI's[8]. All National Nature Reserves (NNRs)[9], terrestrial Ramsar sites[10], Special Protection Areas (SPAs)11 and European Sites (future Special Areas of Conservation)[12] are also SSSI's under the 1981 Act. In the debate on the Habitat Regulations, the Government pointed out that most European sites were already SSSI's because they were among the most important areas in nature conservation terms and would have been notified in due course if they had not been already[13].

The Government has confirmed that it believes it to be appropriate to continue the distinction between sites of international importance, which meet very specific criteria and requirements, and other sites of national importance[14]. The additional protection afforded to sites which are also designated under international or Community law is considered separately in Chapters 2 and 3. As for sites which do not have additional designations, the Government has proposed making it clear that they are all of "national importance" rather than drawing distinctions for example in relation to the power to make nature conservation orders (which has now been repealed, see further below). Some have queried whether this would be useful given that all sites must be of special scientific interest or the duty to notify them would not have arisen in the first place

The Role of SSSI's

In its 1998 Consultation Paper on SSSI's, the Government outlined the importance of SSSI's, as a "central means to deliver nature conservation in England and Wales, by highlighting a number of ways in which they promoted various conservation objectives: appropriately managed, SSSI's would significantly assist in the delivery of biodiversity targets; SSSI's provided a framework for the protection of nature conservation within the planning system and underpinned delivery of international obligations under EC law and under the Ramsar Convention; the sites served as a

[8] Consultation Document, paragraph B: 2 states that the SSSI series should embrace all sites worthy of European and international recognition, alongside other sites which are nationally important (page 16).

[9] On NNRs see Chapter 5 - Part I(NNRs).

[10] As to Ramsar sites, see Chapter 2 - Part I.

[11] SPAs are designated pursuant to obligations under the wild birds directive, see further Chapter 2 - Part I.

[12] On SACs under the habitats directive, see Chapter 3 - Part I.

[13] Hansard, House of Lords Debates, 17 October 1994, Col 108.

[14] Consultation Document, May 1998 (paragraph B:4 1998)

refuge and reservoir for wildlife from which some species might recolonise the wider countryside; they provided examples of ecosystems which themselves could respond naturally to environmental changes and thus provided opportunities for observing such changes and undertaking research into conservation management[15]. The Government also set out the objectives which the SSSI series should fulfil: it should comprehensively cover the major conservation interests in England and Wales, in terms of the best examples of the full range of natural and semi-natural ecosystems and should include the sites "necessary to support viable populations of vulnerable, endangered or nationally scarce species in natural surroundings[16]. It also stated that the sites should have a broadly comparable value for nature conservation. In the new Code of Guidance, it is stated that the purpose of SSSI's in relation to nature conservation is to safeguard for present and future generations, the diversity and geographic range of habitats and species. The sites included within the series of SSSI's are intended collectively to comprise the full range of natural and semi-natural habitats and should include all of our most valuable nature conservations sites. The notification, effective management and conservation of sites is also said to be a critical element in meeting the targets set out in the 1994 UK Biodiversity Action Plan (as to which see Chapter 6 - Part I) [17].

Evolution of the SSSI System

The law relating to the protection of SSSI's dates back to the 1949 National Parks and Access to the Countryside Act and has been revised a number of times, most recently in Part III of the Countryside and Rights of Way Act 2000[18]. The current system is set out in the 1981 Wildlife and Countryside Act. A brief overview of the earlier changes to the system for designation and protection of SSSIs is followed by a discussion of the recent changes.

The first major reform of the system took place as a result of the 1981 Act. Although the notification and protection of SSSI's is now dealt with under Part II of the Wildlife and Countryside Act 1981, a statutory system for the notification of areas of special scientific interest was originally

[15] Ibid, paragraph A:14, page 14.

[16] Ibid, paragraph B:2, page 16.

[17] SSSI Code of Guidance 2003 paragraph 1.

[18] Section 75(2) of the 2000 Act cancels any existing old SSSI notifications made under the 1949 Act-most of which were re-notified under the 1981 Act and remain valid under that Act.

established under the 1949 Act. The system operating under the 1949 Act, however, came to be regarded by Government and others as seriously flawed and in need of a major overhaul. Introducing the Wildlife and Countryside Bill into the House of Commons, the then Secretary of State for the Environment, Michael Heseltine, commented in relation to the system of notification under the 1949 Act that "for all the practical effect that it had such notification need never have taken place"[19]. During the Bill's committee stage in the House of Commons, the Environment Minister, Tom King, described the then existing regime as "an inadequate botched up system"[20]

The primary reason for the loss of credibility of the 1949 system was the discovery that significant numbers of sites were being damaged and destroyed. The scale of the damage had been revealed in surveys carried out by the Nature Conservancy Council. It was recognised at that time that there was nothing in the existing legislation to prevent this from happening because the 1949 Act provided simply for the notification to the local planning authority of areas identified as being of scientific interest. Whilst this system enabled the authority to take account of the presence of the site when preparing development plans and considering proposals for development which might affect the site, there was no provision for statutory protection nor was there even any requirement for the owner or occupier of the site to be notified about the scientific interest of their land. Clearly such a system afforded no protection whatsoever from the effects of activities falling outside the town and country planning system, most importantly most agricultural and forestry activities[21].

The key changes introduced by the 1981 Act included provision for the notification of the sites special interest to the owner and occupier, as well as local planning authority and the Secretary of State, and the introduction of a system whereby a list of operations that might damage or destroy the features of interest had to be specified in the notification[22]. Restrictions were then placed on the carrying out of such operations by the owner or occupier, although whether these restrictions were stringent enough to afford real protection was to remain a matter of debate: ultimately, the owner was only subject to a delay in carrying out the operations unless the power for compulsory purchase of those sites considered to be of Anational importance was used (which was to occur rarely in practice). Subsequently, further important changes were introduced by the Wildlife

[19] Hansard, House of Commons, 27 April 1981.
[20] Hansard, House of Commons, 4 June 1981.
[21] See further chapter 6 on Planning and Chapter 7 on agriculture.
[22] Sites were renotified after the entry into force of the 1981 Act

and Countryside (Amendment) Act 1985 which sought to close a number of loopholes which had come to light in the 1981 provisions: protection of the site was extended so as to take effect upon notification rather than from the date of confirmation of the notification so as to afford interim protection to sites (unscrupulous owners having been free up until this change to destroy notified sites pending confirmation of the order)[23].

In 1994, the National Audit Office produced a report "Protecting and Managing SSSI's" which revealed 869 cases of loss and damage to SSSI's in England alone. In the ensuing debate about the inadequacies of the existing system strong doubts were expressed about the chances for success of a system which depended to such a large extent on the voluntary cooperation of landowners ("the voluntary principle"). A key issue which emerged in the debate on reform was the extent to which some form of compulsion, as opposed to the voluntary approach favoured by the then Government, could be introduced in order to safeguard SSSI's.

Advocates for reform of the SSSI system, including the Government itself, also tended increasingly to focus as much on the need to promote the positive management of sites as on the need to protect sites from damage, though this remained identified as an important area for improvement[24]. In this context, attention increasingly centred on the way in which agriculture was regulated and financed under the Common Agricultural Policy[25]. The importance of the level of resources available to deliver the objectives of the legislation was also recognised and remains a critical issue. In November 1997 a large number of conservation NGOs including Friends of the Earth, the RSPB and the Wildlife Trusts brought forward a Wildlife Charter which called on the Government to introduce better protection for SSSIs and suggesting ways to address the fundamental causes of ongoing damage to sites[26]. The newly amended system for the notification and protection of SSSI's emerged from these criticisms and proposals

[23] See 1985 Parliamentary Committee report.

[24] The Government described the section on management as the key section in its 1998 Consultation Document and commented that sympathetic management of SSSI's was crucial to the long-term survival of their special nature.

[25] Consultation Document, note 1 supra, paragraph A:12, page 14, pointing out that as of 1998, spending on agri-environment measures accounted for just 3% of CAP spending. See further Chapter 7 - Part I.

[26] See Friends of the Earth press release dated 17 November 1997 www.foe.co.uk_and the copy of the Charter linked to the release.

The System for the Designation and Protection of SSSI's

Criteria for selection of sites as SSSI's

Where English Nature or one of the other territorial conservations agencies (formerly the Nature Conservancy Council)[27] are of the opinion that "any area of land is of special interest by reason of any of its flora, fauna, or geological or physiographical features[28], it shall be the duty of the Council to notify that fact to the local planning authority in whose area the land is situated; to every owner and occupier of any of that land and to the Secretary of State" (section 28(1) WCA 1981). In a change introduced in the 2000 Act, the Council must also publish its opinion in at least one local newspaper[29]. The special interest of the site may be *potential* special interest but that must be made clear on notification, *the Bolton MDC case* (see below). Guidance on the criteria to be applied in selecting sites is laid down in "Guidelines for Selection of Biological SSSI's" originally published by the Nature Conservancy Council in 1989. The Government's support for common standards such as those laid down in the 1989 Guidelines is reaffirmed in the 2003 Code of Guidance.[30]

In 1998 the Government stated that it saw no justification for introducing a formal system of scientific review of sites, as had operated in Scotland since 1992, but would ask the agencies to undertake peer review of their processes for notification[31]. JNCC publishes a selection guidelines on behalf of and prepared by the Country Agencies.

Notification

During consultation on the reform of the SSSI system in 1998, the Government took the view that there was no need for substantive changes to the notification system as the system had reached equilibrium and the SSSI network was basically established. Whilst further sites might need to be notified from time to time, the Government accepted that the existing position was approaching equilibrium and recognised that resources increasingly needed to be deployed on securing positive management for

[27] By virtue of s73 of the 2000 Act the Nature Conservancy Council for England is to be known instead as English Nature.
[28] A Geological Conservation review was carried out in an attempt to redress the imbalance between the biological importance of sites and their geological importance which had received less attention.
[29] Section 28(2).
[30] Paragraph 14.
[31] B:11, note 1 supra.

existing sites rather than identifying and notifying new ones (considered further below)[32]. In addition to the new focus on public consultation, the Government proposed introducing a duty on owners to notify new owners about SSSI notification and requiring the inclusion of a statement of the Council's views as to management of the land. It was also proposed to clarify the Council's powers to vary and denotify SSSIs. All these changes have now been introduced in the 2000 Act. The definition of occupier has been amended to include commoners (persons with rights in common)[33].

A notification under section 28(1) must specify the time (which must not be less than three months from the date of the notification) within which and the manner in which, representations or objections to the notification may be made. The Council is required to consider any representation or objection duly made (section 28(3)a, requirement introduced by 1985 Act). This is, in any event, also a requirement under the general administrative principles of natural justice, *Bolton MDC case* (see below). The notification must specify the features by reason of which the land is of special interest (s28(4)(a)) and also, in contrast to the requirements for notification as originally laid down in the 1949 Act, any operations appearing to the Council to be "likely to damage the flora or fauna or those features."(s28(4)(b)). In 1998, the Government confirmed that it intended to retain the concept of lists of potentially damaging operations [34]. A further requirement introduced by the 2000 Act is that the notification must contain a statement of the Council's views about the management of the land[35]

In relation to notification of the features of special scientific interest, it was held in *R v The Nature Conservancy Council ex parte Bolton Metropolitan Borough Council*[36], that where the Council had not made the basis for a notification sufficiently clear to allow the owner to make full and effective objections, there was a breach of natural justice and the decision to confirm the notice would be quashed. In that case, the question was whether it was clear in the notification that the site was being designated for current interest as well as for its potential for regeneration.

As to the scope of any "operations" appearing to the Council to be likely to damage that flora or fauna or those features (s28(4)(b)), a fairly

[32] Sites of Special Scientific Interest: Better Protection and Management, A consultation document for England and Wales, September 1998, DETR, A.2 at page 11.

[33] See paragraph 5(4) of Schedule 9 to the 2000 Act amending section 52 of the 1981 Act.

[34] Consultation Paper (p 29), note 1 supra.

[35] See further section 28(4) final paragraph. This should be a simple statement of how the land is to be managed, Code of Guidance 2003 paragraph 16.

[36] [1994] Env LR 237 QBD, CO/1453/93.

broad view has been taken by the courts. In *Sweet v Secretary of State for the Environment and another*[37], which concerned a challenge to an order under section 29(3) of the 1981 Act[38], Mr Justice Schiemann held that the reference to an "operation" in s 29(3) was wide enough to cover agricultural activities including cultivation, application of fertiliser, grazing and mowing. He rejected an argument, put on behalf of the applicant owner of the land in question, to the effect that an operation is an activity which results in some physical alteration to the land, which has some degree of physical permanence to the land itself. Nor did he find that planning law (which distinguishes operations from a material change of use) was of any assistance in construing the term. In the *R v Nature Conservancy Council ex parte London Brick Company*[39], which also concerned the scope of potentially damaging operation for these purposes, the Court held that it was not irrational to include in a notification, as potentially damaging, an operation which is also of a type which must be carried out, in a controlled way, for the maintenance of the special interest of the site. In that case, English Nature had included drainage as a potentially damaging operation in relation to a site which required pumping to maintain the required water levels. The Court held that there was nothing irrational in such circumstances in a notification listing drainage and the changing of water levels as potentially damaging operations, thereby achieving such measure of control as "the toothless section" affords over drainage.

Confirmation or Withdrawal of the Notice

Following notification, the Council has nine months (calculated from the date on which the Secretary of State was notified) in which either to withdraw the notice or to confirm it with or without modifications (s28(5) of the 1981 Act as amended). In making any modifications however, the Council may not add to the list of potentially damaging operations specified in the notice or extend the area to which the notice applies (s28(7) of the 1981 Act as amended). A notice lapses on notice of withdrawal to any of the persons originally required to be notified, or at the end of nine months if it is not withdrawn of confirmed by the Council (s28(6) as amended). If modified, a notice takes effect in its modified form upon service of the modified notice on the owner or occupier of the land (s28(8) as amended). A notification is a local land charge (section 28(9) as amended).

---

[37] [1989] 2 PLR 14.
[38] Now repealed.
[39] [1994] Env LR 1 QBD; [1996] JPL 227, CO/104/94, 22 November 1994.

In *the London Brick Company case*, English Nature's policy of confirming notification where the special interest existed at the date of the confirmation and unless the continued existence of the special interest was "doomed" was held to be reasonable and in conformity with the legislation (the Court took the view that there was a discretion rather than a duty to confirm notification under s28,but that where special interest does exist, that will be a strong reason for confirmation). It was further held that it was not unreasonable, nor a failure to have regard to a relevant matter, to apply a policy which identified the site in the hope that the notified owner would cooperate with the conservation of the special interest, for example by entering into a management agreement.

The *London Brick Company case* concerned a clay pit, which, as a result of pumping which kept the water level low and affected the salinity of the water, had become a suitable environment for a rare water beetle. In order to maintain that environment, it was necessary to continue to pump the water at the same level. At around the time when English Nature notified the site under s28 however, pumping ceased. The company concerned objected to the notification in part on the basis that English Nature had failed to take account of the artificial nature of the conditions at the site and that, with the cessation of pumping, the pit would gradually revert to a large freshwater body with loss of the habitat and species for which it had been notified. In subsequent proceedings for judicial review of the decision to confirm the notification, it was held, refusing the application, that English Nature were entitled to hold on the evidence available that the special interest continued at the time of the confirmation (as water levels had risen only slightly) and that, although a management agreement was not in place, it was not unreasonable to confirm the notification in the hope of securing the company's cooperation in the conservation of the special interest in the future. This case illustrates the way in which the system prior to the changes introduced by the 2000 Act did not adequately address the need for positive management of sites in order to maintain special interest.

In *R (On the application of Aggregate Industries UK Ltd) v English Nature and another*[40], the owner of a site notified by English Nature as an SSSI challenged the confirmation of the notification, in part under the Human Rights Act 1998. The company which owned the site argued that English Nature, as a public body, had violated its right to a fair hearing under Article 6 of the European Convention on Human Rights. The claim

[40] [2002] EWHC 908 Admin.

was based on the assertion that the company's civil rights (to use and enjoy its land) were engaged by the decision to confirm the notification and that the procedural guarantees required under Article 6, in particular the right to have a determination of one's civil rights heard by an independent tribunal, had not been met. The claimant relied on the *Oerlemans* decision of the European Court of Human Rights in bringing its claim. The High Court accepted that Article 6 was engaged by the decision (noting however that in so far as the decision affected development plan policies it was not directly decisive of civil rights since these would only be directly determined by individual decisions on planning permission.) The Court went on to consider whether or not English Nature constituted an independent and impartial tribunal for the purposes of Article 6 and ruled that it did not (given its close involvement in the original decision to notify) but that the availability of judicial review- meant that there was no violation of Article 6 since the decision was subject to the scrutiny of a court with full jurisdiction. In relation to the issue of the scope of the court's jurisdiction, the Court held that in this type of case, where the decision under dispute involved judgments of policy as well as findings of fact, it was sufficient for the court to have jurisdiction to apply the usual public law principles. The claimant was unsuccessful on the other grounds of challenge.

In *R(on the application of The Hon Patrick Fisher and others) v English Nature*[41], the owners of a site which English Nature had confirmed as an SSSI sought unsuccessfully to challenge that decision[42]. The claimants had argued that the site should have been classified only as an SPA, which they considered to be a less restrictive regime, and not also as an SSSI. In dismissing the challenge, the Judge noted that section 28(1) of the Act "affords scope for judgment: it affords no scope for discretion" and went on to hold that if English Nature, having notified the site, continued to be of the opinion that the statutory criteria were satisfied, its discretion (to confirm) could only lawfully be exercised one way by confirming the notification. The judge also dismissed an argument that the decision violated the claimant's rights under Article 1 of first protocol to the ECHR.

Variation, Notification of Additional Land, Enlargement and Denotification of the SSSI

Following the changes introduced by the 2000 Act, the Council now has express powers to vary notices (although the area of land cannot

[41] Case No CO/3788/2001 Judgment dated 4 July 2003.
[42] The case is under appeal to the Court of Appeal .

be varied under this power), to notify additional land adjacent to the SSSI and to enlarge sites (sections 28A-C of the 1981 Act as amended). The approach taken to the distinction between sections 28B and 28C is that 28B deals with the addition of an area of land which has the same features as the original SSSI whereas the power under 28C in addition to being used for adding land can also add interest features. In the first case, there is no effect on existing owner occupiers who do not need to be notified. In the second case they do, because there are additional features which may occur on the already notified land (but which are not sufficient to merit notification on their own) and which may affect the OLD list[43]) It also has the power to denotify them where the Council is of the opinion that all or part of the SSSI is no longer of special interest (section 28D of the 1981 Act as amended)[44] . In each case, the Council is required to notify the local planning authority, the owner and occupier of the land concerned and the Secretary of State. Where a site is denotifed, the Environment Agency and every relevant undertaker and internal drainage board whose activities may affect the land in question must also be notified of the denotification.

Where a notice is varied or additional land is notified, or a denotification is served, the modified notice takes effect when it is served on the owner and occupier of the affected land. In the case of enlargement of an SSSI under section 28C, no enlargement notice may be given until notice has been given confirming (with or without modification) the original SSSI under section 28(1) or (2). Once the enlargement notification has been served on the owner and occupier of the land concerned, the original SSSI notification cease to have effect (section 28C(5)). In relation to variation of a notice under section 28A, the Council then has nine months from the date of service on the owner and occupier to confirm (with or without modification) or withdraw the notice. In the case of denotification under section 28D, the Council has nine months from the date of service on the Secretary of State either to withdraw the notice or to confirm it, or to confirm it in relation to a smaller area of land (if it does none of these, the denotification notice ceases to have effect. The Council must also publish a denotification in at least one local newspaper.

---

[43] Official comment.

[44] The Secretary of State has recommended that English Nature produce guidelines on the denotification of SSSI's (paragraph 22) and expects the power to be used only in exceptional circumstances (para 24).

Protection of the Site

The Voluntary Approach

Most SSSIs are privately owned[45]. In its consultation on the reform of the SSSI system, the Government acknowledged that the approach taken under the 1981 Act was to rely strongly on the commitment of landowners to maintain the conservation interest, the so-called "voluntary approach"[46]. The Government described the SSSI system as essentially triggering two important consultation processes: in relation to development proposals covered by the planning system which may affect the special interest of the site and in relation to the management and use of the land in other cases, including agricultural activities not covered by the planning system[47]. Prior to the amendments brought in by the 2000 Act however, the scope for prohibiting an owner from destroying the special interest or for stopping development which would have that effect was quite limited (see below). The extent to which the changes introduced by the 2000 Act have adequately addressed those limitations is examined below.

Adequacy of Protection

The weakness in the SSSI system had been identified some time before the 2000 Act. The 1994 National Audit Office report on SSSIs was referred to during parliamentary debate on the habitats directive. The NAO had found that, since 1987, 800 reports of damage to SSSI's had been made. Neglect was identified as a significant cause of the damage and the failure to secure appropriate management agreements for sites or to use the statutory power to make a Nature Conservation Order to protect land most at risk contributed to the problem[48]. In 1998 , a statement was agreed by the UK statutory conservation agencies establishing common standards for monitoring and reporting on the condition of designated sites. The adoption of these standards was intended to facilitate an overall assessment of the condition of SSSI's. Applying this system the Government acknowledged in 1998 that the picture was "disappointing"[49] with only 55% of SSSI's in a favourable condition. The problem of damage caused by neglect as opposed to deliberate acts as identified in the NAO Report was also considered during the 1998 consultations on management of SSSIs. The

[45] See Code of Guidance paragraph 102.
[46] Page 28 of the 1998 Consultation Paper.
[47] 1998: C:3.
[48] H/S: col 244.
[49] Consultation Document, note 1 supra, paragraph A.8.

Government had considered giving the conservation agencies default powers to manage the site in question but doubted that these would work satisfactorily and invited ideas on how to secure effective management, perhaps through the use of orders [50].

Prior notification of potentially damaging operations

Protection of a site designated as an SSSI is based on the restriction, by means of a requirement for prior notification, of the carrying out of the potentially damaging operations specified in the notification. Although this has been, and remains, a central feature of SSSI protection since the adoption of the 1981 Act, the appropriate scope of the duty to notify and the consequences of notification itself were both a matter of contention even while the Bill leading up to the 1981 Act was being debated. The evolution of key aspects of the system of notification of potentially damaging operations is considered below, together with an examination of the recent changes introduced by the 2000 Act.

Should all sites be protected?: The 1981 Countryside Bill

The imposition of the requirement to notify potentially damaging operations on owners/occupiers of all sites was one of the most controversial issues during the passage of the Bill leading up to the 1981 Act. The original proposal in the Bill was that owners/occupiers of only the most important areas of special scientific interest would be required to notify the NCC before they carried out operations which might destroy the scientific value of those areas[51]. These would be sites which were particularly threatened or which the Government had a specific international obligation to protect[52]. The operation could then only be carried out if the NCC consented or if the operation was in accordance with a management agreement or after a three month delay which could be extended to 12 months in certain cases. There was also provision for compulsory purchase. This system was intended to protect such sites from the effects of operations which fell outside the planning control system, which essentially meant most agricultural operations.

For all other sites, the initial proposed changes related only to notification of the site to the owner and local planning authority, a system which was intended to prevent inadvertent damage being caused by owners

[50] page 7 of the Consultation Paper.
[51] Hansard, House of Lords, 16 December 1980, col 985.
[52] Hansard, House of Lords, 12 February 1981, col 316.

who would not otherwise have known that the land in question was of special scientific interest.

Critics of this proposal were concerned that this would create a two tier system of protection for SSSI's and would leave the vast majority vulnerable to damage or destruction while protecting only a small number of "Super SSSI's". Lord Gibson, for example, expressed the fear that "by concentrating on super areas we shall automatically downgrade the rest."[53] Reference was made to Government estimates that only 40-50 SSSI's would be made "Super SSSI's"[54]. Much attention was focussed on the reported scale of damage to sites. The NCC had estimated that between 4-5% of sites annually[55] were suffering damage and, in some cases, total destruction. During the passage of the Bill, these figures were revised upwards to 10% of sites suffering damage and, in some counties, the figure was far higher (for example in Dorset the figure was 32%). It was also pointed out that some 57 of the key 735 sites listed in the NCC's 1977 Nature Conservation Review had since been damaged or destroyed[56].

The Government was initially resistant to calls to extend what it regarded as "super protection" to all SSSI'S, considering that this would be draconian but eventually agreed that what was termed "reciprocal notification" should apply to all SSSI's on the basis that this would ensure that the NCC had the opportunity to influence the activities of landowners in order to minimise or indeed obviate the effect on the SSSI. Accordingly, owners or occupiers of all sites were required to give written notice to the relevant conservation body (English Nature for England and CCW for Wales) of any proposal to carry out any potentially damaging operation which was specified in the SSSI notification. The notification had to specify the nature of the proposed operation and the land on which it is proposed to carry it out[57].

When should protection take effect?: the 1985 Amendment Act

One very important feature of the current system, which was originally introduced by the 1985 Amendment Act, is that protection of the site takes effect immediately upon notification rather than, as previously,

[53] Hansard, House of Lords, 16 December 1980, Col 1011.
[54] Hansard, House of Lords, 16 December 1980, Col 1059.
[55] Hansard, House of Lords, 16 December 1980, Col 991.
[56] Hansard, House of Lords, 16 December 1980, Col 992.
[57] Section 28(5) of the Wildlife and Countryside Act 1981 prior to amendment by the 2000 Act.

on confirmation of the notification (during which time some owners of sites could and did damage or destroy with impunity the features giving the site its special interest). During the passage of the 1981 Act, and in response to concern expressed about the possibility that sites would be destroyed during the three month period between notification and designation as SSSI, the Government had said that the problem of the delay between notification and protection could be resolved by a Code of Practice or by orders made under what became s29 [58]. This proved not to be the case however and the Act was amended to close the loophole in the system of protection. The changes introduced in 1985 ensure that, *from the date of notification*, the owner or occupier of any land which has been notified shall not, while the notification remains in force, carry out or cause or permit to be carried out, on that land any operation specified in the notification except in accordance with the fulfilment of certain conditions (as to which see below).

Who should be subject to the duty to notify?

The issue of who is covered by the duty to notify the conservation agency of potentially damaging operations has arisen in several ways. A person coming onto land within a site solely for the purpose of carrying out operations on the land was not an "occupier" of the land within the meaning of section 28(5) of the 1981 Act (now section 28(E)). This was established in the *Southern Water Authority case*[59], where the NCC had brought a successful prosecution against the water authority, which had dredged a ditch on an SSSI at the invitation of the farmers who owned land on either side of the ditch. No notification of the operation had been provided to the NCC. For reasons of expediency, the Council had decided not to prosecute the farmers for causing or permitting the damage and instead proceedings were brought against the water authority. On appeal to the House of Lords, it was accepted that this dredging was an operation falling within the scope of the notification and that it had caused "grave damage to those natural features of the ditch which the notification had been designed to protect." Noting that this was an "act of ecological vandalism", the House of Lords nevertheless took the view that water authority were not occupiers for the purposes of s28(5). In their view, "the occupier is someone who, although lacking the title of an owner, nevertheless stands in such a comprehensive and stable relationship with the land as to be, in company with the actual owner, someone to whom the mechanisms [for notice, agreements etc] can

[58] Hansard, House of Lords, 15 October 1981, col 483.
[59] Southern Water Authority v NCC [1992] 3 All ER 481

sensibly be made to apply.."(page 782) It was pointed out that the whole point of the initiating notice to the Council under s28(5)(a) (now section 28E(1)(a)) was that it was given before the proscribed operation began. This their Lordships decided, was impossible if a transient presence for the purpose of executing works was capable of maturing in the course of time into a sufficient occupation to bring the worker into the grip of the statutory machinery.

The House of Lords also dismissed an argument that, in this particular case, the water authority were caught by s28(5) as owner of the land because they happened to be owners of another portion of the site in question. The Court held that "The accidental feature that the person who comes on to one part of the land to perform proscribed operations at the request of or with the consent of the owner is himself the owner of a different part cannot make him the owner of 'that land' for the purposes of subsection (5)." The House of Lords expressed no opinion on the question of whether persons in the position of the water authority could be charged as co-principals in an offence under s28(5). This problem has now been addressed in the 2000 Act (see below).

A further problem in relation to the scope of the duty to notify the carrying out of potentially damaging operations arose in relation to successors in title. In the 1981 Act, the requirement to notify operations was placed on all owners and occupiers of the land, including successors in title (words "which has been"). However in its 1998 proposals for reform, the Government recognised that the system had not always worked effectively in this regard. It therefore proposed to require owners or tenants of sites to inform successors of the existence of the SSSI and to notify the relevant conservation agency of any change in ownership[60]. This reform was aimed at addressing problems caused where the new owner of a site claimed to be unaware of its status and the site was destroyed by the new owner[61]. Section 28Q of the 2000 Act deals with this issue by requiring the owner of land included within an SSSI to notify the Nature Conservancy Council where either he disposes[62] of any interest in the land concerned or he becomes aware that it is occupied by a different occupier (section 28Q(1) and (2)). The notice must be sent before the end of the period of 28 days following the date of disposal or the date on which he became aware of the

[60] page 19.
[61] The example given was Gwaun Cwm Cownwy SSSI.
[62] "disposes of" is defined in section 28Q(5) and includes sale, exchange or lease or the creation of any easement, right or privilege but excludes mortgages.

change in occupation. Failure without reasonable excuse to comply with this requirement is an offence (section 28Q(4)).

Changes Introduced by the 2000 Act

The limitation in the scope of the duty to notify operations on the part of those who do not qualify as owners or occupiers prompted the introduction, in the amendments introduced by the 2000 Act, of new duties on certain public authorities, to be known as "section 28G authorities". Section 28G authorities include: a Minister of the Crown or Government department; the National Assembly for Wales; a local authority; certain office holders; statutory undertakers and "any other public body of any description"[63]. Section 28G authorities are placed under a duty to take reasonable steps, consistent with the proper exercise of their functions, to further the conservation and enhancement of the features by reason of which the site is of special scientific interest (section 28G(2)). This duty and the corresponding powers of the Nature Conservancy Council are discussed further below.

Possibilities for protection following notification of a potentially damaging operation

Pre 2000 Act

Prior to the reform of the system introduced under the 2000 Act, an owner or occupier of a site, having duly notified the relevant conservation body of a proposal to carry out a potentially damaging operation, could only proceed to carry out the operation if one of three conditions was met. Those conditions were set out in section 28(6) and they were: that the operation was carried out with the Council's written consent (s28(6)(a)); that the operation was carried out in accordance with the terms of a management agreement under s16 of the 1949 Act or s15 of the 1968 Act (s28(6)(b)); or that four months had expired from the giving of the written notice (s28(6)(c)).

In 1985, an amendment was introduced in the form of s28(6A), whereby the owner or occupier giving notice could, before the expiry of the four month period, enter into a written agreement with the Council that, subject to the possibility of terminating the agreement, the four month condition would not apply in relation to the particular operation which

[63] See Section 28G(3(a)-(f)).

was the subject of the notice under s28(5)(a). This had effect both as regards the owner and the occupier of the land. This meant that for the duration of any such agreement, the only conditions under which a notified operation of that type could proceed were that written consent had been granted or that the operation was carried out in accordance with a management agreement.

A toothless regime?

In the view of Lord Mustill in *Southern Water Authority v NCC [1992] 1 WLR 775*, "It needs only a moment to see that this regime is toothless, for it demands no more from the owner or occupier of an SSSI than a little patience." Noting that it was only in rare cases that the extra protection of an order under s29 of the Act was granted , he went on to observe that "..the Act does no more in the great majority of cases than give the council a breathing space within which to apply moral pressure, with a view to persuading the owner or occupier to make a voluntary agreement." (page 778).

After the 2000 Act

Under the provisions of the 2000 Act, the earlier system of prior notification of potentially damaging operations is retained but in a form which affords the EN or CCW (CRoW only applies in England and Wales) greater power to prevent the carrying out of potentially damaging activities by simply refusing consent. Under section 28E, the owner or occupier of any land included within an SSSI shall not, while the section 28(1)(b) notification is in force, cause or permit to be carried out on that land any operation specified in the notification unless one of them has given notice of the proposal to the Council, specifying the nature of the operation and the land on which it is proposed to carry it out and one of the conditions specified in section 28E(3) is fulfilled. Two of the conditions are the same as those which applied under the pre-2000 amendments: that the operation is carried out with the Council's written consent (section 28E(3)(a) or that it is carried out in accordance with the terms of a management agreement concluded under section16 of the 1949 Act or section 15 of the 1968 Act. The third condition is new however: that the operation is carried out in accordance with a section 28J management scheme or a section 28K management notice (as to which see below)[64]. Gone is the possibility,

[64] Under paragraph 8 of Schedule 11 a notice to carry out works given before 30 January 2001 is to be treated as if made under section 28E. In paragraph 9 however, it is provided that where notice was given more than 4 months before that date in

...

criticised by Lord Mustill in the *Southern Water case*, that the owner or occupier need only wait four months before proceeding with the operation in any event.

A consent may be given subject to conditions and for a limited period (section 28E(4)). If the Council does not consent to the operation, it must notify the person who made the notice accordingly and there is provision for the Council to withdraw or modify the consent. A new feature of this strengthened regime is the right of appeal of owners and occupiers under section 28F against a refusal of consent to carry out an operation (or against conditions imposed in a consent or its modification or withdrawal). The appeal is to the Secretary of State who may hold a hearing or cause a local inquiry to be held[65]. The Secretary of State may affirm the Council's decision, direct the Council to give consent, quash any of the terms of the consent or quash any modification or withdrawal (section 28F(5)). There is a power to make regulations concerning such appeals and this has been done in relation to Wales and Regulations in relation to England are expected to be published shortly[66].

Section 28 G Authorities: Duties in Relation to SSSI's

Another new aspect of the regime for protecting SSSI's is the statutory duty to protect SSSI's placed on public bodies. The duty is not framed in absolute terms, nor can the Council veto the carrying out of activities which in their opinion will damage the site but the new provisions do require the public bodies concerned to pay attention to the conservation interest of the sites in carrying out their functions. The duty is underlined in the Code of Guidance which states that the Secretary of States expects all public bodies to take full account of their responsibilities under section 28G whenever their actions may affect SSSI's[67].

Section 28G authorities include: a Minister of the Crown or Government department; the National Assembly for Wales; a local authority; certain office holders; statutory undertakers and "any other public body of

(*Continued*) circumstances where English nature has not consented to the work and it is not covered by a management agreement, the work may proceed (if no nature conservation order was in force) subject to English Nature' power to issue a stop notice (see further Code of Guidance at paragraph 68).

[65] Although it is stated in the 2003 Code of Guidance that it may often be possible to deal with the matter by way of exchange of written representations (paragraph 45).

[66] See The Wildlife and Countryside (Sites of Special Scientific Interest, Appeals) (Wales) Regulations 2002, SI 2001/1772, HMSO and see paragraph 47 of the Code of Guidance.

[67] See paragraph 74 et seq of the Code of Guidance.

any description"[68]. Section 28G authorities are placed under a duty to take "reasonable steps, consistent with the proper exercise of their functions", to further the conservation and enhancement of the features by reason of which the site is of special scientific interest (section 28G(2)).

In addition its general duty under section 28G(2) of the Act, a section 28G authority is under a specific duty, under section 28H, to give notice to the Nature Conservancy Council before carrying out in the exercise of its functions, operations likely to damage any of the features by which the site is of special interest. This duty to notify applies even if the operation will not take place on land included in the SSSI (section 28H(2)[69].

In response to a notice under section 28H(1), the Council may send a notice saying that they do not assent to the proposed operations or else assenting to them, with or without conditions. If the Council do not assent and the s28g authority nevertheless wish to proceed or if the section 28G authority proposes to carry out the operation otherwise than in accordance with the terms of an assent, the authority must notify the Council after the expiry of 28 days beginning with its original notice of the date on which it proposes to start work and how (if at all) it has taken account of any written advice given by the Council in response to its notice (section 28H(5)). The date of commencement of the operation must not be within 28 days of that second notice. The authority must also comply with the requirements set out in section 28H(6) which are that it must carry out the operations in such a way as to give rise to as little damage as is reasonably practicable in all the circumstances (taking into account in particular any advice given by the Council) and that it must restore the site to its former condition, so far as reasonably practicable if any damage does occur. Adverse effects should be "exceptional" in the view of the Government[70]. The Code of Guidance notes that where the body concerned is proceeding with operations contrary to the advice of English Nature, the latter may ultimately have to resort to judicial review of that decision to go ahead with the work.[71]

There is a further duty under section 28I, which applies where the permission[72] of a section 28G authority is required before operations may be carried out[73]. Before permitting operations which may damage the site,

[68] See Section 28G(3(a)-(f)).
[69] See the chart at page 33 of the Code of Guidance
[70] See paragraph 77 of the Code of Guidance.
[71] See paragraph 75 of the Code of Guidance
[72] "Permission" is defined as including authorizations, consents and any other type of permission, section 28I(7).
[73] See the table at page 35 of the Code for Guidance.

the authority must give notice to the Council (section 28I(1)). As with the duty under section 28H, this applies even if the proposed operations are not to be carried out on land within the SSSI itself. The authority must then wait 28 days before deciding whether or not to give its permission, unless the Council has notified it that it does not need to wait until then. The authority must take any advice given by the Council into account in deciding whether or not to permit the operations in question and if it does so, in deciding what conditions if any to attach to the permission. Paragraph 81 of the Code for Guidance notes that the timetable for consultation is inconsistent with a number of statutory review periods for issuing consents but pending harmonisation states that the consultation periods for SSSI's take precedence where the special features are likely to be damaged.

If the Council advise against permitting the operations in question or advise that certain conditions should be attached, but the authority does not follow that advice the authority shall give notice of the permission and its terms to the Council (including a statement of how if at all the authority has taken account of the advice) and shall not grant a permission which would allow operations to start before the end of the period of 21 days beginning with the date of that notice (section 28I(6)).

The Environment Agency and SSSI's

Special duties are placed on the Environment Agency under section 8(1) of the 1995 Environment Act. Where the relevant conservation agency is of the opinion that the special interest of a site may be affected by the activities of the Environment Agency or by activities carried out pursuant to an authorisation given by the Agency, it is required to notify the Agency that the land is of special interest. Where the Agency has received such notification, it must consult the notifying body before carrying out or authorizing works likely to destroy or damage flora and fauna or prejudice conservation except in cases of emergency.

Management of Sites: New Powers

As mentioned above, attention has widened, since the system was established, from a focus on the protection of sites from deliberate or inadvertent damage to the need to ensure that sites are managed so as to conserve their special interest[74]. Policy initiatives in this regard include English Nature's Wildlife Enhancement Scheme and CCW's Berwyn

[74] Consultation Document, note 1 supra, paragraph A.4-5. Page 11 et seq.

Scheme. In its 1998 Consultation Paper, the Government stated that "the key relationship between the agency and the land manager should be in maintaining and enhancing the special interest rather than merely preventing damage."[75] It recognised that simply protecting sites from development and deliberate damage was insufficient to [secure their long term future], positive management was required (p34 1998).

The 2000 Act has introduced a new focus on securing appropriate management of SSSI's. A notification under section 28(1) must now include a statement of the Council's views about the management of the land. (This applies retrospectively to sites already notified by virtue of Schedule 11 paragraph 6 to the 2000 Act) In addition the Council has new powers to draw up management schemes and if necessary to issue management notices to secure management of the site. The new Code of Guidance on SSSI's states that the management of SSSI's should reflect the principles of sustainable development as set out in its strategy document: "A Better Quality of Life" (1999). The Guidance also states that English Nature should take account of its duty under section 37 of the Countryside Act 1968 to have due regard to the needs of agriculture and forestry and to the economic and social interests of rural areas.[76]

Under section 28J, the Council may formulate a management scheme for all or part of an SSSI. Such a scheme is a scheme for conserving the features by which the land is of special interest or restoring those features or both (section 28J(2)). The notice can be served with the initial sections 28(1)(b) notice or afterwards. The notice is to be served on every owner and occupier of the site but only after they have been consulted about the scheme. The notice of the scheme must specify the time within which representations regarding the scheme may be made (which must be at least 3 months) and the manner within which they may be made. The Council is given a power to withdraw or confirm the notice within nine months of the date of service on the owner/occupier. The section provides that a section 16 agreement or a section 15 agreement may provide for any matter which a management scheme provides for. The Guidance states that a management scheme is a statement which sets out clearly and at the appropriate level of detail the measures necessary for conserving or where practicable restoring the features of the land which make it an SSSI and it may cover the whole or part of an SSSI [77]. It is not expected that management schemes will be required for every site. The added value of a management scheme, as

[75] 1998, paragraph C:22.
[76] See paragraph 8.
[77] See paragraph 30.

opposed to a section 16 or 15 agreement, appears to be that it provides a formal step on the way to compelling management for the conservation and enhancement of the site rather than relying on the voluntary agreement. It may be that as the management notice may be seen as a major imposition by site owners, the provision compelling management was only agreed to if a number of procedural hurdles were required to be cleared first.

Management notices may be issued under section 28K where it appears to the Council that an owner or occupier of land is not giving effect to a provision of a management scheme and as a result its features are being inadequately conserved or enhanced. The Council may not serve a notice unless it is satisfied that it is unable to conclude on reasonable terms a management agreement with the owner or occupier. A management notice is a notice requiring the owner or occupier to carry out such work on the land and do other things with respect to it as are specified in the notice and to do so within the time prescribed. The work must appear to the Council to be that which it is reasonable to require in order to ensure that the land is managed in accordance with the management scheme. If the work is not done within the prescribed time, the Council may enter the land and any other land and carry out the work themselves and recover from the owner or occupier any expenses reasonably incurred. The Government has stated in the Code of Guidance for SSSI's that it expects management notices to be used only in exceptional circumstances where dialogue and negotiation have failed and that such notices would comprise only those actions which are reasonable and necessary to maintain the special interest of the site.[78]

A right of appeal against a management notice is provided in section 28L. Any person served with a notice may appeal to the Secretary of State and the notice does not take effect until the time for appealing has expired or until determination of the appeal. The appeal may be on the ground that some other owner or occupier of the land should take all or any of the measures specified in the management notice (or should pay the cost) (section 28L(2)). The Code of Guidance points out that the appeal may address the terms of a management scheme where the notice relates to actions set out in the scheme. The Secretary of State may order a hearing or a local inquiry and on determining the appeal may quash or affirm the management notice in its original form or subject to modifications (section 28L(5)). In exercising his powers he must take into account as between the appellant and any other person cited under subsection (2) their relative interests in the land and their relative responsibility for the state of the land

[78] See paragraph 64 of the Code of Guidance.

which gives rise to the notice as well as the relative degree of benefit from carrying out the requirements of the notice. The Code of Guidance also states that the Secretary of States will have regard to her duty under section 28G of the amended Act as well as to section 37 of the 1968 Act in determining the appeal. Regulations are to be made making further provision for such appeals.[79]

Section 75(3) of the 2000 Act amends section 15(2) of the Countryside Act 1968 so as to extend the conservation agencies' power to enter into agreements with owners and occupiers of land for the purposes of conserving the special features of an SSSI. The agencies may now enter into agreements with owners or occupiers of other land (not necessarily within or adjacent to an SSSI) for those purposes. In the Explanatory Notes to the Act, the example is given of the protection of a water supply some distance from the SSSI.

The third party offence in s 28P(6) also potentially removes one of the loopholes exposed by the Southern water case. As a third party, the company were not subject to s 28 but would have been caught by this provision. There may however be difficulties in securing prosecutions when it is necessary to show intent/recklessness, knowledge that what was damaged was SSSI (in particular) and that the individual concerned caused the damage.

Compensation

Under the pre-2000 system, a key difficulty was the relative lack of resources available to the conservation agencies to pay site owners/ occupiers for the positive management of the sites as compared to the resources available to farmers in the form of agricultural production subsidy via the Common Agricultural Policy. In some cases this led to attempts by the conservation bodies to seek to negotiate the purchase of the site in question by voluntary conservation bodies[80] It has also led to some farmers threatening to plough up SSSIs in an attempt to secure more money from growing subsidised crops such as flax[81] . As was pointed out during the passage of the 1981 Bill: "Any system of site protection, particularly one

[79] These will be known as the Wildlife and Countryside (SSSI's) (Appeals) Regulations 2003, see Code of Guidance paragraph 66.

[80] See Daily Telegraph 25 May 1998 "Farmer's battle over ancient flower meadows", Charles Clover.

[81] Guardian 11.9.98: farmers can earn 10 times more in EU subsidy growing flax than leaving land in natural state See further Chapter 7 - Part I.

which lays emphasis on management agreements, can be effective only if there is sufficient money made available to the NCC."[L Middleton HL Rep c 404 12 March 1981]

Under the pre-2000 system, an owner or occupier who agreed not to carry out a potentially damaging operation could be awarded compensation on the basis of profit foregone for not carrying out the operation. The method for calculating this type of compensation was not specifically made in the legislation but in guidelines issued under s50 of the 1981 Act in 1983[82]. Section 50 dealt in general terms with payments under certain agreements including those made following notice under s28(5) of the Act. The issue of compensation was controversial during the passage of the Wildlife and Countryside Bill. A proposal was put forward that would have limited the possibility for compensation to cases where it could be shown that the operation in question had been carried out in the previous 20 years HL Rep col 440 12 March 1980. The Government rejected this suggestion, arguing that it was not unreasonable for an owner to decide to change the style of management for his land and that they were confident that there were not many opportunists who would seek to abuse the system by claiming compensation for operations which they had no genuine desire to carry out.

In its 1998 Consultation Document, the Government put forward the view that the existing basis for compensation was inappropriate given the national importance of SSSI's and the wider public interest in their protection (page 7) and proposed that conservation agencies should instead be given the power to refuse consent for damaging operations (as to which see above). Following Consultation, the Government announced that this new power would be subject to a right of appeal to the Secretary of State and that guidance on agreements be revised to encourage positive management for which appropriate payment should be made (p7).

The Act as amended by the 2000 Act now provides for payment in certain defined circumstances. Under Section 28M, the Council is required to make a payment to any owner or occupier who incurs a loss due to the modification or withdrawal of a notice under section 28E(6). The Council may if it sees fit make one or more payments to any owner or occupier of land in relation to which a management scheme under section 28J is in force. This indicates the change in emphasis from compensation for profits

[82] DoE Circular 4/83 (Circular 6/83 WO) Financial Guidelines for Management Agreements.

foregone[83] (in order to prevent damage to a site) to paying for positive management of the land. The amount of payment is to be determined in accordance with Guidance given and published by Ministers[84].

It remains to be seen whether the new system with its greater emphasis on payment for management of the site and the power to refuse consent to damaging activities and issue management notices will overcome these difficulties

The Repeal of Section 29 of the 1981 Act

Section 29 of the 1981 Act was repealed by the 2000 Act. Under s29 of the 1981 Act, special protection could be applied by order of the Secretary of State to certain areas of special scientific interest. This section provided stronger protection than was available for SSSI's under s28 of the Act. It was relatively rarely used however, 19 such orders were in force as at 31 March 1996[85], in comparison with a total number of 3,874 of SSSI's as of the same date. A similar power had existed since 1949 but was also hardly used[86].

In order to be made subject to a s29 order, land had to be, in the opinion of the Secretary of State for the Environment, of special interest and the order had to be for one of the following purposes: for securing the survival in Great Britain of any kind of animal or plant or for complying with any international obligation; or, in the case of any land which is, in his opinion, of national importance, for conserving any of its flora, fauna or geological or physiographical features (s29(1)-(2)). In contrast to the protection of SSSI's under s28 of the Act, the protection afforded to a site under s29 was not just directed towards the actions of the owner or occupier of the land but to any person carrying out damaging operations. Where an order was made under s29(3), compensation could be paid under s30(2)[87] to any person having, at the time of making the order, an interest in land to which the order related comprised in an agricultural unit and could show to the Council that the value of his interest was less than what it would have been if the order had not been made. The amount of compensation was to be equal to the difference between the two values. Claims for

[83] The policy of compensating farmers for profits foregone was abandoned by English Nature in 1998.

[84] Guidelines on Management Agreement Payments and Other Related Matters February 2001.

[85] See English Nature's Fifth Annual Report.

[86] It was used twice, c509 HC Cttee 4 June 1981.

[87] Section 30 was also repealed by the 2000 Act, see Schedule 9 para 2.

compensation were governed by the Wildlife and Countryside (Claims for Compensation under section 30) Regulations 1982 SI 1982/1346.

The Government explained its reasoning for repealing section 29 as being that the powers it contained were no longer needed as sections 28-28R of Act as amended give full protection to SSSIs.[88]

Compulsory purchase

Prior to the 2000 Act, there was a power to compulsorily acquire land subject to a special nature conservation order under section 29 of the 1981 Act[89]. This power could be used if, the order having been made, the owner or occupier proposed to carry out a potentially damaging operation and it was not possible to resolve the matter by entering into a management agreement. In practice this power was little used[90], probably because of the lack of resources made available for such purchase and also because of the culture of adherence to the voluntary principle wherever possible

Under section 28N of the Act as amended by the 2000 Act the Council is empowered to acquire compulsorily all or any part of an SSSI in circumstances where the Council are satisfied that they are unable to conclude, on reasonable terms, a management agreement with the owner or occupier of the land or where the Council have entered into a management agreement but are satisfied that it has been breached in such a way that the land is not being managed satisfactorily. Any dispute about whether or not there has been a breach of the agreement is to be determined by an arbitrator appointed by the Lord Chancellor. The Code of Guidance indicates that the Government expects that this power will only be used rarely but there may be circumstances where it is the only means of securing the conservation interest[91] As yet this power has not been used, nor has a management scheme or notice been served.

Where the Council have acquired land compulsorily, they may manage it themselves or dispose of it (or any interest in it) on terms designed to ensure that it is managed satisfactorily.

88 See Explanatory Notes to the Countryside and Rights of Way Bill, paragraph 211.
89 Section 29 was repealed by the 2000 Act, see Schedule 9, paragraph 2.
90 It is difficult to verify the figures but possibly only once.
91 Paragraph 72 of the Code of Guidance.

Section 75(4) of the 2000 Act inserts a new section 15A into the 1968 Act enabling the conservation agencies to compulsorily purchase land outside an SSSI for the purpose of conserving the special features of a site. This power can only be exercised if the agency are satisfied that they cannot reach an agreement for the conservation of the site with owner or if there has been a breach of such an agreement.

Planning and Transport

Planning and nature conservation is considered more generally in Chapter 6 - Part I. As far as SSSIs are concerned, the current position is set out in PPG9 together with the provisions of the 1981 Act. Whilst the majority of SSSI's are on agricultural land, brown field sites may also contain important habitat. One example is Orton Brick Pits where the largest European colony of Great Crested Newts was found. These sites are subject to particular pressure for redevelopment for housing. [92]

PPG9 makes it clear that nature conservation can be "a significant material consideration" in determining a planning application and that this is especially so where the proposed development is in or near an SSSI. Development proposals in or likely to affect an SSSI will be made subject to Aspecial scrutiny[93]. Recently the Government has echoed this by stating that where a development proposal is within or is likely to affect an SSSI it will be subject to "particular scrutiny" ref: 1998. [Omit: Authorities must consult the conservation agencies about proposals on land within, near to or likely to affect SSSIs.] PPG9 also makes it clear that planning permission should not be refused where the use of planning conditions or obligations will prevent damage to designated sites or to other wildlife habitats or important physical features[94]. Nor should permission be refused if Aother material factors are sufficient to override nature conservation considerations. In the case of certain designations however special rules apply: footnote cross refer other chapters] The Secretaries of State will normally call in and determine applications which significantly affect sites of national and international importance (if the local authority is minded to grant permission and the conservation agency advises against it).

Where a development relates to land in an SSSI, the planning authority must consult English Nature before granting permission. If the

[92] See "Wastelands of Britain" past bloom in natural splendour, The Independent 26 October 1996.

[93] PPG9 paragraph 29.

[94] PPG9 paragraphs 27-28.

authority indicates that it is minded to grant permission against the advice of English nature, the latter can consider whether to ask the Secretary of State to call the application. The authority must also consult English Nature if the development is in a consultation area relating to the SSSI or is likely to affect it even if outside such an area[95]. Consultation areas are defined by English Nature, who have been requested to give priority to areas around internationally important sites[96]. Section 28I also now applies.

In the absence of any consultation area, planning authorities must still consider whether to consult in relation to any development in the vicinity of an SSSI and should bear in mind activities such as water abstraction which have effects on a site which is some distance away[97]. Although this is not clear from the guidance it would seem likely that local authorities should also consider the effects of activities outside any consultation area where these are likely to have an effect on the site in question. In cases of doubt the authority is directed to seek advice from English Nature and to inform English Nature about all decisions in relation to land about which they were consulted.[98] (They should also give a second notice giving details of the permission where the second notice requirement under s28I applies.) Certain permitted development rights have been disapplied in SSSI's eg clay pigeon shooting. Such developments then require normal planning application[99] and environmental impact assessment. 1998.

Where the exercise of permitted development rights on an SSSI would constitute a damaging operation covered by a notification, the owner or occupier of the site must apply to English Nature for consent. There is the possibility of appeal to the Secretary of State if English Nature refuse the application or attach conditions. Alternatively the owner/occupier may submit an application for planning permission to the local authority (who must then consult English Nature)[100] Where there is a valid planning permission granted on application for development on an SSSI, the works may proceed without further notification to English Nature[101].

---

[95] PPG9 paragraph 30, consultation areas are notified under article 10(u)(ii) of the 1995 GDPO.

[96] PPG9 paragraph 31 which also sets out the limits for such areas. Boundaries are to be notified by English Nature to the local planning authority.

[97] PPG9 paragraph 32.

[98] PPG9 paragraph 33.

[99] PPG9 paragraph 34.

[100] Code of Guidance paragraph 49.

[101] Code of Guidance paragraph 53.

Under current guidance it is stated that the Secretary of State will normally call in, on the advice of English Nature, applications having significant effects on sites of national importance, namely NNRs and NCR and GCR. In any event planning authorities are advised to Apay particular regard to the national importance of such sites[102]. The Secretary of State will also call in applications relating to other SSSIs if they raise planning issues of more than local importance. This distinction is likely to disappear in the light of proposed reforms which include the recognition that all SSSIs are of national importance.

Proposed Reforms

The Government has proposed in the context of planning that, as with recent proposals for transport, there should be a "strong presumption" against new or expanded infrastructure which would significantly affect an SSSI (page 6). In relation to its policy on transport schemes, it has said that a transport scheme which will significantly affect an SSSI will not go ahead unless "it is clear that the net benefits in terms of other objectives clearly override the environmental disbenefits, there is no better option and all reasonable steps have been taken to mitigate the impact. We expect very few schemes to pass this test."[103]

Where there is no alternative to the development going ahead, compensatory or mitigating measures should be put in place. The Government said in its consultation paper that it was "aware of some disquiet concerning their use" (1998 C:12) but that such measures could prove effective in some instances.

Environmental Impact Assessment

Developments which are projects subject to the EIA regime and are to be situated in or close to an SSSI will normally require an environmental impact assessment[104]. This is considered in Chapter 6 - Part I.

Agriculture and Forestry

See Chapters 7 - Part I for a full discussion of the legal protection of nature conservation interests in the context of agriculture and planning.

[102] PPG9 paragraph 36.

[103] Sites of Special Scientific Interest: Better Protection and Management, C:18 DETR, September 1998.

[104] See The Town and Country Planning ("Environmental Impact Assessment") (England and Wales) Regulations 1999, SI 1999/293.The EIA Regulations 1999 and DETR Circular 02/99.

The Government has said that agricultural activities are responsible for the greatest impact on sites constituting a greater threat than built development[105]. Forestry grants not available for operations which could damage SSSIs (1998 page 41).

Enforcement

In its consultation on proposed reform, the Government stressed that damage to sites was wholly unacceptable and encouraged agencies to be more proactive in taking action against those who deliberately damage special sites (1998 page 45). The offences relevant to the protection of SSSI's are set out in section 28P of the 1981 Act as amended by the 2000 Act. These relate to the duties of section 28G authorities as well as those placed on owners and occupiers of sites. Third parties are also covered by the offence of "without reasonable excuse" intentionally or recklessly destroying or damaging or disturbing (in the case of fauna) any of the features by reason of which the land in question is of special scientific interest, knowing that what was destroyed, damaged or disturbed was within an SSSI (section 28P(6).

Under the 2000 Act the financial penalties for damaging sites and related offences have been increased. The penalty for, without reasonable excuse, contravening section 28E(1) is a £20,000 fine on summary conviction or a fine on conviction on indictment (the previous fine was level 4 on the standard scale, in other words £2,500 at the time of amendment). Similar penalties are in place where section 28G authorities fail to comply with their obligations under sections 28H. In relation to these offences a reasonable excuse is defined in relation to the carrying out of an operation (or failing to comply with a requirement to send a notice about it) where the operation was authorised by planning permission granted under Part III of the Town and Country Planning Act 1990 or was permitted by a section 28G authority which has acted in accordance with section 28I (section 28P(4)), or where the operation in question was an emergency operation particulars of which were notified to the Nature Conservancy Council as soon as practicable after commencement of the operation. In this context, if an operation needs both planning permission and the permission of a section 28G authority, subsection 4(a) does not provide a reasonable excuse unless both have been obtained (section 28P(5)).

In determining the amount of any fine for a section 28P offence, the court is required in particular to have regard to any financial benefit which has accrued or appears likely to accrue to the person convicted in consequence of the offence (section 28P(9)).

105 Ibid, paragraph C:21.

Section 31 of the 1981 Act has been amended[106] so as to allow the court to order restoration of a site where a person has been convicted of damaging or destroying it under section 28P (1) or (6). This power also applies where a section 28G authority has been convicted under section 28P(2) or (3) whether the operation causing the damage took place on or off the SSSI.

Proceedings in England and Wales for an offence under this section can only be brought by a person other than the Council with the consent of the Director of Public Prosecutions (section 28P(10)). The Secretary of State expects English Nature to develop and publicise a strategy for enforcement.[107]

Powers to enter onto land are set out in section 51. English Nature is not expected to exercise these powers unless it has used all other reasonable means to effect entry by agreement with the owner or occupier.[108]

Byelaws

English Nature and the Countryside Council for Wales are empowered to make byelaws for the protection of a site under section 28R of the 1981 Act as amended. Certain provisions of the 1949 Act relating to scope, enforcement and compensation apply to these byelaws as they do to byelaws made under section 20 of that Act for the protection of nature reserves (as to which see chapter 5 - Part I). The Code of Guidance indicates that this power is particularly useful where activities or behaviour cause minor amounts of damage individually but when carried out repeatedly by large numbers of people can damage the special interest of a site. Defra is to draw up model byelaws for this purpose.[109]

Beyond SSSI's

Legal protection for habitats goes beyond the protection of SSSI's and other designated sites and encompasses general protection for various environmental media and features of the landscape as well as specific protection for areas surrounding such sites. These issues are considered further in chapters 6 and 7 - Part I.

[106] See Schedule 9, para 3 of the 2000 Act.
[107] See paragraph 97 of the Code of Guidance.
[108] See paragraph 100 of the Code of Guidance.
[109] See paragraph 59 Code of Guidance.

CHAPTER 2

SPECIAL PROTECTION AREAS (WILD BIRDS) AND RAMSAR SITES

A. Special Protection Areas for Wild Birds

Habitat Protection under the Wild Birds Directive

The wild birds directive predates the habitats directive by over a decade and in many ways the habitats directive is designed to build on and improve the mechanisms adopted in the earlier directive: the staged timetable for the designation of protected sites and the establishment of a coherent network of protected sites (which includes those designated under the wild birds directive) are two key examples of improvements. In other respects the habitats directive has been argued by some to be a retrograde step-in particular the scope for derogation is widened (these changes are also to be applied to sites designated under the wild birds directive).

The continuing importance of habitat protection for the conservation of wild birds is evident in the Commission's Third Report on the application of the wild birds directive,[1] in which the Commission referred to a 1994 study on the conservation status of European bird species conducted by Birdlife International. The Commission noted that the study, the best scientific information available at that time, had indicated that 38% of the 514 species considered had an unsatisfactory conservation status, either because of a marked decline in numbers or because of limited distribution. The Commission went on to note that the decline was mostly due to changes in land use and management techniques, with intensification of agriculture the main, or a, loss factor for 42% of declining species.[2] Another important factor in the decline was destroyed and damaged habitat, particularly wetlands, whilst hunting, capture and killing generally had a more secondary adverse effect on conservation status.

The Structure of the Directive

The origins of the wild birds directive, the first European Community legislative measure dealing with nature conservation, are considered in Chapter 2 - Part II, together with its scope and provisions

[1] COM(2000) 180 final, Brussels 29.03.2000, Update for 1993-95.

[2] On the current efforts to mitigate the effects of intensive agriculture on wildlife see Chapter 7 - Part I.

relating to species protection. The European Court of Justice's interpretation of the species protection provisions of the directive, as set out in the cases discussed in that chapter, is also relevant to an understanding of the habitat protection provisions considered in this chapter since the Court addresses its general scheme and objectives. References to a number of these species protection cases appear in the ECJ's judgments on the directive's habitat protection provisions as indicated below.

As far as habitat protection is concerned, there are two sets of obligation to protect the habitats of wild birds under the directive. The first is a general duty to preserve, maintain or re-establish a sufficient diversity and area of the habitats of all wild birds covered by the directive (Article 3). This obligation is described as a *sine qua non* for achieving the aims of the Directive in the Commission's Third Report. The second, which the Commission refers to as a central element in the Directive, is a duty to take special conservation measures in relation to the habitat both of the bird species listed in Annex I and also regularly occurring migratory birds not listed in Annex I. In relation to the latter, this means breeding, moulting and wintering areas and staging posts along the migration route (Article 4).

In its rulings on the interpretation of Articles 3 and 4, the ECJ has emphasised that Article 4 is a special regime for the protection of the most endangered birds and those which represent a common heritage and that its requirements are to be interpreted as providing more stringent protection than that afforded under Article 3. In the *Santona Marshes case*, Advocate General Van Gerven analysed the relationship in the following way: "Article 3 imposes obligations with regard to all species [of wild birds] ...and Article 4 adds specific obligations with regard to the birds mentioned in Annex I and migratory birds not mentioned in that Annex." He added "it certainly does not follow, merely because additional rules are laid down with respect to those two categories of birds, that the more general provisions are not applicable".[3] The Court, in its judgment in the case, rejected Spain's argument that Articles 3 and 4 merely imposed an obligation as to a result: to secure the conservation of wild birds. The Court accepted the Commission's view, which was that these provisions required Member States to protect habitats as such because of their ecological value. It followed that the obligations under Articles 3 and 4 existed before any reduction in the number of birds was observed or any risk of extinction materialized.[4] These two sets of obligation are considered further below.

[3] Case 355/90 Commission v Spain, Opinion of the Advocate General paragraph 57.
[4] Case 355/90 Commission v Spain, paragraph 15 of the judgment.

The wild birds directive's system for habitat protection under Article 4 was amended in part by the Habitats Directive in relation to those sites classified as Special Protection Areas (SPAs)[5]. The former system of protection remains in place however in relation to any sites which should have been classified as SPAs by Member States but which have not been, *Case 374/98 Commission v France (Basses Corbieres)*[6]. This means that a stricter regime applies to areas which should have been designated as SPAs as the wider derogations in the habitats directive do not apply until such sites have been designated.[7]

Habitat Protection For All Wild Birds Covered by the Directive

Article 3 requires Member States to take the requisite measures "to preserve, maintain or re-establish a sufficient diversity and area of habitats[8] for all the species referred to in Article 1 of the directive". These measures are to be taken in the light of the requirements referred to in Article 2 of the directive, those being: Ato maintain of the population of wild bird species at a level which corresponds to ecological, scientific and cultural requirements, while taking into account economic and recreational requirements, or to adapt the population to that level"[9]. This provision was considered by Advocate General Fenelly in *Case C-44/95 the Lappel Bank case*[10] (discussed below). Noting that Article 3 was the only provision of the directive expressly to refer to Article 2, he said that, given the comprehensive nature of the obligations arising under Article 3 which, in contrast to the obligations under Article 4, applied to all wild birds regardless of any threat to their conservation status, and the fact that the Directive sought a balance between ecological and competing interests: Ait would have been surprising if the Member States had been precluded from taking account of economic and recreational requirements in complying with Article 3-hence it expressly provides that they should do so..." (para 65).

---

[5] See Chapter 3 - Part I.

[6] Judgment of 7 December 2000 at para 47. See also Chapter 3 - Part I.

[7] See Chapter 3 - Part I.

[8] The term "habitat" is not defined in the directive itself but Advocate General Van Gerven has suggested that the definitions of habitat in Article 1(1)(g) of the Bonn Convention should be used as a guide. Similarly with the reference to "area of distribution" (definition of "range")[AGO-Leybucht Dyke page I-904)

[9] As to the ECJ's interpretation of Article 2 and its relationship with the species protection provisions of the Directive, see Chapter 2 - Part II.

[10] Case C-44/95 R v Secretary of State for the Environment ex parte Royal Society for the Protection of Birds [1997] QB 206 Opinion delivered 21 March 1996.

A more specific indication of the types of measures required is given in Article 3(2) which provides that "the preservation, maintenance and re-establishment of biotopes and habitats shall include primarily the following measures: ..creation of protected areas; ..upkeep and management in accordance with the ecological needs of habitats inside and outside the protected zones; the re-establishment of destroyed biotopes and the creation of biotopes. It is worth noting the reference to upkeep and management of habitats *outside* as well as inside protected zones. This, together with the fact that creation of protected areas is but one of the required measures, is an indication that Article 3 of the directive requires measures to be taken in the wider countryside and in other areas relevant to the conservation of wild birds. The protection of the wider countryside is discussed further in Chapter 6 - Part I.

Special Conservation Measures Under Article 4

In addition to the obligation to protect the habitats of all wild birds covered by the directive (Article 3[11]), the directive also requires Member States to take special conservation measures concerning the habitat of the bird species listed in Annex I (Article 4(1)) and to take "similar measures"[12] in respect of regularly occurring migratory species not listed in Annex I (Article 4(2)). In particular, Member States are required to classify "special protection areas" (SPAs) for the protection of these species. SPAs are described as "the most suitable territories in number and size... for the conservation of these species, taking into account their protection requirements in the geographical sea and land area where the directive applies."

It is clear from the language of Article 4 that the duty to take special conservation measures concerning the habitat of Annex I species and non-Annex I migratory species is wider than the specific duty to classify SPAs as such, nevertheless, the classification of SPAs has been described as the most prominent measure required[13] . Furthermore, the extent of the duty to classify SPAs is not contingent on the degree to which other special conservation measures are taken by Member States. Commenting on the requirement imposed on Member States in Article 4(1) to "classify in

[11] For a discussion of how these and other general obligations are implemented outside designated areas see chapter 6 - Part I.

[12] It is clear from the case law of the ECJ that the similar measures include the classification of special protection areas, see for example the *Santona Marshes case*.

[13] By Advocate General Fenelly in his Opinion in the *Lappel Bank case* [AGO Lappel Bank paragraph 66].

particular the most suitable territories" as SPAs, Advocate General Fennelly took the view in *Case 3/96 Commission v Netherlands*[14] that the words "in particular" show that this phrase should be interpreted as meaning that, amongst the measures that Member States are required to take to ensure the survival and reproduction of these endangered species, they must, as a minimum, classify the most suitable territories as SPAs. In his view, it was clear from the *Santona Marshes* judgment that this was an autonomous obligation. He went on to say that, in order to comply with the more general obligation imposed under Article 4(1), Member States may need to take other special conservation measures, such as classifying other territories as SPAs, but the point was that they were under a specific obligation to classify the most suitable areas as SPAs [15]. The Court in its judgment reached the same conclusion and emphasised that the obligation to classify a suitable number and area of SPAs cannot be avoided by taking other types of conservation measure instead[16]. These cases are considered further below.

Classification of SPAs

In contrast to the language of Article 3, Article 4 does not make express reference to Article 2 of the directive. The implications of this difference in language have been considered in a number of cases before the ECJ, the issue being whether Member States were permitted to take into account the economic and recreational requirements referred to in Article 2 when classifying or protecting SPAs under Article 4. On each occasion, the Court has given a negative response, although in the most recent case, *Lappel Bank*, it recognised that the regime for the protection of SPAs under Article 4(4) had changed following the amendment of the relevant part of Article 4 of the wild birds directive by Article 7 of the habitats directive. This amendment allowed social and economic considerations to be taken into account when *protecting* SPAs in certain circumstances as laid down in the directive.[17]

In the first case in which the issue of the relationship between Article 2 and Article 4 arose, *Case 57/89 Leybucht Dyke*[18], the Court, referring to its earlier case law on the species protection measures of the directive, confirmed that Article 2 "does not constitute an autonomous derogation from the general system of protection established by the directive" and accordingly (rejecting arguments put by the UK) economic and recreational

[14] Judgment of 19 May 1998, [1998] ECR I-3031.
[15] See paragraph 32 of the Opinion.
[16] See paragraph 55 of the judgment.
[17] See further Chapter 3 - Part I.
[18] Case 57/89 Commission v Germany [1991] ECR I-883.

requirements could not constitute "exceptional grounds" justifying the reduction in extent of an SPA. The Court followed the same approach in *Case 355/90 Santona Marshes*[19] and in *Case 44/95 Lappel Bank*[20]. These judgments are considered further below.

Criteria for the Selection of SPAs

The degree of flexibility available to Member States when deciding which areas should be classified as SPAs under Articles 4(1) and (2) has been the subject of some controversy. Two main issues have arisen: the extent to which economic interests may be taken into account when classifying an SPA, which was considered in the *Santona Marshes* and *Lappel Bank* cases and, recently, the question of how to determine whether a sufficient number and area of SPAs has been classified overall, which was addressed by the Court in *Case 3/96 Commission v Netherlands*. Before considering these cases, the criteria expressly set out in the directive need to be considered. The Court has confirmed that these are indeed ornithological criteria, *Santona Marshes*[21]. They relate to the species whose habitats require special conservation measures and, in one respect, to the type of habitat to be classified.

Ornithological Criteria in Article 4, Paragraphs (1) and (2)

As regards which species are to be the subject of special conservation measures including the need to classify SPAs, Article 4(1) of the directive refers to those listed in Annex I (currently 175 species) and goes on to state that account must be taken of species in danger of extinction; species vulnerable to specific changes in their habitat; species considered rare because of small populations or restricted local distribution and other species requiring particular attention for reasons of the specific nature of their habitat. The directive requires trends and variations in population levels to be taken into account as a background for evaluations.[22]

Applying these criteria, Member States must then classify "the most suitable territories in number and size as SPAs for the conservation of these species". The purpose of taking special conservation measures is to ensure their survival and reproduction in their area of distribution. In doing so, Member States must take into account their protection requirements in the

[19] [1993] ECR I-4221, see paragraph 19 of the judgment.
[20] See paragraph 25 of the judgment.
[21] See paragraph 26 of the judgment.
[22] The Joint Committe for Nature Conservation (JNCC) has drawn up guidance for the selction of SPAs, considered below.

geographical land and sea area where the Directive applies. In *Lappel Bank*, the Advocate General stated that this language confirms that the criteria governing the application of Article 4(1) are exclusively objective/ornithological in character, and compliance with those criteria is to be evaluated at the level of the Community, that is to say, what is relevant is a species' survival in its area of distribution in the Community as a whole rather than simply in the individual Member State[23]. The position is similar in relation to Article 4(2) species.

Article 4(2) then requires similar measures to those set out in Article 4(1) to be taken for regularly occurring migratory species not listed in Annex I. In relation to migratory species, Member States must bear in mind their need for protection in the geographical land and sea area where the Directive applies, "as regards their breeding, moulting and wintering areas and staging posts along their migration routes".

As regards the particular types of habitat to be classified, the only specification in this regard appears in Article 4(2) relating to migratory species which requires Member States to "pay particular attention to the protection of wetlands and particularly to wetlands of international importance". This last requirement brings obligations under the Ramsar Convention[24] into the scope of the directive. Interestingly, nearly all the cases brought to the ECJ on the interpretation of Article 4 have concerned, at least in part, Ramsar sites.

The reference to protection requirements in the area where the directive applies seems to indicate that Member States must take account of the conservation status and protection requirements for the species across the Community as a whole and not just in relation to their own territory. A duty is placed on the Commission to take appropriate initiatives with a view to ensuring that areas classified under Articles 4(1) and (2) "form a coherent whole" (having received all relevant information from the Member States). There is, however, nothing in the wild birds directive akin to the detailed procedure and timetable for the establishment of the Natura 2000 network of special areas of conservation (SACs) which was subsequently introduced by the habitats directive and which also incorporates special protection areas classified under the wild birds directive[25]. It is not entirely

[23] See para 74 of the Opinion.
[24] See Chapter 2 - Part I.
[25] See chapter 2 - Part I. As indicated in the Commission's Third Report on the wild birds Directive, the UK designated 50 new SPAs during the period 1993-1995.

clear therefore to what extent the status of the species in question in other Member States is relevant to the classification of a Member State's own SPAs. It is arguable that Member States are not obliged to compensate for under-implementation in other states by classifying more SPAs in their own territory. On the other hand, it appears that in considering the range and behaviour of a species, account should be taken of the presence of a species in the Community as a whole.

Selection of SPAs: Economic and Non-scientific Interests

The issue of whether economic requirements may be taken into account in the process of classifying SPAs has been raised before the ECJ in a number of cases. The Court has consistently rejected arguments put by Member States that economic requirements could be taken into account in classifying SPAs under Article 4(1) and (2).

In *Santona Marshes*, the Commission brought infraction proceedings against Spain for violations of Articles 3 and 4 of the wild birds directive. The case involved Spain=s failure to designate or protect the Santona Marshes, a wetland of international importance which hosted both Annex I birds and other migratory species. Spain had designated part of the Santona Marshes as a nature reserve but the Court held that this was not adequate to fulfil the requirements of Article 4 of the directive: the nature reserve did not cover the whole of the marshes nor were the protective measures adopted sufficient. The Court referred to the fact that no management plan had been approved and this meant that potentially damaging activities had not been identified. Article 4(1) and (2) had not therefore been fulfilled[26]. The Court ruled that although Member States did have a certain margin of discretion with regard to the choice of special protection areas: "the classification of those areas is nevertheless subject to certain ornithological criteria determined by the directive...[27]".

These issues were also raised in the *Lappel Bank case*. Lappel Bank was an area of 22 hectares of intertidal mudflat which was geographically part of the Medway Estuary and Marshes. The latter being wetlands of international importance for a range and substantial number of wildfowl and water species including two Annex 1 species. The area was used as a breeding ground and wintering area, and also as a staging post during migration. Lappel Bank itself provided feeding and sheltering grounds for a number of waders and wildfowl (although none listed in Annex I of the

[26] See paragraph 30-32 of the judgment.
[27] Paragraph 26 of the judgment.

directive). The area bordered the Port of Sheerness, the fifth largest commercial port in the UK. In 1993, the Secretary of State for the Environment decided to exclude Lappel Bank from the area to be designated as the Medway Estuary and Marshes SPA. He acknowledged that this had been done in order to allow further reclamation of Lappel Bank and safeguard the continued viability of the Port of Sheerness which was a significant contributor to the economy of the surrounding area, which suffered from high unemployment. He stressed that the decision was an exceptional one. That decision was challenged by the RSPB on the grounds that it contravened the wild birds directive by taking account of economic considerations when classifying an SPA.

The case went all the way to the House of Lords which made a preliminary reference to the ECJ on the issues raised. The House of Lords asked the ECJ to rule on the extent to which, if at all, economic considerations could be taken into account in the decision as to whether a site was to be classified as an SPA under the directive. It also asked the Court to rule on whether economic requirements could be taken into account in more narrowly defined circumstances. The ECJ had previously addressed a similar issue in relation to the protection of SPAs in the *Leybucht Dykes case*[28] (considered below). In the course of the national proceedings in *Lappel Bank*, both sides had argued that the issue was "acte claire" in their favour and in the Court of Appeal, two judges held that it was acte clair one way and a third, acte clair the other. A result the House of Lords found "surprising".

In his Opinion in the case, the Advocate General said that the argument against taking economic requirements into account was based primarily on the general scheme of the Directive. That general scheme: "indicates that bird conservation is the rule, and that Member States may only rely on other requirements to mitigate that rule where expressly so authorised" (para 53). He also noted that: "it is the Directive itself which strikes the balance as regards classification of SPAs, rather than leaving discretion to individual Member States to find their own balance." (Para. 50). He pointed out that, in its previous case law on the interpretation of Article 2 of the Directive, the Court had supported the view that the Directive itself has struck the necessary balance between economic and ecological factors and that to accept the arguments of the UK would amount to interpreting Article 2 as an autonomous derogation which the Court had consistently rejected (para 60). He also pointed out that allowing Member

[28] Case 57/89 Commission v Germany [1991] ECR I-883.

States to take economic requirements into account in classifying SPAs would render the regime for the protection of endangered birds under Article 4 essentially the same as the regime for other wild birds under Article 3 (paragraph 66).

In answer to the first question posed by the House of Lords, the Court followed the conclusion of the Advocate General and ruled that Member States were not authorised to take into account economic requirements when designating SPAs under paragraphs (1) and (2) of Article 4. The ECJ pointed out that the regime laid down in Article 4 was one of special protection for birds which were either the most endangered in the Community (Annex I species) or constituted a common heritage (migratory species). Citing its previous judgment in *C435/92 Animaux Sauvages*[29], it went on to note that Article 2 of the directive, to which Article 4, in contrast to Article 3, did not refer, did not constitute an autonomous derogation within the scheme of the directive. These factors confirmed that the ecological requirements laid down in Article 4 paragraphs (1) and (2) did not have to be balanced against the other interests referred to in Article 2. As it had stated in the *Santona Marshes* judgment, the ornithological criteria laid down in paragraphs (1) and (2) of Article 4 were what should guide Member States in classifying SPAs and nothing else[30].

The second question referred by the House of Lords asked whether economic requirements could be taken into account in more narrowly defined circumstances. First, the Court was asked whether Member States, when classifying SPAs, were permitted to take account of economic requirements where these constituted a general interest superior to that represented by the ecological objective of the directive. The concept of a "superior general interest" was taken from the Court's judgment in the *Leybucht Dykes case*. In that case the Court had ruled that Member States were permitted, under Article 4(4) of the wild birds directive, to reduce the area of a designated SPA in exceptional circumstances in order to protect a general interest superior to that represented by the ecological objective of the directive. The Court had ruled in that case that economic requirements could *not* constitute such an interest. In considering the issue further in *Lappel Bank*, the Court also referred to its ruling in *Santona Marshes* that, in relation to Article 4 taken as a whole, economic requirements could not constitute such an interest. Accordingly, the ECJ ruled in *Lappel Bank* that

[29] C-435/92 [1994] ECR I-67. Other earlier rulings of the Court also found that Article 2 did not constitute an autonomous derogation, see Chapter 2, Part II.
[30] Paragraphs 23-27 of the judgment.

Member States were *not* entitled to take into account when designating an SPA or drawing up its boundaries under paragraphs (1) and (2) of Article 4, economic requirements as constituting a general interest superior to that represented by the ecological objective of the directive. In contrast to the Advocate General, the Court refused to take a view on whether non-economic interests constituting a superior general interest could be taken into account[31] (the Advocate General had said that they could be[32].

In the second part of its second question, the House of Lords had asked the Court to rule on whether Member States could take account of economic requirements to the extent that they reflected "imperative reasons of overriding public interest" of the kind referred to in Article 6(4) of the Habitats Directive (which dealt with the circumstances under which plans or projects having significant adverse effects on an SAC might nevertheless be proceeded with). Once again, the Court ruled that Member States were *not* permitted to take such interests into account in designating or drawing up the boundaries of SPAs. The Court noted that, having regard to its judgment in *Leybucht Dykes*, Article 6(4) of the habitats directive (which by virtue of Article 7 of the habitats directive applied to SPAs) widened the grounds for encroaching on the area of a designated SPA to include economic and social grounds. It also noted however that Article 7 of the habitats directive only amended Article 4(4) of the wild birds directive and had not amended paragraphs (1) and (2) of Article 4, thus economic requirements did not enter into consideration at the stage of classifying an SPA and could only be taken into account in the circumstances set out in Article 6(4) once the site was *already* designated.

Following the *Lappel Bank case*, the UK Government issued a statement acknowledging that the ECJs ruling in Lappel Bank meant that Member States could only take account of scientific matters in selecting SPAs and identifying their boundaries and stating that this also applied to designation of SACs[33].

In both *Santona Marshes* and *Lappel Bank*, it had been argued by the Governments concerned that they had a discretion in deciding which areas were suitable to be classified as SPAs which permitted them not to classify the areas in question. In *Santona Marshes*, the Court ruled that although Member States did have a certain margin of discretion with regard to the choice of special protection areas: "the classification of those areas is

[31] See paragraph 31 of the judgment.
[32] See paragraph 94 of his Opinion.
[33] See Government Statement dated May 1998, available on the EWD website.

nevertheless subject to certain ornithological criteria determined by the directive...[34] " In his Opinion in *Lappel Bank*, Advocate General Fenelly stated that the discretion afforded to Member States under Article 4(1) and (2) is "biological rather than political". This appears to mean that the designation of SPAs is really a determination based on the application of objective scientific criteria rather than the application of the exercise of a political discretion. The Advocate General went so far as to say that, even where two similar sites had been identified as "suitable" under the terms of the directive, Member States were obliged to classify both rather than choose one on the basis that the other was in the vicinity of an industrial development[35]. That this discretion is more akin to a duty to simply determine at the national level which sites are most suitable appears to be confirmed by the Court's judgment in *Case 3/96 Commission v Netherlands* which states that, having applied the ornithological criteria laid down in the directive, Member States are required to classify all suitable sites[36].

The scope of the discretion so far as the wild birds directive is concerned appears therefore to be well settled. So far as the selection of sites under the Habitats Directive is concerned however, the extent to which economic and social requirements can be taken into account, at least at the Community level, is not fully resolved. The judgment of the ECJ in *Case C371/98 Rv Secretary of State for the Environment ex parte First Corporate Shipping Ltd* confirms that such requirements are *not* to be taken into account at the national level when Member States submit a list of eligible sites to the Commission. However, the Advocate General in that case argued that the taking into account of social and economic factors at the second stage of selection (which occurs at the Community level) might be permitted. The Court did not rule on the issue[37].

Sufficient SPAs: Case 3/96 Commission v Netherlands

The question of whether a Member States could be held to have failed to designate a sufficient number and area overall of suitable sites under Article 4(1) arose in *Commission v Netherlands*. The Commission considered that the Netherlands had violated Article 4(1) by failing to classify a sufficient number of SPAs . The Netherlands argued that it had classified a sufficient number of sites, taking into account the balance between conservation interests and economic and recreational interests and that it

[34] Paragraph 26 of the judgment.
[35] See para's 79 and 88 of the Opinion.
[36] Case 3/96 paragraphs 61-62 of the judgment.
[37] See Chapter 2 - Part I.

had also adopted other special conservation measures. The Commission then brought infraction proceedings in the ECJ.

One of the arguments raised by the Commission was that the obligation under Article 4(1) was both quantitative (number and area of SPAs) and qualitative (type of site) and that the Netherlands had not designated sufficient sites in either respect. The Court accepted that Article 4(1) incorporated both types of obligation but said that a complaint about sufficiency of designation under Article 4(1) did not necessarily cover the qualitative aspect of the obligation and as the arguments about qualitative insufficiency (insufficient freshwater sites) had only been raised at the contentious stage of the infraction procedure this part of the case was ruled inadmissible. This indicates that so far as any future proceedings are concerned, any allegation as to qualitative insufficiency must be clearly spelled out and will not be implied into a charge that an insufficient area or number of sites has been classified.

In order to show that an insufficient number and area of sites had been designated, the Commission relied on a scientific report entitled "Inventory of Important Areas in the European Community" published in 1989, AIBA89"[38]. The report had been drawn up for the relevant Directorate General by bird conservation organisations in conjunction with Commission experts[39]. That report had identified 70 sites and a total area of 797, 920 hectares as suitable for classification as SPAs in the Netherlands. The Commission argued that in designating a number of SPAs which fell far below the number proposed in IBA89, the Netherlands had "manifestly exceeded" its discretion under Article 4(1)[40]. Among the arguments presented by the Netherlands in its defence, it argued that it had designated SPAs on the basis of a balance between the interests of conservation and economic and recreational needs. It also relied on the fact that it had taken conservation measures other than designating SPAs.It argued that it was not appropriate for the Court to base its assessment on IBA89 since that report did not form part of the directive.

The Court rejected the suggestion that the adoption of other conservation measures was an alternative to the classification of SPAs and

[38] The Commission had sought to rely on a more recent report, IBA94, but this was excluded as inadmissible since it appeared to relate to a period after the period for compliance with the Reasoned Opinion and it was settled law that the Court could not take account of developments subsequent to that deadline.

[39] See paragraph 68 of the judgment.

[40] Paragraph 42 of the judgment. The Netherlands had designated 23 sites with a total area of 327, 602 hectares.The Commission argued that this was less that half of what was required according to the report.

ruled that where Annex I species were found on a Member States territory, it was obliged to classify SPAs for that species[41] . Otherwise the special protection regime for endangered species would be no different to the general regime under Article 3 of the directive. It also noted that the objective of establishing a coherent network of sites under Article 4(3) would be undermined if the interpretation put forward by the Netherlands were adopted. Referring to its judgments in *Lappel Bank* and *Santona Marshes*, the Court then ruled that economic requirements could not be taken into account in classifying SPAs and that whilst Member States enjoyed a certain discretion in designating sites, this was subject to the ornithological criteria laid down in the Directive.[42] The Court concluded that where it appeared that a Member State had classified a number and area of sites which were manifestly less that the number and area considered most suitable for conservation of the species in question , it would be held to have violated Article 4(1). It was not, as the Netherlands had argued, necessary for the Commission to establish site specific infringements in each case.

As to the legitimacy of relying on IBA89 in order to assess how many sites should have been designated, the Court accepted that the report was not legally binding, but noted that the Netherlands had failed to produce any scientific evidence of its own or to challenge the validity of IBA89 itself. In these circumstances, said the Court, the inventory, by reason of its acknowledged scientific value, could be used by the Court as a basis for reference for assessing the Netherlands' compliance with its obligations[43] . Nor did the Court need to consider whether the application of the ornithological criteria in IBA89 could lead different entities to reach different results since no evidence to this effect had been produced and the mere possibility that it might occur was not enough[44] . Finally, the Court ruled that by classifying as SPAs, territories whose number and area were clearly smaller than the number and area suitable for classification under Article 4(1), the Netherlands had breached its obligations under the directive.

This ruling implies that any Member State wishing to defend itself against a charge that it has violated Article 4(1) in this way will need to present cogent scientific evidence to justify the extent of designation in its territory, and to either challenge any contrary suggestion in an IBA or other report of similar standing. The question then is whether the Member State

[41] Paragraphs 55-56 of the judgment.
[42] Ibid, paragraphs 59-62, see also discussion above.
[43] Ibid paragraph 70. The ECJ confirmed this approach in Case 374/98 Commission v France (Basses Corbieres), judgment 7 December 2000, at para 25 of the judgment.
[44] Ibid paragraph 71.

should be given the benefit of the doubt if there is genuine scientific uncertainty, or whether the Court would apply the precautionary principle and accept the more extensive designation as the one required under Article 4(1). It should be remembered however that in relation to individual sites, the Court has not always accepted the Commission's view that a site ought to have been designated as an SPA, *Case C-166/97 Commission v France (Seine Estuary)*[45].

The Court did not find it necessary to address other arguments raised in the case including the Commission's argument that a decline in certain Annex I species was evidence that an insufficient number of sites had been designated. The Netherlands had said that a decline in population could have occurred for reasons other than insufficient designation. What might be made of such an argument in any future case remains to be seen but again the weight of the precautionary principle raises interesting issues in this regard.

In its Third Report on the application of the directive, the Commission noted that by the end of 1995, only five Member States had designated more than half of the IBAs within their territory[46]. The Commission then brought proceedings against a number of other Member States for failure to classify sufficient SPAs. The Commission, citing *Commission v Netherlands* in support, relied on the IBA inventory as evidence of their failure to designate sufficient sites. Germany, for example was said to have designated only 40% of the area required[47]. A number of these cases have now been brought to a successful conclusion by the Commission, for example in *Case C-378/01 Commission v Italy*[48], the ECJ upheld the Commission's complaint against Italy, in reliance on the IBA, for failing to classify sufficient SPA's, holding that:

"... in view of the scientific nature of the IBA Inventory 89, and of the absence of any scientific evidence adduced by the Italian Republic, tending particularly to show that the obligations flowing from Article 4(1) and (2) of the Directive could be satisfied by classifying as SPAs sites other than those appearing in that inventory and covering a smaller total area, that inventory, although not legally binding on the Member State concerned,

[45] See para 47 of the judgment. In that case it was not sufficient that a site had been included in a national inventory of sites of ornithological interest and the Court also noted that an impact study had concluded that none of the rarest species on the site would be affected by the development at issue.

[46] See COM(2000) 180 final at para 3.3.

[47] See Commission Press Release, IP 99/514, July 15 1999.

[48] Judgment of 20 March 2003.

can be used by the Court as a basis of reference for assessing whether the Italian Republic has classified a sufficient number and area of territories as SPAs for the purposes of the abovementioned provisions of the Directive (see, to that effect, *Commission* v *Netherlands*, cited above, paragraphs 68 to 70)."(paragraph 18 of the judgment)

Protection and Management of Special Protection Areas

As the Commission points out in its Third Report on the directive, the protection of wildlife very often involves management of their habitats and this assumes a good level of knowledge about the factors which influence the presence of a species in a given habitat. Such knowledge is often partial or lacking. The Commission notes the importance in this regard of Article 10 of the directive which requires Member States to carry out research work for the protection and management of bird populations[49]. Work carried out pursuant to Article 10 will clearly be relevant to the implementation of the obligation to manage SPAs under Article 4 in order to avoid their deterioration or disturbance of the species concerned.

The level of protection to be afforded in the SPAs has been strictly construed by the ECJ. It has ruled that Article 4(1) and (2) requires the Member States to provide SPAs with a legal protection regime capable of ensuring both the survival and reproduction of Annex I and migratory species, *Case C-355/90 Santona Marshes*[50]. In *Case C-96/98 Commission v France (Marais Poitevin*[51]*)*, France had defended itself against the charge that it had failed to take adequate steps to protect the site in question by seeking to rely on a number of general measures including legislation relating to the protection of water and certain agri-environment measures. The Court found that these were insufficient: so far as the Water Law was concerned, to the extent that it included provisions relating to water management it was not such as to ensure sufficient protection for the purposes of Article 4(1) and (2). In relation to the agri-environment measures, the Court noted that these were voluntary and purely hortatory and thus incapable of supplementing effectively the protection regime for the SPAs. France had also raised a further argument, which was that the responsibility for the reduction in wetlands rested primarily with the Common Agricultural Policy (CAP) and not solely with the French authorities. The Court said that even assuming that this were the case and that "a certain lack of consistency between various Community policies" were shown, this could still not

[49] COM(2000) 180 final at para 5.1.

[50] See also Case C-166/97 Commission v France (Seine Estuary) 18 March 1999.

[51] C-96/98 Commission v France [1999] ECR I-8531.

authorise a Member State to avoid its obligations under the wild birds directive, in particular under the first sentence of Article 4(4) (which applied here).[52] This indicates that the measures required under Article 4 (arguably also as amended by the habitats directive) must be focused on the protection of the bird species concerned and binding. Nor will undoubted perverse incentives generated by the CAP provide a defence in relation to damage suffered in an SPA or in a site which should have been so classified.[53]

A central issue in the implementation of the directive is of course the degree of protection which must be afforded to an SPA. As with the question of classifying SPAs, a central concern has been whether conflicting interests, particularly economic interests, can ever justify departing from the requirements of Article 4. The measures to be taken to protect SPAs were originally all set out in paragraph (4) of Article 4 of the directive. Article 4(4) has now been amended by Article 7 of the habitats directive so that the first sentence of Article 4(4) of the wild birds directive is replaced by paragraphs (2), (3) and (4) of Article 6 of the Habitats Directive[54]. In considering the effects of the habitat directive amendment on the protection afforded to SPAs, it is notable that whilst the requirements of Article 6(2) are very similar to those of the first sentence of Article 4(4) of the unamended wild birds directive[55], the significant change in provision for protection of SPAs, particularly in the light of the Court's case law on the interpretation of Article 4(4), results from the application of Articles 6(3) and (4) of the habitats directive to their protection and management.

The application of Articles 6(3) and (4) of the habitats Directive to SPAs introduces significant changes to the protection and management of SPAs: an Aappropriate assessment is required for all plans and projects not directly connected with the management of the site and if the assessment reveals that the plan or project will adversely affect the integrity of the site the plan can only be carried out for Aimperative reasons of overriding public interest, which may include economic and social factors. In addition, compensatory measures must be taken and the Commission duly notified. There are stricter requirements for sites hosting priority species or habitats. Article 6 is considered in more detail in Chapter 3 - Part I.

[52] See para 40 of the judgment.
[53] On agriculture and habitat protection see Chapter 7 - Part II.
[54] The deadline for transposition of the habitats directive was 11 June 1994.
[55] As originally enacted, the first sentence of Article 4(4) required Member States to "take appropriate steps to avoid pollution or deterioration of habitats or any disturbances affecting the birds, in so far as these would be significant having regard to the objectives of [Article 4]."

Overall, it would appear that the level of protection for classified SPAs under the amended regime is reduced in that the scope of derogation is wider and encompasses social and economic considerations in certain circumstances. These provisions are considered in Chapter 3 - Part I but it in order to understand the implications of the amendments it is worth considering the interpretation of the unamended Article 4(4) in the light of the Court's judgment in the *Leybucht Dykes case*. This regime will continue to apply to sites which have not been classified as SPAs but which should have been so classified, as confirmed by the ECJ in *Case 374/98 Commission v France.*

Leybucht Dykes and *Santona Marshes* : Protection of SPAs Prior to the Entry Into Force of the Habitats Directive

In the *Leybucht Dyke* case[56] , the Court considered the question as to whether-and if so under what conditions-the Member States were authorised to reduce the size of an SPA and to what extent other interests could be taken into account in doing so. The case concerned infringement proceedings brought against Germany in which the Commission sought a declaration from the Court that, by planning or undertaking dyke-building works detrimental to the habitat of birds in an SPA, Germany had breached Article 4 of the directive.

Germany had argued that the sole purpose of the works was to secure the safety of the dyke and that Article 4(4) of the directive required a balance to be struck between the various public interests likely to be affected by the management of an SPA and that Member States had a wide discretion in this field. The Commission accepted that such works were acceptable in the case of a threat to human life but only on condition that the necessary measures were restricted to the minimum required, which was not the case here. The UK intervened in the case in support of Germany and argued that there would only be a significant effect within the meaning of the first sentence of Article 4(4) if the deterioration in question was such as to threaten the survival or reproduction of a protected species (which was not the case here) and that within the context of Article 4(4), account could be taken of other important public interests including those referred to in Article 2 of the directive.

The Court did not accept the arguments put by Germany and the UK as to the scope of the discretion available to Member States under Article 4(4). Whilst acknowledging that Member States did have a certain discretion

[56] Case 57/89 Commission v Germany [1991] ECR I-883

with regard to choice of the territories which were most suitable for classification as SPAs under Article 4(1), it ruled that "they do not have the same discretion under Article 4(4) of the directive in modifying or reducing the extent of the areas, since they have themselves acknowledged in their declarations that those areas contain the most suitable environments for the species listed in Annex I to the directive." If that were not so, the Court pointed out: "Member States could unilaterally escape from the obligations imposed on them by Article 4(4) of the directive with regard to SPAs"[57].

The Court concluded that "the power of Member States to reduce the extent of an SPA can be justified only on exceptional grounds" These grounds had to correspond to "a general interest which is superior to the general interest represented by the ecological objective of the directive" and the interests referred to in Article 2, namely economic and recreational requirements did not enter into consideration[58].

In relation to the facts of the case, the Court was of the view that the danger of flooding and the protection of the coast constituted "sufficiently serious reasons" to justify dyke works and the strengthening of coastal structures "as long as those measures are confined to a strict minimum and involve only the smallest possible reduction of the SPA". In this respect, the Court accepted the proportionality test argued for by the Commission. It added a caveat to that test, however in relation to cases where there were offsetting ecological benefits. As regarded that part of the project which was influenced by a concern to ensure access for fishing vessels, the Court confirmed that it was in principle incompatible with the directive to take account of such an interest. Nevertheless, as that part of the project had "specific positive consequences for the habitat of birds", the desire to safeguard the fishing port could be taken into account in order to justify the decision on the line of the new dyke because there were "offsetting ecological benefits, and solely for that reason"[59]. The Court did not address the other interests which the Commission alleged had been taken into account, presumably however same principle should apply.

The range of measures which a Member State may be required to take, in order to fulfil its obligations under Article 4(4), is indicated by the *Santona Marshes* case. In *Santona Marshes* the Commission had criticised Spain for failing to prevent a number of development projects and activities which had adverse effects on the site. In relation to the development projects,

[57] See para 20 of the judgment.
[58] See para 22 of the judgment.
[59] See para 26 of the judgment.

which included the construction of a road and the authorization of aquaculture facilities, Spain had argued that these were justified on economic grounds. The Court rejected Spain's economic defences of the projects emphasised, echoing its judgment in *Leybucht Dykes*, that economic considerations could not justify a derogation from the protective requirements of Article 4(4) (paragraph 45). The Court also ruled that Spain was under a positive duty to protect the site from pollution to the extent, where necessary, of providing a system for the treatment of waste which would prevent the pollution of the site. Spain had argued that it was not obliged to do this because the directive did not specifically require it[60]. Given the similar wording, it is likely that the court's case law on the interpretation of Article 4(4) sheds light on the interpretation of Article 6(2) of the habitats directive.

In *Santona Marshes* the Court rejected an argument put forward by Spain that it could not be in violation of Article 4(4) and Article 4(1) and (2) at the same time since the duty to protect a site did not arise until it had been classified[61] The Court noted that the protective objectives of the directive would be undermined if Spain's interpretation were adopted.

UK Implementation of Articles 3 and 4

The UK's implementation of the habitat protection requirements of the wild birds directive is based on SSSI designation under the 1981 Act[62] and development control policies as laid out in planning guidance, currently PPG No 9: Nature Conservation. This is now supplemented by the Habitats Regulations as regards SPAs since they have been incorporated into the Natura 2000 network of European sites[63].

UK SPAs

A list of UK SPAs, giving their size and location, is available on the JNCC website (www.jncc.gov.uk) As at July 2002, there were 237 SPAS in the UK (87 in England) covering 1,250,000 hectares (597,000 hectares in England)[64].

[60] Paragraphs 51-52 judgment.
[61] Paragraph 22 of the judgment.
[62] For a discussion of the relationship between the two designations see The Honourable Patrick Fisher v English Nature CO/3788/2001, judgment of 4 July 2003
[63] See regulation 10(1)(d) of the Conservation (Natural Habitats &c) Regulations 1994 SI 1994/2716 and see further Chapter 3 - Part II.
[64] Figures obtained from the DEFRA website, checked 27 November 2003.

Selection of UK SPAs

Guidelines for the selection of UK SPAs have been adopted by the JNCC (these are available on their website, see above). These set out a two stage process whereby sites likely to qualify are identified and then assessed against further criteria to determine which are the most suitable for classification. Stage One addresses a range of factors including the number or percentage of birds concerned. Stage Two looks at factors such as population size and density, breeding success, naturalness and history of occupancy, among others.

Protection of UK Sites

Following the entry into force of the Conservation (Natural Habitats) Regulations 1994, classified SPAs became "European sites" for the purposes of those regulations[65]. The protective regime applied to European sites is discussed in detail in Chapter 3 - Part I.

[65] Regulation 10(1)(d) of the 1994 Regulations, SI 1994/2716.

B. Ramsar Sites

The Ramsar Convention

The Convention on Wetlands of International Importance, Especially as Wildfowl Habitat was adopted in 1971 at Ramsar in Iran and is commonly known as the Ramsar Convention[1]. Under the Convention, each Party is required to designate suitable wetlands within its territory for inclusion in a list of wetlands of international importance (Article 2(1). Parties must then formulate their planning so as to promote the conservation of the wetlands included in the list and as far as possible the wise use of wetlands in their territory (Article 3.1). Parties must also promote conservation by establishing nature reserves on wetlands whether they are included on the list or not (Article 4). Where a party deletes or modifies the boundaries of any wetlands on the List it must so far as possible take compensatory measures. The UK ratified the Convention in 1976[2].

The EU wild birds directive implements provisions of the Ramsar Convention in the protection it affords to SPAs which are Ramsar sites.

The Countryside and Rights of Way Act 2000

In May 2000, the Government had announced its intention to afford Ramsar sites the same protection as was provided to SACs and SPAs[3]. During the passage of the Countryside Bill, those calling for the introduction of specific statutory provision for Ramsar sites pointed out that whilst Ramsar sites were already designated as SSSI's, and in most cases as SPAs or SACs, the specific interest of the site on which its Ramsar designation was based might be different to its interest as for example an SPA and it was important to protect the full extent of that interest. It was also important to recognise in legislation the international importance of the sites[4] and to ensure that compensatory measures were taken should any destruction of the site be permitted for the purposes of development.

Section 77 of the 2000 Act introduces a new provision into the 1981 Act, section 37a which places Ramsar sites on a specific statutory

[1] The Convention was amended in 1982 by the Paris Protocol and in 1987 by the Regina Amendments.

[2] The Convention entered into force for the UK on 5 May 1976.

[3] See DETR's Policy Statement on Ramsar Sites, May 2000.

[4] See for example Hansard 14 June 2000, col1036 House of Commons.

footing for the first time. Section 37a provides that when a wetland in Great Britain has been designated under Article 2(1) of the Convention for inclusion on the list of sites of international importance, the Secretary of State must notify English Nature and or the Countryside Council for Wales as appropriate. These agencies must in turn notify the relevant local planning authority, the owner or occupier of the site, the Environment Agency and every relevant undertaker and internal drainage board whose works may affect the site.

CHAPTER 3

NATURA 2000 AND SPECIAL AREAS OF CONSERVATION (HABITATS DIRECTIVE)

The Habitats Directive and Natura 2000

The Habitats Directive[1], adopted on 21 May 1992, is now the centrepiece of European conservation legislation. It serves to implement the European Union's international obligations under a number of environmental treaties including the Convention on Biological Diversity and the Berne Convention and has provided a new and strengthened framework for UK law on the conservation of wildlife, in particular in relation to those natural habitats and species listed in the annexes to the directive. The UK has sought to dovetail the requirements of the directive with pre-existing national conservation law rather than reconfigure the whole system. This has made the structure of UK conservation law rather complicated but has ensured that the new protection for habitats sits alongside the protection afforded to SSSI's[2].

The directive is expressly concerned with contributing towards ensuring "biodiversity", although this term is not defined in the directive[3] (Article 2(1)). The mechanisms used are a combination of the traditional, such as site specific protection and the more innovative, in particular the creation of an ecologically coherent network of protected sites and requirements to maintain nature corridors. The directive does not elaborate on some of the more novel implications of protecting biodiversity however, such as ensuring genetic diversity within a species-time will tell whether this can be addressed through traditional measures or whether the legislation needs to focus specifically on such issues[4]: The directive is to achieve its aims through the conservation of natural habitats and wild

[1] Council Directive 92/43/EEC of 21 May 1992 on the conservation of natural habitats and of wild fauna and flora, OJ L No 206/7 as amended by Council Directive 97/62/EC of 27 October 1997 adapting (Directive 92/43)to technical and scientific progress.

[2] See Chapter 1 - Part I.

[3] This appears to be the first reference to biodiversity in Community conservation legislation and probably reflects the use of the term in the Convention on Biological Diversity (CBD). The range of concerns encompassed in the CBD however clearly goes far wider than the scope of the habitats directive including as it does issues such as access to genetic resources as well as more traditional conservation concerns.

[4] The ECJ has addressed the issue of genetic pollution in the case of van Feesten. See chapter 2 - Part I.

flora and fauna: measures taken under the directive must be designed to maintain or restore, at a "favourable conservation status", natural habitats and species of wild fauna and flora (Article 2). Account is to be taken of economic, social and cultural requirements and regional and local characteristics when these measures are taken. In order to achieve its aims, the directive provides for both habitat and species protection[5] measures, but its main innovation is the establishment of "a coherent European ecological network of special areas of conservation" to be known as Natura 2000 (Article 3(1)). This chapter considers the habitat protection provisions of the directive, in particular the establishment of Natura 2000 and the protection afforded to the individual sites which make up the network.

Natura 2000 is to be composed of sites hosting the natural habitat types listed in Annex I and habitats of those species listed in Annex II of the directive (most of the latter are also listed in Annex IV of the directive dealing with species protection). These sites are to be known as "special areas of conservation" (SACs). The habitat types and species marked with an asterisk in Annexes I and II are "priority" species and habitats which are afforded particularly strict protection (see further below).

The natural habitat types in Annex I are grouped into nine main types including coastal, freshwater, grassland and forest habitat among others. These are then subdivided into specific natural habitat types, so that, for example, included under Forests are "Forests of Temperate Europe" and included in that category are "Caledonian forest" (a priority habitat) and "old sessile oak woods with Ilex and Blechnum in the British Isles". In addition to the SACs designated under the habitats directive, the Natura 2000 network will also include the special protection areas (SPAs) classified by Member States under the wild birds Directive[6]. The overall aim of Natura 2000, as stated in Article 3(1) of the directive, is to enable the natural habitat types and habitats of listed species to be maintained or , where appropriate, restored to a "favourable conservation status" in their natural range.

The Directive has been criticised for as being too "static" since it adopts a "no net loss" approach to biodiversity and does not provide for the alteration of site boundaries to take account of environmental change, for example in relation to a dynamically changing coastline. In its Report on UK Biodiversity, the House of Commons Select Committee on Environment recommended that the Government press the European

[5] See Part II on Species Protection.

[6] Council Directive 79/409/EEC of 2 April 1979 on the conservation of wild birds, OJ L 103, 25.4.1979, p.1. See Chapter 2 - Part I.

Commission to amend the Directive so as to reflect the impact of environmental change upon biodiversity[7]. There was also criticism that marine sites had been particularly neglected in the designation of sites for Natura 2000

Favourable Conservation Status

The conservation status of a natural habitat is defined in Article 1 of the Directive as meaning the sum of the influences acting on a natural habitat and its typical species that may affect its long-term natural distribution, structure and functions, as well as the long-term survival of its typical species. "Favourable conservation status" of a natural habitat occurs when its natural range and the areas it covers within that range are stable or increasing; and the specific structure and functions which are necessary for its long-term maintenance exist and are likely to exist for the foreseeable future *and* the conservation status of its typical species is favourable as defined in Article 1(i).

The conservation status of a species means the sum of influences acting on the species concerned that may affect the long-term distribution and abundance of its populations with the territory covered by the directive (as to which see below). Species will be taken as having *favourable* conservation status where population dynamics data indicate that the species is maintaining itself on a long-term basis as a viable component of its natural habitats; its natural range is neither being reduced nor is likely to be reduced for the foreseeable future and there is, and will probably continue to be, a sufficiently large habitat to maintain its populations on a long-term basis[8].

Priority Species and Priority Natural Habitat Types

The directive makes special provision for sites hosting "priority natural habitats" or "priority species". A priority natural habitat type is one which is in danger of disappearance, which is present in the European territory of the Member States to which the Treaty applies and "for the conservation of which the Community has particular responsibility" in view of the proportion of its natural range which falls within that area.

[7] Report on UK Biodiversity (HC 441) November 2000, Select Committee on Environment, Transport and the Regions Twentieth Report, see paragraphs 51-52.
[8] In its First Report on the implementation of the Directive (see further below) the UK commented that it would be helpful if EC-level discussions were held on the interpretation of the concept of favourable conservation status (see Executive Summary).

They are marked by an asterisk in Annex I. Examples of priority natural habitats occurring in the UK include turloughs; limestone pavements; active raised bogs and Caledonian forest.

Similarly, a priority species is one which falls within the endangered category as defined in the directive and for which the Community has particular responsibility in view of the proportion of its natural range which falls within the European territory of the Member States. These species are indicated by an asterisk in Annex II. The only priority species occurring in the UK is the plant, Western Rustwort (Marsupella profunda)

One consequence of a priority listing is that the Commission can initiate a consultation procedure where it considers that a Member State has failed to include such sites in its national list. Where "in exceptional cases", the Commission finds that a national list fails to mention a site hosting a priority natural habitat type or priority species, Article 5 of the Directive requires the initiation of a bilateral consultation procedure between the Member State concerned and the Commission. The Commission must base its view on "relevant and reliable scientific information" (Article 5(1)) and must consider the site to be essential for the maintenance of that priority natural habitat type or the survival of that priority species. If the dispute over inclusion of the site remains unresolved after a maximum of six months, the Commission must forward to the Council a proposal relating to the selection of the site as a site of Community importance (as to which see below). The Council, acting unanimously, must take a decision within three months of the proposal being referred to it. During the period of consultation, the site is subject to Article 6(2) of the Directive which means that the Member State must take appropriate steps to avoid deterioration of the habitat and disturbance of the species concerned, "in so far as these would be significant in relation to the objectives of the Directive.

The Contribution of the Member States to Natura 2000

Each Member State is to contribute to the creation of Natura 2000 "in proportion to the representation within its territory" of the Annex I natural habitat types and Annex II habitats of species (Article 3(2)).

The territorial scope of the directive is described as extending to "the European territory of the Member States to which the Treaty applies". This therefore excludes Member States' territory outside Europe such as the British Virgin Islands. In *R v Secretary of State for Trade and Industry ex parte Greenpeace (No 2)*[9], the question was raised to as the meaning of the reference to "territory" in the Directive and in particular whether this included the continental shelf (see below). The High Court held that the directive did extend to the continental shelf to a limit of 200 nautical miles and thus Member States were required to apply its provisions to the habitats and species present on the continental shelf in so far as these were listed in the Annexes.

Community co-financing is available to assist Member States with the cost of meeting their obligations to conserve and manage sites under Article 6(1) of the Directive.[10] Funds are available under the Financial Instrument for the Environment (LIFE)[11] which contains a component, LIFE-nature, the objective of which is to contribute to the implementation of the wild birds directive and the habitats directive, and in particular the Natura 2000 network[12]. The maximum rate for the co-financing of nature conservation projects is normally 50% (and 100% for what are known as accompanying measures) but is raised to 75% for projects concerning priority natural habitats or species (or bird species considered to be priority species by the wild birds directive committee). Before taking a decision on any funding proposal, the LIFE Regulation Committee must consult the committee established under the Habitats Directive. Examples of LIFE-funded projects in the UK include urgent action for the bittern (1996); the wet woods restoration project (1998) and the Lowland Limestone Pavement Rehabilitation Project (1999).[13] Article 8 also provides for co-financing and although it appears drawn to deal with Member States with disproportionate obligations with regard to priority habitat or species, the Commission appears to be prepared to take a wider view[14].

Timetable for the Establishment of Natura 2000

In contrast to the regime which governs the classification of SPAs under the wild birds directive, the habitats directive sets out a detailed and

[9] R v Secretary of State for Trade & Industry ex parte Greenpeace (No 2) (QBD) 2000 CMLR 94.
[10] Article 8 of the Directive.
[11] LIFE is now established under Regulation (EC) No 1655/2000 of the European Parliament and of the Council of 17 July 2000, OJ L No 192, 28/7/2000 p.0001 which repeals Council Regulation (EEC) No 1973/92 which formerly governed the fund.
[12] See Article 3 of the LIFE Regulation.
[13] See the UK's First Report on the implementation of the Directive, para 1.c.iii, at page 38.
[14] Official comment.

staged timetable for the establishment of Natura 2000 network and the designation of the SAC's which are to form, along with SPA's, the network of sites known as Natura 2000.

The timetable for the establishment of Natura 2000 is set out in Article 4 of the Directive and takes place in four stages: first, national lists of sites proposed for inclusion in Natura 2000 are drawn up by the Member States and sent to the Commission; second, these national lists are evaluated at the Community level and a draft list of "sites of Community importance" is drawn up; third this list of sites is formally adopted by the Commission under the committee procedure laid down in the directive; fourth, following the adoption of the list, Member States must designate the sites of Community Importance as SACs as soon as possible, and within six years at most. In practice the timetable has been subject to some delay as discussed below.

Stage One: Selection of Sites For the National List and Transmission to the Commission

Stage 1 is the drawing up by each Member State of a list of sites proposed for eventual inclusion in the network, indicating which Annex I natural habitat types and which Annex II species that are native to its territory the site hosts. This list was to be transmitted to the Commission, together with information on each site, within three years of the notification of the Directive[15] (before 11 June 1995). The information must include a map of the site, its name, location, extent and the data resulting from the application of Annex III criteria (conservation status)[16]. The national list of sites is to be drawn up on the basis of criteria set out in Article 4(1) and Annex III and "relevant scientific information". The Member State shall indicate which natural habitat types in Annex I and which species in Annex II, that are native to its territory, the sites host.

An Interpretation Manual has been produced setting out agreed common definitions for the natural habitat types listed in Annex I of the Directive. The Manual was drawn up by the Scientific Working Group established by the Habitats Committee[17] and contains descriptive sheets for natural habitat types listed in Annex I. The Manual explains that

[15] The Directive was notified on 10 June 1992.
[16] The format for this information is set out in Commission Decision 97/266/EC concerning a site format for proposed Natura 2000 sites, OJ No L107, 24/4/1997, p0001-0156.
[17] Second Edition EUR 15 (adopted 13.9.96) available on the Commission website.

Annex I was based on the CORINE biotopes project which was the only one existing at a European level at the time[18].

Selection Criteria

The assessment criteria for the selection of sites for the national list are set out in Annex III of the directive. As pointed out by the Advocate General in the *Lappel Bank case*, the criteria set out in Annex III are "entirely conservation related" (paragraph 70). The ECJ has confirmed that other considerations, in particular economic and social objectives, do not enter into account in the process of classifying sites either under the wild birds directive or selecting sites at Member State level for the purposes of the habitats directive[19]. So far as the Habitats Directive is concerned, in *Case C-371/98 R v Secretary of State for the Environment ex parte First Corporate Shipping*[20], the ECJ confirmed that under Article 4(1) of the Habitats Directive, a Member State was not permitted to take account of economic, social and cultural requirements or regional and local characteristics, as mentioned in Article 2(3) of the directive, when selecting and defining the boundaries of the sites to be proposed to the Commission as candidate SACs, eligible for identification as Sites of Community Importance.

In that case, FCS, the statutory port authority for the port of Bristol, sought judicial review of the Secretary of State's indication that he was minded to propose the Severn Estuary to the Commission as a candidate SAC (cSAC). FCS wished to develop port facilties in the area in question and argued that the Secretary of State was obliged to take account of economic, social and cultural requirements (such as implications for local employment), referred to in Article 2(3) of the Directive, when deciding which sites should be proposed. The Secretary of State argued that, in the light of the ECJ's ruling in *the Lappel Bank case*, he was precluded from taking such considerations into account at that stage. Rejecting the interpretation put forward by FCS, the ECJ, on referral from the High Court, ruled that, in order to produce a draft list of sites capable of leading to the establishment of a coherent network of SACs, the Commission had to have available "an exhaustive list of sites" having the relevant ecological interest at the national level. The list had to be drawn up on the basis of the Annex

[18] The UK's First Report on the implementation of the Directive (see further below) states that the Manual contains only general accounts of each habitat type and that in some cases definitions have been modified following discussion (para 1.a.i).

[19] See further below and in Chapter 2 - Part I.

[20] Judgment of 7 November 2000.

III criteria. Only in that way could the objective of the Directive, as set out in Article 3(1), be realised. The Court went on to point out that "favourable conservation status" had to be assessed in relation to the entire European territory of the Member States to which the Treaty applied and that a Member State would not be in a position, when drawing up its national list, to have precise detailed knowledge of habitats in other Member States[21].

The Court did not address the question (it was not asked to do so) of whether the Commission in considering the national lists and drawing up the list of sites of Community importance, was entitled to take economic and social considerations into account. In his Opinion however, Advocate General Leger, having taken the view that during the first stage of selection, preparation of national lists, consideration of social and economic factors was precluded, went on to say that it was not excluded that "in the second stage [the selection at Community level of the list of SCI's], economic and social requirements may justify a site... not being selected as an SCI, and consequently not being designated as an SAC"[22]. He went on to say, that at that stage, the approach of the Commission and the Member States, observing the objective of sustainable development and the principle of integration of the environmental dimension, must consist of assessing the interests concerned, assessing whether or not the maintenance of human activities in the area concerned may be reconciled with conservation, "and drawing the necessary consequences" as regards the setting up of an SAC. This raises the further issue of the content of the supporting information sent to the Commission with the SAC list. Should it include socio-economic information to inform the Commission when selecting SCIs to be agreed with the Member State? No public position on this issue appears to have been taken by either the Commission or the UK authorities on this point as yet.

Some further guidance on selection is also provided in Article 4 of the directive which states that, for animal species ranging over wide areas, these sites shall correspond to the places within the natural range of such species "which present the physical or biological factors essential to their life and reproduction". For aquatic species which range over wide areas, "such sites will be proposed only where there is a clearly identifiable area representing the physical and biological factors essential to their life and reproduction[23]".

---

[21] See para's 22-23 of the judgment of 7 November 2000.
[22] See Opinion dated 7 March 2000.
[23] In its First Report on the Directive, the UK notes that selection of sites for wide-ranging acquatic species such as the Harbour porpoise poses particular difficulties and is still the subject of discussion at the Community level, para 1.a.i.

Annex III refers to the two-stage process involved in establishing the list of sites of Community importance. In relation to stage one, paragraph A deals with the site assessment criteria for natural habitat types listed in Annex I and paragraph B lists the criteria for the habitats of species listed in Annex II.

In relation to natural habitat types, the criteria include the degree of representivity, the area of the site covered by the natural habitat type, the degree of conservation of the structure and functions and restoration possibilities and a global assessment of the value of the site for conservation of the natural habitat type concerned. The UK approach is that designation on the basis of restoration possibility is only specifically undertaken in relation to the feature "degraded raised bog" (for obvious reasons). However, given that the Annex III criteria are relative and that judgments as to FCS appear to be trend based it may be found, following selection that a site is not contributing to the favourable conservation status of the habitat or species for which it has been selected with restoration being required until it does so[24].

In relation to habitats of species, the criteria include the size and density of the population present on the site in relation to the populations present within national territory[25]; the degree of conservation of the relevant features and possibilities for restoration, the degree of isolation of the population in relation to its natural range and a global assessment of the value of the site for the conservation of the species concerned.

Under Paragraph C of Annex III, Member States are required to classify the proposed sites according to their relative value for the conservation of the habitats and species concerned.

Paragraph D states that the list will show the sites containing priority habitats and species on the basis of the criteria set out in paragraphs A and B. This appears to mean that, whilst the levels of protection may be stricter for priority habitats and species, the criteria for classification are to be the same for all sites at this stage (but see below as to the automatic inclusion of priority sites in the draft Community list).

It appears that the list of sites is not to be regarded as static in that Article 4(1) provides that where appropriate, "Member States shall propose adaptation of the list in the light of the results of the surveillance of the

[24] Official comment.
[25] This is based on specialist judgment rather than statistical analysis, official comment.

conservation status of habitats and species required under Article 11". There does not appear to have been any proposal for such adaptation so far. Adaptations to the list so far, have been to make good deficiencies identified by the Commission. This does only appear to apply to the listing stage. Nowhere does the Directive appear to provide for amending the suite of designated sites. This raises difficulties in relation to eg mobile habitats such as eroding coastlines. It may be that the Commission may devise ways of allowing site boundaries to be amended and new sites to be added. There is express provision for declassification warranted by natural developments[26].

In October 1994 the application of the Stage 1 criteria was discussed at a meeting held in Edinburgh of the Commission and the Member States with territory in the Atlantic Biogeographical Region, which includes the UK, and agreement was reached on their interpretation.

Stages 2 and 3: Establishment and Adoption of a List of Sites of Community Importance

Stage 2 of the timetable for the designation of Special Areas of Conservation involves the establishment by the Commission, in agreement with each Member State, of a draft list of "sites of Community importance" drawn from the Member States' lists (a process known as moderation). The Commission evaluates the list received from each Member State to see whether any further sites need to be added. The directive defines "site of Community importance" as a site which, in the biogeographical region or regions to which it belongs "contributes significantly to": the maintenance or restoration at a favourable conservation status of an Annex I habitat type or Annex II species; the coherence of Natura 2000; and/or the maintenance of biological diversity within the biogeographic region or regions concerned[27]. That list must identify those sites which host one or more priority natural habitat types or priority species. The criteria to be applied in drawing up the list are set out in the second part of Annex III of the directive. The list of sites of Community importance is to be adopted by the Commission in accordance with the committee procedure laid down by the directive within six years of notification of the directive

Annex III indicates that *all* sites identified by Member States as containing priority habitats or species will be included in the draft list. In relation to other sites, Annex III requires the Commission to consider sites'

[26] Official comment.
[27] Article 1(k)of the directive.

contribution to the favourable conservation status of the species or habitat concerned and/or to the overall coherence of Natura 2000. In this context, it then sets out a number of specific criteria to be considered including: the relative value of the site at the national level; the geographical situation of the site in relation to the migration routes of Annex II species and whether it forms part of a continuous transboundary ecosystem within the Community; the total area of the site; the number of Annex I natural habitat types and Annex II species present on the site. As with natural habitat types, the Commission must also consider the global ecological value of the site for the biogeographical region concerned and/or for the whole of the European territory to which the Directive applies. This global value relates both to unique characteristics and the way they are combined

In order to make the necessary evaluation, the Commission, in conjunction with the Nature Topic Centre of the European Environment Agency, organized a series of seminars in the various biogeographical regions identified in the directive at which representatives of the Member States and independent scientific experts participated. The evaluation consisted of a technical analysis of the information received from Member States followed by an assessment of the representivity of the candidate sites and the selection of sites for the list. For non-priority species and habitats, four criteria were applied: uniqueness; high value; high diversity and network coherence (for example a site's importance as migratory route). The list would then be forwarded to the Habitats Committee for approval before being submitted to the Commission for formal adoption under the procedure laid down in Article 21 of the directive (the third stage towards adoption of the network.[28] [1] lists have been adopted so far covering the Macaronesian region.[29] The Decision makes provision for the alteration of the list, in so far as it relates to reefs, in the light of further knowledge and research (Article 2)

As discussed above, in *the First Corporate Shipping Case*, the Advocate General, took the view that it was permissible to take into account social and economic considerations when drawing up the list of SCI's. The ECJ did not pronounce on the matter.

[28] For a detailed description of this process see the Natura 2000 Newsletter Issue 6 (June 1998) available on the nature conservation page of the Europa website.
[29] Commission Decision of 28 December 2001, OJ L 5/16 9.1.2002.

Sites of Community Importance

As soon as a site is placed on the list of sites of Community Importance adopted by Commission a number of the Directive's protective provisions apply to the site (Article 4(5): steps must be taken to avoid significant deterioration of habitats or disturbance of species (Article 6(2)); and an appropriate assessment is required of any plan or project not directly connected with the management of the site. If this results in a negative assessment of the implications of the project or plan for the site, the plan or project may be only be carried out in the absence of alternative solutions and for "imperative reasons of overriding public interest" and compensatory measures to protect the coherence of Natura 2000 will be required (Article 6(3) and (4) of the directive). The only protective provision which does not apply to the site at this stage is the requirement in Article 6(1) for "necessary conservation measures" involving if necessary "appropriate management plans". That requirement is only applied once the site has been designated as an SAC by the Member State (see below). As to whether some protection may be required at an even earlier stage, see the discussion of the *Inter-Environment Wallonie* case below.

Stage 4: Designation of Special Areas of Conservation

Once a site of Community importance has been adopted within the Commission list, the Member State concerned must designate that site as a "special area of conservation" (SAC) as soon as possible, and within six years at most (ie by 5 June 2004). In doing so, the Member State must establish priorities for designation in the light of the importance of the sites for the maintenance or restoration, at a favourable conservation status, of a natural habitat type in Annex I or a species in Annex II and for the coherence of Natura 2000, and in the light of the threats of degradation or destruction to which those sites are exposed (Article 4(4))[30]. Member States may designate SACs through a "statutory, administrative and/or contractual act" (Article 1(j)). SACs are therefore the sites of Community importance designated by Member States where "the necessary conservation measures" are applied for the maintenance or restoration, at a favourable conservation status, of the natural habitats and/or populations of species for which the site is designated.

[30] Implemented in regulation 8 of the habitats regulations.

Implementation at the National Level

A 1996 WWF report on implementation of the directive stated that there was a "general and unacceptable delay" in meeting their obligations under the directive on the part of most of the EU Member States[31], including the obligation to transpose the directive into national law (before 5 June 1994) and to communicate the national list of sites to the Commission (by 5 June 1995). The report also criticises the Commission's response to these delays as being "too weak and too slow". Even though the Commission had initiated infraction proceedings against a number of Member States for non-transposition of the directive, the report noted that in practice those states would still have about two years before the Commission would decide whether to take the cases to the ECJ (the average time it takes an infraction case to reach the Court) and could avoid proceedings by adopting legislation, albeit belatedly, during that time.

In 1997, the Commission issued Reasoned Opinions against 10 Member States including the UK for failing to meet their obligations to notify a complete list of proposed sites by the deadline set down in the directive. The UK had sent a partial list and UK authorities had indicated to the Commission that the remaining sites would be forwarded by mid-1998[32] In 1998 the Commission went on to make applications to the ECJ in respect of France, Finland, Denmark, Germany, Luxemburg, the Netherlands and Ireland on the basis that a complete list had still not been received from those Member States[33].

In September 2001, the ECJ ruled that France, Germany and Ireland were all in breach of their obligations under the Habitats Directive by failing to transmit to the Commission, within the period prescribed, the list of sites required under Article 4(1) of the Directive, together with the information on those sites required under the second subparagraph of Article 4(1)[34]. The Court rejected the argument put by both Germany and France that the obligation to forward the list of sites was conditional on the adoption of the format for the information (which had only been notified on 19 December 1996[35]). The Court held that the format was not the first

[31] "Spotlight on the Habitats Directive - II" May 1996 WWF European Policy Office, page 12.

[32] See Commission Press Release IP 97/889 dated 17 October 1997.

[33] See Commission Press Release IP 98/352 dated 14 April 1998.

[34] See Cases C-220/99 Commission v France, C-71/99 Commission v Germany and C-67/99 Commission v Ireland, judgments dated 11 September 2001, ECR [2001] I-5831.

[35] In the form of Commission Decision 97/266/EEC, see further above.

text to have defined the information on which the selection of sites was to be based, the criteria for selection being set out in Annex III to which Article 4(1) of the Directive referred. Moreover, although Member States enjoyed a certain margin of discretion in identifying eligible sites, the fact remained that site proposals had to be based on the criteria set out in the directive. In order to produce the draft list, said the Court citing its judgment in the *First Corporate Shipping Case* (see below), the Commission had to have available an exhaustive list of the sites which at the national level, had an ecological interest relevant from the point of view of the directive's conservation objective, bearing in mind that the habitats might lie across one or more frontiers inside the Community[36]. The Court also noted that the Commission had allowed extra time for compliance during the preliminary stages of the infraction proceedings (by issuing a fresh an additional letter of formal notice). Similar points were made in the judgment in the case against Ireland. In each case those sites which had been forwarded did not represent to the complete list required under the directive.

In August 2001, the Commission announced that it was to refer Portugal to the ECJ and to send Reasoned Opinions to the Netherlands, Italy, the UK and Germany for having inadequate national legislation to implement the Habitats Directive[37].

Protection and Management of SACs under the Directive

The protection and management of SACs is considered in more detail in the section on UK implementation below (in certain respects the UK affords sites greater or at least earlier protection than that required by the Directive). Article 6 of the Directive sets out the obligations of Member States in relation to SACs as considered below. Articles 6.2 – 6.4 apply to SPAs as from the date of implementation of the habitats directive or the date of classification or recognition by a Member State under the wild birds directive, where the latter date is later (Article 7 of the habitats directive).

It should be noted that, as confirmed by the ECJ in *Case C-374/98 Commission v France* in relation to SPAs, the provisions of Article 6(2)-(4) of the Habitats Directive only apply to SPAs which have been classified as such. So far as areas which have not been classified (but which should

[36] See Case C-71/99, judgment of 11 September 2001, paras.25-28, [2001] ECR I-5811.

[37] Commission Press Release dated 6 August 2001, IP/01/1192.In Case C-256/98 Commission v France the Court found that France had failed adequately to transpose Article 6 paragraphs(3)and(4) into national law (judgment of 6 April 2000).

have been) are concerned, the provisions of Article 4(4) of the wild birds directive will continue to apply. In the same case, the Court accepted that the protection afforded to SPAs under Article 4(4) of the wild birds directive was stricter that that laid down in Articles 6(2)-(4) of the Habitats Directive. This meant that areas which were not classified as SPAs in violation of the birds directive would be more strictly protected under Community law than those which were classified (and thus fell subject to the provisions of the Habitats Directive by virtue of Article 7 of that Directive). The Court went on to note that this duality of protection provided Member States with an incentive to carry out classification of SPAs in so far as this would enable them to have recourse to a procedure allowing for the adoption of a plan or project with adverse effects on an SPA under the conditions laid down in Article 6 of the Habitats Directive[38].

Management Plans

Article 6(1) requires that Member States establish "the necessary conservation measures" involving "if need be" appropriate management plans. These can either be specifically designed for the site or integrated into other development plans. Member states should take "appropriate statutory, administrative or contractual measures" which correspond to the ecological requirements of the natural habitat type or species concerned.

Protection

In language similar to that contained in Article 4(4) of the wild birds directive (which it replaces, see Chapter 2 - Part I, Member States are required under Article 6(2) of the habitats directive to take appropriate steps to avoid the deterioration in SACs of natural habitats and the habitats of species, as well as the disturbance the of species for which the area has been designated "in so far as such disturbance could be significant in relation to the objectives of the Directive". It can be argued that in the light of the precautionary principle, on which Community environmental policy is based[39], Member States should be cautious about permitting disturbance even where the effects on species are not clear.

[38] C-374/98 Commission v France [2000] ECR I-10799, see paras. 56-57.
[39] See Article 174 of the EC Treaty.

Assessment of Plans and Projects

A key requirement in the scheme for the protection of SACs is that plans and projects likely to have a significantly effect on the site must be subject to "appropriate assessment" of the implications of the plan or project for the site's conservation objectives (Article 6(3)). This only applies to plans and projects which are not directly connected with or necessary to the management of the site (for nature conservation, in accordance with the objectives of the Directive). The likelihood of significant effects must be considered, not only in relation to an individual plan or project, but also on the basis of its effects in combination with other plans or projects. It was acknowledged by the ECJ in *Case C-256/98 Commission v France* that the meaning of "plan" was somewhat unclear (para. 38 of the judgment). In that case the Court found that it could not be established that French legislation which required an assessment in the case of development projects and town planning was in breach of the Article 6(3) requirement to assess plans.

The requirement for an appropriate assessment under the habitats directive is distinct from any requirement for an environmental impact assessment under the EIA Directive, although both may be required in relation to a particular project. In relation to the EIA Directive, proximity to an SPA/SAC is one of the factors listed in the annexes as indicating a need for EIA. Paragraph 39 of PPG9 states that "EA would normally be required where a Ramsar site or a potential or classified SPA, or a candidate, agreed or designated SAC could be affected" There are a number of important differences between the two types of assessment. These include, in relation to scope, the fact that an appropriate assessment for the purposes of the Habitats Directive may be required for any type of plan of project not directly connected with the management of the site, whereas EIA is required only in relation to projects of the types listed in the Annexes to the EIA directive. Also, the appropriate assessment is limited in its scope to the implications for the Natura 2000 site (its European features of interest) rather than wider environmental considerations. The appropriate assessment is made by the competent authority rather than the proposer of the scheme (unless a CA is proposing)

In relation to the implications of the assessment, EIA assessment does not dictate the outcome of the decision-making process (the outcome of the assessment must be taken into account by the body which is considering whether to consent to the project), whereas a negative assessment under the Habitats Directive restricts the power of the competent authority to decide to go ahead with the project. Subject to the exceptions set out in Article 6(4) of the habitats Directive, the competent national authorities may only agree to the plan or project after having ascertained as a result of the assessment that "it will not adversely affect the integrity of the site concerned" and "if appropriate" after having obtained the opinion of the general public. Guidance on the methodological approach to the implementation of Articles 6(3) and (4) of the directive has been issued by the Commission [complete][40].

Imperative Reasons of Overriding Public Interest

It could be argued that the effectiveness of the directive in protecting habitats, at least those designated as SACs, will best be measured by looking at the way in which Article 6(4) is operated by the relevant authorities. This is the provision which seeks to ensure that the conservation objectives of the directive continue to be met in the face of the development pressures on land use. Article 6(4) of the directive provides for the possibility of proceeding with a plan or project even where there has been a negative assessment of its implications for the site in certain limited circumstances but *only* where there is no alternative solution. The rules governing whether or not the development may go ahead are different as between priority species and habitats and others. In relation to species and habitats *other* than those with a priority listing, the plan or project may be carried out "for imperative reasons of overriding public interest, including those of an economic or social nature". The Member State must take all compensatory measures necessary to ensure the overall coherence of Natura 2000 and must inform the Commission about these measures.

In relation to priority species and habitats however, the scope for proceeding with a plan or project following a negative assessment is narrowed. In these cases, the *only* considerations which may be raised as constituting imperative reasons of overriding public interest are those relating to human health or public safety, to "beneficial consequences of primary importance for the environment" or, *further to an opinion from the Commission*, to other "imperative reasons of overriding public interest".[41] There appears to be some uncertainty as to whether this requirement is capable of extending to SPAs. The Commission has been reported as stating that it does apply by virtue of Article 7 of the habitats directive[42] but agreed

[40] Available on www.europa.eu.int.

[41] See for example OJ No C 178, 1995, page 3 Draft Commission Opinion of 27 April 1995 on the planned A20 motorway (Germany).

[42] See 1996 WWF Report on the Habitats Directive at page 20 which refers to the use of Ornis Committee criteria.

that amendment was necessary to address this). Although Article 6.4 applies to classified SPAs by virtue of Article 7 there is nothing for the provision relating to priority habitat and species to apply to, as none are listed in the Birds Directive. An additional point here is that the Commission's guidance (Managing Natura 2000 sites, the Provisions of Article 6, April 2000) suggests that the more restrictive provision applies only where the priority feature is actually affected rather than where it is merely a feature of a site that is affected. This is not, of course what either the Directive or the Regulations say. The Commission apparently takes a broad view however of the scope of Article 6(4), arguing that the obligation arises in relation to any species or habitat mentioned in the national list or which *should have been included* on the list, on the basis of the Annex III criteria. The Commission's position in this regard appears to be consistent with the approach taken by the ECJ in the *Santona Marshes* Case in relation to the application of Article 4 of the wilds bird directive[43]. The Commission accepts however that an Article 6(4) Opinion is not legally binding.

The level of scrutiny applied by the Commission to plans and projects in cases where it is required to give an opinion under Article 6(4) has been the subject of criticism. In an article on the issue, Andre Nolkaemper[44] examines opinions issued by the Commission under Article 6(4) in 1995 which related to a proposed German motorway. He criticises the Commission for taking an insufficiently rigorous approach to the scrutiny of projects, in particular as to the availability of alternatives[45] and argues that use of the term "overriding" in the directive clearly indicates that Article 6(4) requires something more than a mere balance of interests in favour of the project.

Protection Under the Wild Birds Directive compared with protection under the Habitats directive

One way of assessing the scope of protection afforded to sites under the Habitats Directive, is to compare the relevant provisions of Article 6 of the habitats directive with those of Article 4 of the wild birds Directive[46] which it supersedes in part. Article 7 of the habitats directive replaces the protective obligations of the first sentence of Article 4(4) of the wild birds directive with the obligations under Article 6(2), (3) and (4) of the habitats Directive.

[43] See Chapter 2 - Part I.
[44] "Habitat Protection in European Community Law: Evolving Conceptions of a Balance of Interests", Journal of Environmental Law Volume 9 Number 2 1997.
[45] See page 279 of Article.
[46] See Chapter 2 - Part I.

The key differences between the two regimes relate to the requirement for positive management of protected sites under the habitats directive under Article 6.1 and the scope for derogation under the Habitats Directive, which permits, in the absence of alternative solutions such derogation on economic and social grounds where these constitute an overriding public interest. Thus the habitats directive appears to offer less protection to designated sites than did the unamended wild birds directive as interpreted by the ECJ in the *Lappel Bank Case*[47] This is very clearly illustrated by the *Commission v Germany, (Leybucht Dykes)*, case which suggested a very limited range of circumstances in which derogation from the obligations of the first sentence of Article 4.4 would be permissible. In that case it was the potential flooding of the town[48]. On the other hand, the timetable for designation of SACs, the requirements for the management of sites and the need to provide compensatory measures where damaging development is permitted to proceed go some way towards mitigating the difference in protection.

The Implications of the Inter-Environment Wallonie Case: From what point should sites be subject to protection under the habitats directive?

Article 4(5) of the Habitats Directive appears to indicate that no protection of a site is required under the directive until that site is placed on the Commission's formal list of sites of Community importance[49]. On the other hand, a judgment of the Court of Justice suggests that sites may attract some degree of protection at an earlier stage.

Following the ECJ's judgment in *Case C-129/96 Inter-Environment Wallonie*[50], a case which concerned the implementation of Community waste legislation, it now appears that Members States may not take measures which would make it difficult or impossible to attain the objectives of the habitats directive, for example by destroying a site which is on the national list (unless perhaps the conditions for such provided in the directive are fulfilled). The case raised the question of whether Article [10 ex5] of the EC Treaty precluded Member States from adopting a provision contrary to the waste framework directive before the period for

---

47 See Chapter 2 - Part I.

48 The case, with its rather strict approach to Article 4.4 appears to have been one of the reasons a more "flexible" approach was provided for in the Habitats Directive, official comment.

49 Article 4(5) cross refers to the third subparagraph of Article 4(2) which deals with the formal adoption of the Commission's list.

50 Case C-129/96 [1997] ECR I-7411, paragraph 26.

transposing the directive had expired. Advocate General Jacobs accepted that a Member State would be in breach of its duty of cooperation under Article 10 ex 5 of the Treaty if it were to adopt measures during the period for implementation of a directive which were liable to jeopardise the attainment of the aims of the directive by the appointed date and would also be in breach of its more specific duty under Article 189 to implement the directive. He went on to agree with the United Kingdom that such a breach would occur if a Member State adopted measures which rendered the attainment of the objectives of the directive "impossible or unduly difficult"[51]. The Court of Justice took a very similar approach and ruled that it followed from Article 5 and 189 that Member States, during the period between adoption of a directive and the deadline for its transposition, "must refrain from taking any measures liable seriously to compromise the result prescribed."[52]

An analogy can clearly be drawn between the type of situation under consideration in *Wallonie* and Member States' obligations as regards the protection of sites prior to the adoption of the list of Sites of Community Importance (at which point Article 4(5) applies). Both situations concern Member States' conduct prior to the materialisation of a Community legal obligation. In *Wallonie* the deadline for transposition had not yet expired when the relevant conduct occurred whereas in relation to the habitats directive, the issue is rather whether Member States have any obligation to protect sites which meet the Annex III criteria and may or may not have been included on the national list but are not yet included on the Commission's list of sites of Community Importance. The *Wallonie* judgment would seem to imply that no measure should be taken (and this might include a failure to act) which is liable seriously to compromise the protection of sites which are due to be designated as Special Areas of Conservation. Such action might include allowing a development to proceed which would destroy the habitats for which the site might have been designated or alternatively, failing to protect a site from the irreversible effects of neglect.

UK policy as to candidate SACs (cSACs) is set out in PPG956[53]: Sites which the Government and the Commission have agreed as Sites of Community importance which are to be designated in due course as SAC's, attract the same legal protection as if they had already been designated.

[51] See paragraphs 39 and 40 of the Opinion dated 24 April 1997.
[52] See paragraph 45 of the judgment dated 18 December 1997.
[53] From February 2000 it became more than policy, see further below although the amending regulations apply in England only).

The position is less clear however as regards sites which are merely under consideration or which should have been put forward as cSACs but have not been. In such cases it can be argued in the light of *Wallonie* that these too require protection.

This issue might be raised in a case where local residents or an environmental group are seeking to protect a site which is not a cSAC but which appears to fulfil, at least potentially, the criteria for inclusion on the lists of Sites of Community Interest. The implications of the *Wallonie Case* would be relevant to any application for interim relief and the national court would have a duty to take account of the fact that a refusal to grant such relief in the absence of a cross undertaking in damages on the part of the claimants might mean that a site is destroyed before final judgment is given in the case (as occurred in the *Lappel Bank Case*)[54] .

UK Implementation "a missed opportunity?"

The UK has implemented the Habitats Directive in Great Britain by means of the Conservation (Natural Habitats) Regulations 1994 (SI 1994/2716) as amended by the Conservation (Natural Habitats &tc) (Amendment) Regulations 1997 (SI 1997/3055) (the Habitats Regulations)[55] and The Conservation (Natural Habitats) (Amendment) (England) Regulations 2000. The UK Government's approach in implementing the directive was to integrate its provisions into the legal framework for protection of sites which was already in place, rather than to institute a completely new system. In presenting the draft regulations in the House of Lords, the Minister of State, Lord Ullswater [HL 17 October 1994 col 85] explained that they introduced new provisions arising specifically from the directive but also embraced existing provisions of the 1981 Wildlife and Countryside Act and other legislation, with modifications where necessary. This would result in a single body of legislation for sites and species of European importance covered by the directive. The existing law, in so far as it applied to sites and species outside the scope of the directive, remained in force in unamended form.

Critics of this approach expressed the view that the opportunity to improve the existing provisions across the board had thereby been missed, in particular in relation to inadequacies in the provision for marine sites and an over reliance on the voluntary approach which resulted in damage

[54] As to which see Chapter 2 - Part I.
[55] The Conservation (Natural Habitat &tc) Regulations (Northern Ireland) 1995 which entered into force on 13 November 1995 implement the Directive in Northern Ireland.

through neglect of sites as well as deliberate acts[56]. The Government confirmed that its intention was to maintain the status quo as far as possible, saying that: "the voluntary principle continues to be an underlying principle of this Government's approach to nature conservation. These Regulations represent the minimum that is necessary to implement the directive"[57]. It is notable that recent changes to domestic legislation have had to address both the protection of marine sites and the limitations of the voluntary approach[58].

The importance attached to the Regulations implementing the Habitats Directive was indicated by the fact that they were made subject to the affirmative resolution procedure by which a statutory instrument can only be adopted once a draft has been approved by both Houses of Parliament[59] There was some criticism of the fact that primary legislation had not been used to implement the directive[60] and thus that there had not been any opportunity to debate the so-called "Henry VIII powers" to make special orders to protect vulnerable sites[61] in the Delegated Powers Scrutiny Committee. The Government responded that the power to make special nature conservation orders laid down in regulation 22 was subject to the provisions of Schedule 1 which required the Secretary of State, in relation to orders which were opposed, either to hold a local inquiry or provide an opportunity for the objections to be heard. The Government also pointed out that much of what was in the regulations simply repeated what was already in the 1981 Act.

As to the relationship between SACs and other designations, the Government stated in its consultation paper on the Regulations that an SAC would already have been notified as an SSSI (under the 1981 Act or Habitats Regulations (the Regulations don't themselves provide for a notification but that any s 28 of the 1981 Act notification in force shall have effect for the purposes of the Regulations)) and that the "vast majority" of such sites were already confirmed as SSSI's. Thus the SAC network was "a development of an existing nature conservation programme."[62]. The

[56] For criticism of the voluntary approach to the protection of SSSI's, see Chapter 1 - Part I.
[57] Hansard , House of Lords, 17 October 1994, Col 109.
[58] See Chapter 1 - Part I.
[59] In practice, most statutory instruments are made subject to the negative resolution procedure by which they enter into force unless a negative resolution is adopted in both Houses.
[60] Hansard House of Commons, 19 July 1994, col 242.
[61] HL col 106, note 62 infra.
[62] Hansard, House of Lords, 17 October 1994, Col 86

Government was keen to "dispel any notion that we are starting from scratch"[63].

The Structure of the Regulations

Part I of the Regulations sets out definitions and provides for a number of general duties to comply with the directive: a general duty is placed on "nature conservation bodies"; a similar duty is placed on competent authorities and relevant authorities in relation to marine areas; finally "every competent authority" (as defined in regulation 6) is to have regard to the requirements of the directive.

Part II of the Regulations provides for the selection, designation, management and protection of sites for inclusion in Natura 2000. These sites are to be known as "European sites". Part III deals with species protection[64].

Part IV of the Regulations implements Article 6 of the directive in respect of various statutory development control schemes, including the town and country planning system, which may give rise to development likely to have a significant effect on a European site. An appropriate assessment is required to be made of the implications for a European site of those plans or projects likely to significantly affect it. Also Under Part IV, decisions pre-dating the later of the 1994 Regulations or the site becoming a European site and made by a competent authority to undertake, consent, permit or authorise a plan or project which would be likely to have such an effect are subject to review by that competent authority by way of an "appropriate assessment" An obligation to carry out appropriate assessment of proposals to carry out certain notified operations arises under regulation 20 and regulation 24.

General Duties to Comply with the Directive

It is important to note that, in addition to laying down detailed rules implementing the specific requirements of the directive (considered below), the Habitats Regulations also create certain general duties which have the effect of reinforcing the more specific provisions and requiring a broad range of public authorities and those carrying out public functions take account of the directive as a matter of UK law. The general duties are of two types and the first is in stronger terms than the second.

[63] Ibid.
[64] See Chapter 3A - Part II.

Regulation 3(2) of the Regulations places a duty on the Secretary of State, the Minister of Agriculture, Fisheries and Food and the "nature conservation bodies" to comply with the Habitats Directive. These bodies *must exercise their functions* (which includes powers and duties) *under enactments relating to nature conservation so as to secure compliance with the directive*. These enactments are specified as including, in England and Wales, Part III of the National Parks and Access to the Countryside1949 Act; s15 of the Countryside Act 1968; Part I and s28-38 of the 1981 Act and s131-134 of the Environmental Protection Act 1990. It is also provided, in regulation 3(3) that in relation to marine areas, any competent authority having a function relevant to marine conservation *must exercise those functions so as to secure compliance with the requirements of the Habitats Directive* (see Marine sites section).

There is also a more general duty, under regulation 3(4), placed on every competent authority (as defined in regulation 6), in the exercise of any of their functions, to *have regard to* the requirements of the Directive "so far as they may be affected by the exercise of those functions". Regulation 6 defines a competent authority as including any Minister, Government Department, public or statutory undertaker, public body of any description or person holding public office. This was described as "a cornerstone provision" of the Regulations in debate in the House of Commons[65]. This is a very widely drawn duty and any competent authority falling within the inclusive definition in regulation 6 will need to ensure that it has had regard to the directive's requirements and presumably be able to demonstrate that it has done so if decisions affecting sites or species protected under the directive are to withstand legal scrutiny An example of how this general duty has affected the policy of a competent authority relates to the way the Regulations, at Regulation 47, appear to provide an exhaustive list of matters to which Reg 48 etc shall apply. There are matters which would fall within the wide approach that the Commission would wish to see taken to the interpretation of "plans or projects" and which are not listed in Regs 54 to 85. Competent authorities have though, relying on their general duties, applied the provisions of Reg 48 to matters which are not listed. Some have, in fact, gone to Public Inquiry. Examples include Harbour Revision Orders, Water Abstraction Licences[66] and Licences required by the Food and Environmental Protections Act.

---

[65] Hansard House of Commons, col 241-19 July 1994.

[66] Although an amendment is soon to be made to the Regulations to specifically include these.

European Sites

Selection of European Sites

In its First Report on the implementation of the Directive, the UK stated that 76 Annex I habitats (including 22 priority types) and 51 Annex II species (including one priority species) had been recorded in the UK. As of June 2001, a total of 555 sites had been submitted to the European Commission as candidate SACs. [67] Lists of UK sites have been sent to Commission in a series of "tranches": the first tranche being sent on 20 June 1995. The 17th and most recent tranche was sent on 8 June 2001 and the final 18th tranche was due to have been sent by 8 July 2001[68]. In presenting the draft regulations to the House of Commons on 19 July 1994, the Government made it clear that it was committed to preliminary consultation on the selected sites with all owners and occupiers and other affected interests before submission of the national list to the Commission.

In its First Report the UK stated that the task of selecting Annex I sites had not been straightforward "due to inherent weaknesses in the Annex I classification used to form the basis for Annex I habitats" which caused considerable debate about the occurrence of some of the habitats within the UK.[69] The main source of data on the distribution and extent of Annex I habitats was the National Vegetation Classification[70] and on species, the Biological Records Centre at the Centre for Ecology and Hydrology. Data on the distribution and extent of Annex I habitats and the range and population of Annex II species in the UK was published by JNCC in "Handbook on the UK Status of EC Habitats Directive interest features".[71] In some cases surveys were carried out to obtain essential information on which to base site selection. The UK states in its First Report that "it is likely that future advances in knowledge will reveal additional high-quality sites for some habitats and species."[72]

[67] First Report by the UK under Article 17 on the implementation of the Directive from June 1994 to December 2000,published by DEFRA October 31 2001, figures given in the Executive Summary to the Report.

[68] According to the DEFRA website (checked 25 November 2003) in the UK, 567 candidate SACs have been forwarded to the European Commission covering approximately 2,160 000 hectares. 219 of these sites are wholly, or partly in England.

[69] See para 1.a.i of the Report.

[70] Rodwell 1991 et seq cited in the Report.

[71] Jackson and McLeod, 2000. See the JNCC report "The Habitats Directive: Selection of Special Areas of Conservation in the UK" for a description of the selection criteria and process.

[72] Para 1.a.i.

The UK received a Reasoned Opinion (dated 19 December 1997) in which the Commission alleged that the complete list as referred to in Article 4(1) of the directive had not been transmitted. In a press release dated 8 September 1997, the UK Government stated that "those sites submitted represented about 3/4 of the anticipated final list and the target for completion was the summer of 1998". The Commission responded by saying (press release) that "transmission of a partial list cannot be considered as meeting the obligations under Article 4(1) since the list is comprehensive neither in geographical terms nor in terms of the habitat types and species habitats which need to be addressed and since the site information does not cover every site and/or is not provided in required format". By June 1999 the UK had submitted what was intended to be the final national list with the exception of two sites[73]. No court action has since been taken against the UK by the Commission on this issue.

Basis for Selection

In its First Report on the implementation of the Directive the UK sets out the way in which it has applied the selection criteria laid down in the Directive. It states for example that in general preference has been given to selecting the largest examples of each Annex I type and to sites which hold a significant proportion of the total habitat resource in the UK (para 1.a.i). In relation to Annex II species, the largest populations have been prioritised for selection, especially any sites holding more than 10% of the total UK population. Account has also been taken of special UK responsibilities where certain habitats or species are more common in the UK than in other Member States, for example Caledonian forest (endemic) and the grey seal *monachus grypus*. The Report also points out that selection was not limited to sites with existing statutory conservation designations and that the UK list contains a significant number of sites which were not notified as SSSI/ASSI at the time they were identified as possible SACs. The Report adds that in all but a few cases, SSSI notification has however been used to support SAC designation. Some of the Annex III criteria are qualitative and rely heavily for their evaluation on the use of best scientific judgment.[74]

The UK has stated that it is committed to widespread consultation during the selection process and that owners and occupiers of potential sites as well as other interested parties and the public will be consulted[75].

[73] See First Report, para 1.a.i at page 19.
[74] See para 1.a.i at page 16 of the Report.
[75] See First Report at page 20 and see also Figure 1 in the UK's First Report which sets out a summary of the UK selection process (page 18 of the Report).

As soon as sites are submitted to the EC they are known as candidate SACs (cSACs) and attract a degree of protection (see further below)[76].

Planning Policy Guidance No 9: Nature Conservation[77] (PPG9) states that, when consultations take place in relation to potential SPAs or candidate SACs, local planning authorities will be asked to consider all extant planning permissions which may affect the proposed area (those which have not been implemented and those which have not yet been completed) and to inform the Government if the implementation of the permission is likely to have a significant effect on the ecological value of the site[78]. The purpose of considering the effect of implementing planning permissions at this stage was apparently so that the Department could consider whether they should be a factor in deciding the boundaries of the site under the requirements of the wild birds directive or the habitats directive (para C3)[79]. Following the judgment of the ECJ in the *Lappel Bank case* however, the Government confirmed that "it is clear that Member States may only take account of scientific matters in selecting SPAs under the Wild Birds Directive and identifying their boundaries" and that furthermore, it considers that the Habitats Directive also requires the selection of SACs and determination of their boundaries "to be undertaken on the basis of scientific criteria".[80] This view was confirmed as correct as far as it relates to the national list following the ECJ's ruling in the *First Corporate Shipping Case* in 2000 (see further above).

European Site Boundaries: the Cairngorms Case

In 1998 the WWF and the RSPB challenged decisions made by the Secretary of State for Scotland in relation to the designation of the Cairngorms cSAC/SPA[81]. One of the issues raised was the way in which the boundaries of the Cairngorms cSAC /SPA had been drawn up[82]. WWF argued that the Secretary of State for Scotland was obliged to include within the site all such habitats and species territories which were "contiguous or geographically linked" to the site and that he had breached the habitats directive, as implemented by the regulations, in failing to do this. The Court rejected this argument, finding that whilst they had to base their

[76] From February 2000, Regulation 48 applies as a matter of law to those sites that have been submitted.
[77] Published October 1994, currently being revised, HMSO.
[78] See para C2.
[79] See para C2.
[80] See Government Statement available on DETR website [see reference below].
[81] See WWF v Secretary of State for Scotland [1999] 1 CMLR 1021.
[82] The other issues raised included the conduct of the assessment.

decisions on scientific judgment, national authorities had a discretion as to the drawing up of site boundaries and were not obliged to include contiguous sites. The Court was referred to a number of ECJ decisions relied on by the RSPB/WWF in support of the argument that national authorities did not have a discretion as to the delineation of the boundaries of SACs. The Court accepted that the decisions in these cases, including *Lappel Bank* and *Commission v Netherlands*, confirmed that national authorities were bound to determine such boundaries on the basis of ornithological criteria but held that none of them was concerned with the issue of whether Member State's discretion extended to boundary delineation.

The Court accepted the view of both sets of parties, that the relevant provisions of the birds directive and habitats directive should be interpreted in such a way as to yield mutually consistent results, thus the approach to classification of "the most suitable territories" as SPAs under Article 4(1) of the wild birds directive should be interpreted so as to be substantially the same as the obligation in Article 4(1) of the habitats directive to prepare a list of sites as candidate SACs. The Court held that, in either case, a "location" only became a "territory" or a "site" for the purposes of the Directives once, inter alia, its boundaries have been established (an approach which does not appear to be consistent with that of the ECJ in the *Santona Marshes case*). The Court found that identification of the boundaries was an integral part of the identification of the territory or site, thus rejecting the two stage process contended for by the WWF and RSBP, and noting, in relation to the assessment criteria set out in Annex III Stage 1 (A and B) of the habitats directive, that a process of evaluation was involved. The discretion to determine such matters as the size of the site concerned was only limited by the requirement, recognised in the case law of the ECJ, that the exercise of discretion had to be governed by ornithological criteria alone. The Court pointed out that the Annex III assessment criteria, for example as to representivity of the natural habitat type, were all expressed in relative terms, requiring a qualitative approach similar to that required by the less specific terms of Article 4(1) of the wild birds directive. In this context, and alluding to the need to have regard to the complexity of nature, the Court held that it was not part of the "complex and sophisticated" scientific exercise to be carried out by Member States that all contiguous or linked qualifying habitats or species populations had to be included.

Nor did the Court accept that the Government had fettered its discretion by using SSSI designation as a starting point in considering the designation of SACs/SPAs. Whilst it recognised that the criteria for the establishment for SSSI's under s 28 of the Wildlife and Countryside Act 1981 were "by no means identical" with those for SPAs or SACs, there was no conflict between them. The Court also pointed out in this context that under regulation 3(2) of the 1994 Regulations, the Secretary of State and SNH were required to exercise their functions so as to secure compliance with the habitats directive. The Court could find nothing wrong in using the boundaries of an existing SSSI as an aid to deciding in due course, "along with other relevant considerations" where the boundary of the European site should be drawn, provided that there was scope for altering the boundary of the SSSI. This approach can be contrasted with that of the Commission, as expressed in a booklet on Natura 2000[83], which took the view that the SACs designation should have added value rather than just involve the designation of sites already protected under national law.

The Court found that SNH had been entitled to take into account the presence of skiing facilities in drawing up the boundaries and to take into account their effects on local habitats and species and that this did not constitute unlawfully taking into account "economic and recreational" matters. As the Court pointed out, to have ignored the presence of the facilities would have been a failure to perform the exercise in a properly scientific way.

Stage 2 of the Selection Process

This was initiated for the Atlantic Biogeographical Region (of which the UK forms part) at a meeting in Ireland on 6-8 September 1999[84]. Following discussions at Community level it was accepted by the UK that the UK list was incomplete in that: there was inadequate coverage of the geographical range or ecological variation shown by some habitats and species; in some cases the proportion of the total national resource was too low; and the UK had only listed selected habitats and species as SAC interest features instead of listing every Annex I habitat and Annex II species occurring on a site. Accordingly the UK's statutory conservation agencies carried out a review of the cSAC series. The Government announced details of the revised proposals in June and July 2000 and further sites have since been submitted in tranches as indicated above.

[83] Natura 2000 booklet.
[84] See First Report, para 1.a.i at page 20 et seq.

A final seminar for the Atlantic region was organised by the Commission in June 2002 and it is expected that the remaining lists of sites (including for that region) will be adopted during the course of 2004.[85]

Notification and the Register of European Sites

A register of European sites is established under regulation 11 of the Regulations and is available to public inspection. The Secretary of State must notify the appropriate nature conservation body of entries on and changes to the register including the inclusion of new sites or the removal of an entry (regulation 12). Regulation 13 then requires the nature conservation body in turn to notify every owner or occupier of land within the site concerned as well as the relevant local authority and such other persons that the Secretary of State directs.

The Register includes: sites of Community importance as soon as they are placed on the list adopted by the Commission under Article 4(2) of the directive; any site hosting a priority habitat or species in respect of which consultation is initiated pursuant to Article 5 of the Directive ; SAC's as soon as they are designated and SPAs classified under the wild birds directive[86] and cSACs following 2000 amendment to Regs 10 and 11 (England only)

The Register may be amended and SAC entries shall be removed if declassified by the Commission under Article 9 of the Directive. Entries will also be removed if they otherwise cease to fall within the relevant category, for example if a site which has been subject to consultation under Article 5 is agreed to be placed on the Commission list by decision of the Council in which case it will become a site of Community importance.

Management and Protection of European Sites

Protection of Candidate SACs

Before examining the way in which the Directive's requirements for the management and protection of SACs have been

[85] See Natura 2000 Newsletter (May 2003) on the Europa website (Commission Environment).

[86] SPAs are included as soon as they are classified or, if classified before the Regulations entered into force, as soon as practicable. This reflects the possibility that further SPAs may be classified. It should be noted that the wild birds directive, in contrast to the habitats directive, contains no timetable for classification of SPAs beyond the need to comply with the directive's obligations from the deadline for transposition.

implemented in the UK, it should be remembered that when the Regulations were adopted the UK Government decided as a matter of policy that, for planning and all other consent regimes, the UK Government would treat cSACs as if they were already fully designated as SACs. Subsequently in 2000, an amendment was made to the Regulations (England only) in order to put the protection of cSACs on a statutory footing by amending the definition of "European Sites" to include sites which have been proposed by the Secretary of State and submitted to the Commission until such time as the site is either not included in the Commission's draft list or is included in the list finally adopted[87].

The UK's First Report states that action taken to avoid deterioration and disturbance on cSACs takes two forms: changes in management (by means of management agreements) and review of notifications and consents for SSSI's (under regulation 21 see below)[88].

Management and Protection of European Sites

The UK has implemented the requirements for managing and protecting sites under Article 6 of the habitats directive by building on the type of protection afforded to SSSI's. The Government stated at the time of implementation that the existing SSSI system and the protection enshrined in it would continue to be the bedrock of nature conservation in Great Britain. Nature conservation agencies would be able to amend their existing SSSI notifications for European sites. There would however be two important additional features to the system for protection of such sites: provision would be made for the assessment of the effects for sites of plans and projects (in order to implement Article 6(3)-(4)) and also for the making of special nature conservation orders (SNCOs) in order to guarantee the protection of sites where the voluntary approach which underlay SSSI protection appeared unlikely to secure the protection of the site.

In relation to the management of European sites, the provisions of the Habitats Regulations [are] modelled on s15 of the 1968 Countryside Act (dealing with SSSI's) and s16 of the 1949 National Parks and Access to the Countryside Act (dealing with nature reserves). As far as protection is concerned, Article 6(2) of the Directive requires Member States to avoid, in SACs "the deterioration of natural habitats and the habitats of species as well as disturbance of the species..." In order to achieve this in UK

[87] The amendment was made by the Conservation (Natural Habitats) (Amendment) Regulations 2000, SI 2000/192 HMSO, which entered into force on 28 February 2000.
[88] See para 1.b.ii at page 28.

legislation, reliance is placed on the duty to notify proposed operations and the restriction on the carrying out of potentially damaging operations under regulations 18-19. This system operates in a similar way to the system of SSSI protection operated under s28 of the 1981 Act (prior to its amendment in the 2000 Countryside and Rights of Way Act); the power to make an SNCO under regulation 22 (similar in some respects to s29 1981 Act which was repealed by the 2000 Act) and the power to make byelaws (regulation 28). Thus the Regulations provide both for negative powers to prevent harm and positive powers to secure management of the site. It could be argued that the obligation to review extant consents in Regulation 50 also contributes to avoiding deterioration.

The importance of monitoring in detecting damage and ensuring that the necessary action is taken to protect the site was underlined during parliamentary debate on the Regulations[89]. The Government said that monitoring of sites was carried out by various bodies such as the BTO.

Management of European Sites

Whilst Article 6(1) of the directive only requires the establishment of appropriate management plans "if need be", the widespread need for such measures appears to be well established[90]. Moreover, the fulfilment of the obligations arising under Article 6(2) of the directive may in itself require positive management of the site. The WWF report emphasises the need for measures to encourage positive land management and says that simply prohibiting damage is not enough to implement the requirement in Article 6(2) to avoid deterioration. During debate on the Regulations, there was criticism that the Regulations did not require a management scheme to be adopted for each SAC. At that time, the Government anticipated that, for the great majority of European sites, existing management agreements would continue unchanged[91]. In the event, existing and any new management agreements entered into are relied on. There are also powers in the post - Countryside and Rights of Way Act /Wildlife and Countryside Act to secure positive management. There are no management plans, as such, specifically prepared for the purposes of Article 6.1 save that "management schemes" are being established, in relation to European marine sites, for the purposes of Regulation 34.

[89] Hansard, House of Lords, 17 October 1994, Col 111.
[90] See Wildlife Link Report "SSSI's: A Health Check" which identified neglect as the greatest long-term threat to the sites.
[91] Hansard Col 108.

The provision in regulation 16 for the appropriate nature conservation body to have the power to enter into management agreements with every owner, lessee and occupier of land forming part of a European site or land adjacent to such a site is modelled on earlier provisions under the 1968 Act and 1949 Act dealing with the management of SSSIs and nature reserves respectively. The Habitats Directive does not specify what form management plans for SACs should take and provides that they may be specifically designed for the site or integrated into other development plans. In the UK the latter approach is generally taken. Existing management agreements in relation to SSSIs or nature reserves which become European sites are preserved by virtue of regulation 17.

In its First Report on the implementation of the Directive, the UK sets out the way in which such plans and agreements are developed in the UK and notes that the conservation agencies have responsibility for preparing and ensuring the implementation of plans for the National Nature Reserves which they manage, as well as the responsibility to prepare short management statements or briefs on those sites which are designated as SSSIs or ASSIs, including Natura 200 sites. This process is reported to be substantially complete as far as England is concerned. These statements are then reviewed regularly to consider their effectiveness against the objectives set for the site concerned[92]. The Report states that English Nature uses three categories of agreement: compensatory, made in the light of restrictions placed on the land; positive, for achieving wildlife gain and wildlife enhancement agreements which support conservation management. The Report also notes that management agreements have been prepared for Natura sites as SSSI agreements and that whilst it is not possible to guarantee that the agreement is aimed at the Natura interest of the site it is anticipated that over the next few years these agreements will be reviewed and additional requirements identified as necessary[93].

Control of Potentially Damaging Operations

The system for controlling potentially damaging operations is based on the system operating under s28 of the Wildlife and Countryside Act 1981(prior to its amendment by the 2000 Act[94]).

Notification: In the first place, any SSSI notification under s28 of the 1981 Act as to the special interest of the site and the operations which

[92] See para 1.b.1 at page 25.
[93] Report at page 30.
[94] As to which see Chapter 1 - Part I.

are likely to damage that interest which is in force in relation to a European site has effect for the purpose of the Habitats Regulations (regulation 18(1)). This means that SSSI protection is preserved for SSSIs which are also European sites under the Regulations. The Regulations expressly provide for the amendment at any time of the SSSI notification in relation to either the special interest of the site or the potentially damaging operations, for the purpose of securing compliance with the Habitats Directive (regulation 18(2)). Read with the general duty set out in regulation 3(2), it appears that nature conservation bodies are under a legal duty to be proactive in ensuring that existing notifications are sufficient for delivering the objectives of the Habitats Directive in relation to the site. Notice of amendments to notifications must be given to every owner and occupier of the site who, in the opinion of the nature conservation body, may be affected by the amendment, and to the local planning authority. No figures are available for the number of such amendments made by nature conservation agencies but some entirely new sites have been notified to underpin terrestrial cSACs. Any such amendment will be also be a local land charge, as under s28(11) of the 1981 Act.

Restrictions: The system for restricting the carrying out of operations notified in relation to a European site is very similar to the system for restricting the carrying out of potentially damaging operations in relation to SSSIs under s28 of the 1981 Act prior to its amendment by the 2000 Act. The owner or occupier of a European site is prohibited from carrying out or causing to be carried out any of the operations specified in a regulation 18 notification unless written notice has been given to the appropriate nature conservation body (specifying the nature of the operation and the land on which it is proposed to carry it out) and unless one of the three conditions set out in paragraph (2) of regulation 18 is fulfilled. The three conditions are that: either written consent has been obtained from the appropriate nature conservation body, or that the operation is carried out in accordance with a management agreement, or that four months has expired from the giving of notice by the owner or occupier.

It is offence to contravene paragraph (1) "without a reasonable excuse". Regulation 18(4) provides that it is a reasonable excuse that the operation in question was an emergency operation particulars of which were notified to the appropriate nature conservation body as soon as practicable or that the operation was authorised pursuant to planning permission under Part III of the TCPA 1990. The penalty on summary conviction is a fine not exceeding level (4) on the standard scale. Proceedings may only be brought by the appropriate nature conservation body but may only be brought by any other person with the consent of the DPP in England and Wales (regulation 18(6)).

Appropriate Assessment of Operations: In relation to applications for consent to carry out a regulation 18 operation, an appropriate assessment is required where the operation forms part of a plan or project which is not directly connected with or necessary to the management of the site and is likely to have significant effect on the site (either alone or in combination with other projects or plans). The appropriate nature conservation body must make an appropriate assessment of the implications of the operation for the site in view of the site's conservation objectives (regulation 20(1)). In the light of the assessment, the nature conservation body may only give consent for the operation after having ascertained that the plan or project will not adversely affect the integrity of the site. These provisions do not apply to sites which are only European sites by virtue of the fact that they are the subject of consultation under Article 5(4) of the Directive. Guidance on appropriate assessment of plans and projects (dealt with under regulation 48) and other related matters has been provided in a series of Habitats Regulations Guidance Notes issued by English Nature and discussed below. Of particular relevance in this context is HGN4 on the meaning of "alone or in combination" as regards significant effects.

Where consent is refused but the conservation body considers that the operation may be carried out anyway, or in any other case where it fears that an operation to which it has not given consent will be carried out, it must notify the Secretary of State of this and must ensure that such notification is given at least one month before the four month period under regulation 19(2)(c) expires (giving the Secretary of State one month in which to act before the operation may go ahead in any event)(regulation 20(4)-(5)). This gives the Secretary of State the opportunity to decide whether an SNCO should be made (see below).

Similar provision for assessment is made elsewhere in the Regulations: in relation to sites subject to an SNCO under regulation 22, here the obligation to make an assessment arises in relation to an application for consent to carry out an operation specified in the order (regulation 24); and also in regulations 48-49, in relation to assessment of plans or projects governed by certain development control legislation, including the town and country planning system. Assessment of plans and projects in the context of the Habitats Regulations is discussed further in the section on Part IV below. The provisions in the Regulations relating to notice and consent are the subject of draft amendment Regulations currently with

Defra. The intention being to reconcile the provisions with the post Countryside and Rights of Way Act notice and consent provisions of the 1981 Act. There are currently and confusingly, two sets of provisions for a similar but different process which may apply to the same area of land. A single consent or refusal with right of appeal etc would appear to be preferable, with English Nature's discretion fettered by consideration of the "tests" in the Regulations in considering whether to grant or not (where the land is both SSSI and European site).

Review of Notifications and Consents under Regulation 21

Regulation 21 preserves existing notifications and consents made under s28 of the 1981 Act, but requires the appropriate nature conservation body to review any such consent as regards its compatibility with the conservation objectives of the site (regulation 21(2)). Notice of any modification or withdrawal of consent must be given to every owner or occupier of land within the site who is likely to be affected by it and comes into force on notice being given. Modification or withdrawal shall not affect anything done in reliance on the consent before notice is given. Where an operation ceases to be covered by a consent by virtue of a modification or withdrawal, the period after which it may be carried out in accordance with regulation 19(2)(c) is four months. As with refusal of consent for an operation under regulation 20, the nature conservation body must notify the Secretary of State if it considers that there is a risk that the operation will be carried out despite the modification or withdrawal (regulation 21(6)).

In the UK's First Report on the implementation of the Directive it is stated that the timetable for review of consents is likely to last until the end of March 2010[95].

Special Nature Conservation Orders

Described by the Government as "the nuclear option" during debate on the Regulations in the House of Commons, SNCOs are a modified, strengthened version of the Nature Conservation Order (NCO) which was available pursuant to a power under s29 of the 1981 Act but which was repealed by the 2000 Act. The Government made it clear when the Habitats Regulations were adopted that it continued to prefer the voluntary approach and expected that, where management was necessary, most of the conservation needs of designated sites would be delivered

[95] See para 1.b.ii at page 29.

through voluntary management arrangements negotiated between owners and occupiers and the nature conservation agencies[96], and that it would prefer not to use its powers of compulsory purchase. In a departure from the voluntary principle however, an SNCO can be made which has the effect of extending indefinitely the period during which an operation may not be carried out (regulation 22). It can therefore prohibit damaging operations indefinitely unless a management agreement is negotiated, or consent is given on overriding grounds. Some MPs expressed concern about the erosion of the voluntary principle represented by the introduction of the SNCO but this was clearly necessary in order to secure the level of protection required under the directive. The SNCO does not however address the problem of positive management referred to above, this must be addressed in the normal way, through the SSSI system/regulation 16.

The Secretary of State has the power to make an SNCO, after consultation with the appropriate nature conservation body, in respect of any land (which includes land covered by water) within a European site. The order specifies the operations which appear to him to be likely to destroy or damage the features of the land which are the basis for its designation as a European site. Schedule 1 to the Regulations governs the making, confirmation and coming into operation of such orders as well as their amendment and revocation. SNCOs are local land charges. S29 Orders made under the 1981 Act which applied in relation to land which on or after the commencement of the Regulations was within a European site are to have effect as if made under regulation 22 of the Regulations (Regulation 27). Consents given under s29(5) of the 1981 Act were to be reviewed as regards their compatibility with the conservation objectives of the site (regulation 27(3)) and notice of any modification or withdrawal of consent given to every owner or occupier of land within the site who may be affected by it.

The effect of an SNCO is that no person shall carry out on any land within a European site in respect of which an order is in force any operation specified in the order unless the appropriate nature conservation body has been given written notice of the proposed operation (including its nature and the land on which it is proposed to carry it out) and one of two conditions is satisfied (regulation 23). These conditions are either that the relevant nature conservation body has given its consent to the operation or that the operation is carried out in accordance with a management agreement.

[96] Hansard 242.

It is an offence to contravene regulation 23(1) without a reasonable excuse. The prescribed penalty is greater than for a contravention of regulation 19, namely a fine not exceeding the statutory maximum on summary conviction, or a fine on indictment. It may seem surprising that the same "reasonable excuse" defence available under regulation 19 in relation to European sites generally, also applies to offences under regulation 23, given that these sites are more strictly protected and the purpose of the order is to protect a site thought to be at risk of damage or destruction Moreover, the same two situations are specified as constituting a "reasonable excuse": an emergency or that the action was authorised by planning permission. In the former case, perhaps it is logical to have the same defence. In the case of the second, it is important to bear in mind the modifications to the planning process made by the Regulations[97] and also set out in planning guidance, in particular PPG 9. These modifications are intended to bring the planning system into line with the requirements of the directive so that the defence is not as extensive as might at first appear.

Regulation 26 provides that a court by which a person is convicted under regulation 23 may make an order requiring the person concerned to carry out such operations for the purpose of restoring the land to its former condition as may be specified in the order. It is an offence to fail without reasonable excuse to comply with such an order, liable to a fine of level 5 on summary conviction and if the failure continues the person may be proceeded against for a further offence from time to time until the order is complied with (regulation 26(5)).

The first SNCO related to drainage works to be carried out in the Peak Moors Special Protection Area. English Nature obtained an injunction to prevent the works within 24 hours of discovering the damage (March 1998).

Appropriate Assessment: Plans or projects likely to have a significant effect on a site which is subject to an SNCO must be made subject to an appropriate assessment under regulation 24[98]. There are a number of differences between the provisions for assessment in relation to ordinary European sites and those subject to an SNCO. The requirements are similar to those contained in regulation 20 relating to European sites generally but go further. The scope of the requirement to carry out an assessment and

[97] These changes are considered further below in the section on Part IV of the Regulations

[98] This requirement does not apply to sites which are only European sites by virtue of regulation 10(1)(c)(sites protected under Article 5(4).

the obligation to only give consent where the plan or project "will not adversely affect the integrity of the site" are the same as in regulation 20. In the case of an assessment relating to an SNCO site however, the nature conservation body is expressly required to give *reasons* for a decision to refuse consent (regulation 24(3)). In addition, in the case of a site which is subject to an SNCO, the owner or occupier may require the nature conservation body to *refer the matter to the Secretary of State* if either consent for the plan or project is refused (he must act within two months) or if no decision is received within three months of an application for consent being made (regulation 24(4)).

If the Secretary of State considers that, there being no alternative solutions, the project must be carried out for "imperative reasons of overriding public interest" he may direct the nature conservation body to give consent. The type of reasons on which such a direction may be based differ according to whether or not the site hosts a priority natural habitat type or priority species. If the site does *not* contain a priority species or habitat, such reasons may be of a social or economic nature. If however the site *does* contain priority species or habitat, the reasons must be those relating to human health, public safety or beneficial consequences of primary importance to the environment or other reasons which, in the opinion of the European Commission, are imperative reasons of overriding public importance (regulation 24(6)).[99]

Compensatory measures: Where the Secretary of State does direct that consent be granted, compensatory measures are required in order to ensure that the overall coherence of Natura 2000 is protected (regulation 24(7)).

Compensation: There is provision for compensation to be paid, under regulation 25, to any person having an interest in land comprised in "agricultural unit" which comprises land to which an order relates. An agricultural unit is land which is occupied as a unit for agricultural purposes, including any dwelling house or other building occupied for the purpose of farming. The claim for compensation must be made to the appropriate nature conservation body and must shown that the value of the interest is less than it would have been had the order not been made.

[99] These concepts are discussed further above.

Compulsory Purchase

The making of a SNCO may not in itself be sufficient to secure that a European site is managed so as to ensure that the conservation objectives of the directive are met. The order will specify what may not be done without consent but will not mandate the management of the site. In certain circumstances, the absence of effective management may be addressed through the exercise of the power to purchase land compulsorily under regulation 32. Where the relevant nature conservation body is satisfied either that they are unable to conclude a management agreement for land within a European site on terms appearing to them to be reasonable or that there is a breach of a management agreement which prevents or impairs the satisfactory management of the site, the nature conservation body may acquire the interest in land compulsorily. In the case of a breach, where the act or omission constituting the breach is capable of remedy, notice must have been given by the nature conservation body requiring remedy of the breach and a reasonable time in which to remedy the breach must have elapsed before the power may be exercised (see regulation 32(2)). Any dispute as to whether there has been a breach of a management agreement is to be determined by an arbitrator appointed by the Lord Chancellor (see regulation 32(3)). In practice there had been criticism in the past that the power to effect compulsory purchase under the 1949 Act had been little used because of the bureaucracy and resources required.

Byelaws

Regulation 28 gives nature conservation bodies the power to make byelaws for the protection of a European site under s20 of the 1949 Act (which relates to nature reserves). Paragraph (3) sets out some of the kinds of byelaws which may be made, including prohibition or restriction of the entry into or movement within the site of persons, vehicles, boats and animals. Regulation 29 provides for certain limitations on the effects of such byelaws however: they may not interfere with the exercise by any person of a right vested in him as owner, lessee, occupier of land within a European site, or any such surrounding or adjacent area as covered by regulation 28(4). Nor may byelaws interfere with any right of way, the exercise of any functions of statutory undertakers, internal drainage board, district salmon board or the running of any telecommunication code system (see regulation 29). Compensation is payable, under regulation 30, where the exercise of any right of a person, whether by reason of his being entitled to any interest in land, or by virtue of any licence or agreement, is prevented or hindered by such byelaws. Existing s20 byelaws in relation to land which is a European site are to continue in effect as if made under regulation 28.

Byelaws are potentially useful as a means of controlling third party activities.

Part IV of the Regulations: Adaptation of Planning and Other Controls

As described above, under Part II of the Habitats Regulations, restrictions are placed on the carrying out of operations notified as likely to damage a European site (regulation 19). These restrictions are placed on the owners and occupiers of land within a European site. Where a European site is subject to an SNCO under regulation 22, no person may carry out any operation specified in the order unless they obtain consent or act in accordance with a management agreement. In practice, the types of operation notified under regulations 18 and 22 are often related to agricultural practices, other typical operations include those relating to river management for fisheries or upland shooting estates. In both cases, where there has been a contravention of these rules, it is a reasonable excuse for a person to carry out an operation if the operation was authorised by a planning permission granted under Part III of the Town and Country Planning Act 1990[100]. Clearly, in order to afford European sites the full protection required under Article 6 of the habitats directive, further provision was required to address the issue of the relationship between the planning system and the protection of European sites and also to take account of other forms of development, outside the planning system, which may have an impact on the site and which are not operations covered by notification under regulation 18. These issues are dealt with under Part IV of the Regulations.

Types of Development Covered by Part IV

In addition to planning controls under the town and country planning legislation, Part IV also covers a number of sectors of development which fall under other statutory regimes: the construction and improvement of highways and roads, cycle tracks, certain consents under the Electricity Act 1989; certain pipeline authorisations under the Pipelines Act 1962; certain orders under the Transport and General Works Act 1992; and certain environmental authorisations and consents under the Environmental Protection Act 1990, the Water Resources Act 1991 and the

[100] Or if the operation was an emergency operation.

Control of Pollution Act 1974. The requirements for assessment of plans and projects and review of existing consents are applied to these sectors in the terms set out in Part IV.

Part IV makes provision for those competent authorities covered by that Part to carry out appropriate assessments of the implications for a European site of plans and projects with which they are concerned and which are likely to have a significant effect on the site (regulations 48 and 49) and also requires them to review existing decisions and consents for such plans or projects by making an appropriate assessment of their implications for the site, although in the latter case, nothing in the regulation requiring review is to affect anything done in pursuance of the consent or permission before the date on which the site becomes a European site or, if later, the commencement of the regulations (regulations 50 and 51). Coordination is required where more than one competent authority is involved, meaning where a plan or project is undertaken by more than one authority, or requires the consent or permission or other authorisation of more than one competent authority, or is undertaken by one or more competent authority and requires the consent etc of one or more other authorities (regulation 52). The requirements of regulations 48-51 are applied to the various development control regimes in the manner set out in regulations 54-85. Guidance on the conduct of appropriate assessment under regulation 48 and related matters has been provided in a series of Habitats Regulations Guidance Notes issued by English Nature[101].

Criticisms have been made that Part IV does not cover all the relevant types of development Neither would it appear to satisfy the Commission's desire[102] to see a broad approach taken to the interpretation of "plan or project". Amendments are proposed to the Regulations to specifically add water abstraction licences to the list of matters to which Regulation 48 etc shall apply but it is difficult to see how an ad hoc approach to amending the list will be satisfactory. Although Regulation 3(4) "only" requires competent authorities to "have regard" to the requirements of the Directive, it has been relied on to take a wider view (see above) . One additional sector now covered by the requirements of the

[101] HRGN1 deals with the appropriate assessment under regulation 48; HRGN2 deals with the review of existing planning permissions and other consents; HRGN3 addresses the determination of likely significant effect; HRGN4 deals with the meaning of "alone or in combination" and HRGN6 deals with the conditions imposed on permitted development (HRGN5 on the determination of "not directly connected with or necessary to the management of the site" is currently being drafted).

[102] (Managing Natura 2000, para 4.3)

directive is offshore oil and gas production. The Offshore Petroleum Activities (Conservation of Habitats) Regulations 2001[103], which entered into force on May 31 2001, implement the Habitats Directive in relation to offshore oil and gas activities carried out wholly or partly on the UK Continental Shelf. The need to implement the directive in relation to activities taking place on the Continental Shelf was established in the *Greenpeace (No 2) Case* in which the High Court accepted arguments put by Greenpeace that the reference to territory in the Directive included protection of habitats and species occurring on the UKCS.

It should be remembered that the general duty set out in regulation 3(4) which requires competent authorities, in the exercise of any of their functions to "have regard to the requirements of the Habitats Directive in so far as they may be affected by the exercise of those functions", applies to all competent authorities covered by the definition in regulation 6, regardless of whether they are among those specifically covered by Part IV. It may be argued that such a general duty cannot substitute effectively for the more specific obligations placed on particular authorities under Part IV and that the phrase "have regard to" does not clearly bind competent authorities to achieve the same level of protection for sites as is achieved under Part IV. It is arguable however that the end result should not, in most cases, differ according to whether an authority is acting in accordance with Part IV or under simply the general duty in regulation 3(4), given the Community law obligation to interpret any national provision, such as regulation 3(4) so as to be in accordance with the directive so far as possible.

Assessment of Plans and Projects Under Part IV of the Regulations

Regulation 48 governs the assessment of the implications of those plans and projects[104] covered by Part IV. It requires the competent authorities concerned to carry out an appropriate assessment of the conservation implications for the site of certain plans or projects, before deciding to undertake, or to give any consent, permission or other authorisation for those plans or projects. Those plans or projects requiring such assessment are any which are likely to have a significant effect on the site (either alone or in combination with other plans or projects) and which are not directly connected with or necessary to the management of the site . English Nature has issued guidance on issues relating to appropriate

[103] SI 2001/1754.

[104] The question of what constitutes a plan or project for these purposes was raised in R (On the application of Beevers and others) v Environment Agency in the context of the operation of a tidal barrage, but it was not resolved as the parties agreed terms on the basis of undertakings given by the Agency, CO/358/2000.

assessment in a series of Habitats Regulations Guidance Notes as referred to below. HRGN 1 notes that in all but the most clear cut cases, competent authorities are likely to need advice from English Nature or other conservation agencies as to whether a plan pr project is likely to have significant effects on a European site and thus require appropriate assessment (para 6). Furthermore it is stated that the competent authority would be expected to follow English Nature's advice and normally to decide the case in accordance with English Nature's recommendations or be prepared to explain its reasons (para 16). PPG 9 also suggests this[105].

Guidance on the determination of likely significant effect is provided in HRGN 3 which states that the significance test "acts as a coarse filter" for all proposed plans and projects which are not directly connected with the management of the site[106] For example, it is stated that very short lived impacts would generally only require only minimal further consideration provided there were no persistent or cumulative effects but the guidance goes on to point out that even here there will be exceptions - a brief disturbance to a seabird colony may have a lasting effect on the population (para 4.2). It is also stated that permanent reductions in habitat area or species populations are likely to be significant unless they are very small scale (para 4.4) but in some cases such as limestone pavements any further loss may be unacceptable. HRGN 4 clarifies the meaning of "alone or in combination" with other plans or projects-a test which appears in regulations, 20, 24, 48 and 60.

A person applying for a consent or other authorization covered by regulation 48 is required to give such information to the competent authority as it may reasonably require for the purposes of the assessment. A competent authority carrying out an assessment under regulation 48 must consult the appropriate nature conservation body and "have regard" to any representations made by the body within such reasonable time as the authority may require. The competent authority may also "if they consider it appropriate" consult the general public (regulation 48(4)). Nothing in regulation 48(1) (or regulation 50(2) dealing with review see below) requires a competent authority to assess any project or plan which would be more appropriately assessed under that provision by another competent authority (regulation 52(2)).

[105] Annex C9.
[106] See para 2.1.

In the light of the conclusions of the assessment, and subject to the issue of alternative solutions and considerations of overriding public interest (regulation 49), the competent authority shall agree to the plan or project only after having ascertained that it will not adversely affect the integrity of the site. HRGN 1 states that an adverse effect on integrity is likely to be one which prevents the site from making the same contribution to favourable conservation status for the relevant feature as it did at the time of its designation (para 22). HRGN 1 also states that a precautionary approach should be taken in considering effects on integrity, in line with the UK Government's principles for sustainable development (para 23). Regulation 48 does not apply to sites which are only European sites by virtue of the fact that they are the subject of consultation under Article 5(4) of the directive. In the Cairngorms case, Lord Nimmo ruled that many inter-related factors required to be considered in deciding whether or not a plan or projet would adversely affect the integrity of a European site. He adopted the definition of integrity set out in [SNH] Circular 6/1995 (also in PPG 9 and, with slight variation in wording Commission guidance, Managing N2K) which referred inter alia to the coherence of the site's ecological structure and function. He rejected the petitioners argument in that case that there had to be an absolute guarantee that the integrity of the site would not be affected and said that the most that could be expected of a planning authority or nature conservation body involved in the assessment was that they identify potential risks and put in place a legally enforceable framework with a view to prevent these from materialising. It was on this basis he added that regulations 48(6) and 54(3) referred to the use of planning conditions[107]. It might be argued that in general terms this ruling does not place sufficient emphasis on the need to secure the integrity of the site under the directive-for example where there appears to be a strong risk of damage through non-compliance with any conditions (perhaps based on a developer's previous record) it is certainly arguable that the authority should make a negative assessment. Also, on the question of what is required by Regulation 48(5) see *ADT Auctions v Secretary of State for Environment Transport and the Regions and Hart District Council* (CO 4040 2000). In amongst lengthy discussion about the remit of a reopened Planning Inquiry with a different inspector the judge found that the approach required by Regulation 48(5) was relevant both where the decision maker thought there would be an adverse effect on the site or where he was undecided.

[107] Page 104 of the judgment transcript.

The requirement to carry out an assessment can apply to plans and projects located in or outside sites. During discussion of the draft regulations, one concern expressed in the House of Lords concerning the operation of regulation 48, was the question of how it would be possible to determine whether a project outside a site would have an effect on it. In order to ensure that relevant plans or projects are assessed consultation zones may been set up, within which English Nature or the relevant conservation body is consulted as to whether assessment will be required (PPG9 para C10). In HRGN 1 English Nature states that in relation to significant effects, these may occur even if the plan or project is some distance away from the designated area and even outside any consultation area defined by English Nature[108].

Type of Assessment

As indicated above, the appropriate assessment under the habitats regulations does not correspond to an environmental impact assessment (although as there are broad similarities, the information obtained for one type of assessment may also be relevant to the other) see PPG 9 at Annex C. The decision-maker needs to assess the implications of the project for the site's conservation objectives so as to ascertain whether or not it will adversely affect the integrity of the site. The "integrity of the site" means the coherence of its ecological structure and function, across its whole area, that enables it to sustain the habitat, complex of habitats and/or levels of populations of the species for which it was classified. The developer must (there is no requirement to in the Reg 48 but PPG 9 and other guidance, eg that of the EA suggests that it is good practice consult English Nature if he is not sure whether the plan or project will have a significant effect on the site. If English Nature considers that it will, the developer must undergo assessment. The scope of the assessment will depend on the location, size and significance of the proposed project. English Nature will advise on this on a case by case basis[109].

Adverse Effects

Regulation 48(5) provides that the authority will agree to the plan or project "only after having ascertained that it will not adversely affect the integrity of the European site". In making this determination however, regulation 48(6) provides that the authority is to have regard to "the manner in which it is proposed to carry out the plan or project" and to any conditions

[108] See HRGN 1 at para 5.
[109] See further PPG 9.

or restrictions subject to which the authority proposes that the consent, permission or authorisation should be given. The relationship between these two parts of regulation 48 was considered in the *Cairngorms case* referred to above.

In the *Cairngorms case*, the WWF and RSPB argued that, in the light of regulation 48(5), conditional planning permission could not be granted for a project which was likely to have a significant effect on a European site (page 88) and the ascertainment of the effects under paragraph (5) had to be to the standard of an absolute guarantee of legal certainty that the project would not adversely affect the integrity of the site. In support of this argument they referred to ECJ authority including *Case C No 435/92 Association pour la protection des animaux* in which the Court had found that a standard of complete protection was required in relation to the fixing of closed seasons for the hunting of wild birds[110]. In this and other cases the ECJ had ruled that a "complete system of protection" was required under the wild birds directive. The conservation groups argued that it followed that, under the Habitats Directive, a similar level of protection for sites was required and that to leave the determination to an administrative discretion constituted a breach of this requirement. This would be the case if reliance were placed on the statutory Agreement and Visitors Management Plan which had been drawn up for the development.

The Plan set out the conditions under which planning permission was granted and under which the development was to operate. WWF argued that there was uncertainty about the impact of the large number of visitors likely to visit the area and this made it impossible to have the necessary guarantee of protection for the site. Scottish Natural Heritage (SNH) argued that regulation 48(5) did not require an absolute guarantee and pointed to the general duty to secure compliance with the directive under regulation 3(2) in the exercise of their functions. They also pointed out that under regulation 48(6) the planning authority was required to have regard to any conditions or restrictions subject to which the permission should be given. The Court (page 104) did not accept that an absolute guarantee that the integrity of the site would be adversely affected was required. The most that could be expected of a planning authority or conservation body was that it would identify the potential risks, so far as reasonably foreseeable, and put in place a legally enforceable framework with a view to prevent these risks from materialising. That was why provision was made in regulation 48(6) and 54(3) (grant of planning

[110] See further Chapter 2 - Part II.

permission) for the use of conditions and Counsel had not argued that the use of conditions was contrary to the directive. The Court would not accept arguments that the bodies concerned might not enforce these conditions- there was nothing in this case to take that possibility outside the realm of theory and anyway the general duties under regulation 3(2) and (4) governed the actions of SNH and the planning authority (the Judge appeared to take the view that they would have a duty rather than a discretion to take enforcement action in circumstances where the site might be damaged).

The approach of the Court in *Cairngorms* places a great deal of reliance on the general duties which bind competent authorities under regulation 3. It can be argued that such an approach can only be consistent with the requirements of the Habitats Directive if in fact those general duties are interpreted strictly by courts in order to ensure that a "complete system of protection" is achieved. Subsequent cases may serve to clarify the extent to which courts will enforce those general duties where this level of protection is not achieved.

The question of alternative solutions also arises in this context. The issue was considered briefly in the case dealing with the dredge of Harwich Haven to increase the capacity of Felixstowe docks to take larger ships . In summary, the proposal was to increase capacity in the port of Felixstowe to take larger vessels and they couldn't get into the port any other way. In the case of a review of a planning permission at Barksore Marshes in Kent the applicant's case fell at this stage. There were found to be alternative solutions. In general it could be argued that an applicant might seek to narrow the scope of the objectives of their plan or project to make it easier to satisfy this question. This is balanced though by the need to find imperative reasons etc. Defining the scope narrowly might help with the alternatives question but a developer would have to guard against talking themselves out of the public interest in so doing

.

Imperative Reasons of Overriding Public Interest

The prohibition in regulation 48(5) on granting consent for plans and projects where there has been a negative assessment is not absolute. Where there are considerations of overriding public interest at stake it may be possible to grant consent for the plan or project despite a negative assessment of the implications of the plan or project for the site in question. The conditions under which this may be done are set out in Regulation 49.

Regulation 49 transposes Article 6(4) of the habitats directive[111] and provides that if they are satisfied that there are no alternative solutions, and that the plan or project must be carried out for imperative reasons of overriding public interest, the competent authority may agree to the plan or project notwithstanding a negative assessment. What may constitute such reasons depends on whether or not the site hosts a priority natural habitat type or priority species. If the site does not contain a priority species or habitat, such reasons may be of a social or economic nature. If however the site *does* contain priority species of habitat, the reasons must be those relating to human health, public safety or beneficial consequences of primary importance to the environment or other reasons which, in the opinion of the European Commission, are imperative reasons of overriding public importance (regulation 24(6)). These concepts are discussed further in the section on the directive.

Concern was expressed about the extent of the power to derogate from the protective provisions of the directive afforded to the Secretary of State under regulation 49 during debate on the Regulations in Parliament. Critics referred to the "Henry VIII powers" to permit development to go ahead if there are considerations of overriding public interest. It was said that it would be "remarkably easy to wriggle out of the obligations if the Secretary of State feels like it". There was also concern about what criteria the Commission would use in order to determine whether, in relation to priority species and habitats, "other reasons" are acceptable[112], and it was argued that this rendered the habitats directive weaker than wild birds directive. This was identified as a "key area where the legislation weakens the nature conservation protection that is available today"[113]. As pointed out by one critic :"in certain areas [the legislation] puts Henry VIII powers in the hands of the Secretary of State and collective college of the cardinals of the European Commission". This criticism was accompanied by complaints about the confidentiality of Article 169 infraction correspondence which made it impossible to tell what the basis for decisions under regulation 49 had been.[114]

In practice, the publication of the Commission Opinions under Article 6 (where priority species or habitats are concerned) may go some way to render transparent the basis for accepting in a particular case that there are imperative reasons of overriding public interest which justify

[111] Article 6(4) is discussed above.
[112] See HC col 252.
[113] See HC col 253.
[114] There is though the Government's outline position statement of May '98 on the Birds and Habitats Directive which deals among other things with imperative reasons.

proceeding with a project. So far as the UK decision-making process is concerned, where a competent authority other than the Secretary of State proposes to agree to a plan or project under regulation 49 they must notify the Secretary of State. They must then wait 21 days before agreeing to the plan or project unless the Secretary of State tells them that may go ahead (regulation 49(5)). The Secretary of State has the power to direct the authority not to grant consent for the plan or project, either indefinitely or for a specified period. This power is without prejudice to any power he has in relation to the decision in question. In determining whether a plan or project should be agreed to under regulation 49(1), a competent authority other than the Secretary of State is required to seek and have regard to the views of other any other competent authorities involved. In relation to sites hosting *priority* species or habitats, where a competent authority other than the Secretary of State, desires to obtain the opinion of the European Commission as to whether reasons for granting consent are to considered imperative reasons of overriding public interest they must submit a written request to the Secretary of State identifying the matter on which an opinion is sought and accompanied by any documents or information which may be required (regulation 49(3)). The Secretary of State may "if he thinks fit" seek the opinion of the Commission and if does so must transmit the opinion to the authority when it is received.

Review of Existing Decisions and Consents under Part IV of the Regulations

Regulation 50 governs the review of existing decisions and consents. The Government explained why it was necessary to make provision for the review of existing permissions when the regulations were being considered by Parliament. As was pointed out, the only derogations permitted under the directive are those contained in Article 6(3)-(4): "It follows that any existing permissions must be assessed, in terms of Article 6(3) to see whether the project meets the criteria in that paragraph". The Government was of the view that "relatively few permissions should need to be reviewed and in even fewer cases should further action need to be taken". ... "Modification, revocation or discontinuance should be exceptional"[115].

[115] See col 108 HL. Barksore Marshes is the one example. The Environment Agency have a project in place to review their consents for the purposes of Reg 50.

Originally the scope of the obligation to review consents under the Regulations did not extend to potential SPA's and candidate SAC's until such time as they were placed on the list of sites of Community Importance as, until that stage, they were not "European sites" within the meaning of regulation 10 (see above). In 1998 the Government announced that, as a matter of policy: "it may be appropriate in some cases to commence an initial review once the site becomes a candidate SAC, ie when it is sent to the Commission."[116]. Furthermore, PPG9 notes that some SSSI's are potential SPAs (subject to further consultation or survey work before a decision is made) or candidate SAC's (identified on the list sent to the Commission) and provides: "For the purpose of considering development proposals affecting them, potential SPA's and candidate SAC's included in the list sent to the European Commission should be treated in the same way as classified SPAs and designated SAC's". This policy has now been superseded by the amendment made to the Regulations by the Conservation (Natural Habitats &c) (Amendment) (England) Regulations 2000, which extend the definition of "European site" in regulation 10 so as to include candidate SACs sent to the Commission (England only)[117].

Regulation 50 applies to existing decisions and consents which relate to a plan or project to which the requirement for assessment under regulation 48(1) would apply if the decision were to be reconsidered. Regulation 50 provides that where, before the date on which a site becomes a European site or, if later, the commencement of the regulations, a competent authority have decided to undertake, or give any consent, permission or other authorisation the authority shall "as soon as reasonably practicable" review their decision, permission, authorisation or consent as the case may be. The authority must then affirm, modify or revoke the decision in the light of the review

The review is based on an assessment of the implications for the site in view of the site's conservation objectives and the provisions of regulation 48(2) to (4) apply "with the appropriate modifications" to the review. The review is either to be carried out under existing statutory procedures or, where none exist, in accordance with any directions issued by the Secretary of State. Generally the competent authority responsible for the consent is the authority which identifies the consents to be reviewed[118].

[116] See Statement "The Birds and Habitats Directives: Outline Government Position" dated to be read together with PPG9, available on DETR website, English and European Wildlife Issues (May 1998).
[117] The Conservation (Natural Habitats &c) (Amendment) Regulations 2000, SI 2000/192 HMSO, entered into force on 28 February 2000.
[118] HRGN 2 at para 5.

Nothing in regulation 50 is to affect any thing done in pursuance of the decision before the date on which the site became a European site or if later, the commencement of the Regulations.

Regulation 51 sets out the way in which the authority should approach the review and further guidance is provided in HRGN 2. Subject to certain additional considerations set out in regulation 51, the provisions of regulation 48(5) and (6) apply as does regulation 49 (discussed above). This means that in the light of the assessment, the competent authority may affirm the decision only after having ascertained that the plan or project will not adversely affect the integrity of the site and in considering whether this is the case, the authority must have regard to the manner in which it is proposed to carry out the plan or project and any conditions or restrictions to which the consent or permission will be subject. In addition, if the competent authority consider that there is no likelihood of that part of the project which would adversely affect the integrity of the European site being carried out or continued, they do not need to speed further with the review for so long as this remains the case[119].

In addition, the decision may be affirmed notwithstanding a negative assessment, if there are no alternative solutions and the authority is satisfied that the plan or project must go ahead for imperative reasons of overriding public interest in accordance with the conditions laid down in regulation 49. The additional considerations laid down in regulation 51 relate to the situation where the integrity of the site may be protected by other action taken by that authority or by another authority. Regulation 51(3) provides that the decision or consent under review may be affirmed if it appears to the authority that such other action "will secure that the plan or project does not adversely affect the integrity of the site", the regulation goes on to provide that where that object may be attained in a number of ways, the authority or authorities concerned shall seek to secure that the action taken is the least onerous to those affected. Regulation 48(4) provides for the possibility of guidance in this area in particular as to the order of application of other controls and the extent to which account should be taken of the possible exercise of other powers. HRGN 2 deals with review procedures. Any modification or revocation effected in pursuance of regulation 51 is to be carried out under existing procedures where these exist. This may include provision for monetary compensation as provided for in the Town and Country planning legislation, *Barksore Marshes case* If none exist, the Secretary of State may give directions as to the procedure to be followed.

[119] See HRGN 2 at para 19.

Compensatory measures

Where, in accordance with regulation 49, a plan or project is agreed to despite a negative assessment or, following a review under regulation 50, a decision is affirmed despite a negative assessment, regulation 53 requires that compensatory measures be taken in order to ensure the overall coherence of Natura 2000. The Secretary of State has a duty to secure that this is done. The Government has said that, in accordance with the polluter pays principle, the cost of these should, where-ever possible, be borne by the developer. The Government has also said that where recreation or restoration is ordered as a compensatory measure, it would expect the site to become in time, of a quality to secure the coherence of the Natura 2000 network.

Some commentators have criticised the Commission for insufficient scrutiny of proposed compensatory measures and pointed to the considerable uncertainties in assessing adequacy of compensatory measures. The Government's May '98 statement sets out some principles as does the Commision's Managing Natura 2000guidance. Attempts are being made to identify principles relating to proximity to damaged habitat, quality, how to deal with technical uncertainty. There are practical difficulties being experienced including securing land. The question also arises as to how to proceed where compensation can not be secured. There was some suggestion in the Barksore case that the plan or project couldn't proceed.

Compensation

The issue of withdrawal of permitted development rights without compensation (contrary to the normal position under an Article 4 Direction) was raised during debate in the House of Commons[120]. The Government responded by saying that existing compensation arrangements under the town and country planning legislation would apply. The amount of compensation is to be determined by the Lands Tribunal unless the Secretary of State indicates otherwise.

Planning Permission and European Sites

During debate on the Regulations the Government stated that the Secretary of State would normally call in for decision planning applications which were likely significantly to affect a European site.[121].

[120] Hansard House of Lords, 17 October 1994, col 92.
[121] HL col 110 ibid.

When permissions are reviewed (having identified relevant permissions during consultation on the site), the local planning authority must ascertain whether implementation is likely to have a significant effect on the site which would adversely affect its integrity. If so, and if the permission does not fulfil the conditions under which a new development proposal would be approved, "the authority must take the appropriate action to remove the potential for harm, unless there is no likelihood of the development being carried out or continued."

The local planning authority must invite the developer to enter into planning obligation to safeguard integrity of site if possible, and if not, modify or revoke the permission or issue a discontinuance order.

Regulation 55(5) exempts planning permission granted by Act of Parliament

Permitted development is development which requires planning permission but is generally deemed to be non-controversial and usually acceptable and is therefore granted a general planning permission by the Secretary of State under the provisions of the General Permitted Development Order 1994[122] Under regulation 60 of the Habitats Regulations, it is a condition of any planning permission granted by general development order that in circumstances where the development is likely to have a significant effect on a European site and is not directly connected with or necessary to the management of the site, the development shall not be begun until the developer has received written notification of the approval of the local authority under regulation 62. Similar provision is made in relation to development begun but not completed before the entry into force of the Regulations. During the debate on the regulations, in relation to regulations 60-63, the Government was asked if they were subject to regulation 48 so as to require the local planning authority to take social and economic factors into account. The Government responded that they were[123].

If developers proceed with a development in or near a European site on the assumption that it is covered by a permitted development right and without checking whether or not it is likely to have significant effects on the site, they risk finding that they have undertaken the project without planning permission (as the requisite condition has not been complied

[122] See HRGN 6 at para 2.1.
[123] Hansard House of Lords, 17 October 1994, col 110.

with) and could face enforcement action. If developers are uncertain as to whether development will have a significant effect they are urged to seek an opinion from English Nature[124]. HRGN 6 makes it clear that as a matter of policy regulation 60 should also be applied to pSPA and Ramsar sites (para 6.1)

Regulation 61 provides for the giving of an opinion by the relevant nature conservation body as to whether the development is likely to have a significant effect. HRGN 6 notes that if English Nature gives an opinion that the permitted development is not likely to have a significant effect on the site, that opinion is conclusive for the purposes of the Regulations (para 9.1) and satisfies the condition. If they conclude that the development is likely to have significant effects approval must be sought from the local planning authority under regulation 62. This is not an application for planning permission it is an application to enable the development to proceed as permitted development (HRGN 6 para 10.2). The planning authority must then make an appropriate assessment and approve the development only after having determined that it will not adversely affect the integrity of the site. If the authority does not make such a finding and the developer wishes to proceed he must apply for full planning permission and regulations 48-49 of the Regulations apply in the normal way. HRGN 6 makes the point that the Regulations apply the precautionary approach and if the effects of a development are uncertain, the condition for permitted development is not satisfied and a full planning application is required (para 14.2).

[124] HRGN 6 at para 3.2 referring to PPG9.

CHAPTER 4

MARINE SITES

Introduction

Marine sites are of particular importance to the protection of biodiversity within the British Isles. It is estimated that 50% of the biodiversity of the UK is found in the seas,[1] with the UK exhibiting almost all the major marine habitat types. The protection of marine conservation sites poses different problems to those encountered in protecting terrestrial sites. These problems stem from legal, physical, managerial and knowledge based differences. Despite these differences, no separate mechanism for the protection of marine sites existed in British law until the Wildlife and Countryside Act 1981 ("1981 Act"). Whilst statutory mechanisms for the protection of marine sites do now exist, they are widely regarded as weak and insufficient to address the particular problems faced in relation to the marine environment.

One particular problem relating to marine conservation is the problem of insufficient knowledge. Marine research tends to be more costly than land-based research and subject to practical difficulties that are not experienced on land. As a result, scientific knowledge of the marine environment has tended to lag behind scientific knowledge of terrestrial environments. This is a particular problem for marine environments further from the coast, one recent report described the 3 nautical mile limit from shore as an 'information watershed'.[2] Although developments in technology provide answers to some of these concerns, the relative lack of knowledge creates difficulties in appropriately targeting conservation strategies. Similar problems attend monitoring and assessment of a site once a regime is in place.

In addition to the problems faced by the physical environment, marine protection also faces particular legal problems. The use of marine sites is more likely to be subject to commitments in non-environmental regimes of international law than is the case with land-based sites. International commitments relating to areas such as fisheries and

---

[1] Laffoley and Bines *Protection and Management of Nationally important Marine Habitats and Species* (English Nature, 2000)

[2] DEFRA, *Review of Marine Nature Conservation – Interim Report* (March 2001) para 83.

navigation may restrict the ability of the state to create protected areas that exclude particular activities. These concerns have led to related difficulties concerning the extent to which particular obligations apply to the marine environment. The most prominent UK example of this problem is the Greenpeace case[3] where the High Court decided that the application of the Habitats Directive extended to 200 nautical miles, as opposed to the 12 nautical mile limit that the Government had applied in implementing the Directive. These difficulties add complexity and confusion to attempts to regulate the marine environment.

Differences in the domestic legal framework also pose problems for marine regulation. Whilst the terrestrial conservation regime has been built upon concepts of private property rights and planning jurisdiction, these concepts have less relevance in the marine environment. In the marine environment, only the soil of the foreshore and the seabed is capable of ownership: the water itself if subject to general public rights of fishery and navigation. Similarly, the jurisdiction of planning authorities tends to extend only to the mean low water mark, excluding the marine environment. These differences mean that terrestrial regimes cannot simply be extended to cover the marine environment.

Perhaps as a consequence of these difficulties, marine protection has tended to lag behind terrestrial protection, leading to a neglect of marine conservation. As a result, the current legal structures have been criticised as inadequate to protect and manage the marine environment

Wildlife and Countryside Act 1981

Prior to 1981, no special regime existed for the protection of marine sites. Indeed, the question of marine conservation was only introduced into the Wildlife and Countryside Bill at a late stage due to pressure from lobby groups and within the Lords. The timing of the introduction of the relevant provisions, together with the controversial nature of the proposals, meant that the legislative scheme was relatively weak. As a result, the provisions have rarely been used.

SSSIs and Marine Sites

The backbone of habitat protection under the 1981 Act (as amended) is contained in the provisions on SSSI designation.[4] These provisions,

[3] *R v Secretary of State for Trade and Industry ex parte Greenpeace Ltd* (No 2) [2000] Env LR 221. For discussion see Chapter 3 - Part I.
[4] See chapter 1 - Part I.

however, have little impact in relation to the marine environment. Although the SSSI regime may apply to land covered by water, the conservation agencies have taken the view that this does not extend to marine sites, save for inter-tidal sites. This view is largely due to the close relationship between the origins of the SSSI regime and the planning regime. As the jurisdiction of the local planning authority generally extends only to the mean low water mark, their jurisdiction does not extend to marine sites outside of the inter-tidal area. Consequently marine protection under the 1981 Act depends on the special provisions discussed below.[5]

Marine Nature Reserves: Designation

The principal means of protecting marine sites in the 1981 Act is found in the creation of Marine Nature Reserves (MNRs).[6] The provisions for creating MNRs have been used infrequently partly due to weaknesses in the legislation itself and partly due to the policy of requiring the consensus of all interested parties employed by successive Governments since the introduction of the 1981 Act.

MNRs can be created to protect areas of land covered (continuously or intermittently) by tidal waters or parts of the sea that are landward of the baselines for measuring the territorial sea or are to a distance of three nautical miles from the baselines.[7] The process of designation is initiated by the national conservation authorities[8], which make an application for designation to the Secretary of State. Such designation can be made for the purposes of:

(a)conserving marine flora or fauna or geological or physiographical features of special interest in the area; or

(b) providing, under suitable conditions and control, special opportunities for the study of, and research into, matters relating to marine flora and fauna and the physical conditions in which they live, or for the study of geological and physiographical features of special interest in the area,[9]

Once such an application is received, the Secretary of State is under a duty to publicise the application and to serve notices on those with a

[5] See further L. Warren ' Law and Policy for Marine Protected Areas' in C. Rodgers (ed.) *Nature Conservation and Countryside Law,* (1996, University of Wales Press).

[6] ss36-37 1981 Act.

[7] s36(1) 1981 Act.

[8] English Nature, Countryside Council for Wales and Scottish National Heritage.

[9] *Ibid* .

vested interest in or right over the land affected. Should objections and representations be made and not withdrawn, a local inquiry must be held.[10] If the application is successful, the area will be designated as an MNR, empowering the relevant conservation authority to manage the site for either or both of the purposes set out in s36 (1) above. This power includes a power to mark the existence and extent of the site,[11] and, more importantly, allows the conservation authority to propose byelaws for the protection of the site.

Marine Nature Reserves: Byelaws

The primary means of protection for an MNR is through the provisions allowing byelaws to be made in respect of the site.[12] Such byelaws are created by the national conservation authorities with the consent of the Secretary of State. At first sight, the powers for the creation of byelaws are relatively broad. Byelaws may be created for the purposes of restricting or prohibiting: the entry of persons and vessels into the reserve; killing, taking, or disturbing of animals or plants in the reserve; interfering with the sea bed; damage or disturbance to any object in the reserve; or depositing of rubbish in the reserve. These provisions can be made to apply generally to the MNR or may be limited to particular parts of the reserve or to particular times of the year. Provision is also made for the granting of permits to do things otherwise prohibited by the byelaws.[13]

Despite the apparent breadth of these provisions, their effectiveness is limited by the wide exceptions contained in the Act. The first restriction is that relating to access by vessels. The Act provides that byelaws may not restrict the right of passage of any vessel other than a pleasure boat. The term vessel is not defined by the Act, but even this limited exception is further weakened by the concession granted under lobbying from the Royal Yachting Association, to the effect that even pleasure boats may not be denied access to the reserve for the whole year.[14] Second, byelaws may not be used to render unlawful the discharge of any substance from a vessel, not to regulate anything done more than 30 meters below the seabed, nor anything done for securing the safety of the vessel, preventing damage to the vessel or its cargo or saving life.[15]

---

[10] Schedule 12 to the 1981 Act.
[11] s36(5) 1981 Act.
[12] s37 1981 Act.
[13] s37(2) 1981 Act.
[14] s37(3) 1981 Act.
[15] s37(4) 1981 Act.

Third, the 1981 Act explicitly states that no byelaw may interfere with the exercise of function by a relevant authority; nor with functions conferred by or under an Act of Parliament (whenever passed); nor with the right of any person (whenever vested).[16] For these purposes, a 'relevant authority' includes any local authority, the Environment Agency, the Scottish Environment Protection Agency, water and sewerage undertakers, navigation, harbour and lighthouse authorities, district fishery boards and local fisheries commissions.[17] This list includes authorities whose functions can have a serious impact on the marine environment and seashore. This exclusion limits the impact that byelaws may have in practice by allowing a wide range of interests to prevail over MNR protection.

Marine Nature Reserves in Practice

MNRs have been little used in practice. Indeed only two MNRs have been designated in Great Britain under the Act.[18] It is now widely acknowledged that the MNR regime has failed to achieve significant protection for marine sites.[19] This failure is due in part to the weakness of the legislation providing for MNRs and the lengthy processes required before a site can be designated. It is, however, also due to the policy position that agreement between all interested parties must be achieved before an MNR can be put in place. This policy originates in a statement made by the Government during the passage of the 1981 Act.[20] Given the wide range of parties that may be interested in a particular site, any such consensus is difficult to reach and provides a substantial impediment to the designation of new sites in practice.

The Habitats Directive

The Habitats Directive[21] is designed to protect 'biodiversity' through a network of protected areas known as Natura 2000. Natura 2000 is composed of sites representing habitat types listed in Annex 1 of the Directive and habitats of species listed in Annex II. This protection is not

[16] s36(6) 1981 Act.
[17] s36(7) 1981 Act.
[18] Lundy was designated in 1986 and Skomer and the Marloes Peninsular in 1990. A third, Strangford Lough, has been designated in Northern Ireland. The Menai Straits were initially proposed in 1988 and are still under consideration for designation as an MNR.
[19] DEFRA 'Review of Marine Nature Conservation – Interim Report' para 55.
[20] HL col 524, 15 October 1981 (Lord Avon).
[21] Directive 92/43/EEC of 21 May 1992, as amended by Directive 97/62/EC. For a discussion of the purpose and operation of the Habitats Directive and Natura 2000 see Chapter 3.

limited to land based sites but also covers a range of marine sites. Annex I lists a number of marine habitat types including coastal lagoons, large shallow inlets and bays and reefs. Similarly, Annex II covers a number of marine species such as common and grey seals, bottlenose dolphins and harbour porpoises.

The Habitats directive is implemented in Great Britain through the Conservation (Natural Habitats &tc) Regulations 1994.[22] The 1994 Regulations provide protection to 'European Sites' including those designated as 'special areas of conservation' ('SACs') under the Habitats Directive, and those sites proposed as SACs. The 1994 Regulations make special provision for European Marine Sites. The Regulations define European Marine Sites as European Sites covered (continuously or intermittently) by tidal waters or any part of the sea in or adjacent to Great Britain up to the seaward limit of territorial waters.[23] In an important case, the High Court has ruled that this definition does not correctly transpose the obligations of the Habitats Directive.[24] Instead the Court held that the Habitats Directive extends to the limits of the continental shelf and to adjacent waters to the 200 nautical mile limit. The ruling has been given effect to in relation to oil and gas through the Offshore Petroleum Activities (Conservation of Habitats) Regulations 2001.[25] DEFRA has also consulted on the introduction of regulations to extend the application of the 1994 Regulations so as to comply with the ruling. In addition, Darwin Mounds, a cold coral reef 185 km off the coast of Scotland, has been identified as a candidate for protection with DEFRA initiating a consultation on its designation as a candidate SAC.

European Marine Sites: Obligations on Public Bodies

The first means of protection for European Marine Sites is through the imposition of obligations on public authorities. Regulation 3(3) requires public bodies with functions relevant to marine conservation to exercise those functions so as to 'secure compliance with the requirements of the Habitats Directive'. The obligation is placed on all 'competent authorities' including those exercising powers in relation to specific statutory provisions including those relating to fisheries, pollution, harbours and marine nature

[22] SI 1994/2716, as amended by SI 1997/3055 and SI 2000/192. See Chapter 3 - Part I.
[23] Reg 2(1) 1994 Regulation.
[24] *R v Secretary of State for Trade and Industry ex parte Greenpeace Ltd* (No 2) [2000] Env LR 221. For discussion see Chapter 3 - Part I.
[25] SI 2001/1754.

reserves.[26] This means that a wider range of authorities are placed under an obligation to 'secure compliance' with the Directive in relation to marine sites than in relation to land based sites where most authorities are subject to a less onerous duty to 'have regard to' the Directive.

Conservation authorities are also placed under additional obligations in relation to marine sites. In particular, they are obliged to inform a wide range of relevant authorities about the conservation objectives for a site and any operations which may be potentially damaging to that site.[27] 'Relevant authorities' cover bodies with a wide range of functions including sewerage and water undertakers, navigation and harbour authorities and local fisheries committees.[28] As with MNRs, the conservation authorities have the power to install markers to indicate the existence and extent of a European Marine Site.[29]

European Marine Sites: Management Schemes

A further power given to 'relevant authorities' is the power to establish management schemes in relation to European Marine Sites.[30] Whilst land based sites will frequently be subject to existing management agreements through the SSSI legislation, this will not be the case for marine sites. As a consequence, the provisions for the creation of management schemes are more likely to be used to draw up new schemes in relation to marine sites than land based sites.

Only one management scheme may be created in relation to each European Marine Site. This creates an incentive for relevant authorities to co-operate in the creation of the management scheme. This can require co-operation between a significant number of bodies. Of the 12 pilot sites studied by the UK Marine SACs Project,[31] seven had ten or more relevant authorities with one site being covered by 27 relevant authorities. Although the 1994 Regulations only empower relevant authorities to create a management scheme, government guidance recommends that other groups such land owners, residents industry and interest groups are involved in

[26] Reg 3(3) and 6, 1994 Regulations.
[27] Reg 33(2), 1994 Regulations.
[28] Reg 5, 1994 Regulations.
[29] Reg 33(1), 1994 Regulations.
[30] Reg 34, 1994 Regulations.
[31] A project run in partnership by English Nature; Scottish Natural Heritage; Countryside Council for Wales; Environment and Heritage Services Northern Ireland; Joint Nature Conservation Committee and the Scottish Association for Marine Science. The project ran from 1996-2001 and studied 12 pilot sites in detail. See www.ukmarinesac.org.uk.

developing the scheme.[32] In order to achieve this objective, it suggests the creation of advisory groups and the use of regular consultation. Should agreement fail, a reserve power is granted to the relevant Minister to require any relevant authority or relevant authorities to produce a management scheme for a marine site.

Once a management scheme is in place the functions of the relevant authority are required to be exercised so as to 'secure compliance' with the Directive: this is the same standard that is imposed on competent authorities under the Regulations.

European Marine Sites: Byelaws

The 1994 Regulations empower conservation authorities to make byelaws for European Marine Sites under s37 of the Wildlife and Countryside Act 1981 which empowers the making of byelaws for MNRs.[33] This power is subject to the same limitations as apply to the making of byelaws for MNRs. These limitations expressly include the limitation that the byelaws may not interfere with the exercise of any functions of a relevant authority, any functions conferred by or under an enactment (whenever passed) or any right of any person (whenever vested).[34] These limitations considerably weaken the power of the conservation authorities to protect the site.

European Marine Sites in Practice

The most pressing concern in relation to European Marine Sites has been the limited applicability of the regime. This concern has been addressed to some extent by the Greenpeace ruling and the resulting governmental recognition that the application of the Habitats Directive extends beyond the territorial sea. Nevertheless, there are concerns that the habitats and species listed in Annexes I and II are too limited in relation to the marine environment.[35] As a consequence, a significant number of marine sites in the UK are not eligible for protection under the Habitats Directive.[36]

---

[32] DETR *European Marine Sites in England and Wales: A guide to the Conservation (Natural Habitat &c.) Regulations 1994 and to the preparation and application of management schemes* (June 1998).
[33] Reg 36(1) 1994 Regulations.
[34] Reg 36 (3) 1994 Regulations.
[35] House of Commons Environment, Transport and Regional Affairs Committee, UK Biodiversity, 20th Report of 1999-2000 HC 441 paras 53-54.
[36] DEFRA 'Review of Marine Nature Conservation – Interim Report' para 52.

Even for those sites that are covered by the Habitats Directive, important questions remain as to whether the legislation is strong enough to provide the necessary protection. The provisions relating to byelaws suffer from the same weaknesses that exist in relation to MNRs. As a consequence, the success of the regime is likely to depend on the success of management schemes. If they are implemented successfully, management schemes have the potential to create integrated protection designed to meet the needs of the particular site in question. There is, however, a danger that the reliance on voluntary action and compromise between various interests will be insufficient to deal with the sensitive complexities of marine conservation. To date, some 65 marine sites have been proposed as SACs and are classified as European Marine Sites.[37] Many of these sites have implemented management schemes, although it is perhaps too early to assess whether these schemes have achieved their objectives.

The Future of Marine Protection

In recognition of the deep concern over the protection of the marine environment, the Government launched the Review of Marine Nature Conservation in 1999. The working group conducting the Review produced an interim report in March 2001. The interim report concluded that there were weaknesses in the current legislation, in particular the failure of MNRs and the limited range of habitats and species protected by the Habitats Directive. In response, the report recognised the need for an integrated and scientifically based approach to marine protection, taking account of the need to protect the seas beyond the 12 nautical mile limit. The report suggested a framework of marine conservation with specific objectives for the whole sea within UK jurisdiction, the regional seas, ecological units within those regional seas, and particular areas of national importance. Although the report did not suggest a detailed regulatory framework at this stage, it proposed a pilot study to analyse the effect of different conservation strategies at the regional seas level. This pilot study was implemented in the Irish Sea. The final report, detailing the outcome of the pilot study and proposals for the future, is expected in March 2004.

In addition to the Review, in May 2002 the Government produced the 'Marine Stewardship Report: Safeguarding our Seas', setting out proposals for the future regulation of the marine environment. In view of the continuing Review of Marine Nature Conservation, the report did not make any detailed proposals for a new regulatory regime. It did, however, recognise the failures in the current system and the need for an integrated,

[37] Joint Nature Conservation Committee. Information correct at 24 October 2003.

eco-system approach to marine conservation. In particular it re-iterated the commitment made at the 5th North Sea Conference, to identify and designate protected marine sites belonging to a network of well-managed sites by 2010.

In view of these developments and the increasing recognition that the current regime for marine conservation is not sufficient, it is likely that proposals for a more appropriate form of regulation will be made in the near future.

CHAPTER 5

NATURE RESERVES AND NATIONAL PARKS

A. Nature Reserves

The Purpose of Nature Reserves

Statutory nature reserves are established for one or both of two purposes: study and research or conservation. Their establishment and management are governed by Part III of the 1949 Act and, in the case of National Nature Reserves, by s35 of the Wildlife and Countryside Act 1981.

For land[1] to be included in a statutory nature reserve under Part III of the 1949 Act, it must be managed for one or both of the purposes set out in s 15 of the 1949 Act:

- the provision, under suitable conditions and control, of special opportunities for the study of, and research into, matters relating to the fauna and flora of Great Britain and the physical conditions in which they live, and for the study of geological and physiographical features of special interest in the area; or

- the preservation of flora, fauna or geological or physiographical features of special interest in the area.

The essential characteristic of a National Nature Reserve is therefore that it is being primarily used for nature conservation[2]. They are established to protect the most important areas of wildlife habitat (and geological formation) in Britain[3].

Under Part III of the 1949 Act, nature reserves may be established either by means of a management agreement, entered into between the relevant Nature Conservancy Council[4] and every owner, lessee and occupier of the land, (s16) or by means of compulsory acquisition of the land concerned by the Council (s17). There is also provision in Part III for the establishment of local authority nature reserves (s21). In addition, marine

---

[1] Land is defined, in section 114(1) as including land covered by water and, in Scotland, as including salmon fishings.

[2] See PPG 9 Nature Conservation, Annex A paragraph A14

[3] See English Nature's website at www.english-nature.org.uk.

[4] Under section 73 of the Countryside and Rights of Way Act 2000, the Nature Conservancy Council for England is to be known as English Nature.

nature reserves can be designated by the Secretary of State on application by the NCC under s36 of the Wildlife and Countryside Act 1981 (see marine protection chapter). The island of Lundy is a designated MNR.

In 1998, in its Consultation Paper on SSSI's, the Government emphasised that NNR's have a different role from SSSI's and other sites of international importance and said that they have a continuing role as sites where the conservation and enhancement of the natural heritage becomes "the primary aim" [paragraph B:8] As at March 2000, there were approximately 2000 National Nature Reserves in England covering over 80,000 hectares[5].

National Nature Reserves

A nature reserve may be declared by the NCC to be a National Nature Reserve where the NCC is satisfied that the land concerned is "of national importance" and is being managed as a nature reserve. Such declarations may be made in respect of land managed as a nature reserve under an agreement with the NCC (as under s16 of the 1949 Act) or held by the NCC and managed as a nature reserve or held by "an approved body", such as a wildlife trust, and managed as a nature reserve (section 35 of the 1981 Act). A declaration by the NCC that any land is a national nature reserve will be conclusive to that effect. Where the nature reserve is one managed by an approved body, the Council may make byelaws for the protection of the reserve on the application of the body concerned. The provisions of s20 and s106 of the 1949 Act apply to such byelaws.

English Nature has been criticised for the "back door privatisation" of NNRs, in other words making increasing use of s35 agreements which means that, in contrast to those established under s16 of the 1949 Act, other organisations are responsible for their management and difficulties over funding etc[6]. This allegation has been refuted by English Nature.[7]

Compulsory Acquisition of Land

The relevant Nature Conservancy Council has the power under s17 of the Act to establish a nature reserve by means of compulsory acquisition of the land. As with the power to enter into management

---

[5] See English Nature's website at www.english-nature.org.uk which provides details of locations etc.

[6] See article "Beyond 2000-will it deliver" Trevor Lawson 1997 ECOS (3/4) 57, 59.

[7] "English Nature's Response to articles by Trevor Lawson and Peter Marren" ECOS 18 (3/4) 61.

agreements under s16 (see further below), the Council must be satisfied that it is "expedient in the national interest" that the land be managed as a nature reserve. It may only acquire an interest in the land, however, where it is satisfied that it is unable, as respects that interest, to conclude on reasonable terms a management agreement under s16 to secure the satisfactory management of the land as a nature reserve. Interest is defined to include any estate or right over the land, whether exercisable by virtue of ownership or by licence and includes, in particular sporting rights (s114(1)). The Council may only exercise its power under s17 on being authorised to do so by the Secretary of State (s103(1).

Section 108 of the 1949 Act gives persons authorised in writing by the Minister, or the Council, the power of entry onto land for the purpose of surveying land in connection with acquisition of the land or an interest in the land, whether by agreement or compulsorily. This power also applies to local authorities acting under s21 of the 1949 Act (see below).

Evidence that Land is a Nature Reserve Under s16 or s17

A declaration by the NCC that any land is the subject of a management agreement under Part III of the 1949 Act or has been acquired and is held by them is provided to be sufficient evidence of that fact unless that contrary is proved. Furthermore, a declaration by the Council that such land is being managed as a nature reserve will be conclusive of the matters declared (section 19 of the 1949 Act). Where land ceases to be managed as a nature reserve or ceases to be held by the NCC, a declaration to that effect must be made and will be conclusive of the matters declared. Such declarations must be published in the manner best suited for informing the persons concerned (s19(4)).

Protection of Nature Reserves

As far as voluntary agreement is concerned, section 16 of the 1949 Act gives the Council the power to enter into an agreement which may impose restrictions on the exercise of rights over the land by the persons who can be bound by the agreement. Those restrictions must be expedient for the purposes of the agreement. The precise form and terms of such agreements are not prescribed by the Act but section 16(3) provides that such agreements may provide for the management of the land, the carrying out of work and the doing of "such other things" as may be expedient for the purposes of the agreement and may provide that such management, work etc be carried out by or the cost defrayed either by the Council or by the owner or other persons bound by the agreement or partly one or the other. Section 16(3) also provides for the making of payment pursuant to the agreement, including compensation by the NCC for restrictions on the exercise of rights imposed by the agreement.

It is provided that, what is now s5 of the Forestry Act 1967, shall apply to any agreement entered into under s16, this means that where the agreement concerns land devoted to forestry by agreement with the Forestry Commissioners, the Council may enforce those parts of the agreement relating to restrictions as mentioned in s16.

Management of Nature Reserves

Management agreements bind the parties to the agreement and, where s79 of the Law of Property Act 1925 applies (providing that the burden of a covenant is to run with the land unless the contrary intention is expressed), will bind subsequent owners of the land.

The Council have a further sanction at their disposal should there be a breach of the agreement which prevents or impairs the satisfactory management of the land as a nature reserve. Under s18 of the 1949 Act, they may then acquire the interest to which the agreement relates compulsorily. A breach is not to be treated as having occurred by virtue of any act or omission capable of remedy unless it is not remedied within a reasonable time after notice requiring remedy has been given. Disputes under s18 are to be settled by arbitration, by an arbitrator appointed by the Lord Chancellor, or in the case of Scotland by the Lord President of the Court of Session.

In addition to agreeing the management of the land under a management agreement or by managing the land themselves, the Council may secure the protection of the nature reserve against the acts of third persons by making byelaws (see below, although these will not have effect unless a section 19 declaration has been made and published in respect of the nature reserve).

Powers of Entry

Under section 51 of the 1981 Act (as amended by section 80 of the Countryside and Rights of Way Act 2000), powers to enter land are laid down for a range of purposes including for the purpose of determining whether or not to enter into any agreement under section 16 of the 1949 Act or to ascertain whether a term of an agreement under section 16 of the 1949 Act has been complied with. The power is that of a person authorised by the relevant authority which, in the case of s16 agreements, is the Nature Conservancy Council[8]

Byelaws

The power to make byelaws under s20 of the 1949 Act is a general one but subsection (2) indicates the type of provision that is envisaged. Among the prohibitions and restrictions indicated are those on entry into the reserve of persons, vehicles, boats or animals; the prohibition or restriction on the killing, taking molesting or disturbing of any living creatures of any description or of their eggs or the taking or interferences with any vegetation or the doing of anything which will interfere with the soil or damage any object in the reserve; the prohibition or restriction of the shooting of birds within such area surrounding or adjoining the reserve as appears requisite for the protection of the reserve[9]; the prohibition or restriction of the lighting of fires or the depositing of rubbish. It is also provided that byelaws may provide for the issue of permits authorising entry or the doing of anything which would otherwise be unlawful.

The byelaws may relate to the whole or part of the reserve and, in the case of restrictions on the shooting of birds, to any area surrounding or adjoining a reserve as appears requisite for the protection of the reserve. Different provision may be made for different parts of the reserve (s20(2)(g)).

The limits of the byelaw-making power are set out in the final paragraph of s20(2) which provides that such byelaws shall not interfere with the exercise by any person of a right vested in him as owner, lessee or occupier of land in a nature reserve. This means that where the exercise of such rights may prejudice the management of the reserve, provision must be made to address this in a management agreement or, if necessary, by means of the compulsory acquisition of the land or an interest in the land under the powers in Part III described above.

Further limitations are also set out in s20: byelaws may not interfere with exercise of any public right of way or of any functions of statutory undertakers or with the running of telecommunications code system or with the exercise of any right conferred by or in accordance with the telecommunications code on the operator of such a system.

[8] Section 51(2) of the 1981 Act as amended by section 80 of the 2000 Act.

[9] An example of a "buffer zone" provision, see chapter 6 - Part I.

Where the byelaws have the effect of preventing or hindering the exercise of any right vested in a person, either because they have an interest in land or by virtue of a licence or agreement, subsection (3) provides that that person is entitled to receive compensation from the Council. Disputes relating to claims for compensation under s20 of the 1949 Act are determined by the Lands Tribunal (s107(2)).Byelaws made under the 1949 Act shall apply to Crown land if the appropriate authority consents (section 101(8)of the 1949 Act).

The Nature Conservancy Council has the authority to enforce any byelaws which it makes under the Act (s106(3)[10]).

Local Nature Reserves

Local authorities have the power to establish nature reserves on any land in their area which is not already managed as a reserve by agreement with the NCC or held by the NCC as a nature reserve (section 21 of the 1949 Act) and which, in their opinion is land which it is "expedient, in the interests of the locality" that it should be managed as a nature reserve. This is aimed at protecting habitat of special interest locally. PPG9 encourages local authorities to identify and record sites of local importance. Local authorities in England are required to consult English Nature about the establishment of such a reserve[11] . As at November 2002, there were over 600 local nature reserves in England covering over 29,000 hectares.[12]

The provisions of Part III of the 1949 Act relating to management agreements, compulsory acquisition, declarations and the making of byelaws also apply to local authorities, who must exercise their functions under Part III in consultation with the NCC. Local authorities may enter into agreements with drainage authorities for the exercise by the drainage authority of any power of doing work exercisable by the local authority under s21.

Sections 236-238 of the Local Government Act 1972 apply to byelaws made under the Act (section 106(1)).

[10] See SI 1975/1970 and SI1984/918.
[11] See PPG 9 paragraph A22.
[12] See www.enlish-nature.org.gov.uk.

Relationship with Other Designations

All National Nature Reserves were re-notified in 1987 as SSSI's under s28 WCA 1981.

If the land in question is a European site under the Habitats Regulations, a management agreement under s16 1949 Act has effect as if entered into under regulation 16 of the Habitats Regulations relating to management agreements(regulation 17(1) of the Habitats Regulations). This means that any other thing done or deemed to have been done under Part III of the 1949 Act in respect of any land prior to that land becoming land within a European site, or adjacent to such a site, shall continue to have effect as if done under the corresponding provisions of the Habitats Regulations (17).

B. National Parks

National Parks and Areas of Outstanding Natural Beauty are not designated solely or even primarily for their wildlife interest. Nor do these designations offer the same level of protection for wildlife as those such as SSSI's or SACs which are specifically aimed at wildlife conservation[1]. In recent years however the emphasis on wildlife conservation has been strengthened by amendment of the statutory regime for the designation of National Parks and AONBs and the introduction of new statutory requirements for management of the land. It will often be the case that parts of land designated as a National Park or AONB will also benefit from designation as an SSSI or other wildlife habitat designation. In relation to land which is not otherwise protected however, these two designations do offer some more limited protection for wildlife, in particular in the context of planning restrictions, the making of moorland and heath protection orders (in the National Parks) and in the requirements for management of the land concerned.

National Parks came into being under Part II of the National Parks and Access to the Countryside Act 1949. National Parks are not established solely for the purposes of wildlife conservation[2] but, as will be seen, nature conservation has always been part of their purpose through the concept of preserving (now conserving) and enhancing "natural beauty". This term is defined in s 114(2) of the 1949 Act[3] as including references to the preservation of flora, fauna and geological and physiographical features of an area. A direct link with wildlife conservation was introduced by the Environment Act 1995 which also required the National Park Authorities to take account of the economic and social needs of local communities.

Selection of National Parks

The purposes to be fulfilled by National Parks are set out in s 5(1) of the 1949 Act, as amended by s61 of the Environment Act 1995. Those purposes are "conserving and enhancing the natural beauty, wildlife and cultural heritage of the areas specified" and "promoting opportunities for the understanding and enjoyment of the special qualities of those areas by

---

[1] See Chapters 1-3.
[2] This was primarily addressed in Part III of the 1949 Act which provides for Nature Reserves, see Chapter 5 - Part I.
[3] As amended by the Countryside Act 1968.

the public." Originally, s5(1) provided simply for the preservation and enhancement of natural beauty and the promotion of their enjoyment by the public.

The areas in question are "those extensive tracts of country in England, as to which it appears to the [Countryside Agency[4]], that by reason of their natural beauty and opportunities for open air recreation, having regard both to their character and to their position in relation to centres of population, it is especially desirable that measures be taken for the purposes [in s5(1)]."

By virtue of s4A of the 1949 Act (introduced by the Environment Act 1990), Part II of the 1949 Act applies to land in Wales as it applies to land in England, with the functions of the Countryside Agency carried out by the Countryside Council for Wales. In Scotland, National Parks are governed by the National Parks (Scotland) Act 2000[5]. Scottish National Parks have now been established in Loch Lomond and the Trossachs and the Cairngorms.

The purposes substituted by the 1995 Act come into effect in relation to a particular National park from the time when a National Park authority (as to which see below) becomes the local planning authority for the Park (s61(4) of the 1995 Act). The purposes specified in s5(1) as originally enacted are "original purposes" and those substituted by the Environment Act are "substituted purposes".

Designation

There are currently 11 National parks in England and Wales, (including the Broads)[6]. National Parks are designated by means of an order made by the Countryside Agency[7] under s7 of the 1949 Act. Before making the Order, the Countryside Agency is required to consult every joint planning board, county council, county borough council and county district council whose area includes any land in the area to be designated a National Park (in accordance with s7). The Countryside Agency must

[4] The 1949 Act established a National Parks Countryside Agency, renamed the Countryside Agency in the 1968 Act which also introduced amendments to the provisions for National Parks.

[5] The Act received Royal Assent on 9 August 2000.

[6] Eight National Parks are in England, the proposed New Forest and South Downs National Parks (see text infra) will be the ninth and tenth.

[7] Or the Countryside Council for Wales in relation to Wales.

make copies of the order available for public inspection (s76)). The Minister may, after consultation with the Countryside Agency and the relevant authorities in accordance with the Act vary the order designating the National Park.

South Downs

The South Downs was one of the twelve areas originally proposed for designation in the 1940s but was dropped from the list proposed for designation under the 1949 Act, as were the Norfolk and Suffolk Broads. The latter were eventually given equivalent status in 1989 however[8]. The Sussex Downs Conservation Board was set up in 1992 with a more limited remit-the right to be heard in planning issues. On 14 November 2002, the Countryside Agency announced that it had agreed to create a South Downs National Park and that a South Downs National Park Designation Order would be published in January 2003 for consultation and submission to the Secretary of State for confirmation[9].

Protection and Management of National Parks

The key elements of the statutory system for protecting and managing the National Parks are the general, mainly advisory, role of the Countryside Agency; certain modifications to the planning system in relation to development affecting a National Park; the making of moorland and heath protection orders under section 42 of the Wildlife and Countryside Act and the drawing up of byelaws. The establishment of National Park Authorities under the 1995 Act has also reinforced the provisions for their protection and management.

The Countryside Agency has general duties in relation to the protection and management of the National Parks, as laid down in section 6 of the 1949 Act. These include a duty to consider what action is required to ensure that purposes set out under section 5 are fulfilled. It must also give advice to planning authorities as to arrangements for administering an area as a national park and assist them with formulating proposals as to the exercise of their powers (s6(4)). The Countryside Agency must give advice to the Minister about development proposals in the National Park and where the local planning authority consults them about the development plan or about any application for planning permission. The

[8] See the Norfolk and Suffolk Broads Act 1988.

[9] See www.countryside.gov.uk/news.

Countryside Agency may make recommendations to Minister (or others as appropriate) about any proposals for the development of land in a National Park which appears to "be inconsistent with the maintenance of the area as a National Park". If in any case the Countryside Agency is not satisfied that effect will be given to their recommendations or advice as to any matter...it must refer the matter to the Minister and advise him of exercise of powers of direction or enforcement conferred by 1949 Act or Planning Acts

National Park Authorities

National Park Authorities were introduced by s 63 of the 1995 Act. They may be established by order of the Secretary of State either for existing Parks or for any new Parks[10]. The 1995 Act aimed to give National Park Authorities the opportunity to take a strategic view of biodiversity in the parks and operate within the framework of a new Protocol between what is now the Countryside Agency, the Countryside Council for Wales and English Nature.

The functions of the authorities include general duties under s 37-38 of the 1968 Act relating to the protection of interests such as agriculture and the avoidance of pollution and also include powers to do anything which, in the opinion of the authority, is calculated to facilitate, or is conducive or incidental to, the accomplishment of the purposes set out in s5(1) of the 1949 Act as amended or the carrying on of functions under any other enactment. Those powers do not include the power to do anything in contravention of any restriction imposed by virtue of that part of the 1995 Act or to raise money (s65).

Within three years of their establishment, National Park Authorities were required to prepare and publish a National Park Management Plan, formulating policy for the management of the Park and for the carrying out of its functions in relation to that Park (s66). The Plan is to be reviewed every five years. In publishing, adopting or reviewing any plan, the NPA must give notice to every principal council whose area is wholly or partly comprised in that Park and to the Countryside Agency, English Nature and or the CCW and take into consideration any observations made by those bodies.

---

[10] See Schedule 7 of the 1995 Act.

Planning and the National Parks

National Park authorities are the local planning authority in relation to the Park (certain functions are exercised concurrently with the district council see s 4A(4) of 1990 Act as inserted by 1995 Act) including carrying out the functions of a mineral planning authority. National Park Authorities also have functions under the 1981 Act as respects any land in any National Park for which that authority is the local planning authority.

Local Planning Authorities are required to consult the Countryside Agency about development plans including alterations for any area including the whole or part of a national Park (s9) and take into consideration the Countryside Agency's observations. They also have a general power under section 11 to take action necessary for the accomplishment of the purposes laid down in s5(1) in relation to their area within a National Park.

Section 11 does not, however, apply in relation to any National Park Authority. Instead, s11A, as inserted by s62 of the Environment Act 1995, applies. It places a duty on the NPA, in pursuing the purposes under s5(1) of the 1949 Act, to seek to foster the economic and social well-being of local communities within the National Park "but without incurring significant expenditure in doing so" and shall for that purpose co-operate with local authorities and public bodies whose functions include the promotion of economic or social developments within the area of the National Park.

Section 11A also provides that if, in performing any of its functions in relation to land in a National Park, it appears that there is a conflict between the purposes set out in s5(1), the NPA is to attach greater weight to the purpose of conserving and enhancing the natural beauty, wildlife and cultural heritage of the area comprised in the National park.

Moorland and Heath Protection Orders

Moorland and heath in National Parks may be afforded special protection by order under s42 of the 1981 Act. Ministers may apply an order if satisfied that it is expedient to do so. Section 42 Orders provide that no person shall plough up or otherwise convert into agricultural land[11],

[11] Agricultural land does not include land used for rough grazing for livestock but not otherwise used as agricultural land, s52.

land which has not been agricultural land at any time during the preceding 20 years [ignoring any unlawful conversion contrary to the 1949 or 1968 Acts]. Nor may any person carry out any other agricultural operations or forestry operations specified in the order which appear likely to affect the lands' character or appearance. An example of such an order is that relating to Dartmoor[12]. It is an offence to infringe an order without reasonable excuse.

The restrictions in the order do not apply if the owner or occupier of the land in question has, after its entry into force, given the local planning authority written notice of the proposed operation, its nature and the land on which it is proposed to carry it out and either the local planning authority consents to the operation, or if it neither consents nor refuses, 3 months have passed, or where consent is refused, 12 months have passed. Notifications of proposed operations must be sent to the Minister, English Nature or the Countryside Council for Wales and the Countryside Agency.

Byelaws

Local Authorities may make byelaws under s90 of the 1949 Act, inter alia for the prevention of damage and they may appoint park wardens (under section 92).

The Environment Agency

Section 8 of the Environment Act 1995 makes provision for consultation between National Park Authorities or Broads Authorities and the Environment Agency. National Park Authorities or Broads Authorities are under a duty under section 8(2) of the Act to notify the Environment Agency if they consider that any area of land in a National Park is land in relation to which matters under s6(1) (water) and 7 (general environmental duties) of the 1995 Act are of particular importance and may at any time be affected by schemes of the Agency or an authorisation given by the Agency. Where the Environment Agency has received such notification, it is required[13] to consult the notifying body before carrying out or authorising any works, operations likely to destroy or damage flora or fauna or geological or physiographical features by reason of which the land is of special interest or which are likely to significantly prejudice anything "the importance of which is one of the reasons why the matters mentioned in subsection (2) above are of particular importance in relation to that land."

[12] See SI 1991/1616.

[13] Save in an emergency, see subsection (4).

Areas of outstanding Natural Beauty

Areas of Outstanding Natural Beauty were established under s 87 of the 1949 Act and are now governed by Part IV of the 2000 Act[14]. AONBs are designated by order of the Countryside Agency or the Countryside Council for Wales and are any area in England and Wales, not in a national park, which appears to the Agency or Council to be of such outstanding natural beauty that it is desirable that the provisions of Part IV of the 2000 Act, (formerly of the 1949 Act), relating to such areas should apply[15]. Any reference in Part IV to the conservation of the natural beauty of an area includes reference to the conservation of its flora, fauna, geological and physiographical features[16].

There are some 41 AONBs in England and Wales ranging in size from 16 square kilometres (the Isles of Scilly) to over 2000 square kilometres (the Cotswolds).

Designation

The Countryside Agency or Council must consult every local authority whose area includes any part of area proposed for designation and then, before making the order, publish in the London Gazette and one or more local newspapers, notice that they propose to make the order, indicating the effect of the order and time within which representations may be made. They must consider nay representations duly made (s83 of the 2000 Act).

The Order must be submitted to and confirmed by the Secretary of State for Environment, Food and Rural Affairs in the case of England or the National Assembly in the case of land in Wales. The Countryside Agency or Council must forward local authority observations and any other representations other than any to which the order gives effect. The Secretary of State or Assembly may confirm the order either with or without modifications. If the order is refused or modified, the Secretary of State or Assembly must consult the Countryside Agency or Council and the relevant local authority. Copies of the order should be available for public inspection. Orders may be revoked or varied by subsequent orders (section 83 of the 2000 Act).

---

[14] The provisions of Part IV entered into force on 1 April 2001, see the Countryside and Rights of Way Act 2000 (Commencement No 1) Order 2001, SI 2001/114.

[15] Section 82 of the 2000 Act

[16] See section 92(2) of the 2000 Act.

Protection

Under section 84 of the 2000 Act, certain provisions of the 1949 Act governing National Parks also apply in relation to AONB: the duty on the Agency or council to give advice on development matters (section 6(4)(e) of the 1949 Act); consultation on development plans (section 9); consultation in connection with access agreements and orders (sections 64 and 65).

Under section 84(4), local authorities are given a general power to take such action as is expedient for the accomplishment of the purpose of conserving and enhancing the natural beauty of the area.

Section 85 of the 2000 Act places certain public bodies under a general duty in carrying out their functions in relation to, or so as to affect, land in an AONB, to have regard to the purpose of conserving and enhancing the natural beauty of the AONB. Public bodies include Ministers of the Crown, any public body such as a county council, any statutory undertaker or any person holding public office.

Section 86 introduces the possibility of establishing conservation boards for AONB's[17]. The power is that of the Secretary of State of National Assembly. The functions and purpose of such boards are described in section 87 which provides that the boards are to have regard to two purposes: to conserve and enhance the natural beauty of the AONB and to increase public understanding and enjoyment of the area. If there is a conflict between the two the former is to prevail (section 87(1)). Conservation boards, while having regard to these two purposes, are to seek to foster the economic and social well-being of the local communities within the AONB (section 87(2)). Conservation boards are placed under the general duties to protect the interests of the countryside and avoid pollution set out in sections 37-38 of the Countryside Act 1968.

A new emphasis on management is introduced in section 89 of the 2000 Act, which requires a management plan to be prepared and published for each AONB. This will be the responsibility of the local authority concerned, unless a conservation board has been established. This requirement is modelled on the requirements for National Parks introduced by the Environment Act 1995.The management plan is subject to consultation in accordance with section 90.

[17] The procedure for making such orders is contained in section 88 which provides for the affirmative resolution procedure.

CHAPTER 6

THE WIDER COUNTRYSIDE: BEYOND DESIGNATED SITES, LIMESTONE PAVEMENTS AND HEDGEROWS

A. The Wider Countryside

The Wildlife and Countryside Bill was criticised for doing nothing for the basic fabric of the countryside, the "everyday things such as ponds, hedges, hedgerow trees and small woodlands".[1]. Nearly twenty years later, the necessity for "a broader and more integrated approach to conservation" incorporating site protection and wider measures beyond those areas was acknowledged by the Government in a 1998 Consultation Document[2]. This chapter examines in outline a number of areas where the law seeks to address the need to protect wildlife habitats outside designated areas and in the wider countryside including through land use planning and the protection of landscape features important for wildlife, measures taken in relation to agriculture are considered in Chapter 7 - Part I. Clearly most, if not all, environmental law is at least indirectly relevant to the protection of wildlife habitats in that it protects the environmental media in which wildlife exists. This chapter is concerned with those aspects of the law which seek to protect wildlife habitat more specifically. Some of the measures considered in this Chapter are aimed at supporting the protection of specially designated sites whilst others are aimed simply at protecting wildlife in the wider countryside generally. The importance of such measures in protecting biodiversity is evident when it is remembered that only around 10% of UK land is within an SSSI.[3]

General Requirements for the Protection of Habitat in the Wider Countryside

Underpinning the site specific measures discussed elsewhere[4], are general legal requirements under international and European law which give rise to a duty on the part of states to protect wildlife habitat in the wider countryside. More recently, a general duty to protect biodiversity

[1] Hansard House of Lords, December 1980, col 994.
[2] Sites of Special Scientific Interest: Better Protection and Management, A Consultation Document for England and Wales, September 1998, DETR.
[3] House of Commons Select Committee on the Environment, Report on UK Biodiversity (HC441) see paragraph 60, ((November 2000).
[4] See in particular Chapters 1 and 2 - Part I.

has been incorporated into domestic law. The most important effect of these general duties is probably to raise the profile of conservation as a policy objective and strengthen the case for greater resources to be allocated to it. From a legal point of view, a binding obligation to, for example, produce a plan for biodiversity, is something which is in principle enforceable. There might also be circumstances where the duties discussed below might be invoked in the appropriate fora to secure protection for areas outside specially protected sites, particularly where widespread deterioration of types of habitat or landscape feature can be demonstrated.

The Convention on Biological Diversity

At the international level, the need to look beyond the protection of specially protected areas in undertaking *in-situ* conservation[5] is recognised in the Convention on Biological Diversity (CBD). Article 8 of the Convention requires Parties "as far as possible and as appropriate" to look beyond protected areas in a number of ways. Under Article 8(c), Parties are to regulate or manage biological resources important for the conservation of biodiversity *whether within or outside protected areas* with a view to assuring their conservation and sustainable use (emphasis added). Article 8(d) of the Convention then requires Parties to "promote the protection of ecosystems, natural habitats and the maintenance of viable populations of species in natural surroundings" (again, not just in protected areas).

UK Biodiversity Action Plans

Article 6 of the CBD requires parties to develop national strategies for the conservation and sustainable use of biodiversity and to integrate biodiversity considerations into all activities. In 1994 the UK adopted its overall Biodiversity Action Plan and from 1995 began to adopt specific action plans for particular species and habitats. Each plan documents the current situation for the habitat/species concerned, defines targets for improvement and lists actions required to support those targets. Reporting on the progress made with each plan is carried out. Originally the plans had no statutory basis, but following provision made in the Countryside and Rights of Way Act 2000, some statutory underpinning has been provided-although this does not explicitly refer to the plans themselves.

Section 74 of the 2000 Act relates to the conservation of biological diversity and creates a statutory duty to have regard to the purpose of

[5] In-situ conservation is defined as "the conservation of ecosystems and natural habitats and the maintenance and recovery of viable populations of species in their natural surroundings..."

conserving biological diversity in accordance with the Convention. That duty is imposed, in carrying out their functions, on Ministers, Government Departments and the National Assembly for Wales. The duty is qualified "so far as is consistent with the proper exercise of those functions".

There is also a specific duty to draw up and publish a list of the living organisms and types of habitats which are of principle importance for the purpose of conserving biological diversity. In England the "listing authority" is the Secretary of State for Environment, Food and Rural Affairs and, in Wales, the Welsh Assembly[6]. Under section 74(3) the listing authorities are under a duty to take such steps as are reasonably practicable to further the conservation of the listed habitats and species and to promote their conservation by others.

The background to the concerns which led to the adoption of section 74 is set out in a House of Commons Select Committee Report on Biodiversity. In its report on UK Biodiversity, the House of Commons Select Committee on Environment, Transport and Regional Affairs considered the question of whether the UK Biodiversity Action Plans should be put on a statutory footing and concluded that Government Departments, Executive Agencies, Non-Departmental Public Bodies, Utility Regulators and the Regional Development Agencies should be required to further the aims of the biodiversity action plans (paragraph 29)[7]. It expressed concern that in amendments to the Countryside Bill such a duty was not placed on bodies other than Ministers and Government Departments. The Committee noted that there was concern as to the disappointing rate of progress in implementing Habitat Action Plans as compared with that for some of the Species Action Plans (paragraph 18). It noted English Nature's observation that successful Habitat Action Plans were those where suitable land was owned by statutory or conservation bodies or lay within an SSSI (paragraph 19). The Committee also noted that non-governmental organisations were strongly in favour of a statutory duty being placed on Government Departments and Non Department Public Bodies to further the plans (paragraph 26). English Nature believed that there should be some statutory underpinning of the plan process. This would provide permanence, clarity of responsibility and a profile for resourcing. DETR was concerned that statutory underpinning would risk alienating the bodies involved in the process. The Committee also noted that, among those in favour of statutory

---

[6] Section 74(2) of the 2000 Act.

[7] Select Committee on Environment, Transport and Regional Affairs, UK Biodiversity (HC 441) 22 November 2000.

provision, there was a consensus that it should not take the form of making the plans themselves statutory since they were dynamic. Instead the general view was in favour of a duty to further biodiversity or the plans themselves. In the event, as indicated above, the former approach was taken.

This change reflects a more general trend in favour of the introduction of statutory general duties to protect the environment, or aspects of it, in UK environmental law and to give a legal basis to important policy initiatives. In this case, the effectiveness of such a shift may be able to be measured to some extent by the accelerated progress which might be expected particularly in relation to Habitat Action Plans. This new duty may also go some way to meeting the charge that the implementation of the Habitats and Birds Directives in the UK had focussed on designating sites to the exclusion of implementing obligations to protect the wider countryside.[8]

European Union Legislation

European Union legislation also acknowledges the importance of general protection as well as site specific protection for wildlife, for example, there is a general duty, under Article 3 of the European Union's wild birds directive, to take the requisite measures to preserve, maintain or re-establish a sufficient diversity and area of habitats for all species of naturally occurring wild birds in the relevant European territory. This duty includes primarily the creation of protected areas, upkeep and management in accordance with the ecological needs of habitats *inside and outside* protected zones; the re-establishment of destroyed biotopes and the creation of biotopes. Article 4 of the Directive then makes provision for special conservation measures in relation to the habitat of birds listed on Annex I and migratory birds, including the classification of special protection areas[9] but Article 4(4) also requires Member States to strive to avoid deterioration or pollution of habitats "*outside* these protection areas".

There is also recognition of the need to protect the wider countryside in the European Union's Habitats directive which, although it focuses on the sites to be included in Natura 2000 network[10], also takes account of landscape features of major importance for wild flora and fauna outside the designated sites. This requirement is discussed further below.

[8] See HC Select Committee on the Environment Report on UK Biodiversity (HC441) at paragraph 55, November 2000.
[9] See further Chapter 2 - Part I.
[10] See further Chapter 3 - Part I.

The Planning System

In the UK, the protection or otherwise of wildlife habitats, both inside and outside designated sites, is dependent to a great extent on the operation of the planning system. As discussed below, planning authorities are required to take account of the need to protect wildlife when considering specific development projects and also when drawing up development plans. In the case of specially protected areas, the rules are more stringent and these are discussed in Chapter 1, 2 and 3 of Part I. This section is concerned with the protection of habitat outside designated areas.

As might be expected, specific attention is given to nature conservation objectives within the planning system. Whether sufficient weight is given to protection of wildlife remains a matter for debate however. There is particular pressure on planning authorities to consent to development in areas such as housing and transport infrastructure where development may have major impacts on wildlife habitat inside and outside protected areas. In 2000, the House of Commons Select Committee on Environment found that it was apparent that biodiversity concerns had not been adequately integrated into planning policy and noted the importance of the upcoming review of Planning Policy Guidance Note No 9 on Nature Conservation (PPG9). In particular, the Committee recommended that a revised PPG9 should encourage local plans to reflect the Biodiversity Action Plans priorities, emphasise the importance of local wildlife sites and give guidance on the potential benefits of planning gain for biodiversity generally and habitat provision in particular[11]. Proposals for a revised PPG have yet to be published.

Wildlife Inside and Outside Designated Sites

So far as the current position is concerned, PPG9 reminds planning authorities that "...the protection of wildlife is not an objective which applies only in SSSI's; it depends on the wise use and management of the nation's land resources as a whole. The Government looks to local authorities to keep themselves informed of the state of the natural environment locally, and to take account of nature conservation decisions wherever relevant to local decisions."

PPG9 goes on to point out that: "Our natural wildlife heritage is not confined to the various statutorily designated sites but is found throughout the countryside and in many urban and coastal areas...Many

[11] HC 441 paragraph 92.

urban sites for nature conservation have an enhanced local importance as a consequence of the relative lack of wildlife sites in built up areas. Endangered species protected under the 1981 Act may be found in many places not notified as SSSI's".[12] Other planning policy guidance notes also refer to the need to protect wildlife, for example PPG12 on Development Plans refers at paragraph 4.3 to guidance contained in the document "Planning for Sustainable Development: Towards Better Practice 1998", chapter 5 of which deals with nature conservation and states that planning policies should protect and enhance habitats and wildlife corridors in the wider countryside as well as in urban areas.

According to Government policy guidance, the planning system as a whole and the preparation of development plans in particular, "is the most effective way of reconciling the demand for development and the protection of the environment" and thus plays "a key role" in contributing to the Government's strategy for sustainable development[13]. The contribution of nature conservation policies to sustainable development is identified in guidance as: "increasing wildlife habitats, safeguarding biodiversity, including species and habitats at risk, as well as providing opportunities for recreation and enhancing the quality of life generally"[14].

The Government has stated that its objectives for nature conservation are to ensure that its policies "contribute to the conservation of the abundance and diversity of British wildlife and its habitats, or minimise the adverse effects on wildlife where conflict of interest is unavoidable, and to meet its international responsibilities and obligations for nature conservation."[15] It should be remembered of course, as pointed out in guidance, that the planning system "embraces a more diverse range of objectives than solely environmental protection", therefore environmental factors, including nature conservation, represent just one material consideration to be taken into account in reaching a decision on whether or not to grant planning permission for a development. Recent guidance has however emphasised the need for a holistic approach in which the interaction of policies, including the environmental and social implications of policies for economic growth, are considered: "planners should integrate a site based approach with a more broadly based concern with

[12] PPG9 page 6

[13] See PPG 1 General Policies and Principles 1997, paragraph 39.

14 Planning for Sustainable Development: Towards Better Practice (1998), chapter 5 of which deals with nature conservation,

[15] PPG 9 Nature Conservation 1994, paragraph 2.

biodiversity"[16]. PPG9 also calls on local authorities to identify "positive opportunities" for improvements to the nature conservation of an area or site and points out that these can be linked to site specific land allocated for development in a development plan.

Aside from the more general obligations on planning authorities described above, the relationship between land use planning controls and legal protection for nature conservation has a number of aspects which might be said to provide "the bottom line" in relation to development projects which may have an impact on wildlife and on habitats. First, nature conservation and the protection of wildlife are required to be taken into account during the decision-making process which determines the grant of planning permission for and the siting of development generally. Second, there are specific rules relating to planning applications which affect or may affect protected sites[17]. Third, the existence of planning permission may provide the basis for a defence to a potential breach of a number of protective provisions in UK conservation legislation[18]. This chapter first looks at the first of these parts of the relationship and then in outline at the second. Chapters 1, 2 and 3 - Part I deal with the second and third.

Development Plans and Planning Policy Guidance

The statutory development plan provides "the primary basis" for making decisions on development proposals[19], although other material considerations must also be taken into account (see below). Nature conservation objectives must be taken into account both during the drawing up of development plans and also as a material consideration to be considered as part of the decision-making process on individual planning applications and appeals. As discussed below, there are a number of specific references to conservation in the planning legislation, but one of the main (legal) mechanisms by which Government policy on nature conservation is incorporated into the planning system is through the guidance contained in various Planning Policy Guidance Notes (PPGs)[20]. PPG's set out the Government's policies on different aspects of planning and local planning

[16] PPG12 at paragraph 4.3 refers to Planning for Sustainable Development: Towards Better Practice 1998, chapter 5 of which deals with nature conservation.

[17] These are discussed in Chapters 1-3 on specially protected sites.

[18] See, for example in relation to the protection of SSSI's s28(8)(a) and s29(9) of the 1981 Wildlife and Countryside Act (before amendment by the 2000 Act).

[19] See PPG 12, (1999) paragraph 1.6

[20] See Chapter 3 as to the way in which the Habitats Regulations impact on the planning system in so far as European sites are concerned.

authorities must take their contents into account in preparing their development plans. The guidance may also be material to individual planning decisions. A number of PPGs address nature conservation in the context of planning. Principal among these is PPG9 on Nature Conservation but as is pointed out in PPG9 itself, other PPGs may also be relevant including: PPG7 (The Countryside Environmental Quality and Economic and Social Development); PPG12 (Development Plans); PPG13 (transport); PPG17 (planning for open space sport and recreation); PPG20 (coastal planning) and PPG21 (tourism).

Regional Planning Guidance (RPG's) also includes coverage of nature conservation issues but the form of that guidance means that the issue is addressed very generally[21]. Local authorities should aim to ensure that regional nature conservation issues are brought before the regional planning conferences.[22] RPGs must incorporate quantified targets including those relating to the protection and promotion of biodiversity.[23]

As stated above, the local planning authority must take the contents of PPGs into account in drawing up its development plans.[24] PPG9 states that nature conservation objectives should be reflected in structure plans, unitary development plans and local plans.[25] It also states that: "Nature conservation objectives should be taken into account in all planning activities which affect rural and coastal land use, and in urban areas where there is wildlife of local importance." PPG9 also states that "Nature conservation issues should be included in the surveys of local authority areas required by s11 and 30 of Town and Country Planning Act 1990 to ensure that the plans are based on fully adequate information about local species, habitats, geology and landform." "Plans should be concerned not only with designated areas but also with other land of conservation value and possible provision of new habitats. They should take account of locally prepared nature conservation strategies, which should in turn be consistent with development plan policies.".

Structure plans[26], which set out key strategic policies and provide a framework for local plans, and part I of Unitary Development Plans,

[21] See PPG 11 Regional Planning (October 2000).
[22] PPG9 page 6.
[23] Paragraph 16 of PPG 11.
[24] See Annex A to PPG 12 on Development Plans for a description of the different types of plan and the areas to which they relate.
[25] PPG9 see paragraphs 19 et seq.
[26] These are drawn up by County Councils, some unitary authorities and National Park authorities.

which have a similar function in relation to part II of Unitary Development Plans, must contain a written statement of general policies on development and use of land. The general policies are required to include policies on the conservation of the natural beauty and amenity of the land and improvement of the physical environment[27].

Local plans and Part II of Unitary Development Plans contain more detailed policies to guide development in a particular local authority or unitary area[28]. They must include a map and a conservation policy. If objections are made to the plan a local inquiry must be held. The local planning authority may then adopt the plan with or without modifications. The Secretary of State can call the plan in for approval. Local plans must be in general conformity with the structure plan (1990 Act s36(4)), but provisions of the local plan prevail unless the structure plan authority has stated that the local plan is not in conformity with the structure Plan.

The detailed policies in local plans (and in part II of unitary development plans) should conform to the nature conservation framework contained in the structure plan (or in part I of the unitary development plan)[29]. They should identify relevant international, national and local nature conservation interests, ensure that the protection and enhancement of those interests is properly provided for in development and land-use policies and place "particular emphasis on the strength of protection afforded to international designations." PPG9 also states that plans should give "reasonable certainty to developers, landowners and residents alike about the weight that will be given to nature conservation interest in reaching decisions"[30] They may include detailed proposals for specific sites. PPG9 makes it clear that both local plans and part II of Unitary Development Plans should identify key sites of nature conservation importance such as SSSI's; NNR's; SPA's; SAC's and Ramsar sites, in order to "establish a strategic framework and exemplify the particular characteristics of nature conservation interest in the plan area in their national and international context". The Guidance goes on to say that "Policies to be applied to these sites should reflect their relative significance and place particular emphasis on the protection of internationally important sites[31]. Local plans must be in conformity with the structure

[27] 1990 Act s31(3)-introduced by the Planning and Compensation Act 1991.
[28] These are drawn up by District Councils, some unitary authorities and National Park authorities.
[29] Ibid, paragraph 22.
[30] Ibid, paragraph 24.
[31] Planning Policy Guidance No 9 Nature Conservation, paragraph 22 (October 1994).

plan and similarly part II of a UDP must be in conformity with part I[32]. In the event of a conflict between the local plan and the structure plan, the former will prevail unless the structure plan authority has stated that the local plan is not in general conformity and it has not been revised (see paragraph 6.5 PPG 12 1999). Thus development plans must pay heed both to designated sites and also to wildlife outside such areas.

Under the planning system, local authorities must consult on draft plans before they are deposited. In relation to structure plans, there is a list of statutory consultees whereas in relation to local plans, guidance is given as to those who should be consulted. A number of the consultees to whom reference is made are those specifically concerned with nature conservation and wildlife. In the case of structure plans, consultees include the Secretary of State for the Environment, local authorities within the plan area and adjacent areas and English Heritage as well as English Nature, the Countryside Agency and the Environment Agency. In the case of local plans, Annex C of PPG12 sets out those consultees who should be consulted if their interests will be affected by the proposed plan. The list is broad and includes a number of Government Departments as well as other bodies representing utilities and public and commercial interests. Among the public bodies included in the list are the Environment Agency, English Nature, the Countryside Agency and the Forestry Commission. Also included are environmental groups at the national, regional and local level including the CPRE, RSPB, Friends of the Earth and the wildlife trusts who are to be consulted on environmental issues and their relationship to other policies and proposals. In all cases, local Agenda 21 Groups should be consulted. Consultation provides an opportunity for the local authority and those objecting to aspects of the draft plan to try and negotiate a solution. Matters which remain unresolved can be dealt with by the Planning Inspector at the local inquiry. Conservation issues may, and often are, therefore raised at the consultation stage.

The local planning authority can amend the structure plan but must have regard to planning guidance, regional and strategic given by the Secretary of State[33] Before it adopts or alters the structure plan, the local planning authority must hold an examination in public of the matters to be examined. The Secretary of State may call the plan in for his approval. Once adopted, the local planning authority must inform the authorities

[32] See further PPG 12, paragraph 6. 1 et seq.
[33] 1990 Act s31(6).

responsible for local plans and state whether any existing local plan is in conformity with the structure plan or not.[34]

Minerals and Waste

Minerals and waste local plans should also take account of nature conservation interest, especially in respect of designated sites. Mineral Planning Guidance Notes, especially No's 1,2,6,7 and 10 require the interests of wildlife to be taken into account. Proposals likely to affect SSSI's "should be the subject of the most rigorous examination" and English Nature must be consulted on such applications[35]. "The need for the mineral must be balanced against environmental and other relevant considerations ". Particular attention must be paid to the proposed end-use of the site in framing planning conditions and special considerations apply if the site enjoys international designation. The possibility for creating new habitat should also be examined.

Peat

Special consideration is afforded to proposals for the working of peat. Peat is formed from the accumulated remains of plants growing in waterlogged conditions. Generally it is found in lowland areas, in distinctive and rare habitats. Peatlands are listed under the habitats directive and some have priority status. Large areas of such habitats are often drained for agriculture or cut for domestic purposes.

MPG 13 on peat extraction requires sites of raised bogs and other peatlands of key nature conservation importance to be identified in development plans[36]. The Guidance states that peat extraction from bogs with a high nature conservation interest will only be permitted in exceptional circumstances and identifies those types of sites in relation to which applications will normally be called in[37].

Planning Applications

Nature Conservation as a "Material Consideration"

The local planning authority must have regard to the provisions of the development plan and any other material considerations in deciding

[34] 1990 Act s35C.
[35] PPG9 paragraph 40.
[36] Paragraph 52.
[37] Paragraph 57.

whether to grant planning permission[38]. Under s54A of the 1990 Act (as amended by Planning and Compensation Act 1991) an application for planning permission or an appeal is to be determined in accordance with the plan unless material considerations indicate otherwise.

PPG9 makes it clear that nature conservation can be a significant material consideration in determining many planning applications, especially in relation to development in or near SSSI's where there are statutory requirements to consult English Nature[39]. However it goes on to state that local planning authorities should not refuse permission for development if "development can be subject to conditions that will prevent damaging impacts on wildlife habitats or important physical features, or if other material factors are sufficient to override nature conservation considerations."[40] This does not appear to offer wildlife particularly great protection given the pressures on development in areas such as housing. As discussed in Chapter 3, the position is somewhat better in relation to designated sites, in particular European sites. It should be noted that the environmental information generated by an environmental impact assessment has become a material consideration.

The presence of a protected species is a material consideration when a local planning authority is considering a development proposal which, if carried out, would be likely to result in harm to the species or its habitat.[41] English Nature should be consulted before permission is granted. Conditions or obligations should be considered under which the developer would take steps to secure protection of the species particularly if it is listed on annex iv of the habitats directive. It should be noted that there is special protection for badger setts, see s10 (1)(d) of the 1992 Act discussed in Chapter 3 - Part II.

In *R v Poole Borough Council Ex parte Beebee,*[42] an objector argued that in considering a planning application, the local planning authority had failed to take into account a relevant consideration, namely that the proposed development would affect an existing SSSI but the court found that the authority had taken into account the substance of what was required so planning permission not quashed.

[38] 1990 Act s70(2).
[39] PPG 9 paragraph 27.
[40] Paragraph 27, ibid.
[41] PPG9 paragraph 47.
[42] Queen's Bench Division, [1991] 2 PLR 27, [1991] JPL 643, 21 December 1990.

Development Affecting European Sites

The Habitats Regulations regulate the granting of planning permission for development which is likely significantly to affect an SPA or SAC. PPG9 gives further guidance on development control for SPAs and SACs. These controls are discussed further in Chapter 3 - Part I but essentially, regulation 48 of the Habitats Regulations requires the planning authority to carry out an "appropriate assessment" of the implications for the site of any plan or project which is likely to have a significant effect on a European site in Great Britain (either alone or combination with other plans or projects). PPG9 elaborates further on how the assessment is to be done. This does not apply to plans or projects not directly connected with or necessary to the management of the site however. Accordingly, the authority must first determine whether an assessment is required by ascertaining whether the plan or project is directly connected with, or necessary to, the management of the site in question for nature conservation and if not, whether it is likely to have a significant effect on the site "in terms of the ecological objectives for which the site was designated" either alone or in combination with other plans or projects. The authority must take account of the advice of English Nature and if the initial assessment is inconclusive, PPG states that "a fuller assessment will be needed to establish the effects of the proposed development on the site".[43]

Once the authority has determined that a plan or project unconnected with the conservation management of the site is likely to have significant effects, they must assess its implications in the light of the site's conservation objectives in order to ascertain whether the plan or project will adversely affect the integrity of the site. PPG9 describes the integrity of the site as "the coherence of its ecological structure and function, across its whole area, that enables it to sustain the habitat, complex of habitat and/or the levels of populations of the species for which it was classified"[44]. PPG9 states that the scope and content of an assessment under regulation 48 will depend on the location, size and significance of the proposed project.

The appropriate nature conservation body must be consulted for the purposes of the assessment and regard must be had to any representations which it makes (within such reasonable time as the planning authority may specify). In the light of the assessment, the planning authority may agree to the plan or project only after having ascertained that it will not adversely affect the integrity of the site. In considering whether

[43] PPG9 Annex C page 17.
[44] Paragraph C10 of PPG9.

the plan or project will adversely affect the site, the authority must have regard to the manner in which it is proposed to carry it out and to any conditions or restrictions subject to which it proposes that the permission or authorisation be given. This means that where for example a mitigation package has been negotiated perhaps in the form of a s106 planning agreement, it is the effect of the development subject to the mitigation package which is considered.

In certain cases, where there is no alternative and there are considerations of overriding public interest the plan or project may be carried out despite a negative assessment. This is governed by regulation 49 of the Habitats Regulations.

Should the assessment be inconclusive, a fuller assessment will be needed to establish the effects of the proposed development on the site[45]. The Secretary of State will normally call in planning applications which are likely to significantly affect sites of international importance (including SPAs and SACs). Where the application is not called in and the authority proposes to allow the development to go ahead, the Secretary of State must be notified in advance[46].

The General Development Order

The Secretary of State may grant planning permission by means of a development order either for general classes or specific case of development[47]. The General Development Order is subject to the requirements of the Habitats Regulations, regulations 60-63. In particular, where development is likely to have a significant effect on a European site and is not directly connected with or necessary to the management of the site (see above), it may not be begun until the developer has received written notification of approval from the local planning authority under regulation 62 of the Regulations. Under Regulation 61 the opinion of the relevant nature conservation body may be sought as to whether the development in question is likely to have a significant effect.

Provision is also made in the Regulations for development covered by special development orders, simplified planning zones and enterprise zones (regulations 64-66). Essentially, planning permission under these

[45] PPG9, Annex C.

[46] PPG9 Annex C paragraphs 9-10.

[47] 1990 Act s59. In relation to Wales the Secretary of State's functions have been transferred to the Welsh Assembly, SI 1999/672, art 2 Schedule 1.

schemes for development which would significantly affect a European site is withdrawn or will not be granted. Provision for compensation is made in regulation 67.

Planning Conditions and Obligations

Planning permission may be, and normally is, granted subject to conditions. In relation to applications which may affect nature conservation objectives, PPG9 states that local planning authorities should not refuse planning permission if development can be subject to conditions that will prevent damaging impacts on wildlife habitats or important physical features, or if other material factors are sufficient to override nature conservation considerations[48]. Where there is a risk of damage to a designated site, the local planning authority should consider the use of conditions or planning obligations in the interest of nature conservation, for example conditions requiring areas to be fenced off to protect them or to restrict operations or uses to specific times of year. Planning obligations can accompany permissions in order to secure long-term management of an area, provide funds for management, or to provide for compensatory nature conservation features.

In relation to planning permission which relates to the working of minerals, PPG9 states that where planning permission is given conditions will normally be required. These may relate to the winning and working of the minerals themselves and to restoration and aftercare of the site.[49] The Guidance also points out that mineral working may also provide an opportunity for habitat creation and enhancement, and that mineral planning authorities and companies should bear this in mind.

Under regulation 37 of the Habitats Regulations (see below), planning policies in respect of conservation are to include policies encouraging the management of landscape features which are of major importance to wild flora and fauna. In practice this is achieved in large part by means of suitable planning conditions and obligations.

Absence of planning controls for agriculture

By virtue of s55(2)(e)of the 1990 Act, the use of any land for the purposes of agriculture or forestry (including afforestation) and the use for

---

[48] PPG9 page 7 para 27.
[49] PPG9 paragraph 40.

any of those purposes of any building occupied together with land so used does *not* fall within the scope of development for the purposes of planning control. The planning controls discussed above therefore have very little role in protecting wildlife from the impact of agriculture. Environmental legislation such as that regulating water quality and the use of pesticides clearly has a role to play in protecting wildlife from the impacts of agriculture but the absence of planning controls raises the question as to how much the law provides a real framework for protecting the wildlife interest of agricultural land. The scope of protection afforded by measures outside the planning system is considered in Chapter 7- Part I.

Environmental Impact Assessment

Environmental impact assessment is required under the Environmental Impact Assessment Directive[50] for certain types of development project. The types of projects covered by the Directive are listed on Annexes I and II. Those listed in Annex I always require assessment whereas those listed in Annex II require assessment only where they are likely to have significant effects on the environment, including on flora and fauna . In relation to the latter, the selection criteria in Annex III must be applied in making a determination as to the likely effects of the project and these include a consideration of the location of the project. Regard is to be paid to the areas likely to be affected and particular attention must be given to effects on SPAs classified under the wild birds Directive and SACs designated under the Habitats Directive. In many cases the specific requirements for appropriate assessment under the Habitats Regulations will overlap with obligations under the EIA Directive[51]. Relevant authorities and the public are to be consulted during the assessment process. The outcome of the assessment does not dictate whether or not the project will receive consent from the relevant authority but the information and consultations received as a result must be taken into consideration by that body in reaching its decision[52].

A full consideration of the requirements of the Directive lies beyond the scope of this book but environmental impact assessment plays an important role in protecting wildlife from the adverse effects of development, both inside and outside protected areas.

[50] Council Directive 85/337/EEC on the assessment of the effects of certain public and private projects on the environment OJ No L175 5.7.85 p 40 as last amended by Council Directive 97/11/EEC OJ No L73 14.3.97 p5.

[51] For a further consideration of the relationship between the two regimes, see Chapter 3 - Part I.

[52] Article 8 of the Directive as amended.

In 2001 the Strategic Environmental Assessment Directive was adopted[53]. This requires the assessment of certain plans and programmes. The plans and programmes are those adopted in a wide range of sectors including agriculture, forestry, industry, transport and planning and which set the framework for future development consents for the projects listed in the EIA Directive or which have been determined to require assessment under the Habitats Directive. The outcome of the process must be taken into account in preparing the plan or programme concerned and before its adoption or submission to the legislative procedure[54]. The SEA Directive is also an important general measure contributing to the protection and conservation of wildlife.

Management Agreements outside Designated Areas

During the passage of the Wildlife and Countryside Bill, Lord Sandford lamented the relative lack of further action to establish management agreements elsewhere in the countryside (outside National Parks etc), in particular by district councils. Such concerns led to the adoption of further provision for the conclusion of management agreements.

Under s39 of the Wildlife and Countryside Act 1981, a relevant authority can, for the purpose of conserving or enhancing the natural beauty or amenity of any land which is both countryside and within their area or of promoting its enjoyment by the public, make an agreement with any person having an interest in the land with respect to the management of the land during a specified term or without limitation for duration of term. "A relevant authority" means the local planning authority, or the relevant planning authority where the land is in a National Park (s39(5)). The power is a general one but subsection (2) gives an indication of the type of provision that is envisaged, referring to restrictions on the method of cultivation or its agricultural use; the imposition of obligations to carry out works or agricultural or forestry operations. Management agreements may also confer on the relevant authority the power to carry out works for performing their functions under the 1949 Act or 1968 Act. Management agreements with a person with any interest in land are be binding on persons deriving title under or from that person and are enforceable against those persons by the relevant authority unless the agreement provides otherwise (s39(3)).

[53] Directive 2001/42/EC of the European Parliament and the Council on the assessment of the effects of certain plans and programmes on the environment (27 June 2001).
[54] Article 8 of the Directive.

Local Authorities

As part of their duty under s11 of the Countryside Act 1968 to have regard to the desirability of conserving the natural beauty and amenity of the countryside, local authorities should consider entering into management agreements with owners of occupiers of land under under s39 of the 1981 Act and the giving of loans or grants. They should also manage their land so that account is taken of its wildlife interest for example in the sympathetic treatment of roadside verges, open spaces and parks.

Nature Corridors and Buffer Zones

"Statutory and non-statutory sites, together with countryside features which provide wildlife corridors, links or stepping stones from one habitat to the another, all help to form a network necessary to ensure the maintenance of the current range and diversity of our flora, fauna, geological and landscape features important to wildlife."[55]

Nature corridors, such as hedgerows and verges, and other landscape features which allow species to travel, are important ecologically in maintaining healthy populations of species. They help to prevent communities of species from becoming fragmented and thus more vulnerable to pressures on their habitat. During debate on the Habitats Regulations in the House of Lords, it was said to be clear "that for most and perhaps all the listed species and habitats which occur in the UK the protection and management of SACs will not be enough to obtain favourable conservation status. Species such as the otter travel great distances and are not confined to particular sites. Consequently new and more effective policies are needed for the wider countryside...The Government is wrong to rely on existing schemes because most are purely voluntary and [we] need something stronger.[56] The importance of these features has been highlighted in a number of recent UK Government plans and reports. The UK's Biodiversity Action Plan refers to local authority strategies to maintain green corridors such as river valleys[57]. The UK's First Report on its Implementation of the Convention on Biological Diversity points out that rivers and streams provide a wildlife corridor link between fragmented habitats in intensively farmed areas.

---

[55] PPG9 page 6.
[56] Hansard, House of Lords, 17 October 1994, col 101-102.
[57] UK AP.4.82.

Also important is the establishment of so-called buffer zones around protected sites which go some way to reduce the adverse effects on protected areas of off-site activities. It has also been pointed out that in drawing up boundaries of protected areas, account should be taken of the possible effects of climate change (by designating larger areas)[58]. Whatever the scale of those effects may prove to be, it seems clear that ensuring the survival of nature corridors and providing buffer zones is likely enhance the resilience of the ecosystems within protected sites.

The importance of both these types of features has increasingly been recognised in conservation legislation. Article 10 of the Habitats Directive requires Member States to endeavour "where they consider it necessary" in their planning and development policies and with a view to improving the ecological coherence of Natura 2000, to encourage the management of landscape features of major importance for flora and fauna. Despite the qualified language the inclusion of this provision in the Directive is important since the protection of nature corridors and buffer zones represents a more sophisticated approach to habitat protection than the traditionally exclusive focus on discrete protected areas.

Nature Corridors

Although the term "nature corridor" does not appear in the directive [or the implementing legislation], the Habitats Directive makes special reference to landscape features such as rivers or field boundaries which are of major importance to wildlife in particular for migration and dispersal and so on. The thirteenth recital to the Habitats Directive states that "land use planning and development policies should encourage the management of features of the landscape which are of major importance for wild flora and fauna."

Article 10 of the Directive then requires Member States to "endeavour, where they consider it necessary, in their land use planning and development policies and, in particular, with a view to improving the ecological coherence of the Natura 2000 network, to encourage the management of features of the landscape which are of major importance for wild fauna and flora."Such features are those which by virtue of their linear and continuous structure (such as rivers with their boundaries or the traditional systems for marking field boundaries) or their function as stepping stones (such as small ponds or small woods), are essential for the migration, dispersal and genetic exchange of wild species."

[58] The IUCN handbook on the CBD, page 40.

Clearly this is a softer obligation, to "endeavour to encourage" rather than to protect outright,) than those relating to the protection of special areas of conservation in Article 6 of the directive (although any such features found within SAC's would of course be covered by the stricter protection afforded to such sites). Nevertheless, the requirement does draw attention to the ecological importance of these features for wildlife and must be taken into account by decision-makers as a matter of European law.

Implementation of Article 10 in the UK

In the UK, Article 10 has been implemented by Regulation 37 of the Habitats Regulations which introduces the concerns of Article 10 into certain planning enactments. Regulation 37 provides that, for the purposes of the planning enactments to which it refers, policies in respect of the conservation of the natural beauty and amenity of the land shall be taken to include policies encouraging the management of features of the landscape which are of major importance for wild flora and fauna (describing these in the language of Article 10 of the Directive). Those enactments are: the Town and Country Planning Act 1990 12(3A) (unitary development plans); s31(3) (structure plans); s36(3) (local plans) and the equivalent Scottish legislation.

The protection of such features is also referred to in PPG9, which refers to regulation 37 of the Habitats Regulations and Article 10 of the Directive, and notes that "suitable planning conditions and obligations may serve to promote the management of landscape features of major importance for wild flora and fauna" (paragraph 23).

The UK's implementation of Article 10 has been criticised by conservation organisations such as Plantlife[59]. The House of Commons Select Committee on the Environment in its Report on Biodiversity recommended that all types of traditional field boundaries including banks, ditches and dykes (and not just certain hedgerows) should be protected so as to ensure the continued presence of habitats for some species and corridors for others.[60] In this context a power for English Nature to negotiate management agreements outside SSSI's was also seen as very important to securing the protection of such features. This has been introduced by section 75(3) of the 2000 Act , which amends section 15 of the 1968 Act so as to allow English Nature to enter into management agreements with

[59] HC 441 at paragraph 64 et seq, note 3 supra.
[60] HC 441 paragraph 65, note 3 supra.

owners of land outside an SSSI for the purpose of protecting the special interest of the SSSI.

Buffer Zones

The issue of the extent to which areas surrounding protected sites should themselves be protected is addressed in a number of ways in nature conservation legislation...

At the international level, Article 8(e) of the CBD requires Parties "as far as possible and as appropriate" to promote environmentally sound and sustainable development in areas adjacent to protected areas with a view to furthering protection of these areas. As to what is possible or appropriate in this regard, concerns have been expressed, for example in the debate on the Habitats Regulations in the House of Lords, about the "penumbra effect" where off-site activities that might just be considered damaging to an SAC will be caught in the list of proscribed activities creating uncertainty for landowners who would not then know where they stood in relation to what or was not permitted activity near such sites[61].

The case of *Sweet v SOSEnv and NCC*[62] might be seen to raise the issue of buffer zones, although the term was not used in argument. In *Sweet*, the High Court rejected an application for judicial review of a decision to make a special nature conservation order under section 29 of the 1981 Act (that section was repealed by the 2000 Act). The owner of the land subject to the order argued that the part of the land concerned was not of national interest and could not therefore be made subject to an order under section 29 (it was not disputed that another part of the land was of national interest). Mr Justice Schiemann decided however that the inspector's finding in the local inquiry that the whole of the order land constituted a single environment and was to be treated as such was one to which he was entitled to come on the evidence. It followed that the Secretary of State had been entitled to draw the boundaries as he had done, protecting the site as a whole as being of national interest. Although the particular statutory power under consideration has now been repealed, this case illustrates a purposive approach to the legislation which is sensitive to what might be called the environmental realities of trying to protect particular habitats contained within a wider environment. In such cases, areas outside those of immediate interest may have to be protected if the interest of the site is to be maintained. This approach may still be relevant in cases involving the designation of specific sites.

[61] Hansard, House of Lords, 17 October 1994, col 96.
[62] [1989] JPEL 927.

B. Limestone Pavements

Limestone pavements have had specific statutory protection since the adoption of the 1981 Wildlife and Countryside Act. This habitat may have received such particular attention because of its distinctive features and also because of the very specific threat it faced(removal of the stone for use in garden landscaping, see further below). Limestone pavements are defined in s34 of the 1981 Act as "an area of limestone which lies wholly or partly exposed on the surface of the ground and has been fissured by natural erosion." The First UK Government Report under the Convention on Biological Diversity[1] described them as a scarce and non-renewable resource of both geological and biological importance, rich in vascular plants, bryophtes and lichens. They have a complex pattern of crevices (grikes) between which are massive blocks of worn limestone (clints). The habitat is widely scattered in Britain totaling less than 3,000 hectares, with the largest areas in North Yorkshire and Cumbria, and smaller areas in Lancashire, Wales and Scotland. The UK holds a significant proportion of limestone pavement habitats within the EU and limestone pavements are listed as a priority natural habitat type under Annex I of the habitats directive (for priority habitats see further Chapter 3 - Part I.[2]

Limestone Pavement Orders

Section 34 of the Wildlife and Countryside Act 1981 affords special protection to those limestone pavements considered to be of special interest and which are made subject to a statutory order.

When the Wildlife and Countryside Bill was originally introduced in 1980, limestone pavements covered about 5000 acres in England and Wales. It was recognised at that time that they were threatened by despoliation, principally to provide rock for garden rockeries[3] [97% of limestone pavements were said to be damaged (c399)]. During the Bill's Second Reading in the House of Lords, it emerged that there were doubts about the extent to which the removal of limestone from limestone pavements constituted "development" and was therefore subject to

---

[1] UK 1st CBD Report.

[2] A number of sites comprising limestone pavements have been put forward to the Commission as SACs for example Ingleborough Complex in North Yorkshire, English Nature Press Release June 1998.

[3] Hansard, 16.12.80 col 986.

planning control. There were particular concerns that, in contrast to removal by mechanical means, simple removal of the limestone by hand or crow bar was not subject to planning control[4]. Accordingly, the Government proposed a new order-making power which would protect limestone pavements by prohibiting any removal or disturbance of limestone.

There was some discussion as to who should make the proposed orders as there was clearly a landscape interest as well as a botanical/ physiographical interest. The question of a possible role for the Countryside Commission was raised. This was resolved by providing that either the relevant Council or, in relation to England, the Countryside Commission could notify the special interest of a limestone pavement to the local planning authority (s34(1)).

About half of limestone pavements are SSSI's[5] but the scope of protection under a s34 order was, in one important respect at least, wider than that afforded to SSSI's [prior to the changes introduced by the 2000 Act]. The Government introduced an amendment to what became s34 making it an offence for "any person" to remove or disturb limestone on any land subject to an order. This was in order to close a loophole which would otherwise exist in relation to persons who were not the owners or occupiers of the land in question [col384]. The same potential loophole was not closed in relation to SSSI's however until the 2000 Act (see chapter 1 - Part I).

In relation to England, English Nature and the Countryside Commission are under a duty to notify the local planning authority of any land comprising a limestone pavement, which in their opinion, is of special interest. Special interest may relate to the flora, fauna or geological or physiographical features of the land.

Where it appears to the Secretary of State or to the relevant local planning authority (as defined in s34(6)) that the character or appearance of any such land is likely to be adversely affected by the removal or disturbance of limestone, the Secretary of State of the local planning authority may make an order designating the land and prohibiting the removal or disturbance of limestone on or in it. The procedure for making such orders is governed by Schedule 11 of the 1981 Act which states that

[4] Hansard House of Lords 12, February 1981, col 376.
[5] Some also have other designations-Ingleborough Complex is also a National Nature Reserve, see further Chapter 5 - Part I.

orders take effect on their being made. There is provision for publicity to be given to orders and where orders are opposed, the Secretary of State may call for a local inquiry or afford any person objecting to the order the opportunity of being heard.

Orders may only be amended or revoked by the relevant planning authority or the Secretary of State after consultation with the Council or the Commission (and the planning authority if the order was made by the authority and is being amended or revoked by the Secretary of State) (see s34(3)).

Enforcement

It is an offence, punishable by the statutory maximum fine on summary conviction or an unlimited fine on indictment, for any person, without reasonable excuse, to remove or disturb limestone on or in any land subject to a limestone pavement order.

There was some debate during the passage of the Bill concerning the defences which should be available. In the end a proposal for a general agricultural use defence was dropped. Section 34(5) provides that it is a reasonable excuse if the removal or disturbance was authorised by planning permission.

In 1998, in the context of its consultation on the protection and management of SSSI's, the Government invited views on how limestone pavements might be more effectively protected. In particular, the Government wanted to know whether the owner of the land should be made responsible for the protection of the areas covered by an order (to address third party theft). However this proposal was not taken up. Increased protection has been afforded through the imposition of higher fines however. Section 78 of the Countryside and Rights of Way Act 2000 amended the provision for fines to be imposed for removing or disturbing limestone in order to match the increased penalties available for damage caused to SSSI's.

Hedgerows in the UK

The UK's hedgerow network has been estimated at 400,000 km in length and constitutes an important refuge for biodiversity in the rural landscape[1]. The same report estimated an annual loss of 5% of hedgerows[2]. One of the most notable findings of the 1990 Countryside Survey related to the loss of field boundaries. Between 1984 and 1990, it was estimated that the length of hedges declined by about 23% resulting in the adoption of several steps to reverse or slow the pace of change.[3] These measures included ancient and/or species-rich hedgerows being included as a Priority Habitat in the UK Biodiversity Action Plan in 1995 with a target to halt the loss of all such hedgerows by 2005; to achieve favourable management of 50% of these hedges by the same date; and to maintain the overall numbers of hedgerow trees. Hedgerows in England and Wales were given statutory protection under the Hedgerow Regulations of 1997[4]. According to the 2000 Countryside Survey , the decline in length of hedgerow reported in the earlier survey has been halted and there is some evidence that losses in the early 1990s have been reversed. [5]

The Hedgerow Regulations 1997 [SI 1997/1160][6]

Section 97 of the EPA 1995 gave the appropriate ministers the power to frame regulations for the protection of important hedgerows in England and Wales.[7] These Regulations came into force on 1st June 1997 and apply

---

[1] UK 1st Report CBD.
[2] UK 1st Report CBD, page 22.
[3] See Countryside Survey 2000, DEFRA website http://www.defra.gov.uk /wildlife-countryside/cs2000/04/01.htm).
[4] SI 1997/1160.
[5] http://www.press.dtlr.gov.uk/0011/0734.htm.
[6] Under Article 10 of the EC Habitats Directive, member states are required to encourage the management of hedges and other linear features in their land use and development policies, with a view to improving their ecological coherence. This requirement has been incorporated into UK legislation through the Conservation (Natural Habitats etc.) Regulations 1994., see further Chapter 3 - Part I.
[7] According to the Departmental Explanatory note to the regulations, in order to facilitate the protection of these important hedgerows, the regulations apply to a wider class of hedgerows as is described in Regulation 3.

to any hedgerow or any stretch of hedgerow forming part of a hedgerow,[8] growing in, or adjacent to, any common or protected land, or land used for agriculture, forestry or the breeding or keeping of horses, ponies or donkeys, if it has a continuous length of 20 metres[9] or more; or a continuous length of less than 20 metres where both ends meet (whether by intersection or junction) another hedgerow.[10] However, the regulations do not apply to any hedgerow within the curtilage of, or marking a boundary of the curtilage of, a dwelling-house.[11]

Important hedgerows

The criteria for determining "important hedgerows" for the purposes of section 97 of the EPA and the Regulations is that the hedgerow or the hedgerow of which it is a stretch have existed for 30 years or more and satisfy at least one of the criteria set out in Part II of Schedule I.[12]

Regulation 5 prohibits the removal of a hedgerow subject to the ['permitted work' exceptions in regulation 6] unless – (1) the local planning authority in whose area the hedgerow is situated or, where it is situated in the area of more than one such authority, the authority where the greater part of the hedgerow is situated, has received from an owner of the hedgerow a 'hedgerow removal notice' together with the required plan and evidence; and[13] (2) either the authority gives its written consent to the removal or the specified period [14] has expired without the authority having given to that person a hedgerow retention notice[15] stating that the work may not be carried out[16]; and (3) the removal is carried out in accordance with the proposal specified in the hedgerow removal notice; and (4) finally that the hedgerow is removed within the period of two years beginning with the date of service of the hedgerow removal notice.[17]

Anyone who intentionally or recklessly removes, or causes or permits another person to remove, a hedgerow in contravention of the above provisions is guilty of an offence.[18]

[8] The Hedgerow Regulations 1997, Regulation 3(2).
[9] For the purposes of ascertaining the length of any hedgerow, any gap resulting from a contravention of the regulations, and any gap not exceeding 20 metres, is to be treated as part of the hedgerow. ibid, Regulation 3(5).
[10] ibid, Regulation 3(1) (a) & (b).
[11] ibid, Regulation 3(3).
[12] ibid, Regulation 4 and Schedule 1, Part II.
[13] ibid, Regulation 5(a).
[14] ibid, Regulation 5(6).
[15] ibid Regulation[5.
[16] ibid, Regulation 5(1)(b).
[17] ibid, Regulation 5 (c) & (d).
[18] ibid, Regulation 7(1).

A local planning authority,[19] upon receiving a hedgerow removal notice, must decide within 42 days whether or not to give notice to that person, in the form of a 'hedgerow retention notice'.[20], stating that the work or, where the hedgerow removal notice refers to more than one hedgerow, so much of the work as may be specified by the authority in its notice, may not be carried out, A local planning authority shall not give a hedgerow retention notice in respect of a hedgerow which is not an important hedgerow[21] and must give such a notice in respect of an important hedgerow unless satisfied by the reasons given in the hedgerow removal notice, that there are circumstances which justify the hedgerow's removal.[22] A hedgerow retention notice must specify each criterion which applies to the hedgerow to which the notice relates except where regulation 8(4) applies (the hedgerow was planted pursuant to a notice). A hedgerow retention notice may be withdrawn at any time by the local planning authority by giving written notice of the withdrawal to the person to whom the hedgerow retention notice was given. Where a hedgerow retention notice has been given stating that work relating to the hedgerow may not be carried out, and that notice has not been withdrawn, removal of the hedgerow consisting of or including any such work is prohibited.

The removal of any hedgerow is permitted if it is required for any of the following purposes:[23] making a new opening in substitution for an existing opening which gives access to land,[24] ;obtaining temporary access to any land in order to give assistance in an emergency; obtaining access to land where another means of access is not available or is available only at disproportionate cost; national defence; carrying out development for which planning permission has been granted or is deemed to have been granted (subject to certain exceptions essentially relating to permitted development, regulation 6(1)(e)); carrying out work for the purpose of flood defence or land drainage; [25] preventing the spread of, or ensuring the eradication of any plant pest or any tree pest[26]; the carrying out by the

[19] Where a hedgerow in respect of which the local planning authority has received a hedgerow removal notice is situated in a parish in England for which there is a parish council, or in a community in Wales for which there is a community council, that authority must consult that council (or, where there is more than one such council, each of them) on the proposal to remove that hedgerow, ibid, Regulation 5(3).

[20] ibid, Regulation 5 (2).

[21] ibid, Regulation 5(5)(a).

[22] ibid, Regulation 5(5)(b).

[23] ibid.Regulation 6(1).

[24] The person removing it shall fix the existing opening by planting a hedge within 8 months of the making of the new opening. Regulation 6(2).

[25] This work is to be carried out, pursuant to, or under, the Land Drainage Act 1991, the Water Resources Act 1991 or the Environment Act 1995. Regulation 6(1)(f).

[26] Both Plant and Tress Pests are defined in Regulation 6(1)(g).

Secretary of State of his functions in respect of any highway for which he is the highway authority or he has the same powers under the Highways Act 1980 as the local highway authority[27]; carrying out any felling, lopping or cutting back required or permitted to prevent obstruction of or interference with electric lines and plant or to prevent danger;[28] or the proper management of the hedgerow. The fact that work is permitted under these provisions does not affect any prohibition or restriction imposed by or under any other enactment or by any agreement.[29]

Replacement of hedgerows.

Except where the local planning authority is the owner of the hedgerow[30], where it appears to the local planning authority that a hedgerow has been removed[31], the authority may (whether or not proceedings are instituted) give a notice to the owner, requiring him to plant another hedgerow or, where the hedgerow has been removed by or on behalf of a relevant utility operator, give a notice to that operator requiring it to plant another hedgerow.[32] Such a notice must specify the species and position of the trees and/or shrubs to be planted and the period within which the planting is to be carried out.[33]

A hedgerow planted in compliance with a notice must be treated for the purposes of the Hedgerows Regulations and for the period of 30 years beginning with the date of substantial completion of the planting, as if it were an important hedgerow.[34]

Appeals

Except where the local planning authority is the owner of the hedgerow[35], a person to whom a hedgerow retention notice or a notice under Regulation 8(1) requiring the planting of a hedgerow is given may, by notice given within 28 days from the date on which the notice was given to him (or such longer period as the Secretary of State may allow), appeal to the Secretary of State against the decision to issue the notice.[36] The notice of

[27] Regulation 6(1)(h).
[28] Regulation 6(1)(1).
[29] Regulation 6(3).
[30] Regulation 15.
[31] In contravention of Regulations 5(1) or (9).
[32] Regulation 8(1).
[33] Regulation 8(2).
[34] Regulation 8(4).
[35] Regulation 15.
[36] Regulation 9.

appeal must state the grounds for the appeal and a copy of the same must also be served on the local planning authority which gave the hedgerow retention notice or the notice under regulation 8(1).[37] Before determining the appeal, the Secretary of State must afford to the appellant and the local planning authority an opportunity of being heard by a person appointed by the Secretary of State for the purpose.[38] In determining the appeal the Secretary of State may allow or dismiss it, in whole or in part; and must give any directions necessary to give effect to his decision, including directions for quashing or modifying any notice, and he must notify the appellant and the local planning authority of this decision.[39] The Secretary of State may cause a local inquiry to be held in connection with an appeal.[40]

Records

Each local planning authority must compile and keep freely accessible to the public a record containing a copy of every hedgerow removal notice received by them, every hedgerow retention notice issued by them; every notice issued by them to the person who gave the hedgerow removal notice stating that the hedgerow maybe removed and every determination notified to them under regulation 9(3).[41]

Injunctions

Where a local planning authority considers it necessary or expedient for an actual or apprehended offence[42] under the Hedgerows Regulations to be restrained by injunction, the authority may apply to the High Court or the county court[43] for an injunction, whether or not it has exercised or is proposing to exercise any of its other powers under the regulations.[44] On such an application being made, the court may grant such an injunction as it thinks appropriate for the purpose of restraining the offence.[45]

[37] Regulation 9(2).
[38] Regulation 9(4).
[39] Regulation 9(3).
[40] Regulation 9(5). For further powers of the Secretary of State in this regard see Regulation 9(6) and (7).
[41] Regulation 10.
[42] the offences are defined in Regulation 7.
[43] Regulation 11(3).
[44] Regulation 11.
[45] Regulation 11(2).

Power of entry

Regulation 12 provides for rights of entry for authorized persons for the purpose of: surveying it in connection with any hedgerow removal notice received by the authority; ascertaining whether an offence under the regulations has been committed; determining whether a notice requiring the planting of a hedgerow should be given[46], if there are reasonable grounds for entering for the purpose in question. In addition, any person duly authorised in writing by the Secretary of State may enter any land for the purpose of surveying it in connection with an appeal under the regulations, if there are reasonable grounds for entering for that purpose.

There is provision for notice to be given and any right to enter any land must be exercised at a reasonable hour. No right to enter may be exercised in relation to land which adjoins that in respect of which a hedgerow removal notice has been given or an appeal made; and is occupied by a person other than the person who gave the hedgerow removal notice or made the appeal, unless at least 24 hours' notice of the intended entry has been given to the occupier of that adjoining land.[47] Where the hedgerow is or is to be removed by or on behalf of a relevant utility operator from land of which it is not the owner[48], no right to enter any land by virtue of regulations 12(1)(a) or (2) above may be exercised unless at least 24 hours' notice of the intended entry has been given to the occupier of the land.[49]

If it is shown to the satisfaction of a justice of the peace on sworn information in writing (a) that there are reasonable grounds for entering any land for any of the purposes in regulation 12(1) or (2) ; and (b) that (i) admission to the land has been refused, or a refusal is reasonably apprehended; or (ii) the case is one of urgency, the justice may issue a warrant authorising any person duly authorised in writing by a local planning authority or, as the case may be, the Secretary of State to enter the land.[50] The warrant authorises entry on only one occasion and that entry must be within one month from the date of the issue of the warrant; and at a reasonable hour, unless the case is one of urgency.[51]

[46] Regulation 8

[47] Regulation 12(3) &(4)

[48] Regulation 5(10)

[49] Regulation 12(5)

[50] Regulation 13(1). For the purposes of this provision admission to land shall be regarded as having been refused if no reply is received to a request for admission within a reasonable period. Regulation 13(2)

[51] Regulation 13(3)

A right of entry[52] is construed as including power to take samples from any hedgerow on the land and samples of the soil. A person authorised to enter land in the exercise of such a right must, if so required, produce evidence of his authority and state the purpose of his entry before entering. He may take with him such other persons as may be necessary; and on leaving the land must, if the occupier is not then present, leave it as effectively secured against trespassers as he found it.[53] Any person who wilfully obstructs a person acting in the exercise of a right of entry is guilty of an offence and liable on summary conviction to a fine not exceeding level 3 on the standard scale.[54] If any damage is caused to land or chattels in the exercise of a right of entry, compensation[55] may be recovered by any person suffering the damage from the authority who gave the written authority for the entry or, as the case may be, the Secretary of State.[56]

Local planning authorities as owners of hedgerows.[57]

Where a local planning authority is the owner (whether alone or jointly with others) of a hedgerow, regulation 15 applies. Notwithstanding provisions relating to the arrangements for the discharge of functions by local authorities[58], a hedgerow removal notice may not be considered either by a committee or sub-committee of the authority concerned if that committee or sub-committee is responsible (wholly or partly) for the management of the land in which is situated the hedgerow to which the notice relates; or (2) by an officer of the authority concerned if his responsibilities include any aspect of the management of the land in which is situated the hedgerow to which the notice relates.[59]

Criticism of the Regulations

The Hedgerow Regulations 1997 were designed to protect exceptionally species rich hedgerows and those of landscape, archaeological and historic importance, there are however many hedgerows

---

[52] Regulation 14 (1)defines the power conferred by virtue of Regulations 12 or 13 to enter land – "a right to entry."
[53] Regulation 14(2)
[54] Regulation 14(3)
[55] Any question of disputed compensation is to be referred to and determined by the Lands Tribunal. Regulation 14(5) and (6)
[56] Regulation 14(4)
[57] Regulation 16 contains particulars relating to hedgerows on ecclesiastical property.
[58] Particulars of which are set out in Sec. 101 of the Local Government Act, 1982. Regulation 15(1)
[59] Regulation 15(2)

which do not meet these criteria but are nevertheless important habitats that need preserving. This has resulted in the criticism of the Regulations by several bodies including the Council for Protection of Rural England (CPRE) as being too little, too late.

The definition of "important" used in the regulations means that only a small percentage of hedges qualify for protection.[60] Further the Regulations only protect hedges in farmland, not those in parkland and gardens. Hedges if they are less than 30 years old are automatically disqualified from protection. Furthermore work by the UK Biodiversity Steering Group points out that poor management, such as ploughing very close to the hedge margin or very heavy pruning at the wrong time of year, is resulting in more hedge loss than direct removal. The Regulations do nothing to protect against such threats. The local authorities who enforce the Regulations, were not given any extra resources to carry out this task. In a survey of all local authorities in England, the CPRE found that only 19% of local authorities had found the Regulations easy to use. It was also noted that in Environmental Impact Assessments carried out since 1997, the Regulations are often referred to but survey work has not been carried out to see if the hedges meet the criteria.

A number of these criticisms and concerns about the regulations were addressed in the CPRE's Report "Hedging Your Bets." The Report was a result of a unique survey of 133 local authorities responsible for implementing the 1997 legislation. It showed that across England overall less than 1 in 4 hedges were protected and there was an alarming variation in the degree of protection from region to region .[61] The results of this survey came out at a critical time. Michael Meacher, on taking office as Minister for the Countryside gave a commitment to review and improve the Hedgerow Regulations. In May 1997 the Government announced that

[60] To be 'important' a hedgerow must be at least 30 years old and meet at least one of eight set criteria:

i. marks a pre-1850 parish or township boundary;
ii incorporates an archaeological feature;
iii. is part of, or associated with, an archaeological site;
iv. marks the boundary, or is associated with, a pre- 1600 estate or manor;
v. forms an integral part of a pre-1845 field system;
vi. contains certain rare plants or animals;
vii. includes a certain number of woody species over a given length; and
viii. runs alongside a public right of way and contains a minimum number of woody species. These criteria fail to address the landscape importance of hedgerows or reflect the diversity of hedgerow types across the country.

the Hedgerow Regulations 1997 would be reviewed by a Group to see how they could provide stronger protection for important hedgerows.[62]

Recommendations by the group which carried out the review were published in July 1998. Some of the recommendations required amendments to primary legislation: making provision for local authorities to decide which hedgerows are important and extending the definition of hedgerows.[63] Subsequently Michael Meacher gave evidence to the House of Commons Environment Sub-Committee enquiry, The Protection of Field Boundaries (July 1998) stating that he was committed to effective regulation.

Other issues

DEFRA also administers two agri-environment schemes to tackle the issue of hedgerow loss through neglect, by promoting the conservation and restoration of hedgerows in England: the Environmentally Sensitive Areas (ESA) scheme provides incentives to farmers to protect the landscape, wildlife and historic interest of 22 areas of the country considered to be of national environmental significance and the Countryside Stewardship scheme[64] similarly provides incentives to protect, enhance, restore and recreate priority landscapes, their wildlife habitats and historical features in areas of England outside ESAs. Farmers receive payments for entering 10 year management agreements.

[61] More than 90% of all hedgerows in the North East and North West lack legal protection and even in East Anglia, with the highest degree of protection of any region, less than 40% are protected.

[62] Announcing the creation of the Hedgerows Review Group to assess the failings of current legislation protecting hedgerows (Hedgerows Act 1995) in May 1997, Michael Meacher MP said: 'The Regulations, laid by the previous Government to protect countryside hedgerows of significant historical, wildlife or landscape value, are but a first step in safeguarding these important features. We are determined to have an effective system which provides strong protection.' See http://www.cpre.org.uk/press/rel2000/011.htm.

[63] The executive summary of the report is available at ://www.defra.gov.uk /wildlife-countryside/hedgerow97/index.htm).

[64] SI 2000 No. 3048, The Countryside Stewardship Regulations 2000.

CHAPTER 7

AGRICULTURE AND HABITAT PROTECTION

Clearly most of the conservation legislation covered in this book, in particular relating to species and habitat protection, will have significant implications for agricultural land use and practices. This section outlines some of the conflicts that can arise between agricultural land use and conservation and then examines the ways in which current legislation on agriculture seeks to address the structural conflicts between agriculture and conservation.

The Impact of Agricultural Land Use on the Conservation of Biological Diversity

"Agriculture dominates the land use of the UK and farming presents the greatest threat to biodiversity while also being the sector that can contribute most to its conservation."[1]

In the UK agricultural ecosystems currently make up about 70% of land area. The increasing intensification of agriculture since the 1950s has generally led to a less diverse landscape-one of the factors likely to have led to decreases in the biodiversity of agricultural ecosystems[2] Awareness of the impact of agricultural practices on biodiversity has led to a growing recognition that radical reform of the agricultural system is required if the decline of biodiversity is to be halted and reversed. This concern forms part of a general reappraisal of the European Union's Common Agricultural Policy. Specific reforms intended to start the process of "greening the CAP" have been adopted by the European Union and these are considered further below, together with some of the programmes adopted at the national level. Historically, agricultural legislation was aimed at promoting food production[3] and this did not change with the advent of the Common Agricultural Policy, which the UK acceded to when it joined the European Community in 1973. The recognition that farming was important for reasons other than food production however, dates at least as far back as the Scott Report of 1943[4]. The Report took the view that prosperous farming was essential for "social and aesthetic" reasons as well as in order to secure food production reasons (majority view). The need to integrate environmental concerns into the system of food production is now

---

[1] UK First National Report to CBD, December 1997, page 14.

[2] UK First National Report to the CBD, December 1997, at page 22.

[3] For example the 1947 Agriculture Act places emphasis on agricultural production, s17 Agriculture Act-intensification of land use.

[4] The Report of the Committee on Land Utilisation in Rural Areas.

acknowledged by the UK Government[5]. In the 2000 White Paper "Our Countryside: The Future" the Government stated that, in the future, the intention was that: "Farming's main task will still be to produce the food we eat"[6] but also that there would be increasing recognition of the role of farmers and land managers in maintaining "an attractive and diverse" countryside. The Government hoped that many more farmers would "turn a positive approach to the environment to their own economic advantage" with payments for environmental goods such as a flourishing wildlife[7].

The current law regulating agricultural practices in the UK now derives principally from the European Community's Common Agricultural Policy (CAP). The UK pays £3-3.5 billion in the form of EU and domestic support to UK agriculture each year[8] The CAP has been heavily criticised for the way in which it encourages intensive farming practices which harm the environment, in particular by subsidising farming practices which have an adverse effect on conservation[9]. Conversely the CAP has also tended to render more environmentally-friendly practices uneconomic:

"The Common Agricultural Policy is a major influence and too small a proportion of its resources are channelled towards achieving environmental objectives through appropriate land management. The forthcoming reforms of the CAP should lead to a more market oriented policy and greater emphasis on measures designed to secure specific environmental goals".[10]

In their report of 2002, the Government-appointed Curry Commission on Food and Farming took the view that, without substantial change, farming and the food industry in England were unsustainable from an environmental, as well as an economic point of view[11] and went on to make a series of recommendations for reform, discussed further below.

An example of the impact which agricultural practices may have on biodiversity was provided to the House of Lords during an inquiry into sustainable development. NERC noted that the correlation between changes

[5] In its first Report to the CBD, the UK Government highlighted the need to produce food efficiently, at affordable prices, "in ways that are consistent with a thriving rural economy and conservation of the countryside and wildlife".

[6] The White paper describes farming as the bedrock of the UK Food Chain worth £57 billion each year and 3.3 million jobs, chapter 8, paragraph 8.1.1.

[7] "Our Countryside the Future, A Fair Deal for Rural England" published 28 November 2000, Chapter 8 "The Future-what we want to see".

[8] Our Countryside: The Future Chapter 8, para 8.2.1.

[9] "Our Countryside the Future" para 8.2.2.

[10] UK 1st CBD Report page 27.

[11] "Farming and Food, a Sustainable Future" January 2002, see Chapter 4 page 67.

in species abundance and changing agricultural practices made it possible to deduce that there was a relationship between the two, but observed that there were relatively few examples where a causal relationship had been proved. One such example however was that of the Corncrake which had suffered a drastic decline in recent decades. RSPB field studies had shown the transition from haymaking to intensive silage production as the main means of growing animal fodder to be the single main cause of this decline. Silage was cut earlier than hay, often with multiple cuts within one growing season and this resulted in drastic losses of nests and chicks. Conversion of grassland to arable land and of silage/hay meadows to permanent grazing may also have contributed[12].

Other direct problems arising from the impact of the current agricultural system include the effects on wildlife of the intensive use of pesticides and fertilisers. The need to address these problems, for example by providing resources for management agreements with farmers, was raised during the parliamentary debate on the Habitat Regulations in 1994:

> "All of us know how this country suffered from the Industrial Revolution-and we are still trying to clear up the results of it after countless years...What we must avoid is that we do not have the same situation from the agricultural revolution which is now taking place."[13]

Another aspect of the problem arises more indirectly from the way in which the Common Agricultural Policy favours intensive practices through the system of subsidies, creating perverse incentives against practices which are less harmful to biodiversity and rendering certain forms of farming simply uneconomical. One example of this problem is the reversion of grassland and heathland to scrub through neglect. This issue was also raised during the debate on the Habitat Regulations:

> "...many of the land management systems which have produced internationally important wildlife habitats such as lowland heath are no longer economical. Substantial financial support may be needed if landowners are to continue to operate uneconomic farming systems or to restore such systems where they have been lost for nature conservation purposes..." [14]

---

[12] House of Lords Report on Sustainable Development page 301.
[13] Lord Underhill [c429 HL Committee].
[14] Hansard, House of Commons, 19 July 1994, col 249.

A well-publicised example of the damaging effects of such perverse incentives occurred in 1997 when a farmer in Sussex ploughed up an ancient meadow in order to sow flax. The EC subsidy for growing flax in 1997 was nearly £600 per acre as compared with £100 per hectare to maintain ancient grassland. The problem was particularly acute in relation to the flax subsidy because the subsidy could be claimed on any farmland no matter how great its conservation importance, whereas generally subsidies were only available to registered arable land.[15] In the end, the meadow was reinstated when potential purchasers of the raw flax indicated that they would not accept flax cultivated on unsuitable sites.

Overgrazing is also a major problem in some areas. According to English Nature, more than ¼ million hectares of England's SSSI's have been damaged by overgrazing and over-intensive sheep management as a direct consequence of CAP livestock subsidies.[16]

Integrating Environmental Concerns into the CAP

The objectives of the CAP are currently set out in Article 33 (ex Article 39) of the EC Treaty and include: increasing agricultural productivity by promoting technical progress; ensuring a fair standard of living for the agricultural community; stabilizing markets and assuring both the availability of supplies and that supplies reach consumers at reasonable prices.

These objectives should of course be read within the context of the Treaty as a whole, Article 6[17] (ex Article 3c) of which requires environmental protection requirements to be integrated into the definition and implementation of other Community policies (those referred to in Article 3), including the common policy on agriculture, in particular with a view to promoting sustainable development. Set out below are some of the ways in which the Community may be said to be attempting to meet this obligation in the context of the CAP[18].

The UK has expressed support for integrating environmental concerns into the CAP: "[The] actual total of payments to farmers remains low in

[15] "EU subsidies spawn threat to ancient grasslands", Independent 29 October 1997 Oliver Tickell.

[16] Cited in the Curry Commission Report at page 74.

[17] The requirement for integration of environmental protection requirements was first introduced into the Treaty in 1987 under the Single European Act.

[18] For a comprehensive examination and critique of integration see the IEEP report to the Commission, DG Agriculture "Environmental Integration and the CAP" of September 2002, available at www.europa.euint/comm/agriculture/environment/report/ieep.

comparison to the overall size of the UK's agricultural economy and in comparison with the total expenditure of the European Common Agricultural Policy. Options for reducing agricultural subsidies and for increasing environmentally-led payments need to be pursued."[19]

Calls to "Green the CAP" are not new. The House of Lords considered the issue in 1992[20]. It heard evidence from a number of environmental organisations calling for various reforms to the operation of the CAP. The CPRE for example, called for the introduction of environmental criteria for payments for set aside. [The RSPB pointed out that: "Agriculture is central to the management and conservation of much of our countryside and the biodiversity it contains; approximately 130 bird species in the UK depend largely on farmland, of which 40 are considered conservation priorities.".[21]

In 1992 a number of reforms to the operation of the CAP were introduced including a move away from price support towards "area payments" which are unrelated to individual yields, the intention being that this would remove artificial incentives for arable intensification and the ploughing up of grass land. In addition, a number of Community instruments were adopted which sought to integrate environmental concerns into the operation of the CAP through support for positive measures. These tended to focus on environmental protection generally rather than singling out nature conservation, although the protection of biodiversity was a key concern.

Council Regulation (EC) No. 2078/92[22] set up a Community aid scheme promoting a number of environmentally-friendly measures: the use of farming practices which would reduce the polluting effects of agriculture; environmentally favourable extensification of crop farming and sheep and cattle farming, including the conversion of arable land into extensive grassland and environmental set-aside. Under that Regulation, schemes could include aid for farmers who undertook to adopt or continue with a number of environmentally beneficial practices. The need for real improvements was later reinforced in Commission Regulation (EC) No 746/96, which provided that the aid granted to farmers had to have a "positive impact on the environment and countryside" and contribute to

[19] UK 1st Report CBD.

22 Environmental Aspects of the Reform of the CAP HL Session 1992-93 & 14 Report

[21] RSPB Memo page 1 HL agric

[22] Council Regulation (EC) No 2078/9218 on agricultural production methods compatible with the requirements of the protection of the environment and the maintenance of the countryside (OJ L No 215 30/07/1992 page 85). The validity of the Regulation, now repealed was recently upheld by the ECJ in Case 336/00 Austria v Huber, judgment of 19 September 2002.

an improvement in good farming practice. Those practices included, among others: the substantial reduction of the use of fertilizers and/or plant protection products; the introduction or continuation of organic farming; the change-over to more extensive forms of crop including forage; the set-aside of farmland for at least 20 years with a view to its use for purposes connected with the environment, in particular for the establishment of biotope reserves or natural parks of for the protection of hydrological systems. In order to ensure the achievement of the objectives, Member States were to determine conditions for granting aid; the amount to be paid and terms and conditions under which it was to be paid.

These measures have recently been updated in the light of further reform as part of the Agenda 2000 initiative. Agenda 2000[23] set out the EU's programme for reform of the CAP as it moved towards enlargement in central and Eastern Europe. It referred to rural development policy as the "second pillar" of the CAP alongside markets policy and one of the aims of reform was to ensure that a greater proportion of agricultural expenditure went towards "nature conservancy". Included within that second pillar therefore were the agri-environment measures already in place[24]. Council Regulation 2078/92[25] was repealed and replaced by Council Regulation (EC) 1257/99[26], which is the current basis for EU agri-environment measures. Regulation 1257/99[27] establishes the framework for Community support for sustainable rural development. Chapter VI deals with agri-environment measures. Article 22 states that support for agricultural production methods designed to protect the environment and to maintain the countryside (agri-environment) "shall contribute to achieving the Community's policy objectives regarding agriculture and the environment". Normally, support is to be granted to farmers who give agri-environment commitments for at least five years and the

[23] "Agenda 2000: For a Stronger and Wider Union" is based on a Commission Communication to the Member States and was intended to set out a framework for a range of policies to take the EU into the 21st century. The adoption of the measures concerned was completed by the end of 1999. See further www.europa

[24] On EU agricultural law and policy see further www.europa.eu.int/comm/agriculture

[25] In 1998, the Commission carried out an evaluation of the agri-environment schemes operated under Regulation 2078/92 and found that "substantial environmental benefits" had been shown particularly for nitrate reduction and nature protection and that at just 4% of the agricultural budget, the programmes represented good value, see DGVI working document VI/7655/1998 available at the europa website.

[26] Council Regulation (EC) No 1257/99 of 17 May 1999 on support for rural development from the EAGGF and repealing and amending certain regulations (the Rural Development Regulation)OJ L 160/80 26.6.1999.

[27] See also Commission Regulation 1750/99 laying down detailed rules for the application of Council Regulation 1257/99.

commitments must involve more that the application of good farming practice.[28]

Cross Compliance

A key feature of the reforms heralded by Agenda 2000 is the use of cross-compliance, the mechanism whereby where Member States make payments under agricultural support schemes dependent on compliance with certain environmental requirements[29]. This is distinct from the agri-environment schemes described above where farmers are specifically paid for taking on certain positive environmental commitments. The legal basis for cross compliance is Article 3 of Regulation 1259/1999[30] which requires Member States to take measures to ensure that agricultural activity within the scope of the Regulation is compatible with environmental protection requirements.[31] Article 3 provides that such measures may include support for agri-environmental commitments; general mandatory environmental requirements and "specific environmental requirements as a condition for direct payments" to farmers under CAP support schemes (under the "Guarantee" section of the EAGGF, except in relation to those provided under the rural development support schemes). Member States may provide for a reduction or, where appropriate, cancellation of the benefits accruing from support schemes concerned if such specific environmental requirements are not respected.

In 2000 the House of Commons Select Committee on the Environment called on the Government to make maximum use of cross compliance mechanisms to ensure that high environmental standards were maintained in return for the payment of subsidies[32]

Measures Operated in the UK

The UK operates a range of agri-environment schemes and is currently reviewing their application. In 2000, the UK Government launched the

[28] Article 23 of Regulation 1257/99.

[29] Support for the use of cross-compliance was expressed by the Curry Commission in its report of 2002, see Chapter 4 page 73.

[30] Council Regulation 1259/1999 of 17 May 1999 establishing common rules for direct support schemes under the common agricultural policy OJ L 160 26.6.1999 page 113

[31] For a discussion of cross compliance see the IEEP report to the Commission, DG Agriculture "Environmental Integration and the CAP" of September 2002, available at www.europa.euint/comm/agriculture/environment/report/ieep, pages 66 et seq and pages 80 et seq.

[32] Report on UK Biodiversity (HC 441) at paragraph 80.

seven year English Rural Development Programme. Similar programmes have been put in place in Wales, Scotland and Northern Ireland. The ERDP awards £1.6 billion to include additional funding for agri-environment schemes[33]. A number of these schemes operated before its introduction and derive from earlier EU agri-environment measures dating from the 1990's. The largest scheme is the Countryside Stewardship Scheme, followed by the Environmentally Sensitive Areas Scheme, covering about 10% of agricultural land between them. Others include the Organic Farming Scheme and the Woodland Grant Scheme. Under the Countryside Stewardship Scheme, farmers are paid for adopting environmentally friendly practices such as cutting back on weed killer and creating buffer zones between crops and field edges allowing for grater diversity and protecting perimeters from crop sprays.

The Curry Commission (see below) noted that the existing agri-environment schemes had had positive effects and recommended that the existing schemes be streamlined and simplified. The Commission took the view that whilst the existing schemes were well suited to targeting specific areas of countryside, a broader approach was also needed which would encourage good environmental practice across a much wider area of the countryside and involve larger numbers of land managers[34]. This "broad and shallow scheme" would assist in attempts to reverse the decline of species such as the skylark and the brown hare. A simpler set of targets for this wider scheme would cut down on the need for site inspections and reduce running costs. The Environment Agency should regulate the operation of such schemes. The Commission supported proposals from the RSPB, English Nature and others for prescriptions for lowland arable and livestock farms covering conservation issues such as the retention of grass margins at field boundaries.

The Curry Commission

In 2001, the Government appointed a Policy Commission to look into the issue of a sustainable future for farming and food. The Commission, chaired by Sir Donald Curry, produced its report "Farming and Food, a sustainable future" in January 2002[35]. As part of its investigation, the Commission examined the environmental impact of the food industry and farming, noting the continuing decline of many wildlife species once common on farmland as well as other environmental impacts such as water pollution. The Commission argued for public support for the provision of

[33] "Our Countryside: the Future" see note 7 infra, Chapter 8.
[34] Curry Commission Report, page 79.
[35] Available at www.cabinet-office.gov.uk/farming

environmental public goods and stressed the importance of securing environmental benefits across the countryside at large rather than retaining "environmental theme parks"[36].

Pending significant reform of the CAP, the Commission noted that there were two national policy initiatives open to the UK government which would go some way towards improving the situation: reforms to the way in which the UK allocated CAP grant for the production of sheepmeat (the sheep envelope) so as to create more environmental incentives and the use of "modulation". The latter involved Member States transferring CAP resources from direct production payments towards the securing of real public goods as permitted under the Rural Development Regulation (up to a maximum of 20%). The UK was already using such funds to contribute towards the ERDP but the schemes operated under the ERDP were oversubscribed[37]. Among the recommendations made by the Commission was that the rates of modulation across the UK should be increased to 10% from 2004, with further increases to the maximum level of 20% if substantial CAP reform was not achieved in 2006-7[38]. The Commission also recommended that spending on agri-environment schemes should be substantially increased, initially through modulation, and that existing schemes should be merged to become the upper tiers of a new stewardship scheme which would also encompass a broad and shallow entry level scheme open to as many farms as possible[39].

The Government accepted this recommendation in its Strategy for Sustainable Farming and Food, published on 12 December 2002[40]. New broad and shallow agri-environment schemes are to be introduced in 2005-6 having first been piloted for two years in four areas[41]. The Strategy also makes provision for continued expansion of schemes such as the Countryside Stewardship scheme.

The Ways in which Conservation Legislation Addresses Agriculture

As has already been noted, the general provisions of habitat and species protection in conservation legislation such as the Wildlife and

---

36 Curry Commission Report, page 70.
37 Curry Commission Report, see page 76.
38 Curry Commission Report, page 77.
39 These recommendations were welcomed by the CPRE, see further Policy Position Statement on Farming, November 2002 available at www.cpre.org.uk.
40 See DEFRA press release dated 12 December 2002.
41 See DEFRA press release dated 14 November 2002.

Countryside Act 1981 and the Habitats Regulations 1994 will have a direct effect on agricultural land use and these provisions are considered in Chapters 1,2 and 3 - Part I. There are also a number of provisions in conservation legislation which specifically focus on agriculture, in particular on the awarding of agricultural grants, and these are considered below.

The Sandford amendment: s32 of the 1981 Act

The need to address the impact of agriculture on wildlife proved to be one of the most controversial issues which arose during the passage of the Wildlife and Countryside Bill through Parliament[42]. Lord Sandford highlighted the inadequacies in this regard of the general duty imposed on Ministers and government departments to have regard to the conservation of natural beauty under section 11 of the 1968 Act. Lord Sandford argued that a more specific measure was required and put forward an amendment to the Bill designed to ensure that, in awarding agricultural grants, Ministers took proper account of the needs of conservation. The proposed new clause related to schemes under the Agriculture Act 1970 in National Parks and other areas. Under the proposed clause, Ministers would be under a duty not to agree to such schemes if they would lead to adverse effects. The proposal concerned the management of the countryside as a whole rather than nature conservation alone. In response to the proposal, the Government brought forward its own amendment and this was eventually incorporated into the Bill, its scope having been extended to include all SSSIs. Section 32 provided that where an application for farm capital grant was made for the purposes of activities on an SSSI or land subject to a special nature conservation order the Minister responsible for determining the application was under a duty "so far as may be consistent with the purposes of the grant provisions" to exercise his functions so as to further the conservation of the features by reason of which the land had been designated[43]. In cases where the Nature Conservancy Council objected to the award of the grant because of the damaging effects of the activities in question on the site, the Minister could not make the grant unless he had considered the objection and consulted the Secretary of State. Where the application was refused as a result of an objection, the conservation body was required to offer to enter into a management agreement imposing restrictions on the activities and providing for the making of payments to the applicant. A similar provision, relating to European sites, is contained in the Habitats Regulations.

[42] See 12 March 1981 col 480.

[43] Section 32 was amended by the Countryside and Rights of Way Act 2000 so as to remove provision for land covered by a section 29 order.

At the time the 1981 Act was passed, the Government was unable to accept that agricultural grants themselves should be available for diversification as originally proposed. It took the view that as other parts of the Bill safeguarded conservation, the mandatory offer of management agreements to secure conservation benefits was unnecessary. In recent years the idea that there should be a statutory basis for agreeing positive measures to manage the countryside as part of farming practice has taken hold, as discussed in this chapter.

The Habitats Regulations

The general protection afforded to European sites under the Habitats Regulations has implications for agricultural activities, for example where activities which may adversely affect those sites constitute potentially damaging operations the carrying out of which by owners or occupiers of land within a European site is restricted under regulation 19 of the Regulations or where the management of agricultural land becomes of the subject of a management agreement for a European site drawn up under the regulation 16.[44]

There is also specific provision concerning the duties of agriculture Ministers in relation to European sites. Regulation 88 of the Habitats Regulations provides that where an application for a farm capital grant[45] is made in respect of activities on land within a European site, the Minister responsible for determining the application is under a duty "so far as may be consistent with the purposes of the grant provisions" to exercise his functions so as to further the conservation of the flora, fauna or geological or physiographical features by reason of which the land has been designated as a European site.. In cases where the relevant nature conservation body has objected to the award of the grant because of the damaging effects of the activities in question on the site, the Minister may not make the grant unless he has considered the objection and, in the case of land in England, consulted the Secretary of State Where the application is refused as a result of an objection by for example, English Nature, the conservation body must offer to enter into a management agreement imposing restrictions on the activities and providing for the making of payments to the applicant. The level of such payments is to be determined in accordance with guidance given by the relevant Minister depending on where the land is situated, in England this would be the Minister for Agriculture.[46]

[44] See Chapter 3 - Part I.

[45] A "farm capital grant" means a grant under the Agriculture Act 1970 or under European Community regulations, see regulation 88(3).

[46] See Regulation 89.

Planning Controls and Agriculture

Planning legislation does not generally provide a means of addressing the tensions between agricultural land use and conservation since most agricultural activity is excluded from planning control[47]. Section 55 of the Town and Country Planning Act 1990 defines development for the purposes of planning control. Subsection (2) lists operations or uses of land that shall not be taken, for the purposes of the Act, to involve development of the land and includes "the use of any land for the purposes of agriculture...and the use for any of those purposes of any building occupied together with land so used". (s55(2)(e)). In so far as some agricultural-related activities are covered by planning controls (the putting up of farm buildings for example), the impact of planning controls on wildlife conservation generally is considered in Chapter 6 - Part I.

Environmental Impact Assessment of Certain Agricultural Projects

Environmental impact assessment is required under the Environmental Impact Assessment Directive[48] for certain agricultural activities, in particular projects for the use of uncultivated land and semi-natural areas for intensive agricultural purposes[49]. Such projects are listed on Annex II (paragraph 1) of the Directive and assessment is therefore required in circumstances where the project is likely to have significant effects on the environment, including on flora and fauna[50]. In making such a determination the selection criteria in Annex III must be applied and these include a consideration of the location of the project. Regard is to be paid to the areas likely to be affected and particular attention must be given to effects on SPAs classified under the wild birds Directive and SACs designated under the Habitats Directive.

This requirement of the Directive is implemented in England by the Environmental Impact Assessment (Uncultivated Land and Semi-Natural Areas) Regulations 2001[51]. These Regulations do not apply to

[47] See further Chapter 6 - PART 1.

[48] Council Directive 85/337/EEC on the assessment of the effects of certain public and private projects on the environment OJ No L175 5.7.85 p 40 as last amended by Council Directive 97/11/EEC OJ No L73 14.3.97 p5.

[49] Paragraph 1 of Annex II of the amended Directive also refers to other agricultural activities including the restructuring of rural land holdings and certain water management projects involving irrigation and drainage.

[50] Insert reference to other Cameron May publication on environmental impact assessment for fuller discussion of the subject.

[51] SI 2001/3966. In Wales the requirement is implemented by the Environmental Impact Assessment (Uncultivated Land and Semi-Natural Areas)(Wales) Regulations 2002, SI 2002/2127.

projects to which other regulations dealing with the assessment of forestry or land drainage projects apply, nor to projects falling within the scope of the Town and Country Planning (Environmental Impact Assessment) (England and Wales) Regulations 1999.

The Regulations[52] provide that no person is to carry out such projects without first obtaining a screening decision from the Secretary of State (regulation 4). A screening decision determines whether the project in question is likely to have significant effects on the environment (in accordance with the selection criteria set out in Schedule 1 to the Regulations) and therefore requires assessment before it can be undertaken (regulation 5(4). Such a project is known as a relevant project under the regulations. Under regulation 6, no person may begin or carry out such a project without first obtaining consent from the Secretary of State. Under regulation 5 which sets out the screening procedure, a project which the Secretary of State decides is likely to have a significant effect on a European site (protected under the Habitats Regulations implementing the Habitats Directive[53]) either alone or in combination with other projects, and which is not directly connected with or necessary to the management of the site, must be treated as likely to have a significant effect on the environment.

Provision is made in the Regulations for a person requiring consent to undertake a relevant project to request a scoping opinion from the Secretary of State on the information to be provided in the environmental statement (regulation 7). The Statement must include information on aspects of the environment likely to be significantly affected by the project including flora and fauna to the extent that this is reasonably required to assess the environmental effects of the project and which the applicant can reasonably be required to compile. The regulations then go on to set out the procedure for applying for consent to the Secretary of State. In making her decision on the application, the Secretary of State must consider, in the light of the environmental statement, any additional environmental information provided under the regulations together with any representations received from the public, relevant consultation bodies and EEA States (where these have been consulted under regulation 11). The Secretary of State may not grant consent for a project which would involve doing anything which would be unlawful under regulations 39, 41 or 43 of the Habitats Regulations (which does not include anything for which a regulation 44 license has been granted).

[52] The Regulations entered into force on 1 February 2002, those for Wales on the 19 August 2002.
[53] See further Chapter 3 - Part I.

Subject to the exception set out in the Regulations, where the project is one which is likely to have a significant effect on European site, the Secretary of State may only grant consent for the project only if she has considered its implications for the European site and is satisfied that the project will not adversely affect the integrity of that site. The consideration leading to such a determination is to involve an appropriate assessment of the implications of the project for the conservation objectives of the site (regulation 13(6)). The exception is where (in accordance with the requirements of the Habitats Regulations), the Secretary of State is satisfied, there being no alternative solution, that the project must be carried out for imperative reasons of overriding public interest[54], she may grant consent for the project notwithstanding a negative assessment of the implications for the European site. There is also provision for compensatory measures to ensure the coherence of Natura 2000[55]. Further provision is made for review and appeals and for enforcement of the Regulations, including the issuing of stop notices.

[54] Save where the site hosts a priority natural habitat type or species where the reasons must relate to human health, public safety or beneficial consequences of primary importance to the environment or other reasons which in the opinion of the European Commission constitute imperative reasons of overriding public interest for the site concerned, see further Chapter 3 - Part I.

[55] As to the operation of Natura 2000 see Chapter 3 - Part I.

PART II
SPECIES PROTECTION

SPECIES PROTECTION

The protection of individual specimens of particular species, generally those considered to be rare or vulnerable, is a longstanding feature of conservation law. Such protection generally takes the form of prohibiting the killing or taking of specimens of listed species, subject to certain limited exceptions. This type of provision aims to protect species both from persecution (for example of birds of prey by gamekeepers and landowners) and from over-exploitation (for example the taking of wild bluebells for commercial purposes). This section begins by examining in Chapter 1-Part II on how the law approaches concepts such as species and subspecies.

The protection of certain species of wildlife from taking or killing dates back a considerable time in the United Kingdom but the rationale for these provisions was not that of modern conservation law, essentially acting in the public interest, but to preserve game species for the wealthy elite. Although modern species protection provisions resemble to some degree those earlier laws in so far as they prohibit the taking and killing of listed species, they are now accompanied by provisions relating to inhumane killing and in some cases controls on possession and sale. There is also detailed provision on the granting of licences which derogate from protection. This section examines these types of provisions as they apply to wild birds (Chapter 2 - Part II), wild animals (Chapter 3 - Part II) and wild plants (Chapter 4 - Part II). The regime for wild birds, contained in Part I of the 1981 Wildlife and Countryside Act, derives from the European Wild Birds Directive (Council Directive 79/409/EEC) and has been the subject of extensive judicial consideration at the European level. The regime for wild animals and plants contained in Part I of the 1981 Act predates any European requirements but is now accompanied by the regime contained in the 1994 Conservation (Natural Habitats etc) Regulations which implement the Habitats Directive (Council Directive 92/43/EC) in the UK. The latter affords special protection to "European protected species" of wild animals and plants. There is some overlap between the two regimes, both as to the species covered and in relation to the protection afforded, but in certain respects protection is stricter under the 1994 Regulations. Marine species are covered by all these regimes but are considered separately in Chapter 5 - Part II which examines the specific regimes for whales and seals as well general issues surrounding the protection marine species. Chapter 3 - Part II considered the separate statutory regime for badgers under the 1992 Protection of Badgers Act which is aimed primarily at protection from persecution.

Chapter 6 - Part II examines the legal framework under the 1981 Wildlife and Countryside Act for controlling the introduction of invasive alien species and considers by way of example the controversy surrounding the culling of the ruddy duck. Chapter 3 -Part II considers the way in which the law seeks to protect the welfare of wild animals, in particular wild mammals under the 1996 Wild Mammals Protection Act. Chapter 7 - Part II considers recent legal changes under the 2000 Countryside and Rights of Way Act which underpin positive action for species recovery and also the legal regulation of zoos under the 1981 Zoo Licensing Act as recently amended to bring it into line with the Zoos Directive (Council Directive 1999/22).

CHAPTER 1

WHAT IS A SPECIES?

> *"...the species concept is crucial to the study of biodiversity. It is the grail of systematic biology ."* [1]

The biological concept of a species is generally defined in the following way: "a species is a population whose members are able to interbreed freely under natural conditions"[2] Also of key importance is the recognition that there are two basic levels in the diversity of life: genetic variation within species and differences among species[3]. Until relatively recently, conservation law has not sought to grapple with these issues. It was sufficient if the legislation simply listed the species which were subject to protection. This has begun to change however. The adoption of the 1992 Convention on Biological Diversity, has meant that concepts such as biodiversity now have a legal significance. Article 2 of the Convention defines biological diversity as:

> "... the variability among living organisms from all sources including, inter alia, terrestrial, marine and other aquatic ecosystems and the ecological complexes of which they are part; this includes diversity within species, between species and of ecosystems. "

If states have undertaken to protect biodiversity they must also be able to agree on how that concept may be measured and this involves an appreciation of what is meant by "species". Over time this is likely to lead to refinements in the way conservation legislation is framed. Instead of the traditional focus on species, it may become necessary to frame legislation specifically to address issues such as species richness and variability.It is also the case that, in considering provisions which aim to protect species, courts may have to grapple with issues of scope which require them to analyse the meaning of the term. These two developments are considered further below.

The Concept of Biodiversity

Whilst many conservation instruments use the term "species", none of the international legal instruments concerned with nature conservation

---

[1] E O Wilson "Biodiversity" page 38.
[2] E O Wilson "Biodiversity" page 38.

seek to define it other than, in the case of the CITES Convention, to clarify that it includes subspecies or geographically separate populations[4] Nor is the term "species" defined in Community or UK domestic law. The Wildlife and Countryside Act 1981 avoids use of the term, referring simply to "wild bird", "wild animal", "wild plant" and either, as in the case of birds, applying to any wild bird or referring to those listed in the various Schedules to the Act. The 1992 Convention on Biological Diversity does not define the term species but it does draw new emphasis, in legal terms to the issues of variation within species and between species.

If, as Wilson put it, the species is "the basic unit of biological diversity" and the law is dealing with the preservation of such diversity there is likely to come a time when the law relating to biodiversity/nature conservation will need to involve itself more directly with the concept in determining, for example, whether species richness has been maintained-particularly where species are not already classified and named. This may become particularly relevant where new liability regimes are adopted which seek to impose liability for damage to biodiversity. The European Union is currently in the process of adopting a regime which provide for liability for damage to biodiversity[5]. So far the proposal does not specifically address how damage to species or other components of biodiversity is to be measured. The parties to the CBD are considering the issue of liability for damage to biodiversity pursuant to Article 14.2 of the Convention. At COP6 the Parties adopted a decision agreeing to establish an experts group to carry out further analysis of the issue.[6]

Case C-202/94 Godefridus van der Feesten[7]

In van der Feesten, the ECJ was not asked to define the reference to species in the wild birds Directive but it did have to consider a connected

[3] E O Wilson, ibid page 88.

[4] Article I of CITES provides that for the purposes of the Convention "species" means any species, sub-species or geographicaslly separate population thereof; Article I of the Bonn Convention defines "migratory species" as "the entire poplulation or any geographically separate part of the population of any species or lower taxon of wild animals, a significant proportion of whose members cyclically and predictably cross one or more national jurisidictional boundaries."

[5] See the White Paper on Environmental Liability COM 2000 (66) final dated 9 February 2000.

[6] The decision (UNEP/CBD/COP/6/L.14) requests the Executive Secretary to convene a legal and technical experts group to review information on and conduct further analysis of issues relating to liability and redress in the context of CBD Article 14.2, in particular clarifying and developing relevant definitions and to report to COP-7.

[7] Judgment of 08/02/1996, Criminal proceedings against van der Feesten [1996] ECR I-355.

issue: the application of the law to non-European subspecies of protected species[8]. Case C202/94 Godefridus van der Feesten, arose out of criminal proceedings in the Dutch courts against Mr Van der Feesten for illegal possession of the grey headed goldfinch *carduelis carduelis caniceps* which, unlike the black headed or "European" goldfinch *Carduelis carduelis carduelis*, does not occur naturally in the wild in the territory of the Member States. The parties accepted that the European goldfinch benefited from the protection of the Directive. Mr Van der Feesten, however, contested the charge brought against him on the basis that Dutch legislation, which appeared to include within its scope non-European subspecies of European species of wild bird, did not comply with the wild birds Directive which it was intended to implement and which, he maintained, did not apply to non-European subspecies such as the grey headed goldfinch. The Dutch court therefore asked the ECJ to address the question of whether the provisions of the wild birds Directive applied to a subspecies which, as in this case, did not occur naturally in the wild in the European territory of the Member States[9].

The text of the Directive did not make this clear since Article 1, which sets out the scope of the Directive, provides simply that "This Directive relates to the conservation of all species of naturally occurring birds in the wild state in the European territory of the member States to which the Treaty applies...".

The Court noted that the Directive is intended to provide effective protection for European avifauna and that this protection is centred on the concept of species (paragraph 10). It observed that in avian taxonomy the concept of species includes all of a species' subdivisions, such as breeds and subspecies, consequently "a specimen belonging to a subspecies will always belong to the species comprising the subspecies in question." The Court concluded from this that "if a subspecies occurs naturally in the wild in the European territory of the Member States to which the Treaty applies, the species to which the subspecies belongs must be considered to be a European species and, consequently, all the other subspecies of the species in question including those which are not European, will be covered by the Directive."

[8] Wilson on subspecies: "individuals occupying a paricular part of the range of the species, with genes and natural history distinct from those of other subspecies. Members of different subspecies can freely interbreed. They can arise either as populations adapting to local conditions or as hybrids between subspecies." (W page 67)

[9] For a consideration of the other issue raised in the case, concerning the extent to which Member States may protect such subspecies by taking stricter measures under Article 14 of the Directive, see Chapter 2 - Part II.

The Court's reasoning appears to be based on a pragmatic appreciation of the difficulties which could arise if non-European subspecies were held to be excluded from the scope of the Directive. These difficulties would arise because whilst, in the Court's view, "the concept of species covers a biological entity, the scientific definition of which is generally accepted and is based on characteristics forming part of the genetic heritage of individual members of the species in question", the concept of subspecies "is not based on distinguishing criteria which are as strict and objective as those defining species inter se. Thus it is not rare for there to be disagreements in scientific circles as to how certain subspecies can be identified and distinguished from one another." The Court made reference to the concept of subspecies as designating a population which, within a species, differs from other populations of the same species on the basis of criteria such as morphology, habitat or the behaviour of it members.

The Court concluded that the scope for scientific disagreement as to the identification and distinguishability of subspecies would make it difficult to implement the Directive and might result in the Directive not being uniformly applied within the Member States if non-European subspecies were excluded from the Directive's scope.

Interestingly, Advocate General Fennelly had taken the opposite view in his Opinion on the case. He did not consider that the use of the term species in Article 1 was decisive, finding that in a number of places the term "species" was clearly used to refer to particuluar subspecies from which he concluded that the term "species" "cannot be interpreted in each and every circumstance as necessarily including every subspecies of the species protected under the Directive"(paragraph 33). He also noted that various pronouncements on the Directive made by the Community institutions, including the Council, during its adoption had referred to the threat to and need to conserve the ecological balance in Europe (paragraph 34). He contrasted this with other Community instruments such as Regulation (EEC) No 3626/82 which (at that time) implemented the CITES Convention in the EU and clearly applied to "all species threatened with extinction which are or may be affected by trade."... without regard to their geographical location, including all subspecies and geographically separate populations of such species". The Advocate General concluded that if the term species were universally acknowledged to include all subspecies of a particular species such definitions would be unnecessary (paragraph 35). Finally, he considered that the Court's case law indicated that the Directive was only intended to cover the conservation of European birds.

In contrast to the Court, the Advocate General was also unconvinced by the argument that since it was biologically/practically very difficult to distinguish subspecies the Directive should be interpreted as covering all subspecies. For such an argument to succeed, he concluded the parties would have had to show "it is never, or almost never, possible to distinguish between subspecies" and this had not been shown (paragraph 41).

Following this judgment, it now appears that where any subspecies of a species occurs naturally in the wild in the European territory of the Member State, Member States should ensure that their implementing legislation applies to all subspecies of that species, including non-European subspecies.

In the UK, s 27(1) of the Wildlife and Countryside Act 1981 defines "wild bird" as "... any bird of a kind which is ordinarily resident in or is a visitor to Great Britain in a wild state...". Thus the provisions of the 1981 Act would not appear to cover the case of possession or sale of a specimen of a non-European subspecies which has been captured outside Great Britain. In the light of Van Feesten, it may be argued that UK legislation should not be confined to birds which are ordinarily resident in or visitors to Great Britain, but should in fact cover wild birds occurring in the wild in the Community as a whole. This is probably most relevant to controls on sale and possession rather than taking from the wild (in the UK).

CHAPTER 2

WILD BIRDS

Introduction

The first UK laws which sought to protect species of wild birds for reasons of general nature conservation rather than in order to conserve certain species for sporting/game interests date from the latter half of the nineteenth century[1] Anti-poaching laws prohibiting the killing or capture of certain game species were in place much earlier.

The current legislation protecting wild birds is based on European legislation. Article 5 of Council Directive 79/409/EEC of 2 April 1979 on the conservation of wild birds[2] (the wild birds Directive) requires Member States to establish a general system of protection for all species of birds to which the Directive applies[3] and sets out a number of acts which must be prohibited: deliberate capture or killing by any method; deliberate destruction of, or damage to, nests and eggs and removal of nests; taking eggs and keeping eggs even if empty; deliberate disturbance particularly during the breeding and rearing season where this would have a significant effect on conservation and keeping species, the hunting and capture of which is prohibited. Certain species are subject to special rules concerning their commercial exploitation (Article 6)[4] and hunting (Article 7)[5]. Species listed in Annex I and regularly occurring migratory species are to be the subject of special conservation measures concerning their habitat[6].

This approach, whereby all species of wild bird are protected and activities such as hunting, capture and killing are authorised only under certain conditions reverses the "traditional" approach to conservation law in many Member States under which only certain species were protected.

---

1 The Sea Birds Preservation Act 1871; the Wild Bird Protection Acts of 1880, 1888 and 1894, 1896, 1902 and 1904.

2 OJ 1979 L 103, p1.

3 Namely, all species of naturally occurring birds in the wild state in the European territory of the Member States to which the Treaty applies (Article 1).

4 See further Chapter 2 - Part II.

5 See further Chapter 2 - Part II.

6 See further Chapter 2 - Part I.

The Wildlife and Countryside Act 1981

The current UK law relating to the protection of wild birds by means of species protection measures, is mainly contained in Part I of the Wildlife and Countryside Act 1981. Part I of the Act contains some provisions similar to those contained in earlier legislation, in particular the Protection of Wild Birds Acts 1954 and 1957 which it repealed and replaced, and transposes the wild birds Directive into UK law Opening the debate on the Bill's second reading in the Lords, Lord Bellwin acknowledged that the stimulus for bringing forward the Bill at that particular time was the wild birds Directive, he also referred to the Berne and Bonn Conventions[7] to which the UK was a signatory.

As to the impact of the directive itself, at the time the Wildlife and Countryside Bill was passing through Parliament, the British Government described it as "more a tidying up operation than a sweeping innovation"[8]. It is certainly true that some of its key provisions, such as the general prohibition on killing, injuring or taking any wild bird, are basically the same as those appearing in earlier UK legislation. Nevertheless, certain changes were introduced and, perhaps even more importantly, the fact that these provisions stemmed from obligations under an EC directive meant that their interpretation and application were subject to the surveillance of the Commission and the jurisdiction of the ECJ. In the event, the wild birds directive was to prove to be the most litigated piece of EC environmental legislation and to give rise to a substantial quantity of European case law.

Scope of Protection

The scope of the directive, both as to species and geographical area covered is set out in Article 1, which refers to the conservation of all species of naturally occurring birds in the wild state in the European territory of the Member States. In Case 252/85 Commission v France[9], the ECJ ruled that French legislation which restricted protection to birds which formed part of "the national biological heritage" contravened the directive. The Commission had identified 24 species of migratory bird, which in its view, were covered by the directive but which were excluded from the scope of the French legislation. These were species of migratory bird from other

---

[7] The Berne Convention on the conservation of European wildlife and natural habitats, www.coe.int and the Bonn Convention on Migratory Species of Wild Animals, www.wcmc.org.uk.cms.

[8] Hansard, House of Commons, 27 April 1981, col 526.

[9] [1988] ECR 2243.

Member States which, said the Commission, might at any given time, be found within French territory. The Court, recalling earlier rulings on the directive, stated that: "the protection of migratory species is typically a trans-frontier environmental problem entailing common responsibilities for the Member States. The importance of complete and effective protection of wild birds throughout the Community, irrespective of the areas they stay in or pass through, causes any national legislation which delimits the protection of wild birds by reference to the concept of national heritage to be incompatible with the directive."[10]

Under Part I of the Wildlife and Countryside Act 1981, protection is afforded to any "wild bird", subject to the exceptions provided for. "Wild bird" is defined in s27 as "any bird of a kind which is ordinarily resident in or is a visitor to Great Britain in a wild state but does not include poultry or, except in section 5 (prohibition of certain methods of killing) and 16 (licences) any game bird".

The question arises, in the light of *Case 252/85 Commission v France*, as to whether this definition is too narrow in scope for the proper implementation of the directive. It is not clear from that case whether the issue is simply one of determining whether national legislation is framed on the basis of an incorrect underlying principle (which is likely to have the effect of excluding migratory species which may be present within a Member State "at any given time") or whether a breach can only be established if it can be shown that a particular (probably migratory) species has in fact been excluded from protection. The judgment does not make it clear whether the first is sufficient. The UK legislation would appear to exclude from the protection of the 1981 Act rare vagrants from other Member States. A strict application of *Commission v France* would appear to require that such birds be covered however.

The conservation importance of this issue is perhaps indicated by the Commission's recognition in its second report on the directive that: "peripheral populations play a particularly important role in the process through which species adapt to changes in the environment" In the European context this process is vital.[11]

Deliberate Capture and Killing

Prohibitions or restrictions on the deliberate capture and killing of birds constitute the most long established means by which UK legislation

[10] I[1988] ECR 2243, paragraph 15 of the judgment.

[11] Commission's 2nd Report on the wild birds directive, page 9.

has sought to protect wild birds from decline through over exploitation or persecution and remain a central part of the legal protection afforded to species. Whilst further forms of legal protection have been added to nature conservation legislation as new threats to the survival of species have emerged or been identified[12], provisions on deliberate capture and killing have been retained and have remained largely unchanged from those found in the legislation of the nineteenth century. Introducing Part I of the Wildlife and Countryside Bill for its Second Reading in the House of Lords, Lord Bellwin on behalf of the Government explained that, in relation to the protection of wild birds, the main concern "is not the amateur bird-watcher or egg-collector, although of course egg-collecting has largely been illegal since 1954, but those who make a profit from excessive exploitation of wild creatures, or kill them unnecessarily or without due care..."[13]. The legislation however makes no such distinction and in circumstances where some species are in severe decline even amateur collectors can pose a significant threat to a species' survival.

Section 1 of the Wildlife and Countryside Act renders it an offence for any person intentionally to kill, injure or take any wild bird[14] For the purposes of section 1 a wild bird is defined as "any bird of a kind which is ordinarily resident or is a visitor to Great Britain in a wild state but does not include poultry or any game bird."(S 27(1)). During the passage of the Bill, the Government explained that the word "ordinarily" had been included "so as to exclude from protection escapees of non-native, primarily exotic species such as the ring necked paraqueet" so as to be consistent with the new controls on the introduction of non-native species[15]. Section 1(6) further qualifies the definition of wild bird so as not to include "any bird which is shown to have been bred in captivity". The burden of proving that a bird was bred in captivity therefore falls on the defendant. A bird is not to be treated as bred in captivity under Part I unless "its parents were lawfully in captivity when the egg was laid."(s27(2)). During the passage of the Bill, the Government was asked whether a captive bred bird which was subsequently released into the wild would be covered by s1(6). The Government confirmed that in its view such a bird would be covered.

[12] Protection of eggs introduced for the first time and provision made for the establishment of reserves in the Wild Bird Protection Act 1894. Controls on the plumage trade were introduced to protect birds internationally in the Importation of Plumage (Prohibition) Act 1921.

[13] Hansard, House of Lords, 16 Dec 1980, col 984.

[14] Section 1(1)(a). Article 5 (a) of the wild birds Directive requires Member States to prohibit "deliberate capture or killing by any method".

[15] Hansard, House of Lords, Earl of Avon 12 Feb 1981 col 119.

Formerly, if an offence committed under section 1 related to a bird included in Schedule 1 (as to which see below), the person responsible was liable to a special penalty (s1(4)). The provision for special penalties was repealed by the Countryside and Rights of Way Act 2000[16] This was because of the introduction of tougher penalties for offences generally under Part I of the Act (see further below). However the effect of the special penalties provision has been preserved in relation to sections 3(1)(c) and 7(3)(a) of the 1981 Act.

Defences and Exceptions

Certain defences and exceptions in relation to the killing or taking of wild birds which would otherwise be prohibited under section 1 are available. Specific exceptions are provided for in sections 2 and 4 of the Act (as to the latter see further below). Section 2(1) provides that, subject to the remaining provisions of section 2, a person will not be guilty of an offence under section 1 by reason of the killing or taking of a bird listed in Part I of Schedule 2 (which includes birds such as the Canada Goose and Woodcock) outside the close season or the injuring of such a bird outside the close season in an attempt to kill it. The respective close seasons are set out in subsection (4) and these may be varied by order (subsection 5).

An authorised person does not commit an offence under section 1 by reason of: the killing or taking of a bird listed in Part II of Schedule 2, or the injuring of such a bird in the course of an attempt to kill it, or the taking, damaging or destruction of a nest of such a bird or the taking or destruction of an egg of such a bird (section 2(2)). However as of 1 January 1993, no birds have been listed in Part II of Schedule 2[17] . This follows discussion of the concept of pest species, see Chapteron birds-derogations.

Subsection (3) restricts the extent to which these exceptions apply on Sundays. There is a power (subsection (6)) for the Secretary of State to order further periods of special protection (of up to 14 days) for Schedule 1 Part II or Schedule 2 Part I birds outside the close season where he considers it expedient. These orders may extent to the whole or any specified part of Great Britain.

Penalties

Penalties for all the offences in Part I of the Act are set out in section 21. Offences under section 1 are subject, on summary conviction to

[16] See 2000 Act sections 81(1), 102 and Schedule 16 (Part IV).

[17] The list of species was removed by the Wildlife and Countryside Act 1981 (Variation of Schedules 2 and 3) order 1992, SI 1992/3010, art 2.

a term of imprisonment not exceeding 6 months or to a fine not exceeding level 5 on the standard scale or to both. The power to impose a custodial sentence had long been called for by a number of agencies and non-governmental organisations and was eventually introduced by the Countryside and Rights of Way Act 2000.[18]

Nests and Eggs

All nests are protected while the nest is in use or being built (section 1(1)(b)). The wild birds directive appears to require more comprehensive protection however. In *Case 252/85 Commission v France*[19], the Court ruled that the prohibition on destroying, damaging or removing nests under Article 5 of the Directive "must apply without any limitation in time" since many species re-use each year nests built in earlier years. It was therefore contrary to the Directive for French legislation to afford protection to nests only during the close season[20].

It is also illegal to take or destroy the egg of any wild bird (section 1(1)(c) and "destroy" includes doing anything calculated to prevent the egg from hatching (section 27(1)). A defence is available if the person can show that the egg has not been taken or was taken otherwise than in contravention of the relevant provisions. The Court has ruled that under Article 5 of the directive, eggs must be protected all year round and not just during the close season as France had sought to do (*Commission v France* as above).

Disturbance

Protection from disturbance is only extended to birds listed in Schedule 1[21]. Intentional disturbance of any Schedule 1 bird is prohibited under section 1(5) which renders it an offence for any person intentionally to disturb a bird while it is building its nest or is in, on or near a nest

[18] See for example, the evidence of the Nature Conservancy Council to the HC Select Committee on the Environment (see page 64) in the course of a review of the operation and effectiveness of the WCA in 1984-85. The NCC called for the introduction of an alternative of imprisonment as originally provided for in 1954-67 Acts. For the amending provisions see the 2000 Act, section 81(1) and Schedule 12.

[19] [1988] ECR 2243.

[20] See paragraph 9 of the judgment.

[21] Under Article 5 of the wild birds Directive, Member States are required to prohibit deliberate disturbance of all wild birds covered by Article 1 particularly during the period of breeding and rearing "in so far as disturbance would be significant having regard to the objectives of this directive". Presumably the UK has taken the view that in protecting only those birds listed in Schedule 1 it is meeting that requirement.

containing eggs or young or to disturb the dependent young of such a bird. During the Bill's committee stage in the House of Lords, there was some discussion of the meaning of "dependent". Lord Cranbrook expressed the view that it meant " a young bird before it is capable of looking after itself"[22] It was also pointed out during debate that in the case of some 30 out of 85 species of Schedule 1 birds, the young would leave the nest as soon as they hatched, so the provision was an important one[23]. An attempt to commit any offence under Part I of the Act is in itself an offence and subject to the same penalty.[24]

The offence of reckless disturbance was added by the 2000 Act. The Explanatory Note to the Act explains that by adding the lesser test of reckless disturbance, a prosecutor will have to show that a person either deliberately took an unacceptable risk or failed to notice an obvious risk and thereby caused disturbance. (This being consistent with the fact that reckless disturbance in the context of interfering with a badger sett is an offence under section 3 of the Protection of Badgers Act 1992.)[25]

Schedule 1 of the Wildlife and Countryside Act 1981

In addition to listing the bird species protected from disturbance, (section 1(5)), Schedule 1 is now relevant to the power to extent periods of special protection beyond the close season (to those listed in Part II of Schedule 1). It also restricts the application of the exceptions set out in section 4 (as to which see below), ensuring that Schedule 1 birds receive greater protection than other species. In common with much nature conservation legislation, the criteria for listing species in Schedule 1 of the 1981 Act are not set out in the legislation. The basis for including species in Schedule 1 was discussed during the passage of the Bill, the Government explained that it had taken the scientific advice of the NCC and its advisory committee, species by species, and where there was a clear, if not necessarily unanimous, view that protection is needed for conservation, "we have proposed it."[26]. For the Government is was explained that : "...what we have not been prepared to do is to give protection to a common species because it may be mistaken for a rare one" and that "Schedule 1 should not grow too long and should meet real and not hypothetical needs."

---

22 Hansard. House of Lords, 27 January 1981, Cranbrook (col 637).
23 Hansard col 638.
24 Section 18(1) WCA.
25 See Schedule 12, para 1 of the 2000 Act.
26 Hansard, House of Lords, 2 February 1981, col 959 E of Avon.

There was criticism from some quarters of the omission from Schedule 1 of very rare visitors. Lord Kilbracken proposed the generic inclusion of any bird "that is not ordinarily resident in or is not a regular visitor to Great Britain in a wild state" so as to extend protection to rare breeders and vagrants by way of including them without having to list them all individually. The Government, however, took the view that such birds did not warrant special protection in Schedule 1 and did not want to "devalue" special protection in Schedule 1 by including them. In fact certain rare breeders have been included in Schedule 1, for example the Bewick swan, there is nothing in the wording of the to prevent the inclusion of species which do not breed here but which are regular or scarce winter visitors.

Areas of Special Protection

Although it involves the designation of an area of land, section 3 of the Act is concerned with species protection rather than habitat protection, which is dealt with under Part II of the WCA[27]. As the Government pointed out in discussion of the proposed clause on areas of special protection: "if shooting were a prime threat an order under [section 28] could be made prohibiting shooting over land as an operation likely to destroy or damage its fauna.[28] Section 3 has been very little used in practice.

The Secretary of State may by order declare that a specified area shall be subject to special provisions which may include that any person who, except as may be provided in the order, enters into that area or any part of it at any time or during any period specified shall be guilty of an offence; that any person who within that any area or any specified part of it intentionally kills, injures or takes any wild birds so specified. Provision may also be made in relation to acts relating to the protection of nests, eggs and the disturbance of birds and their young. Specific defences for authorised persons are laid down in subsection (2) and subsection (3) provides that the making of such an order shall not affect the exercise by any person of any right vested in him. Consultation requirements are laid down in subsection (4) and the owners /occupiers of the area are given an effective right of veto under subsection (5).

Section 3(5) of the Act prevents the Secretary of State from making an order unless all the owners and occupiers of any land included in the intended order have either consented or made no objection or any objections

[27] See Chapters 1, 2 and 3 - Part I.
[28] Hansard, House of Lords, 10 march 1981, col 143.

which have been made have been withdrawn. During the passage of the Bill, the Government was criticised for preserving the owner's power of veto which had done "a great deal to emasculate the sanctuary order provisions in the 1954 Act.".[29] Most of the sanctuaries created under the earlier legislation had already been under the control of local authorities or wildlife conservation bodies. Others called for affected owners to be given a right to compensation. The Government said that it regarded voluntary cooperation as "a vital feature of wildlife conservation" and as the best guarantee that protection would be achieved.[30]

The penalties applied to offences under section 3 were amended by the 2000 Act which removed the provision for special penalties. Subsection 3(1) now provides that an offence under the section is to be treated as falling under section 7(3A) of the Act.

Possession Controls

A range of possession controls were introduced under the Wildlife and Countryside Act 1981. These are set out in section 1(2) (as regards live or dead wild birds generally or their eggs) and section 7 of the Act (as regards those bird species listed on Schedule 4). It should be remembered that Article 5(e) of the wild birds directive requires Member States to prohibit the keeping of birds of species the hunting and capture of which is prohibited. Provision for the hunting of certain species is made in Article 7 of the Directive which permits the hunting only of those species listed in Annex II under prescribed conditions. This means that under the directive, and subject to the possibility of derogation in accordance with Article 9[31], the only birds which may be kept are those listed in Annex II. In case C-159/99 Commission v Italy therefore the Court ruled that national provisions which provided for the keeping of three species not listed on Annex II for the purpose of use as decoys were contrary to Articles 5 and 7 and Annex II of the Directive[32].

Eggs

Egg collecting was first made illegal under the 1954 Act but possession was only made illegal under the 1981 Act. The Government explained that the new controls only applied to "eggs taken after the date

[29] Hansard, House of Lords, 27 January 1981, col 674.
[30] Hansard, House of Lords, 27 January 1981, col 677.
[31] See further Chapter 2E - Part II.
[32] See judgment of 17 May 2001 [2001] ECR I-4007.

of the Act which it will be illegal to possess"[33]. Concern was expressed during debate on the Bill about how holders of existing collections, such as museums, would prove their origin, asked whether a sworn affidavit would be sufficient, the Earl of Avon replied that, should a case come to court "we believe that it would be sufficient for a museum to have kept proper records of all eggs received after the enactment of this Bill and to swear an affidavit that all other eggs in its possession were held before the Act's provisions applied to them nor were the eggs taken in breach of the provisions of the 1954-67 Acts."[34] Calls for the compulsory registration of egg collections were not taken up. The NCC also called for the introduction of controls on the movement of fertile captive bred eggs because a lack of controls would create a loophole whereby, it was said, eggs illegally taken from the wild could be claimed to have been laid in captivity. This was addressed in section 27(2) which provides that a bird shall not be treated as bred in captivity unless its parents were lawfully in captivity when the egg was laid.

Section 1(2)

Section 1(2) of the Act provides that, subject to the provisions of Part I of the Act, it is an offence for any person to have in his possession or control (a) any live or dead wild bird[35] or any part, or anything derived from, such a bird; or (b) an egg of a wild bird or any part of such egg. In Kirkland v Robinson[36], the Divisional Court dismissed the defendant's appeal against his conviction under section 1(2)(a), holding that the offence was one of strict liability and it was not necessary for the prosecution to prove that the accused knew that the birds were wild birds within the meaning of the Act.

Section 1(3) goes on to provide that a person shall not be guilty of an offence under subsection (2) if he shows that the bird had not been killed or taken, or had been killed or taken otherwise than in contravention of the relevant provisions. Relevant provisions for these purposes means the provisions of Part I and of orders made under it and the provisions of the Protection of Birds Acts 1954 to 1967 and of orders made under those Acts. Thus for example, a person who can show that she is in possession of a disabled live wild bird, taken solely for the purpose of tending it and

[33] Hansard, House of Lords, 16 December 1980, Earl of Avon col 1091.
[34] Hansard, House of Lords, 27 January 1981, col 633.
[35] A stuffed and mounted bird is still a "dead wild bird" for the purposes of this section, Robinson v. Everett [1988] Crim LR 699.
[36] [1987] Crim LR 643.

releasing it when no longer disabled and provided that the bird was disabled "otherwise than by [her] unlawful act", does not commit an offence under section 1(2) (see further section 4(2)(a) below).

Section 7 and Schedule 4

The possession controls set out in section 7 apply only to those birds listed in Schedule 4 of the 1981 Act. Schedule 4 currently includes a number of birds of prey such as the Golden Eagle, as well as some other species including the Dartford Warbler and Woodlark[37]. Section 7 essentially provides for a system of registration and provides that any person who keeps or has in his possession or control any Schedule 4 bird which has not been registered and ringed or marked in accordance with regulations made by the Secretary of State shall be guilty of an offence. The current regulations are the Wildlife and Countryside (Registration and Ringing of Certain Captive Birds) Regulations 1982 as amended by the Wildlife and Countryside (Registration and Ringing of Certain Captive Birds) (Amendment) Regulations 1994[38].

Furthermore, if any person has within his possession or control a Schedule 4 bird within 5 years of having been convicted of an offence under Part I of the Act (relating to animals or birds) or any other offence involving their ill treatment, he will be guilty of an offence (section 7(3) as amended by the Countryside and Right to Roam Act 2000)[39]. The relevant offences are set out in Section 3A as inserted by the 2000 Act. Similar provision is made in subsection (4) rendering it an offence to "knowingly dispose or offer to dispose of" a Schedule 4 bird within five years of conviction.[40] The penalties for offences committed under section 7 are set out in section 21 of the Act.

In August 2002, DEFRA and the Welsh Assembly published a consultation paper to seek views on the future of the system of bird registration in England and Wales. In the light of the responses to the consultation exercise, it was decided to retain the registration system but to remove the requirement to re-register birds every three years and to introduce a number of other changes.[41] New legislation is expected during the latter part of 2003.

[37] Schedule 4 was last amended by the Wildlife and Countryside Act 1981 (Variation of Schedule 4) Order 1994 (S.I. 1994/1151).
[38] SI 1982/1221 as amended by SI 1991/478 and SI 1994/1152.
[39] See section 81(1) and Schedule 12 of the 2000 Act.
[40] Pursuant to subsection (5) no account is to be taken for the purposes of subsections (3) and (4) of any offence which has become spent for the purpose of the Rehabilitation of Offenders Act 1974.
[41] See report available at http://www.defra.gov.uk/wildlife-countryside/consult/birdreg/responses.htm

Exceptions to Sections 1 and 3

Section 4 creates a number of exceptions to the protection given in sections 1 and 3 as discussed below.

Acts Done Pursuant to Other Legislation

Certain exceptions relate to things done under other legislation relating to agriculture and animal health. Section 4(1)(a) provides that nothing done pursuant to a requirement by the Minister of Agriculture under section 98 of the Agriculture Act 1947, or in the case of Scotland by the Secretary of State under section 39 of the Agriculture Scotland Act 1948, shall be made unlawful by section 1 or in any order made under section 3 of the 1981 Act. These provisions relate to the prevention of damage to crops etc by pests. Section 98 allows the Minister to require the killing, taking or destruction on specified land of, inter alia, wild birds other than those included in Schedule 1 to the Wildlife and Countryside Act.

Section 4(1)(b) of the Wildlife and Countryside Act provides that nothing done under or in pursuance of an order made under sections 21 or 22 of the Animal Health Act 1981 will be unlawful under sections 1 and 3 of the WCA. These provisions of the Animal Health Act concern the destruction of wildlife, including any species of bird, for the purposes of disease control where disease has been or is being transmitted from those species to animals of any kind in an area, and destruction is necessary to eliminate or substantially reduce the incidence of disease in animals in that area. The relevant Nature Conservancy Council must be consulted before an order is made.[42]

Except in the case of a Schedule 1 bird, or the nest or egg of such a bird, nothing done under or in pursuance of an order made under any other provision of the Animal Health Act 1981 shall be unlawful under sections 1 or 3 of the Wildlife and Countryside Act. This exception therefore includes provisions relating to disease control and to the transport, import and export of animals which may include poultry.

An exception relating to the ringing of wild goose and duck was removed during the passage of the Wildlife and Countryside Bill. There were concerns that a loophole would be created and in any event it was suggested that the matter could more properly be dealt with under licences issued under what is now section 16[43].

[42] Section 21(3).
[43] See Chapter 2E - Part II.

Disabled Birds

There are two exceptions relating to disabled birds. The taking of a disabled bird will not be an unlawful act provided that the person shows that the bird was disabled otherwise than by his unlawful act and was taken solely for the purpose of tending it and releasing it when no longer disabled (section 4(2)(a)).

In addition, it will not be unlawful to kill a wild bird if the person can show that the bird had been so seriously disabled otherwise than by his unlawful act that there was no reasonable chance of its recovering (section 4(2)(b)).

Incidental Results of Lawful Operations

An act will not be unlawful under sections 1 and 3 if it is "the incidental result of a lawful operation and could not reasonable have been avoided" (section 4(2)(c)). Concern was expressed about the potential scope of this exception during the passage of the Bill.

It appears from the case-law of the ECJ that such a provision is acceptable provided that it covers only acts which were not intended to cause birds to be killed etc. The authorisation of intentional acts constitutes a derogation from Article 5 of the wild birds directive which must then meet the requirements of Article 9 if it is not to infringe the directive[44].

In *case 412/85 Commission v Germany*[45], the ECJ had to consider German legislation which removed from the prohibitions implementing Article 5 of the directive, acts taking place in the course of "the normal use of land for agricultural, forestry or fishing purposes". The Court held that these provisions constituted an unlawful derogation from Article 5 rejecting Germany's argument that actions performed with the intention of killing and disturbing wild birds cannot be described as forming part of "normal agricultural " activities. The Court ruled that as German legislation did not define "normal use" it could not be assumed that all the acts covered were unintentional and therefore the provision constituted a derogation which did not meet the requirements of Article 9 of the Directive.

[44] See Chapter 2E - Part II.
[45] Judgment of 17 September 1987, [1987] ECR 3503.

Acts necessary for certain purposes

The killing or injuring of a wild bird, other than a bird listed in Schedule 1, by an authorised person will not be an offence under sections 1 or 3 of the Act if the action in question was necessary for a purpose listed in section 4(3) of the Wildlife and Countryside Act. Those purposes are: preserving public health or public or air safety (s4(3)(a); preventing the spread of disease (s4(3)(b)); or preventing serious damage to livestock, foodstuffs for livestock, crops, vegetables, fruit, growing timber, fisheries or inland waters.[46]

During the passage of the Wildlife and Countryside Bill, and in the face of objections to their inclusion (on the grounds that they were unnecessary, would be too readily available and did not comply with directive) the Government explained the intention behind these exceptions and their relationship with the licensing provisions under what is now section 16 of the Act. Lord Sandys said "the Government certainly intend that the normal means of dealing with predictable damage shall be by licensing [under what is now s16]" but considered that the defence was necessary "to ensure that in a genuine emergency a farmer is able to defend his crops without fear of committing an offence, provided he can satisfy the court that his action was necessary."[47] Lord Sandys went on to say that "with the more comprehensive licensing provisions [in section 16], we expect its use to practically disappear". The Government sought to allay concern by reminding critics that ADAS would advise on methods of dealing with such situations and might advise in certain situations that for example, shooting may not be appropriate. Nevertheless, in order to meet some of the concerns expressed the reference to person was changed to "authorised person".

The scope of section 4(3) remained a matter of some controversy however and in 1995 the emergency exceptions in section 4(3)(c) were amended so as to bring them fully into line with the wild birds directive[48]. Following these amendments, an authorised person will not be regarded as showing that any action was necessary unless he shows that "as regards that purpose, there was no other satisfactory solution"(section 4(4)). This provision transposes Article 9(1) of the directive[49] In addition, an

[46] Inland waters were added by the Wildlife and Countryside (Amendment) Regulations 1995, SI 1995/2825. They are defined in section 27 of the Act.

[47] Hansard, House of Lords, 27 January 1981, col 697.

[48] The Wildlife and Countryside (Amendment) Regulations 1995, SI 1995/2825, regulation 2.

[49] See further chapter 2E - Part II.

authorised person is not be entitled to rely on the defence in section 4(3)(c) if it had become apparent before the action was taken that such action would be necessary and a licence under section 16 had not been applied for as soon as reasonably practicable. Nor can the defence be relied on if a licence application had been determined (by implication refused or not granted in wide enough terms to authorise the action taken). This requirement, which had been called for during the debates on the Bill, mirrors section 10(6) of the Act which applies to exceptions to the protection of wild animals. Finally, in order to rely on the defence, an authorised person must notify the agriculture Minister as soon as reasonably practicable after the action has been taken.

A. Protection From Indiscriminate Killing/Taking And Inhumane Treatment

Regulation of Methods of Taking/Killing

Stricter controls on the methods which might lawfully be used to kill, injure or take wild birds were introduced under the 1981 Act. This was no doubt due to the requirements of the Wild Birds Directive, Article 8 of which provides that "In respect of the hunting, capture or killing of birds under this Directive, Member States shall prohibit the use of all means, arrangements or methods used for the large-scale or non-selective capture or killing of birds or capable of causing the local disappearance of a species, in particular the use of those listed in Annex IVa[1] " In addition Member States are required to prohibit any hunting from the modes of transport and under the conditions mentioned in Annex IV (b)[2] . The wording of Article 8 makes it clear that the list in Annex IVa is not exhaustive.

Section 5 of the 1981 Act prohibits a number of methods of killing or taking wild birds. The prohibitions apply to all species of wild bird, although a number of the exceptions relate to particular species (as to which see below). First, s5(1)(a) renders it an offence to set in position any of the articles listed in that subsection, being of such a nature and so placed so as to be calculated to cause bodily injury to any wild bird coming into contact with it. The articles listed are any spring, trap, gin, snare, hook and line, any electrical device for killing, stunning or frightening or any poisonous, poisoned or stupefying substance. In contrast to the other offences created under s5, there is no reference to the purpose of the action in this subsection. It is the nature of the article concerned and the way it is placed which gives rise to the prohibition.

The remaining offences created under section 5 all refer to the use of articles for the purpose of killing or taking a wild bird. Under section 5(1)(b), it is an offence to use any of the articles listed in s5(1)(a), whether or not of such a nature and so placed as to be calculated to cause bodily injury to any wild bird, or to use any net, baited board, bird-lime or substance of a like nature to bird-lime.

---

[1] Annex IV(a) refers inter alia to explosives, nets and semi-automatic weapons.

[2] These include aircraft and motor vehicles and boats driven at a speed exceeding 5 kilometres an hour.

The articles listed in section 5(1)(c) are not specifically designed to kill or take birds but that subsection makes it an offence to use them for that purpose. Those articles are any bow or crossbow; any explosive other than ammunition for a firearm (defined); any automatic or semi-automatic weapon; any shotgun of which the barrel has an internal diameter at the muzzle of more than one and three quarter inches; any device for illuminating a target or any sighting device for night shooting; any form of artificial lighting or any mirror or other dazzling device; any gas or smoke not falling within paras (a) and (b) of section 5 or any chemical wetting agent.[3]

The use of decoys is prohibited under section 5(1)(d), along with the use of any sound recording or any live bird [or] other animal whatever which is tethered, or which is secured by means of braces or similar appliances or which is blind, maimed[4] or injured. It is an offence under s5(1)(e) to use any mechanically propelled vehicle in immediate pursuit of a wild bird for the purpose of taking or killing it.

An important amendment to section 5 was introduced by the Wildlife and Countryside (Amendment) Act 1991. That Act introduced S5(1)(f) which creates an offence of knowingly causing or permitting to be done any of the acts mentioned in s 5(1)(a)-(e) and which do not fall within the exceptions set out in s5(5). The amendment was introduced by means of a private members bill, conceived by the RSPB, which was particularly concerned about the scale of unlawful killings of birds of prey such as the Red Kite. The bill was to strengthen protection in such cases by closing a loophole which had become evident in the 1981 Act and allowing the prosecution of those who directed or allowed others to commit offences of using illegal methods of killing wildlife. Concern had been expressed during the passage of the Wildlife and Countryside Bill that employers were tacitly encouraging gamekeepers to commit offences under the Act. The Government's view at the time was that this would be covered under s35 Magistrates Court Act on aiding and abetting[5].

[3] During the passage of the bill, the rationale for outlawing some of the methods was discussed: "It is just possible that the reason we do not like semi-automatic shotguns is that we think there is something ever so slightly common involved in them." Commented the Earl of Onslow, Hansard col 721 E. The Government assured him that it was simply a matter of what the directive required.

[4] See Holden v Lancashire Magistrates Court (1998) 162 J.P. 789; [1998] C.O.D. 429, in which the Divisional Court held that clipping wing feathers was not maiming because the effect was not permanent, even though the evidence was that the operation was repeated in order to ensure that the birds in question could never fly.

[5] Hansard, House of Lords, 27 January 1981, reference col 725.

An illustration of this loophole was given during debate on the bill on its Third Reading in the House of Commons. Mr Ron Davies MP referred to a case in Scotland where a gamekeeper was prosecuted and convicted for laying poisonous substances that brought about the death of legally protected birds of prey. He informed the court that he had been instructed by his employer to lay the poison, was in fear of his job and so followed instructions. He was found guilty and convicted of the offence but his employer escaped prosecution having committed no offence under the terms of the Act.[6]

Defence/Exceptions

In proceedings under s5(1)(a), it is a defence to show that the article was set in position for the purpose of killing or taking, in the interests of public health, forestry, fisheries or nature conservation, any wild animals which could be lawfully killed or taken by those means and that the accused took all reasonable precautions to prevent injury thereby to wild birds (section 5(4)). The 1991 Amendment Act introduced an equivalent defence in cases of causing or permitting someone to do an act under s5(1)(a) (subsection 4A).

A number of further exceptions are set out in subsection (5). Nothing in subsection (1) shall make unlawful the use of a cage trap or net by an authorised person for the purpose of taking a bird listed in Part II of Schedule 2. It should be remembered however that this is Schedule is currently empty. Nor is it clear why what is essentially a welfare provision should be waived in the case of certain species, even those considered by some to be "pests". The other exception of practical relevance relates to the use of a cage trap or net for the purpose of taking any game bird if it is shown that the taking of the bird is solely for the purpose of breeding (section 5(5)(c)), but nothing in the subsection makes lawful the use of any net for taking birds in flight or the use for taking birds on the ground of the use of any net which is projected or propelled otherwise than by hand.

Welfare of Captive Birds

The welfare needs of captive birds is also addressed to a degree in the 1981 Act. Interestingly these provisions do not derive from the requirements of the wild birds directive. Section 8 makes it an offence for any person to keep or confine any bird whatever in any cage or other

[6] Hansard HC Session 1990-91 vol 22 March 1991 col 574-575.

receptacle which is not sufficient in height, length or breadth to permit the bird to stretch its wings freely. Subsection (2) sets a number of exceptions to this prohibition. The offence does not apply to poultry. Nor does it apply to the keeping or confining of any bird while that bird is in the course of conveyance by an means (section 8(2)(a)); while that bird is being shown in public exhibition or competition (provide the time does not exceed 72 hours) (section 8(2)(b)); while that bird is undergoing examination or treatment by a vet (section 8(2)(c))[7].

It is also an offence, under subsection (3) to promote, arrange, receive money for (and a range of related acts) any event whatever at which birds are liberated by hand or by any other means for the purpose of being shot immediately after their liberation. Owners or occupiers of land who permit such events to take place on their land are also guilty of an offence.

The penalties for these offences are set out in section 21 of the Act. A person guilty of an offence under section 8 shall be liable on summary conviction to imprisonment for a term not exceeding six months or to a fine not exceeding level 5 of the standard scale or to both. The usual multiplier provision applies by virtue of subsection (5) and the court shall order the forfeiture of any bird in respect of which the offence was committed and may order the forfeiture of anything used to commit the offence (section 21(6)).

[7] See RSPCA v Shilton unreported June 30 2003, QBD where the court considered the scope of the exceptions in section 8(2).

B. Hunting

The killing and taking of wild, birds is generally prohibited under European and domestic legislation but hunting is permitted in respect of certain species, at certain times and under certain conditions. The legislation does not seek to define what is meant by hunting, in particular it does not generally distinguish between hunting for recreation or subsistence, although it can be assumed that the vast majority of hunting activity in Europe is primarily recreational[1]. Certain subsistence related activities are dealt with specifically under domestic legislation but this is in the context of collection (of certain birds or birds eggs) rather than hunting[2].

Supporters of hunting often assert that field sports tend to promote conservation. Those who oppose hunting in principle do not usually do so on conservation grounds but on the basis of ethical considerations. From a conservationist perspective, the legal control of hunting is intended to ensure that such activity does not endanger quarry species or others who may be indirectly affected. For those supporting the continuation of field sports, however, changes in the law relating to species protection have tended to arouse suspicion that the opportunity will be taken by their opponents to slip a hunting ban in through the backdoor. During the passage of the Wildlife and Countryside Act 1981, the Government sought to allay such concerns by assuring those concerned that the Act was not intended to increase controls on field sports except where necessary for conservation[3].

Wild Birds Directive

The hunting of certain species in accordance with national legislation is permitted under the wild birds Directive but it is subject to the observance of close seasons and the conservation objectives of the Directive. Article 7(4) of the wild birds Directive requires Member States to ensure that the practice of hunting (including falconry) is carried on in accordance with the national measures in force and in compliance with the principles

---

[1] See Commission Guidance document on hunting, para 2.3.2, discussed further below.
[2] See section 16(2) of the Wildlife and Countryside discussed in Chapter 2E - Part II.
[3] Hansard HL col 527 3R. There was also concern that the Secretary of State might use his power in what is now section 5(2) of the 1981 Act to ban field sports by the back door but it was suggested that the limitation on that power contained in s5(3)(added later) ensured against such a move, Hansard, House of Lords, 2 February 1981, col 912.
[4] See para 2.4.7 of the Commission Guidance (June 2003).

of "wise use and ecologically balanced control" of the species of birds concerned. In particular, species to which hunting laws apply must not be hunted during the rearing season nor during the various stages of reproduction. Migratory species must not be hunted during their period of reproduction or during their return to their rearing grounds. Member States are required to send to the Commission all relevant information on the practical application of their hunting regulations.

The principle of "wise use" is not defined in the directive but its meaning has been considered by the Ornis Committee as reported in the Commission's Second Report on the directive (see below). In recent guidance, the Commission has stated that in the context of hunting, "wise use clearly implied sustainable consumptive use with an emphasis on maintaing populations at a favourable conservation status" and goes on to say that the concept appears to correspond well with the definition of sustainable utilisation given in the Convention on Biological Diversity[4]. That definition refers to the use of components of biological diversity in a way and at a rate that does not lead to the long-term decline of biological diversity, thereby maintaining its potential to meet the needs and aspirations of future generations.[5]

Those species which may be hunted are listed in Annex II to the Directive. The species are those which owing to "their population level, geographical distribution and reproductive rate throughout the Community" may be hunted under national legislation (Article 7(1)).Annex II is divided into two parts: the birds listed in Annex II/1 may be hunted "in the geographical sea and land area where this Directive applies" Article 7(2) , that is to say throughout the Community, whereas those listed in Part 2 of Annex II may be hunted only in the Member States in respect of which they are indicated (Article 7(3)). For example, the pheasant, *Phasianus colchicus*, is listed in Annex II/1 and may be hunted in any Member State where national legislation allows. The turtle dove is listed in Annex II/2 and may only be hunted in the member States indicated, namely Greece, France, Spain, Italy and Portugal where national legislation allows.[6]

[5] Article 2 of the CBD. The Commission Guidance also refers to guidance on the meaning of wise use developed under the Ramsar Convention, para 2.4.8.

[6] There appears to be an anomaly in the listing under the Annexes: the requirement of Article 7(1) that hunting must not jeopardise conservation efforts appears to be at variance with the contents of Annex I and II because some species are included in both Annex I and II/I, for example the partridge. A number of species listed in Annexes II/1 and II/2 are also included in Annex I for example the black grouse and barbary partridge.

Impact of hunting

The impact of hunting is two-fold according to Commission, involving a reduction of the (spring) population size and a reduction of available habitats. These two factors determine a species' ability to adapt to a changing environment. The reduction in available habitats arises because of the disturbance caused by hunting which restricts the use of those habitats where hunting activity takes place. The Commission took the view that it was generally not advisable to subject a species with a declining population status to hunting but in some cases, for sociological rather than biological reasons, it was "beneficial for the conservation status to keep hunting possible" but in such cases it was necessary to compensate with positive measures for habitat management.

In recent guidance (see further below) the Commission has stated that the practice of hunting must not represent a significant threat to efforts for the conservation of both huntable as well as non-huntable species and that the national hunting regime should take into account the potential disturbance caused by hunting.[7]

Evaluating the ecological impact of hunting

The Ornis committee[8] considered the concept of "taking account of economic and recreational requirements" (Article 2 of the directive) in relation to the taking of birds by hunting and capture[9] In relation to migratory birds, they concluded that in respect of population dynamics: low levels of taking had little effect on spring population size; moderate levels were unlikely to cause populations to decline but would reduce the size of the spring population; very high levels of taking would lead to decline in populations "and for most species the level at which this will occur is unknown"[10]. They concluded that better data and modelling of both sedentary and migratory birds subject to taking was needed. "In the absence of such information, high levels of taking should be avoided". This is clearly correct on the basis of the application of the precautionary principle, given the risk of serious irreversible damage in the form of species loss if hunting is permitted at levels which lead to a decline in population.

[7] Para 2.4.2 of the Commission's Guidance g hunting, see further below.
[8] This is the committee of experts which meets under the auspices of the wild birds directive to consider policy and implementation issues relating to the requirements of the directive.
[9] See page 7 of the Commission's 2nd Report on the wild birds directive.
[10] Page 8 ibid.

The Ornis Committee also examined the scope of the principles of wise use and ecologically balanced control underpinning the setting of close seasons as indicated in Article 7(4) of the directive. In relation to all birds, they considered that the entire rearing season is encompassed by the various stages of reproduction and dependence. In relation to sedentary birds, they concluded that "...the period of reproduction and dependence begins when the nesting territory is defended and ends when the young become independent". In relation to migratory birds, the Committee concluded that "during their period of reproduction or during their return to their rearing grounds" meant the period from the beginning of the annual geographical migration towards the reproduction areas until the end of the various stages of reproduction and dependence. For geese these are considered to end with the fledging of the young.[11]

Case 435/92 Association pour la Protection des Animaux Sauvages and Others and Prefet de Maine et Loire, Prefet de Loire-Atlantique

There have been a number of cases before the ECJ concerning the implementation and interpretation of Article 7 of the directive. In 1993, the ECJ gave judgment in Case 435/92 Association pour la Protection des Animaux Sauvages and Others and Prefet de Maine et Loire, Prefet de Loire-Atlantique. The case concerned the compliance of the dates fixed for close seasons under national law with the provisions of the Directive relating to the protection of migratory birds during their return to their rearing grounds.

The ECJ referred to its earlier judgment in *Case C157/89 Commission v Italy* in which it had held that Article 7(4) of the Directive is designed to secure a complete system of protection in the periods during which the survival of wild birds is particularly under threat and that accordingly protection against hunting activities could not be confined to the majority of the birds of a given species, as determined by average migratory movements. Taking account of the principles set out in that judgment, the method consisting in fixing the closing date for hunting by reference to the period during which migratory activity reaches its highest level could be considered to be compatible with Article 7(4) of the Directive. The same was true of those methods which took into account the moment at which a certain percentage of birds had started to migrate and of those which consist in ascertaining the average date of the commencement of pre-mating migration. Thus the Court ruled that, pursuant to Article 7(4) of the Directive,

[11] See page 8 of the Commission's Second Report.

the closing date for the hunting of migratory birds and waterfowl had to be fixed in accordance with a method which guaranteed complete protection of those species during the period of pre-mating migration and that, as a result, methods whose object or effect was to allow a certain percentage of the birds of a species to escape such protection did not comply with that provision[12].

The Court also ruled, referring to earlier judgments, that national authorities were not empowered by the Directive to fix closing dates for the hunting season which varied according to the species of bird (because of the problem of disturbance to other species and the risk of confusion as between species), unless the Member State concerned could adduce evidence, based on scientific and technical data relevant to each individual case, that staggering the closing dates for hunting would not impede the complete protection of the species of bird liable to be affected by such staggering[13].

The matter took on a major political significance, most particularly in France. As the House of Lords Committee noted "The prompt political reaction to the Court's judgment may have been influenced by the imminence of the European Parliamentary elections".[14]

Proposed amendment of the Wild Birds Directive

The response to the Court's ruling in Case C-435/92 was the bringing forward by the Commission of a controversial proposal to amend the wild birds directive. Shortly after that ruling, the Commission adopted a proposal to amend Article 7 of the Directive. The proposal was to set criteria for determining the maximum duration of the hunting season according to the favourable or unfavourable conservation status of the species[15]. It was concerned with the determination of the end of the spring hunting season for [migratory] birds.

The proposal was put before the Environment Council in March 1994, which then submitted it to the European Parliament with a request that it be considered under the urgency procedure. Following the refusal of the European Parliament to treat the proposal as urgent, the proposal was

[12] See [1994] ECR I-00067 paragraph 12-13 of the judgment.
[13] Paragraph 22 of the judgment and see Case 38/99 Commission v France ECR [2000] I-10941 where France was held to have adduced no such evidence to justify staggering the dates and was therefore held to have violated Article 7(4).
[14] The Eleventh Report of the House of Lords Select Committee on the European Communities, 1993-94 Session:"Protection of Wild Birds", Part 2, paragraph 9, page 7).
[15] 5947/94; COM(94)39 final.

considered by the House of Lords Select Committee on the European Communities.

The Select Committee considered oral and written evidence from a number of bodies including the RSPB, the JNCC and the DoE as well as written evidence from the BTO and FACE-UK. In its report[16], the Select Committee criticised the proposal on a number of grounds and recommended its withdrawal. It considered that the proposal would result in complication in that different dates could be set for different species and different parts of the same Member State which would hamper effective enforcement and the protection of breeding stocks. In addition, a number of important terms were undefined, resulting in a lack of clarity, in particular "favourable conservation status". The key criticism, however, was that there was a lack of scientific information on which to determine the likely impact of the proposal, in particular in the ORNIS Database on bird population and migration. The Committee was of the view that "the effect [of prolonging the Spring hunting season] must be to reduce to some extent the total population successfully migrating and breeding"[17] and in such circumstances, the precautionary principle should be applied, requiring no change in the date of the close season unless and until it could be shown that the reduction would not adversely affect the conservation status of the species concerned. The Committee called for the development of ORNIS "as a matter of priority" so that an analysis of the conservation status of each migratory species could be produced and the pattern and timing of migration of each species could be established so that the likely effects of changes in the date of the close season can be determined with reasonable confidence. Only then, and having entered into consultation with interested bodies, should the Commission put forward a proposal for change or a communication indicating why no change is needed.

The Committee remarked that, in order to be effective: "...the law setting the end of the spring hunting season for wild bird species must be simple to apply, clear in intention and in effect, widely supported as reasonable and, consequently, enforceable without too much difficulty. The

[16] The Eleventh Report of the House of Lords Select Committee on the European Communities, 1993-94 Session:"Protection of Wild Birds". See in particular the Committee's opinion set out at pages 10-12.

[17] The RSPB had spoken of "killing the breeding capital"(page 7, oral evidence of RSPB) because in spring hunting (as opposed to autumn hunting) the "natural mortality of birds has already taken place" thus creating a disproportionate impact on the coming breeding population.

proposal under consideration fails these tests comprehensively."[18] In the end the Commission's proposal was not adopted.[19]

Case 182/03 Ligue pour la protection des oiseaux/Premier Ministre et Ministre de l'Amenagement du territoire et de l'Environnment

This reference from the French Conseil d'Etat concerned the interpretation of Article 9(1)(c) of the Directive[20] In answer to the first question posed, the Court, referring to its previous case-law noted that Article 9 of the Directive authorises Member States to derogate from provisions relating, inter alia, to hunting (*Case 247/85 Commission v Belgium* [1987] ECR 3029, paragraph 7). The Court had also accepted the possibility of derogating from the prohibition on hunting species of birds not listed in Annex II to the Directive, to which Article 7(1) refers, in particular for the reason set out in Article 9(1)(c) of the Directive (*Case C-118/94 Associazione Italiana per il WWF and Others* [1996] ECR I-1223, paragraph 21). It followed that the hunting of wild birds for recreational purposes during the periods mentioned in Article 7(4) of the Directive might constitute a judicious use authorised by Article 9(1)(c) of that directive, as might the capture and sale of wild birds even outside the hunting season with a view to keeping them for use as live decoys or to using them for recreational purposes in fairs and markets (see *Case 262/85 Commission v Italy* [1987] ECR 3073, paragraph 38). The answer to the first question was therefore be that Article 9(1)(c) of the Directive permitted a Member State to derogate from the opening and closing dates for hunting which follow from consideration of the objectives set out in Article 7(4) of the Directive.

In answer to the second question referred to the Court, the ECJ ruled that that Article 9 of the Directive was to be interpreted as allowing hunting to be authorised pursuant to Article 9(1)(c) where there was no other satisfactory solution. That condition would not be met, inter alia, if the sole purpose of the derogation authorising hunting was to extend the hunting periods for certain species of birds in territories which they already frequented during the hunting periods fixed in accordance with Article 7 of the Directive. The derogation had to be carried out under strictly supervised conditions and on a selective basis and apply only to certain birds in small numbers. Lastly mention had to be made of: the species subject to the derogations; the means, arrangements or methods authorised for capture or killing; the conditions of risk and the circumstances of time

[18] Paragraph 22, page 10 of the report.
[19] See Commission's Second Report on implementation of wbd COM(93) 572 final.
[20] See further Chapter 2E - Part II.

and place under which such derogations might be granted; the authority empowered to declare that the required conditions obtained and to decide what means, arrangements or methods might be used, within what limits and by whom; the controls which would be carried out[21].

Commission Guidance on Hunting

In the light of the extent of litigation on the subject of the hunting of wild birds[22], the Commission has now issued guidance on the hunting provisions of the directive[23]. The Commission points out that there is already extensive case law on the subject and that the guidance will have to be modified in the light of further decisions of the ECJ. In that guidance, the Commission states that hunting represents a consumptive use of wildlife and therefore "must be seen in the broader context of sustainable use of resources" and continues "The concept of wise use[24] need not necessarily be limited to consumptive use. It must recognise that birdwatchers, nature lovers, scientists and society as a whole also have a legitimate right to enjoy or explore wildlife, as long as they exercise this right responsibly. It is generally accepted that the value of environmental resources includes both use values and existence values."[25] This clearly indicates that hunters are not a privileged group within the scheme of the directive as well as reinforcing the notion that any use must be sustainable and meet the conservation objectives of the directive.

The Guidance goes on to examine the practical application of the principle of wise use to the hunting of wild birds, taking into account the scientific work undertaken on the sustainability of hunting[26] The guidance points out that there is a need for sound, scientifically based monitoring mechanisms to ensure that any use is maintained at levels which can be sustained by wild populations without adversely affecting the species role in the ecosystem[27]. In relation to disturbance caused by hunting, the Commission notes that this is particularly relevant in relation to wetland habitats where large concentrations of wild birds, including huntable species, occur. The Commission goes on to note that the importance of avoiding significant disturbance from hunting is a key objective in the

[21] Paragraph 19 of the judgment.
[22] A list of relevant cases is set out at Annex I to the Guide.
[23] "Guidance document on hunting under Council Directive 79/409/EEC on the conservation of wild birds" June 2003, available on the Europa website.
[24] See further above.
[25] See para 2.4.10 of the Commission Guidance.
[26] See paras 2.4.12-2.4.31 of the Guidance.
[27] Guidance para 2.4.15.

management of any Natura 2000 site[28]. Another issue which needs to be considered in the context of wise use is the environmental pollution from lead shot used as ammunition in hunting. The Commission states that any use of it in SPAs which leads to deterioration of habitats or significant disturbance to birds is incompatible with the protection requirements of these sites[29] The Guidance goes on to deal with a range of issues including game management, ecological control and the fixing of close seasons

The Wildlife and Countryside Act 1981

In the United Kingdom, Part I of the Wildlife and Countryside Act makes provision for the hunting of certain species. Section 2(1) of the Act permits those species included on Part I of Schedule 2 to be hunted outside the close season[30]. The section does not expressly refer to "hunting", instead it creates an exception to certain offences created by s1 of the Act. Under s2(1) a person is not guilty of the offence of killing or taking a listed bird outside the close season for that bird, or the injuring of such a bird outside that season in the course of an attempt to kill it. "Close season" is defined in subsection (4)[31].

During the passage of the Wildlife and Countryside Bill, a number of amendments aimed at rationalising the close seasons were proposed. It was argued that since the setting of close seasons in the 1954 legislation (on which those in the Bill were based) a lot more had been learned about the movements/migratory behaviour of birds[32]. One amendment related to the close season for woodcock and would have had the effect of securing the same close seasons in Scotland as in the rest of Great Britain by reducing the Scottish shooting season by one month. It was suggested that close seasons should be rationalised across Europe so as to afford greater protection to migratory birds. None of these proposals was adopted.[33]

Another proposal during the passage of the Bill was to delete what is now section 2(4)(c). It was argued that the shooting season should end

[28] Guidance paras 2.4.18-19.
[29] Guidance para 2.4.20.
[30] These are all species which feature on Annex II of the Birds Directive. During the passage of the Bill, the Government described them as "sporting birds" and explained that it was not disposed to shorten further the list contained in the directive.
[31] Subsection (4) was amended in relation to Scotland by SI 2001/337 in respect of the Capercaillie as of 4 November 2001. The setting of close seasons has a long legislative history extending back at least as far as the Wildfowl Protection Act 1876.
[32] Col 659.
[33] In Case C-435/92 the Court ruled that it was acceptable in principle for different regions to set different close seasons on condition that complete protection of the species was guaranteed.

everywhere for all species on 31 January as biological evidence showed that shooting after midwinter might increase total mortality and reduce the breeding capacity of waterfowl populations, particularly because of the risk of destroying the bonds between established pairing couples. It was suggested that waterfowl are already paired before they leave their British wintering grounds for their more northern overseas breeding grounds and that the advantage of arriving already paired is to take maximum advantage of the short summers there. It was said that non-quarry species would also be disturbed at a vulnerable time prior to migration[34]. This proposal was also unsuccessful. The Government said that it had taken advice and consulted the Nature Conservancy Council and had not been advised to make any change. It stated that the scientific evidence was not clear and pointed to what was termed the "bad weather clause" (now section 2(6)) as reassurance that measures could be taken where there was evidence of risk to populations[35].

Night shooting

The issue of night shooting was much discussed during the passage of the Wildlife and Countryside Bill. Amendments were proposed to prohibit shooting, for example between the first hour after sunset and the first hour before sunrise[36]. Concerns were expressed that protected birds would be shot by mistake at night and that there would be more wounded birds. Comparisons were drawn with other European countries which banned the practice. Those supporting the interests of wildfowlers were firmly against the proposal. The Government, having taken advice from the Nature Conservancy Council, rejected the proposal on the grounds that there was no conservation case for it[37] and amendment was withdrawn.

Sunday Shooting

The exceptions to section 1 set out in section 2(1) and (2) of the Wildlife and Countryside Act are restricted to some extent on Sundays. By virtue of subsection 2(3) of the Act, the taking or killing of birds included in Part I of Schedule 2 outside the close season, is not permitted on Sundays or Christmas Day in Scotland or in any area of England or Wales prescribed in an order of the Secretary of State. The killing or taking or a bird included in Part II of Schedule 2 (now empty), and the taking, damaging or destruction

[34] Hansard, House of Lords, 27 January 1981, col 664.
[35] Hansard, House of Commons, 19 May 1981, col 103.
[36] Hansard, House of Lords, 27 January 1981, col 641.
[37] Hansard col 647, Ibid.

of the nest of such a bird or the taking or destruction of its egg is also an offence on Sunday or on Christmas Day.

Bad Weather Order

Section 2(6) of the Act was dubbed "the bad weather clause" during the passage of the Bill. It allows the Secretary of State[38] to declare by order any period (which must not exceed 14 days) as a period of special protection for birds. The power may be exercised where it appears to the Secretary of State expedient that any wild birds included in Part II of Schedule 1 or Part I of Schedule 2 should be protected during any period outside the close season for those birds[39]. There was some criticism of what is now section 2(7) which requires the Secretary of State, before making an order under section 2(6), to consult "a person appearing to him to be a representative of persons interest in the shooting of birds of the kind proposed to be protected by the order". The Government defended itself against the charge that this created a lack of balance by pointing out that it was also provided that the Nature Conservancy Council should be consulted, but this latter provision was then dropped.[40]

Relationship with Sales

During the passage of the Wildlife and Countryside Bill, the Government was asked why it had not made the seasons the same for both types of activity. The Government said the sales season should be longer so as to allow persons to dispose of birds legally.

Penalties/Enforcement

The penalties for offences committed under section 1 are set out in section 21(1) of the 1981 Act. These would include cases where someone has not fully complied with the conditions for the hunting exception on section 2. Offences under section 1 are subject, on summary conviction to a term of imprisonment not exceeding 6 months or to a fine not exceeding level 5 on the standard scale or to both. The power to impose

[38] Now the Welsh Assembly in respect of Wales, SI 1999/672.

[39] See for example the DoE press release of January 13 1997 announcing the introduction of an order banning the shooting of wild ducks and geese from January 10 to January 24, 1997, because of the adverse effect severe weather conditions were having on the birds' survival. The ban was tol be reviewed after seven days and wouldl not be lifted until there had been seven frost free days.

[40] Hansard, House of Lords, 27 January 1981, col 669.

custodial sentences for offences under the Act had long been called for by a number of agencies and non-governmental organisations and was eventually introduced by the Countryside and Rights of Way Act 2000.[41]

[41] See for example, the evidence of the Nature Conservancy Council to the HC Select Committee on the Environment (see page 64) in the course of a review of the operation and effectiveness of the WCA in 1984-85. The NCC called for the introduction of an alternative of imprisonment as originally provided for in 1954-67 Acts. For the amending provisions see the 2000 Act, section 81(1) and Schedule 12.

C. Sale and Related Activities

Trade in endangered species is regulated internationally under the CITES Convention which is implemented in the European Union by Council Regulation (EC) No 338/97 on the Protection of Species of Wild Fauna and Flora by Regulating Trade Therein[1]. Trade in many species of wild bird is regulated under the CITES Convention and the implementing European legislation. Those regimes are discussed in detail in Part III of this book. This chapter deals only with the trade controls contained in the wild birds directive and in UK domestic legislation. Essentially, the directive regulates trade in all species of wild birds, prohibiting it in most cases but permitting it under certain conditions in others and UK domestic controls implement these obligations. It should be remembered that the CITES regime, both internationally and at the European level, is focused on the impact of trade on *endangered* species and in principle is not concerned with species which are not likely to be subject to trade, whereas the wild birds regime is concerned with the conservation of wild birds generally and trade controls are a only a part of the regulatory framework which is intended to secure their conservation status. Many European species of wild bird, those which are endangered (or at risk of becoming so) and which are likely to be affected by trade, are covered by both regimes but some are covered only by the directive.

The Wild Birds Directive

Article 6 of the Directive lays down a general prohibition on the "sale, transport for sale, keeping for sale and the offering for sale" of "live or dead birds and of any readily recognisable parts or derivatives" of the bird species referred to in Article 1 of the directive[2]. However two categories of exception are then provided for in paragraphs (2) and (3) of Article 6.

Article 6(2) provides that the activities referred to in paragraph (1) shall not be prohibited in respect of species listed in Annex III/1 provided that the birds have been legally killed or captured. Annex III/1 includes a

[1] See generally Part III of this book.

[2] Article 1 refers to "all species of naturally occurring birds in the wild state in the European territory of the Member States to which the Treaty applies". Article 6 does not refer to eggs, although these are specifically brought within the scope of the directive by Article 1(2) of the directive. It seems doubtful that eggs may properly be described as parts or derivatives of birds.

small number of species of game birds including the partridge and the pheasant[3] Most of these species are also listed on Annex II/1 of the directive which means that they may be hunted throughout the European Union.[4]

Article 6(3) allows Member States, for the species listed in Annex III/2, to allow within their territory the activities referred to in paragraph (1) provided that they make provision for certain restrictions and provided that the birds have been legally killed or captured or otherwise legally acquired. The paragraph lays down a procedure by which Member States wishing to grant authorisations for such activities shall first of all consult the Commission. This is to allow for a joint examination of the conservation implications of the marketing of such specimens across the Community[5] Should the examination, in the view of the Commission show that the intended authorisation may lead to the species concerned becoming or being at risk of becoming endangered, the Commission is required to forward a reasoned recommendation to the Member State concerned, stating its opposition to the marketing of the species in question. The recommendation is to be published in the Official Journal. Member States which grant authorisations under Article 6(3) are required to verify at regular intervals that the conditions governing the granting of such authorisations continue to be fulfilled. Annex III/2 contains a number of species of wildfowl and game birds including the greylag goose and the capercaillie. Most of these species are also listed on either Annex II/1 or Annex II/2 of the directive which means that they may be hunted under the conditions laid down by Article 7 of the Directive (see Chapter 2C - Part II).

Article 6(4) requires the Commission to carry out studies on the biological status of the species listed on Annex III/3 and on the effects of marketing on such status. The Commission was required to submit, at the latest four months before the deadline for transposition, a report on the entry of such species into Annex III/2[6] In 1991, Annex III was amended and the nine species of Annex III/3 were transferred to Annex III/2[7]

[3] See Annex II/1 as amended by Commission Directive 91/244/EEC of 6 March 1991 amending Council Directive 79/409/EEC on the conservation of wild birds *Official Journal L 115 , 08/05/1991 P. 0041 - 0055*

[4] By virtue of Article 7(2) of the Directive, see the chapter on hunting of wild birds.

[5] Specific reference is made to population levels, geographical distribution and reproductive rates of the species concerned.

[6] Pending that decision Member States were to apply existing national rules to such species, without prejudice to Article 6(3).

[7] Commission Directive 91/244/EEC of 6 March 1991 amending Council Directive 79/409/EEC on the conservation of wild birds *Official Journal L 115 , 08/05/1991 P. 0041 - 0055*

The Wildlife and Countryside Act 1981

The sale of live or dead wild birds, their eggs and so on is dealt with under section 6 of the 1981 Wildlife and Countryside Act. Subject to the provisions of Part I of the Act[8], it is an offence under section 6(1)(a) for anyone to sell, offer or expose for sale, or have in his possession for the purpose of sale, or transport for sale any live wild bird other than a bird included in Part 1 of Schedule 3 to the Act. It is important to note that section 6(5) provides that any reference in section 6 to a bird included in Part 1 of Schedule 3 is a reference to any bird listed which was bred in captivity and has been ringed or marked in accordance with regulations made by the Secretary of State[9]. Section 6(1) therefore does not contain an exemption in relation to the sale of certain species of wild birds per se, only in relation to captive bred and marked/ringed specimens of certain species. The same prohibitions apply to an egg of a wild bird or any part of an egg. It is also an offence under section 6(1)(b) to publish or cause to be published any advertisement likely to be understood as conveying that the person concerned buys or sells, or intends to buy or sell any of those things.[10]

Under section 6(2), as amended by the Countryside and Rights of Way Act 2000 (in respect of England and Wales), subject to the provisions of Part I of the Act, any person who sells etc[11] any dead wild bird, other than a bird included in Part II (can be sold dead at all times)[12] or Part III (can be sold dead from 1 September to 28 February)[13] of Schedule 3, or any part of or anything derived from such a wild bird is guilty of an offence (section 6(2)(a)). It is also an offence, under subsection 2(b) to publish or cause to be published any advertisement likely to be understood as conveying that the person concerned buys or sells, or intends to buy or sell any of those things. Section 6(2) was amended to remove the reference to the registration scheme formerly operated under regulations made by the Secretary of State[14]. As a result of a review it was decided to discontinue the scheme in favour of a general licence.

[8] These include section 16 under which licences may be granted, see in particular section 16(4)(a).

[9] The relevant regulations are the Wildlife and Countryside (Ringing of Certain Birds) Regulations 1982, SI 1982/1220.

[10] Section 6(4) which imposed special penalties for any section 6 offence committed in respect of a Schedule 1 bird was repealed by the Countryside and Rights of Way Act 2000 sections 81(1) and 102 and by the Criminal Justice (Scotland) Act 2003 section 86.

[11] The same activities as are listed in subsection 1(a) are covered.

[12] See section 6(6). Currently only the woodpigeon is listed

[13] See section 6(6). Currently lists a number birds also listed on Annex III to the directive.

[14] Subsections (7)-(10)were also repealed accordingly in respect of England and Wales by the Countryside and Rights of Way Act 2000 section 102.

Competitive showing is dealt with under section 6(3) which renders it an offence for anyone to cause or permit to be shown for the purposes of competition, or in any premises in which a competition is being held, any live wild bird, other than a bird included in Part 1 of Schedule 3[15], or any live wild bird one of whose parents was such a bird. During the passage of the Wildlife and Countryside Bill the Government explained that its intention was to restrict the species that could be shown competitively to birds which bred readily in captivity and where there was a sufficient captive population to satisfy demand.[16]

The penalties for offences committed under section 6 are set out in section 21(1) of the 1981 Act. Offences under section 6 are subject, on summary conviction to a term of imprisonment not exceeding six months or to a fine not exceeding level 5 on the standard scale or to both. The power to impose custodial sentences for offences under the Act had long been called for by a number of agencies and non-governmental organisations and was eventually introduced by the Countryside and Rights of Way Act 2000.[17]

---

[15] Lists a number of song birds and the barn owl.

[16] Hansard, House of Lords, 2 February 1981, col 932.

[17] See for example, the evidence of the Nature Conservancy Council to the HC Select Committee on the Environment (see page 64) in the course of a review of the operation and effectiveness of the WCA in 1984-85. The NCC called for the introduction of an alternative of imprisonment as originally provided for in 1954-67 Acts. For the amending provisions see the 2000 Act, section 81(1) and Schedule 12.

D. Licences and Derogations

Conflict of interests

On occasion, the prohibitions on activities such as killing, taking, and disturbing certain species come into conflict with other public or private interests, such as public health or agriculture, or with the wider interests of nature conservation itself. The need to take account of potentially competing interests may be given general expression in the legislation, over and above specific provision for derogation. The European Court of Justice has ruled that Article 2 of the wild birds Directive shows that the Directive takes into consideration, on the one hand, the necessity for the protection of birds, and on the other the requirements of public health and safety, the economy, ecology, science, farming and recreation *Case 262/85 Commission v Italy*[1]. This seems to suggest that the system of protection taken as a whole achieves, or strives to achieve, this balance.

As far as individual cases of conflict are concerned, and in addition to providing for certain specific exceptions to the prohibitions[2], conservation legislation generally addresses the problem by providing, under certain conditions, for the possibility of obtaining derogations from specific prohibitions in the form of licences to carry out activities which would otherwise be prohibited where this is necessary to protect such interests. Of course licences cannot, by themselves, resolve the underlying causes of the conflicts of interest in response to which they are issued. In its memorandum of evidence to the House of Commons Environment Committee in 1984, the National Farmers Union pointed out that, in its view and that of MAFF, licences were "only one part of the solution to problems caused by normally protected species. It is essential that complementary agricultural/ conservation initiatives be taken to provide a long term solution, as killing a few birds or animals usually achieves only short-term [objectives]"[3]. The NFU went on to give examples such as the continued research and help needed with regard to heron and cormorant damage on fish farms. The NFU offered a long-term solution, the provision of alternative feeding areas,

[1] Judgment of 8 July 1987, [1987] ECR 1073. The Court was careful to point out however that Article 2 of the Directive "does not constitute an autonomous derogation from the general system of protection"(para 8).

[2] See for example Article 6(2) of the wild birds directive which provides for the lawful sale etc of certain game birds listed in Annex III/1 and Article 7 which permits the hunting of certain species which are listed in Annex II.

[3] See HC Session 1984-85, Minutes of Evidence, 20 November 1984, page 158.

to the difficulties caused by Brent geese which feed on agricultural crops in certain southern coastal areas. It recommended that the Government give greater priority to projects such as this which complement the existing licence arrangements. Perhaps the most important way in which the tensions between the conservation of wild birds and economic interests need to be addressed is through promotion of more environmentally friendly agricultural practices[4].

Licences

One would expect the grounds on which such licences may be granted and the conditions under which they may be applied to be set out in conservation legislation. Equally important however is the issue of the extent to which such conflicts of interest are inevitable and cannot be resolved by means other than the issue of a licence. This emphasis on the need for a restrictive use of derogations is evident in European legislation and has now been incorporated into the UK provisions for licensing. This restrictive approach is reflected both in article 9 of the wild birds directive and in article 16 of the habitats directive which provide for derogations from the species protection provisions of those two instruments[5]. These provisions indicate that, whilst the legislation recognises that the interests of conservation may not be paramount in every individual case, derogations constitute a last resort and competing economic or social interest will not simply take precedence in every case where a conflict arises.

As regards the licences themselves however, the approach taken to their issue, as indicated both by the terms of the legislation itself and by the policies of the issuing authorities, is of key importance in determining whether the overall conservation objectives of the legislation are being upheld. It is therefore unsurprising that Article 9 of the wild birds directive has generated a significant amount of judicial scrutiny at the European level. Some of key cases will be considered in detail further below.

Article 9 of the Wild Birds Directive

Article 9 of the wild birds directive sets out both the specific grounds on which derogations may be granted "where there is no other satisfactory solution" (Article 9(1)), and also a number of matters which must be

[4] See Chapter 7 - Part I.

[5] See also Article 9 of the Berne Convention, implemented in the European Community by the Habitats Directive, which provides for the possibility of certain exceptions to the protective provisions of the Convention "provided that there is no other satisfactory solution".

specified in the derogations, including the species to which they apply and the conditions of risk and the circumstances of time and place under which such derogations may be granted (Article 9(2))[6]. Member States are required to report annually to the Commission on their implementation of Article 9(Article 9(3)) and the Commission is required to ensure, on the basis of available information, that the derogations granted are not incompatible with the Directive (Article 9(4)). The Court has indicated that where a Member State notifies the Commission of derogations in accordance with Article 9(4) and is willing to reach agreement with the Commission on the detailed rules for application of the derogation and the Commission fails to respond, it is unlikely to uphold a subsequent complaint against the measures by the Commission[7].

The Court summarised its approach to Article 9 in a ruling on a reference from an Italian court in which it concluded that national measures derogating from the species protection provisions of the wild birds directive must refer in sufficient detail to the factors set out in paragraphs (1) and (2) of Article 9. *Case C-118/94 Associazione Italiana per il World Wildlife Fund and others v Regione Veneto*[8] concerned a challenge to Italian legislation which authorised the hunting of birds which were not included in Annex II of the Directive, contrary to Article 7 of the directive. The question then arose as to whether the legislation could be justified as a derogation under Article 9.

The Court, referring to earlier judgments on Article 9[9], ruled that, whilst transposition into national law does not necessarily require enactment in precisely the same words in a specific express legal provision, and "a general legal context may be sufficient if it actually ensures the full application of the directive in a sufficiently precise and clear manner", nevertheless "faithful transposition becomes particularly important in a case such as this in which the management of the common heritage is entrusted to the Member States in their respective territories. The Court then set out three conditions which must be met if a Member State is to rely

[6] Article 9(2) requires derogations to specify: the species which are subject to derogation; the means, arrangements or methods authorised for capture or killing; the conditions of risk and circumstances of time and place under which such derogations may be granted; the authority empowered to declare that the required conditions obtain and to decide what means arrangements or methods may be used, within what limits and by whom and the controls which will be carried out

[7] See Case 252/85 Commission v France, paragraph 31 of the judgment.

[8] Judgment 7 March [1996] ECR I-223.

[9] Case 252/85 Commission v France [1988] ECR 2243; Case247/85 Commission v Belgium [1987] ECR 3029; Case 262/85 Commission v Italy [1987] ECR 3073.

on article 9: the Member State must restrict the derogation to cases where there is no other satisfactory solution; the derogation must be based on at least one of the reasons listed exhaustively in Article 9(1)(a), (b) and (c); the derogation must comply with the precise formal conditions set in Article 9(2) which are intended to limit the derogations to what is strictly necessary and to enable the Commission to supervise them. The Italian legislation did not establish those criteria or conditions and therefore "introduced an element of uncertainty" as regarded the obligations to be observed in granting the derogations. The Court noted that "Although Article 9 therefore authorises wide derogations from the general system of protection, it must be applied appropriately in order to deal with precise requirements and specific situations".[10]

It appears therefore that, whilst it may not be necessary for every requirement of Article 9 to be spelt out in national legislation, there must be no doubt that all the requirements are to be met. Advocate General Da Cruz Vilaca, in his Opinion in *Case 247/85 Commission v Belgium* explained that "An essential concern underlying Article 9 is to limit the scope of the exceptions either by a legal definition thereof or by supervision on the part of the national authorities and the Commission. In order to come within the scope of Article 9, the derogations must be worded and applied in a manner that facilitates rather than impairs such supervision."[11]

Section 16 of the Wildlife and Countryside Act 1981

During the passage of the Wildlife and Countryside Bill, the Government described its general policy as follows: "...licences will be issued in accordance with policies which take account of the extent of damage caused, the conservation status of the species involved and the availability of alternative methods of preventing the damage."[12] The Government rejected the idea of making regulations which would govern the issue of licences as this would restrict flexibility. The power to grant licences to derogate from the protective provisions of sections 1, 5, 6(3). 7 and 8 of the 1981 Act is set out in section 16(1) of the Act (since amended).

General and Individual Licences

Under section 16 of the Wildlife and Countryside Act, the issuing authority is given some flexibility as to the form and scope of licences which may be granted. Subsection (5) provides that, subject to subsections 5A and

10 Paragraph 21 of the judgment.
11 See page 3048 of the report of the Opinion [1987] ECR 3029.
12 Hansard, House of Lords, 16 December 1980, col 984.

6, licences may be "to any degree, general or specific" (s16(5)(a)) and may be granted to "either to persons of a class or to a particular person" (s16(5)(b)). By virtue of subsection (8), the definition of a class of persons "may be framed by reference to any circumstances whatever including, in particular, their being authorised by any person".[13] A general licence, unlike a licence granted to a specific individual, does not need to be applied for, it applies automatically to cover actions carried in accordance with its terms and conditions. Whilst activities carried out under a general licence may be more difficult to monitor, it is always possible to impose a condition obliging those operating under the licence to inform the issuing authority about the scale of activity undertaken. In its Third Quinquennial Review of Schedule 5 to the Wildlife and Countryside Act 1981, the JNCC suggested that a condition, requiring traders to inform the Department about the type and volume of trade undertaken, be attached to the general licence authorising the sale of certain amphibians for example.[14]

During the passage of the Wildlife and Countryside Bill, the Government explained the sorts of circumstances in which general and individual licences would be issued:

> "The general licence will be issued ... where it is known in advance that a group of people will need it. The licence will be limited to that group of people and will be specific as to the species to be killed, the period of time, the area of the country, and the purpose and method of killing for which it is valid."[15]

As for individual licences, these would be issued "in those cases where a general need is not foreseen".[16]

Some were critical of the use of general licences, the RSPB argued that "A general licence would be very little different from placing the bird in Part II of Schedule 2" (listing birds which could be killed or taken by authorised persons at all times, all species have now been removed from this Schedule see below). Lord Donaldson of Knightsbridge was concerned that for example, to give a general licence to allow herons to be destroyed at fish farms would remove from fish farmers the onus to design their farms in

[13] Almost identical language is used in regulation 45 of the Habitats Regulations (see paragraphs (1) and (2).

[14] See paragraph 2.4.1.2.

[15] Hansard col 984 (16 December 1980).

[16] Hansard col 984, Ibid.

such a way as to minimise heron damage[17] The Government defended the use of general licences on grounds of practicality and explained that, in the case of fish farms, it was anticipated that licences would be granted to individual fish farmers and only when other types of deterrent had failed.

Whilst the ECJ has not ruled against the granting of general derogations in principle, it has indicated that derogations may not be so general in nature as to render it impossible for the requirements of Article 9 to be met in full. In case 247/85 Commission v Belgium, the Court upheld the Commission's complaint against Belgian provisions which permitted the removal or destruction of birds nests built against houses and adjoining buildings in contravention of Article 5(b) of the Directive. The Court accepted that Belgium's justification of the provisions: the prevention of fires, flood and disease were of a kind as to justify the removal of nests under Article 9 but went on to point out that it was clear that the removal or destruction of nests was only necessary "in specific cases in which the higher ranking interest of public health and security must override the protection of birds and their habitats." In the Court's view it could not "always be maintained that all nests built against houses and adjoining buildings always represent a danger to health."[18] In contravention of paragraph (1) of Article 9, the Court found that the derogation was not limited to specific situations where there was no other satisfactory solution, nor did the derogation comply with the formal requirements of Article 9(2) in that it did not specify the conditions of risk and circumstances of time and place in which the derogation was granted or the controls to be carried out.

Subsection (5) of section 16 provides that licences may be subject to compliance with any specified conditions (s16(5)(c)) and that they may be modified or revoked at any time by the appropriate authority (s16(5)(d)), subject to which they will be valid for the period stated in the licence (s16(5)(e)).[19] In 1995, following rulings on the interpretation of Article 9 of the wild birds Directive by the ECJ (see above), the UK amended section 16[20] to tighten up the conditions under which licences could be issued. One of the changes made was the introduction of subsection 5A which provides that a licence under subsection (1) which authorises any action in respect of wild birds shall: "specify the species of wild birds in respect of which, the circumstances in which, and the conditions subject to which, the action may be taken"; "specify the methods, means or arrangements

[17] Hansard, House of Lords, 9 February 1981 col 48.
[18] See paragraph 28 of the judgment.
[19] Similar language is used in regulation 45(3) of the habitats regulations.
[20] SI 1995/2825.

which are authorised or required for the taking of the action" and shall, subject to subsection (5)(d), "be valid for the period, not exceeding two years, stated in the licence".[21]

In relation to those licences which authorise any person to kill wild birds or wild animals, section 16(6) requires the licence to specify the area within which, and the methods by which the wild birds or animals may be killed and subject to revocation or modification, shall be valid for a period not exceeding two years as stated in the licence.[22]

Power to grant licences: Issuing authority

The grounds on which licences may be granted and the identity of the authority which may issue the licence are set out in relation to all the species covered by Part I of the 1981 Act in section 16.[23] The question of who should issue the various licences was a matter of some controversy when the Wildlife and Countryside Bill was debated in Parliament. As in earlier legislation, namely the 1954 Protection of Birds Act and the 1975 Conservation of Wild Creatures and Plants Act, responsibility for the issue of licences was divided among a number of authorities depending on the ground on which the licence was issued. Under the Wildlife and Countryside Act, licences were to be issued either by the Secretary of State for the Environment, or by the Nature Conservancy Council or by the agriculture Minister. Some were nervous of licensing powers placed in the hands of the then MAFF, fearing a conflict of interest between securing conservation and protecting the interests of farmers: "I do not think it is right that MAFF should be judge and jury in its own case".[24]

The Government, however, emphasised that all the issuing authorities, including MAFF, would follow the same overall policy and that the NCC were under a duty to provide scientific advice to those issuing licences. The Government explained its approach as seeking to give the licensing authority to that branch of Government which was best equipped to exercise it so that licences, such as those for photography, "based solely on scientific judgment" had been allocated to the NCC, whereas licences for precautions against the spread of disease or the safeguarding of crops

[21] The general licences in respect of birds issued under section 16 are set out on DEFRA's website at http://www.defra.gov.uk/wildlife-countryside/vertebrates/gen-licence.htm
[22] Similar provision is made in regulation 45(4) of the habitats regulations in relation to licences issued under regulation 44 of those regulations.
[23] The issue of licences in relation to species covered by the Habitats Regulations is dealt with in regulations 44 and 45 of those regulations which in general use similar language.
[24] Hansard, House of Lords, 9 February 1981, col 38.

would be the responsibility of MAFF. In addition, the Government sought to allay any concern by pointing to an administrative agreement between the DoE and MAFF that all Schedule 1 birds would be considered by DoE[25] and laid emphasis on the provision for consultation so that "the final licensing decisions should represent the balanced view of all the relevant interests"[26]. The definition of "appropriate authority" for the purposes of licensing under section 16 is set out in subsection (9), which is discussed further below under "UK Licences".

Power to grant licences: Grounds

Article 9(1) of the wild birds directive sets out exhaustively the grounds on which Member States may derogate from the species protection provisions in Articles 5-8 of the directive[27] and these are: in the interests of public health and safety; in the interests of air safety; to prevent serious damage to crops, livestock, forests, fisheries and water; for the protection of flora and fauna (Article 9(1)(a); for the purposes of research and teaching, of repopulation, of reintroduction and for the breeding necessary for these purposes (Article 9(1)(b)). Finally, Article 9(1)(c) allows derogations "to permit, under strictly supervised conditions and on a selective basis, the capture, keeping or other judicious use of certain birds in small numbers". The Court has ruled unlawful, derogations granted for reasons falling outside those set out in Article 9(1): for example derogations on grounds of "local interest" in *Case 247/85 Commission v Belgium;* and derogations for acts taking place "in the course of the normal use of the land for agricultural, forestry or fishing purposes" in *Case 412/85 Commission v Germany.*

Article 9(1)(c)

In contrast to the other grounds for derogation in Article 9, Article 9(1)(c) does not prescribe the precise purpose for which the derogation is granted, simply that the use must be "judicious" and the derogation must

[25] Hansard, House of Lords, 9 Feb 1981, col 40.

[26] In the event, the Bill was amended so as to strengthen the requirements for consultation and section 16(10) requires the agriculture Minister to consult from time to time with each of the Nature Conservancy Councils as to the exercise of his functions under section 16 and prohibits him from granting a licence of any description "unless he has been advised by the relevant Nature Conservancy Council as to the circumstances in which, in their opinion, licences of that description should be granted." Section 16(11) defined the relevant Nature Conservancy Council as the one for the area in which it is proposed to carry out the activity requiring a licence.

[27] The conditions under which the derogations may be granted are set out in paragraphs (2) and (3) of Article 9, see above.

be strictly supervised and permitted only on a selective basis. Clearly this provision is capable of being applied in a wide range of circumstances to accommodate interests which are not reflected elsewhere in Article 9[28], provided that all the conditions in Article 9(1)(c) are met.

The scope of Article 9(1)(c) has been tested in a number of cases before the Court of Justice. In *Case 252/85 Commission v France*[29], the Commission argued that French legislation permitting the use of limes and horizontal nets to capture of thrushes and skylarks (a derogation from Article 8(1) of the Directive) could not be justified on the basis of Article 9(1)(c) since "those means of capture do not constitute selective methods and do not therefore allow 'judicious use of certain birds in small numbers within the meaning of the Directive'." The Court however, applying the approach adopted in *Case 262/86 Commission v Italy*, ruled that it was necessary to examine whether the legislation guaranteed that the derogation was being applied on a strictly controlled and selective basis so that the birds in question are captured only in small numbers and in a judicious manner. The Court rejected the complaint against France, finding that the French rules were very precise and made the grant of authorisation to capture such birds subject to a considerable number of restrictive conditions. In addition, the Court found that the Commission had not shown that the legislation permitted the capture of birds in a manner incompatible with a judicious use of certain birds in small numbers, thus placing the onus of proof firmly on the Commission to adduce evidence that legislation did not comply with Article 9(1)(c)[30].

In relation to the meaning of "small numbers", the Court observed that Article 2 of the directive, in conjunction with the 11th recital to the preamble indicated that the criterion of small numbers was not an absolute criterion but referred to the maintenance of the level of the total population and to the reproductive situation of the species concerned. Subsequently in 1993, the Ornis Committee, established under the wild birds Directives, considered the reference to "small numbers" in Article 9(1)(c) and concluded that in order to determine small numbers, a threshold should be fixed as a given percentage of the total annual mortality of the population concerned,

[28] In the UK it has been used to grant licences for the purposes of falconry, taxidermy and the collection of gulls eggs for human consumption for example.

[29] Please [1988] ECR 2243.

[30] Interestingly, Advocate General Da Cruz Vilaca had recommended that the Court find against France on this point because the method of capture was not selective nor could it be guaranteed that only small numbers of birds were involved, both of which were requirements under Article 9(1)(c). In relation to the latter he noted that the legislation did not contain any restriction on the number of birds which may be captured.

namely the sum of death from natural causes and due to taking under Article 7, if applicable.[31]

As to what the percentage should be, the Committee considered that there were two approaches: the figure had to be lower, at least by an order of size, than the figures characteristic of the taking of birds under Article 7 (1% in their view); or, the taking must have a negligible effect on the population dynamics of the species concerned (1% or less since parameters of population dynamics are seldom known to within less than one percentage point and bird taking of less than 1% can be ignored from a mathematical point of view). The Committee therefore concluded that, small numbers should be considered as being any taking of less than 1% of the total annual mortality of the population concerned (average value) for species which may not be hunted. For species which may be hunted it should be considered as around 1%. Finally, the Committee took the view that for takings exceeding these thresholds, an in-depth scientific analysis would be required by the competent authority granting the derogation to ensure that the derogation is not incompatible with the objectives of the directive[32].

By contrast, in *Case 247/85 Commission v Belgium*, the Court upheld the Commission's complaint and found that Belgium could not rely on Article 9(1)(c) to justify provisions allowing the capture and keeping of certain birds. Whilst the Court acknowledged that the legislation subjected persons authorised to strict rules and controls, it went on to find that those rules did not guarantee that the number of birds to be captured would be limited to small quantities or that the birds would be protected during nesting and rearing (presumably applying the test for judicious use).

The Ornis Committee also later considered the meaning of "other judicious use" and concluded that the concept included "activities which make a vital contribution to improving the efficiency of the general system for the protection of wild birds established by the directive". In addition "it may also include other use provided that this does not jeopardise the general objectives of the directive and it may include hunting using birds of prey in the context of falconry"[33]. On "judicious use" in the context of hunting see

[31] For sedentary species the population concerned is the population of the geographical region in which the derogation applies. For migratory species, it means the population of the regions from which the largest numbers of migratory birds come before passing through the region to which the derogation applies during the period it is in force.

[32] See the Second Report of the Ornis Committee at page 11 (November 1993).

[33] Committee Second Report at page 10.

the ECJ's recent judgment in Case C-182/03 Ligue pour la protection des oiseaux/Premier Ministre et Ministre de l'Amenagement du territoire et de l'Environnment discussed in Chapter 2C - Part II.

As far as the UK is concerned, section 16 was amended in 1995 so as to bring the relevant grounds for issuing a licence under Article 9(1)(c) into line with the requirements of the Directive. Section 16(1A)(b) now requires an authority issuing a licence under section 16(1)(e)-(h) not to do so "otherwise than on a selective basis and in respect of a small number of birds."[34]

UK Licences

Section 16(9) deals with the identity of the appropriate authority in respect of the issue of section 16 licences[35]. Either the Secretary of State for the Environment, in consultation with an advisory body[36] or the relevant NCC may issue licences: for scientific, research[37] or educational purposes (s16(1)(a); for the purpose of ringing or marking or examining any ring or mark on wild birds (s16(1)(b)); for the purpose of conserving wild birds (s16(1)(c)); for the purposes of the repopulation of an area with wild birds or the reintroduction of wild birds, including any breeding necessary for those purposes (s16(1)(ca))[38]; for the purpose of conserving flora or fauna (s16(1)(cb))[39]. The Secretary of State in consultation with the relevant NCC may issues licences for the purpose of protecting any collection of wild birds, which for these purposes includes game birds as defined in section 27 of the Act(s16(1)(d)); for the purposes of falconry or aviculture (the latter being defined in section 27 as the "breeding and rearing of birds in captivity")(s16(1)(e)); for the purposes of any public exhibition or competition (s16(1)(f)) and for the purposes of taxidermy (s16(1)(g)). It is clear from recent amendments to section 16 that grounds (e)-(g) (and also (h) see below) are considered to fall within the "judicious use" exception in

[34] The WCA(Amendment)Regulations 1995 regulation (3).
[35] See further in relation to the exercise of functions under this section by the National Assembly for Wales, by the National Assembly for Wales (Transfer of Functions) Order 1999, SI 1999/672, art 2, Sch 1.
[36] Section 23 gives the Secretary of State for the Environment the power to establish advisory bodies to advise him on the administration of Part I of the Act or otherwise in connection with the protection of birds [or animals or plants].
[37] The reference to research was inserted by the WCA (Amendment) Regulations 1995 SI 1995/2825, regulation 3.
[38] Inserted by the 1995 Amendment Regulations. The terms repopulation and reintroduction are defined simply as having the same meaning as they bear in the Directive, section 16(9A).
[39] Inserted by the 1995 Amendment Regulations.

Article 9(1)(c) of the Directive discussed above (see now s16(1A)(b) as inserted by the 1995 Amendment Regulations).

The Wildlife and Countryside Bill originally included a general power to issue licences for the "provision of food for human consumption" but this met with some concern that such a power was too broad and the Bill was amended so that only certain practices which were "traditional and harmless to conservation" could be licensed[40]. By virtue of s16(2) and (9), the Secretary of State, in consultation with the relevant NCC may issue licences for the purpose of providing food for human consumption in relation to a gannet on the island of Sula Sgeir, or a gulls egg or, at any time before 15 April in any year, a lapwing's egg. These licences can only authorise acts otherwise prohibited under section 1 or 3 of Part I so that, for example, they cannot authorise sale of eggs (which is prohibited under s6). Licences to sell or advertise birds may be issued by the Secretary of State, in consultation with the NCC under (s16(4)(a)).

The relevant Nature Conservancy Council may grant licences for the purposes of photography (s16(1)(h)). It was made clear during debate on this provision that the licence would not give authority to enter land in circumstances in which it would be a trespass.

The agriculture Minister[41] may issue licences: for the purposes of preserving public health or public or air safety (s16(1)(i); for the purpose of preventing the spread of disease (s16(1)(j) or for the purposes of preventing serious damage to livestock, foodstuffs for livestock, crops, vegetables, fruit, growing timber, fisheries or inland waters (s16(1)(k)[42]. The meaning of "serious damage" which is based on Article 9(1)(a) of the wild birds directive, was considered by the ECJ in Case 247/85 Commission v Belgium[43]. The Court ruled that the aim of that provision was not to prevent the threat of minor damage. In that case however, the fact that the Belgian measures in question referred simply to the causation of "damage" was not enough for the Court to conclude that Belgium was not in fact applying the concept consistently with the directive. The same approach was adopted in Case 236/85 Commission v Netherlands[44], although in both cases Advocate General Da Cruz Vilaca took the opposite view asserting that the

[40] Hansard, House of Lords, 30 March 1981 col 34.

[41] The Minister may not grant a licence of any description unless he first received advice from the relevant Nature Conservancy Council as to the circumstances in which, in their opinion such licences may be granted.

[42] The reference to inland waters was inserted by the 1995 Amendment Regulations.

[43] [1987] ECR 3029.

[44] [1987] ECR 3989.

mere reference to the prevention of damage was less restrictive than the language of the directive (see paragraph 16 of his Opinion in case 236/85)

Livestock is broadly defined in s27 of the 1981 Act and includes, amongst others, any animal which is kept "for the provisions or improvement of shooting or fishing" This means for example that a licence could in principle be obtained to protect game birds from predation by birds of prey. Inland waters are also defined in section 27 to mean inland waters within the meaning of the Water Resources Act 1991; any other waters which are within the seaward limits of the territorial sea or controlled waters within the meaning of Part II of the Control of Pollution Act 1974, other than ground waters as defined in section 30A(1)(d).

Alternatives to the Issue of a Licence

Over and above the limitations as to the grounds on which and the conditions under which derogations may be granted by member States, both Article 9 of the wild birds directive and Article 16 of the Habitats Directive permit derogations only where no satisfactory alternative can be found45. Article 9(1) provides that Member States may derogate "where there is no other satisfactory solution".[46]

Section 16 of the Wildlife and Countryside Act which implements Article 9 of the wild birds directive in the UK was amended in 1995 to bring it into line with this aspect of Article 9. Originally the section did not expressly refer to the requirement that there be no other satisfactory solution. In response to a proposal for an amendment which would have inserted express wording on alternatives into what is now s16, the Government explained that in its view such an amendment was unnecessary "as the licence-issuing authority responsible will not issue a licence if it is not required."[47] The Government was also concerned that the onus of showing that no alternative was available should not be placed on the applicant for a licence. As amended, section 16(1A) (a) prohibits a licensing authority from granting a licence "unless it is satisfied that, as regards that purpose, there is no other satisfactory solution". Presumably the licensing authority

[45] Advocate General Fenelly described this as an "essential precondition" in Case 118/94, (paragraph 35 of his Opinion). Similar wording is found in Article 9 of the Berne Convention which concerns derogations from the provisions of that Convention.

[46] Article 16(1) of the habitats directive permits derogations provided "that there is no satisfactory alternative and the derogation is not detrimental to the maintenance of the populations of the species concerned at a favourable conservation status in their natural range.".

[47] Hansard, House of Lords, 9 February 1981 col 44.

will reach a view on all the evidence before it and it will be in the interests of applicants to address this issue in their application for a licence.

Clearly the issue of the availability of alternative solutions is of particular importance in relation to general licences as recognised by Lord Donaldson of Knightsbridge during the debate on the Bill. He was concerned that for example, to give a general licence to allow herons to be destroyed at fish farms would remove from fish farmers the onus to design their farms in such a way as to minimise heron damage.[48] The Government defended the use of general licences on grounds of practicality and explained that in the case of fish farms it was anticipated that licences would be granted to individual fish farmers and only when other types of deterrent have failed. It appears therefore that general licences are only issued where it is apparent that no satisfactory alternative is available to any of those falling within the scope of the licence and this is now clearly a requirement under the amended section 16 (subsection 1A(a)).

The Court, in its decisions on Article 9 of the Directive has repeatedly confirmed that the grant of permits must be conditional upon the absence of any other satisfactory solution.[49]

Amendments to Section 16

In order to bring section 16 fully into compliance with Article 9 of the wild birds directive, it was amended in 1995[50]. A new subsection 1A was introduced which provides that: " The appropriate authority (a) shall not grant a licence for any purpose mentioned in subsection (1) unless it is satisfied that, as regards that purpose, there is no other satisfactory solution; and (b) shall not grant a licence for any purpose mentioned in paragraphs (e) to (h) of that subsection otherwise than on a selective basis and in respect of a small number of birds.".

A further new provision, subsection (5A), provides that: "A licence under subsection (1) which authorises any action in respect of wild birds, (a) shall specify the species of wild birds in respect of which, the circumstances in which, and the conditions subject to which, the action may be taken; (b) shall specify the methods, means or arrangements which

[48] Hansard, House of Lords, 9 February 1981 col 48.
[49] See Case 236/85 Commission v Netherlands paragraph 13; Advocate General Da Cruz Vilaca described the requirement as being "in harmony with the principle of proportionality" (see Opinion in Case 247/85 Commission v Belgium page 3047 of the ECR report.
[50] See SI 1995/2825.

are authorised or required for the taking of the action; and (c) subject to subsection (5)(d), shall be valid for the period, not exceeding two years, stated in the licence."

Section 16(5) provides that, subjection to subsection (6) a section 16 licence may be "to any degree general or specific"; may be granted either to persons of a class or to a particular person, may be modified or revoked any time and shall be valid for the period stated in the licence. Subsection (6) deals with licences to kill wild birds (or animals) and requires the derogation to specify the area within which, and the methods by which the birds may be killed and, subject to revocation, shall be valid for the period, not exceeding two years, specified in the licence.

Penalties and Enforcement

It as an offence under section 17 of the 1981 Act to make a false statement for the purpose of obtaining a licence, punishable on summary conviction to a term of imprisonment not exceeding 6 months or to a fine not exceeding level 5 on the standard scale or to both[51] The general enforcement powers under section 19 of Act are also available, providing for powers of search, seizure and arrest in prescribed circumstances. New powers of entry for wildlife inspectors were introduced by the Countryside and Rights of Way Act 2000 in form of section 19ZA[52]. Another new provision, introduced at the same time, section 19ZB introduces a power to take samples in certain circumstances.

The courts have taken a fairly strict approach to the interpretation of section 16 and the scope of licences granted under it. In the *Royal Society for the Prevention of Cruelty to Animals v Cundey*[53], the RSPCA appealed against the dismissal of its information alleging that the defendant had attempted to kill birds, namely starlings, contrary to section 18(1) of the 1981 Act. The Defendant had maintained that he had acted in accordance with general licences issued by MAFF and DETR under section 16. The RSPCA had contended that the licences were to be read as subject to the condition that the protection offered by the licences was only applicable

[51] Section 21(1) as amended by the Countryside and Rights of Way Act 2000, section 81(1) and Schedule 12. The "multiplier" provision in section 21(5) applies, so that the maximum fine shall be determined as if the person convicted had been convicted of a separate offence in respect of each bird, nest etc involved.

[52] Inserted, in relation to England and Wales, by the Countryside and Rights of Way Act 2000, s 81(1), Sch 12, para 8 (entry into force 30 January 2001).

[53] [2001] EWHC Admin 906; (2002) Env LR 17.

where the reason behind the commission of the wrongful act complied with one of the purposes set out in subsection (1) of section 16. The Administrative court allowed the RSPCA's appeal and held that the DETR licence clearly limited authorisation to those acts carried in accordance with one of the purposes for which the licence was granted and accordingly it offered no protection to the Defendant against prosecution under section 18(1). In relation to the MAFF licence, no specific statement qualified the permission as subject to a statutory purpose but in order to give effect to the operative words of section 16(1), a section 16 licence had to be interpreted as providing authorisation for the killing or taking of birds only where such actions were carried out in accordance with one of the exonerating purposes set out in section 16(1).

In *RSPCA v Shilton*[54] the Administrative Court, considering the dismissal of two informations brought by the RSPCA for use of a trap to catch magpies and of causing unnecessary suffering to a magpie, held that although the defendant's use of the trap was within the terms of a section 16 licence, this did not prevent an offence of causing unnecessary suffering contrary to the section 1(1)(a) of the 1911 Animal Protection Act from being made out.

Notion of "Pest" Species

The Government gave assurances during the Second Reading of the Wildlife and Countryside Bill, that those who make their living from the land "will be authorised to kill pests"[55] Others were keen to point out that the identity of the real pest species was a matter for debate:

> "This Bill, like all other legislation dealing with the claims and welfare of other species, rests upon the doctrine that the interests of the human species are paramount...when other species get in the way we call them pests. But the real pest in the living world is man himself. He is the most destructive creature that was ever brought on to this plant..."[56]

The dangers of labelling particular species as pests were highlighted during the consideration of the proposal to amend the wild birds directive by the House of Lords European Committee. The Committee noted that bird protection organisations warned against using "pest" as a

[54] Unreported June 30 2003 QBD Admin Ct [2003] EWHC 1696 Admin.
[55] Hansard, House of Lords, 16 December 1980, col 984.
[56] Hansard, House of Lords, 16 December 1980, col 1034.

general term for certain species for a number of reasons including that: there may only be a problem at the local level; that the species may be wrongly identified as the source of the problem and that such a label may obscure the need for a better understanding of the role of species in various natural and semi natural processes. The compromise was to put certain species on Annex II (1/2) under certain conditions.

The regularity with which the protection of particular species comes into conflict with other interests has nevertheless earned them the dubious distinction of being regarded, at least by some, as "pest species" and, in the past, rendered solutions other than licensing attractive to the legislator. In earlier UK legislation it was provided that certain bird species such as the magpie, jay and house sparrow could be killed or taken at any time by authorised persons[57]. Authorised persons were defined in the legislation and included the owner or occupier of any land on which the action was taken[58].

The approach of including a pest species schedule in this way was originally repeated, in relation to certain bird species, in the Wildlife and Countryside Act 1981. Section 2(2) of the Act provides that an authorised person shall not be guilty of an offence under section 1 of the Act by reason of, inter alia, the killing or taking of a bird included in Part II of Schedule 2. The thirteen bird species listed in the Schedule included a number of corvide species, gulls such as the herring gull among others. The adoption of this approach, rather than the use of individual licences was criticised during the passage of the Wildlife and Countryside Bill. Following a number of rulings from the ECJ on the interpretation of Article 9 of the wild birds directive however (discussed below), it became clear that the establishment of a pest schedule ran counter to the requirements of Article 9 of the wild birds Directive. The species listed in Schedule II Part 2 were eventually all removed on 1 January 1993.[59]

Case 247/85 Commission v Belgium

In case 247/85 Commission v Belgium, the Court had followed the Advocate General in upholding the Commission's complaint that Belgian legislation which allowed certain persons to capture and kill house sparrows, tree sparrows and starlings and their eggs and nests was in

[57] See section 2 of the Protection of Birds Act 1954.
[58] Section 14 ibid.
[59] See the Wildlife and Countryside Act 1981 (Variation of Schedules 2 and 3)Order 1992, SI 1992/3010. article 2.

breach of Article 9 of the wild birds directive. The Belgian government had sought to argue that the provisions were justified because the species concerned caused serious damage to crops and, in the case of starlings posed a threat to public health due to their presence in towns (both grounds for granting derogations under Article 9).

The Court ruled that, owing to their generality, the derogations contained within the Belgian legislation exceeded the limits set by Article 9 of the directive.[60] In particular, Article 9(1) required a derogation granted under that article to cover specific situations and also to comply with the requirements set out in Article 9(2).The Belgian legislation, the Court found, did not comply with those requirements. Specifically, it did not indicate the reasons for which the derogation had been granted, as required by Article 9(1). The legislation did not explain how the prevention of serious damage to crops or the protection of public health necessitated the granting of a permanent derogation applying throughout Belgium to such a wide category of persons. In addition, the provisions contravened Article 9(2) since they mentioned neither the time nor the place in relation to which they were granted nor the controls which would be required (to ensure that the conditions of Article 9 were met).

In his Opinion on the complaint, the Advocate General had taken the view that, in order to come within the scope of Article 9 of the directive, derogations must be worded and applied in such a manner as to facilitate supervision by the national authorities and Commission and that the Belgian legislation did not meet this requirement. He went on to suggest that in order to justify the absence of any limitations as to time or place, Belgium would have had to provide evidence that such birds *always* caused serious damage to crops *throughout* Belgian territory and that such evidence had not been furnished. He concluded that there was a "manifest disproportion" between the extent of possible damage and the scope of the exception permitted by Belgian legislation[61]. Although the Court did not adopt this line of reasoning expressly, it may provide guidance as to the evidence which would be required to defend a generally expressed derogation of this kind.

---

[60] See paragraph 34 of the judgment at [1987] ECR 3029 page 3066.
[61] See page 3049 of the report.

The UK Response

In the light of this and a number of similar cases brought against other Member States[62] and in response to the initiation of infraction proceedings against the UK by the Commission, the Government agreed with the Commission that the UK would have to alter the way in which it dealt with the pest species contained in Part II of Schedule 2 to the Wildlife and Countryside Act 1981. The UK government agreed to remove all species from Schedule II/2 thus depriving section 2(2) of any effect and adopt, as an alternative, the licensing powers under section 16 of the Act (unless recourse could be had to the "emergency" provisions such as, in relation to birds, section 4(3)).

The Government intended to introduce general licences which would permit the killing or taking of pest birds at all times but the first such proposals were dropped after criticisms that they were overly bureaucratic and burdensome. Revised proposals were put forward in 1992 under which authorised persons would be given the necessary authority to kill pest species. These annual licences would cover broad geographical areas and would specify in general terms the purposes for which pest control would be carried out. The scientific adviser to the Department, the JNCC, would monitor the effect of pest control on the conservation status of the species concerned and where necessary could recommend revocation of the licence to allow the species to maintain a satisfactory conservation status. An Order removing all species from part II of Schedule 2 entered into force in 1993. Details of the current general licences are available on the DEFRA website.

In the meantime, the Commission had sought to address the problem of pest species, at least in part, by proposing an amendment to the wild bird directive which would have added five (corvid) pest species to the Directives hunting annex. The UK opposed this proposal on the basis that was needed instead was a provision which would allow for the unrestricted killing of all UK-recognised pest species throughout the year without the need for licences[63]. Eventually five species of Corvidae were added to Annex II/2[64].

---

[62] See case 252/85 Commission v France [1988] ECR 2043; case 262/85 Commission v Italy; case 236/5 Commission v Netherlands [1988] ECR 2043, [1987] ECR 3989.

[63] See supplementary EM on Com (91)42 Final 5185/91.

[64] Council directive 94/24/ec of 8 june 1994 amending annex to directive 79/409/eec on the conservation of wild birds

CHAPTER 3

WILD ANIMALS

A. General Protection

The main pieces of conservation legislation protecting wild animals in the UK are Part I of the Wildlife and Countryside Act and Part III of the Conservation (Natural Habitats etc) Regulations 1994. Certain species receive protection under separate statutes including badgers which are considered in Chapter 3C - Part II. This chapter is concerned with the general regimes under the 1981 Act and the 1994 Regulations.

The form of protection afforded to wild animals under Part I is very similar to that afforded to wild birds[1], although the scope is narrower in that certain forms of protection such as the prohibitions on killing, injuring and taking and the possession controls only apply to those species of animal listed in Schedule 5 to the Wildlife and Countryside Act rather than simply applying to all wild animals. The prohibitions on certain methods of killing or taking apply to all wild animals however.

Under the Conservation (Natural Habitats etc) Regulations 1994[2] full protection is afforded to those species, known as "European Protected species" listed in Schedule 2 to the Regulations and limited protection, against certain methods of taking or killing, to wild animals of the species listed in Schedule 3 to the Regulations.

Part I of the Wildlife and Countryside Act 1981

In contrast to the protection afforded to wild birds under Part I of the Wildlife and Countryside Act 1981, most of the protective provisions relating to wild animals under Part I apply only to certain wild animals. Section 9 of the Wildlife and Countryside renders it an offence to intentionally kill, injure or take, or to posses or sell any wild animal included in Schedule 5. There are also prohibitions on intentionally or recklessly damaging or destroying shelters used by such animals (discussed in more detail below). The only provisions which apply to any wild animal are those in section 11 relating to prohibitions on certain methods of killing and taking wild animals. "Wild animal" is defined under s27(1) of the

---

[1] See Chapter 2 - Part II.

[2] These entered into force on 30 October 1994.

Wildlife and Countryside Act as "any animal (other than a bird) which is or (before it was killed and taken) was living wild". Schedule 5 to the 1981 Act lists those wild animals which may not be killed, injured or taken and the sale and possession of which are prohibited (under section 9 of the 1981 Act). Schedule 5 is subject to a five yearly review by the Joint Nature Conservation Committee[3] which must advise the Secretary of State for the Environment[4] whether any animal should be added to or removed from Schedule 5 (the same powers and duties apply to the listing of plants under Schedule 8 as to which see below, Chapter 4 - Part I. A copy of this advice is laid before Parliament (section 24(3)).

The criteria for listing species in Schedule 5 (and Schedule 8) are indicated in section 22 of the Act dealing with the power to vary the Schedules. The Secretary of State is empowered to amend Schedule 5 by order, on a representation made jointly by the Nature Conservancy Councils in the following ways: he may add to Schedule 5 any animal which, in his opinion, "is in danger of extinction in Great Britain or is likely to become so endangered unless conservation measures are taken."; he may remove an animal which, in his opinion, is no longer endangered or likely to become so endangered (section 22(3)). The Secretary of State also has the power to amend Schedule 5 for the purpose of complying with an international obligation(Section 22(4)).

These changes can apply generally or be restricted to particular provisions of Part I[5] or to particular times of year and, except where the change is introduced for the purpose of complying with an international obligation, may be limited to particular areas of Great Britain (section 22(3)-(4)).

The JNCC makes its recommendations after consultation with statutory conservation agencies, including the Countryside Commission, the Institutes of Terrestrial and Freshwater Ecology and the Environment

---

[3] See section 133 of the Environmental Protection Act 1990.which had the effect of substituting the Joint Nature Conservation Committee for the Nature Conservancy Council which had previously carried out the review.

[4] Pursuant to section 53 of the Scotland Act 1998, functions such as the making of Orders changing Schedules 5 and 8, as regards Scotland, are now exercisable by Scottish Ministers. In Wales, the National Assembly for Wales (Transfer of Functions) Order 1999 transferred such Order-making powers, as regards Wales, to the National Assembly for Wales.

[5] For example, a number of species of frogs and toads are protected in relation to sale only (section 9(5)).

Agency[6] and NGOs (the latter consultation being coordinated through Wildlife Link).

The Quinquennial Review

The first Quinquennial Review was carried out in 1985 and subsequent reviews took place in 1991,1996 and 2001. The reviews set out reasoned recommendations for listing new species or removing species from the Schedule. The recommendations give a good indication of the range of threats to species and to the various benefits to conservation which are anticipated from listing. Examples of threats to species in the third Quinquennial Review included: predation from introduced species (the water vole threatened by mink); exploitation based on EC quota which are not based on scientific data (the basking shark); loss of habitat and collection (the Stag Beetle); pollution and obstruction of migration routes (the Allis shad); increased trade (the bluebell); modification of habitat (flamingo moss);inappropriate grazing regimes (convoluted cladonia) and global warming (Polar feather-moss). Included among the recommendations in the fourth Review was increased protection for the water vole and full protection for a number of marine fish species. No species were recommended for removal from either Schedule 5 or 8[7].

The JNCC sets out the anticipated benefits of its listing recommendations in its report. The benefits to be derived from listing also vary. In addition to the direct benefits of listing (some recommendations are for listing for certain purposes only such as to prohibit sale) such benefits include the focussing of attention on a species which in turn may encourage habitat management and/or the introduction of a species recovery programme (water vole); the encouragement of further research (basking shark); the need to take account of the species during the planning of developments (Alpne sulphur tresses); the promotion of a flagship species to enhance awareness to manage particular habitats (New Forest Beech-lichen).

In explaining the rationale for its final recommendations at the time of the second Quinquennial Review in 1991, the Joint Nature

[6] The functions of the NRA having been transferred to the Environment Agency.

[7] In practice most of the recommendations have been accepted by the Secretary of State: following the 1985 review, all but two of the NCC's recommendations were accepted and implemented (See QR 1991 page 3). Of the recommendations made in the second review, all but four of the JNCC's 94 recommendations were accepted. Following the third review, only three recommendations were not accepted.

Conservation Committee explained that it had proceeded on the basis that "in danger of extinction" in section 22(3) broadly equated to "endangered" as defined in the internationally recognised IUCN Red Data Book on endangered species and "likely to become so endangered" as "vulnerable"[8] . These definitions state that "endangered" refers to taxa in danger of extinction and whose survival is unlikely if causal factors continue to operate and includes those whose numbers are so reduced to a critical level or whose habitats have been so drastically reduced that they are deemed to be in immediate danger of extinction."; "vulnerable" refers to taxa which are likely to move into the endangered category in the near future if the causal factors continue operating, and includes taxa subject to over-exploitation, extensive destruction of habitat or other environmental disturbance and those with populations that have been seriously depleted and whose ultimate security has not been assured or populations that are still abundant but under threat from severe adverse factors throughout their range." The JNCC indicated that it worked on a timescale of 5-10 years.

Because the number of species meeting these criteria was very large, a qualification was added to the effect that direct legal protection must potentially bring tangible benefits to the species. This approach enabled an initial list of 1000 species to be reduced to 91[9].

In contrast to the Bern Convention therefore[10], the 1981 Act lists endangered and vulnerable species together for conservation purposes (Schedule 6 is welfare oriented rather than conservation oriented and some species, for example of bats, appear in both). The restrictions recommended for Appendix 2 animals in the Bern Convention are matched by a Schedule 5 listing under the 1981 Act. This means that vulnerable species listed on Schedule 5 are protected more stringently than required by Article 7 of the Bern Convention.

The JNCC has also set out eligibility criteria for species to be considered for listing: generally only native taxa are to be considered and their taxonomic status must be well authenticated.[11]

[8] Second Quinquennial Review report page 5.
[9] Third Quinquennial Report at page 6.
[10] Endangered species are alisted in Appendix 2 to the Bern Convention and vulnerable species on Appendix 3.
[11] See Fourth Quinquennial Review report page 7.

In the Third Review, the JNCC acknowledged that, in many cases, implementation of wide-ranging habitat and species action plans[12] is a more suitable means of conserving species than listing them on Schedules 5 and 8. The Committee gave the example of the UK Biodiversity Action Plan for rare species conservation as a more positive and apposite approach than "simply legislating against the damaging activities in s9 and 13 of the WCA"[13].

Dual Listing on Schedules 5 of the 1981 Act and Schedule 2 of the Habitats Regulations

A large number of animal species are listed on both Schedule 5 and on Schedule 2 to the Habitats Regulations. In its Third Review, the JNCC noted that it has been suggested that for administrative reasons it would be better to remove from Schedule 5 all those species which appear in Schedule 2 of 1994 Regulations but that the Department of Environment had advised that the dual listing should be maintained since the protection afforded under the legislation is slightly different[14].

Protection against Deliberate Capture or Killing

Under section 9(1) and subject to the provisions of Part I 9 it is an offence intentionally to kill, injure or take any wild animal included on Schedule 5. In any proceedings for an offence, the animal shall be presumed to have been a wild animal unless the contrary is shown (section 9(6)).

A number of exceptions to section 9 are set out in section 10. These are similar to those covering offences relating to wild birds in section 4 of the Act[15]. Nothing in section 9 shall make unlawful: anything done in pursuance of a requirement by the Secretary of State under section 98 of the Agriculture Act 1947; nor anything done under the Animal Health Act 1981 (section 10 (1)). In addition, a person shall not be guilty of an offence under section 9 by reason of the taking of any animal, if he shows that the animal had been disabled otherwise than by his unlawful act and was taken solely for the purpose of tending it and releasing it when no longer disabled. Nor will a person be guilty of an offence by reason of killing an animal if it was so seriously disabled otherwise than by his unlawful act that there was no reasonable chance of it recovering. Nor is an offence committed if the individual can show that the act was the incidental result

[12] See further Chapter 1 - Part II.
[13] See the Third Quinquennial Review Report at para 2.3.2 3.
[14] See paragraph 1.3.3 of the Third Quinquennial Review Report.
[15] See Chapter 2 - Part II.

of a lawful operation and could not reasonable have been avoided (section 10(3))[16].

Acts done by authorised persons for certain purposes are also exempt (in relation to killing or injuring an animal): if the action in question was necessary for a purpose listed in section 10(4) of the Act. Those purposes are: preventing serious damage to livestock, foodstuffs for livestock, crops, vegetables, fruit, growing timber or any other form of property or to fisheries. An authorised person is not be entitled to rely on the defence in section 10(4) as respects any action taken at any time, if it had become apparent before that time, that that action would prove necessary for the purpose in question and either a licence under section 16 had not been applied for as soon as reasonably practicable after that fact became apparent; or an application for such a licence had been determined.

Possession Controls

Section 9(2) states that subject to the provisions of Part I of the Act, if any person has in his possession or control any live or dead wild animal included in Schedule 5 or any part of or anything derived from, such an animal, he shall be guilty of an offence.

In addition to the defences available under section 10(1) and (3)(see above), a person will not be guilty of an offence under subsection (2) if he shows that the animal had not been killed or taken, or had been killed or taken otherwise than in contravention of the relevant provisions, or had been sold (whether to him or any other person) otherwise than in contravention of those provisions. "Relevant provisions" for these purposes means the provisions of Part I and of the Conservation of Wild Creatures and Wild Plants Act 1975.

Sales Controls

Section 9(5) renders it an offence to sell, offer or expose for sale, or have in one's possession or transport for the purpose of sale any live or dead wild animal included in Schedule 5, or any part of or anything derived from, such an animal. It is also an offence to publish under section 9(5)(b) to publish or cause to be published any advertisement likely to be understood as conveying that the person concerned buys or sells, or intends to buy or sell any of those things. Section 9(6) applies so that there is a presumption

[16] But partly disapplied in relation to bats, see further below.

in any proceedings that the animal in question was wild unless the contrary is shown.

Subsection (3) provides that a person shall not be guilty of an offence under subsection (2) if he shows that animal had not been killed or taken, or had been killed or taken otherwise than in contravention of the relevant provisions or that the animal or other thing in his possession or control had been sold (whether to him or to any other person) otherwise than in contravention of those provisions. Relevant provisions means the provisions of Part I of the Act or of the Conservation of Wild Creatures and Wild Plants Act 1975.

In principle the exceptions in section 10(1) and (3) discussed above also apply to section 9(5) although in practice it is difficult to see how any of these would be applicable to sales offences.

Protection of Structures or Places used for Shelter or Protection

Section 9(4)(a) of the 1981 Act renders it an offence intentionally or recklessly to damage or destroy, or obstruct access to, any structure or place which any wild animal included in Schedule 5 uses for shelter or protection. This provision was amended by the Countryside and Rights of Way Act 2000 so as to include the reference to reckless acts[17]. It is also an offence, under section 9(4)(b), to disturb any such animal while it is occupying a structure or place which it uses for that purpose.

Protection for Bats

Schedule 5 to the 1981 Act includes all species of Horseshoe bats and all species of Typical bats. At the time of the passage of the Wildlife and Countryside Bill, research conducted by the Institute of Terrestrial Ecology had shown that bats had become almost wholly dependent on buildings for roosts. There was also evidence that chemical fluids ("drins") being used to treat wood were causing serious problems for bats. These factors were the basis for making special provision for bats in section 10(5), which qualifies the exception to the disturbance offence in section 9(4) in relation to bats (and the general defence in section 10(3)(c)). In the case of bats, a person shall not be entitled to rely on the defence provided by subsection (2) or (3)(c) of section 10 as respects anything done in relation to a bat "otherwise than in the living area of a dwelling house" unless he has first

[17] Countryside and Rights of Way Act 2000, s81(1), Schedule 12 para 5(a), entry into force 30 January 2001.

notified the Nature Conservancy Council for the area in which the house is situated or, as the case may be, the act is to take place of the proposed action or operation and allowed them a reasonable time to advise him as to whether it should be carried out and, if so, the method to be used (section 10(5)as amended by the 1990 Act).

By 1984, the NCC considered in evidence to a parliamentary committee which was considering amendments to the 1981 Act, that the provisions of the Act had worked well "especially for bats". In the first full year of operation there were 1,336 applications to NCC for advice about bat roosts. The NCC did however recommend the deletion of the word "intentionally" in section 9 of the Act, especially as regarded activities which might adversely affect bats on the basis that many of the most harmful acts (treating wood etc) were not intended to harm bats but did have that effect.

New Protection for Dolphins, Whales and Basking Sharks

Subsection 4A of section 9 was inserted by the Countryside and Rights of Way Act 2000[18]. Subsection 4A provides that subject to the provisions of Part I of the Act it is an offence for any personal intentionally or recklessly to disturb any dolphin, whale or basking shark listed on Schedule 5. In introducing the proposed new provision, Minister for the Environment Michael Meacher explained that it was intended to address disturbance of these species by motorised leisure craft rather than commercial fishing. In the latter case, the exception in section 10(3)(c) (incidental effect of a lawful activity which could not reasonably be avoided) might be applicable. The difficulty with the existing provisions of section 9(4) in this case was that these species did not have readily identifiable places of shelter and thus this kind of disturbance was not caught by the existing offence in section 9(4)[19].

Section 16 Licences

Derogations from the requirements of section 9 may be granted by licences issued under section 16(3) and (4) of the 1981 Act. Subsection (3) refers to anything done under section 9(1), (2), (4) and (4A), whilst subsection (4) of section 16 is concerned with acts covered by section 9(5) (sales etc).

---

[18] Section 81(1) and Schedule 12 para 5(b).
[19] Hansard House of Commons 14 June 2000 col 1040.

The purposes for which a licence may be granted under subsection (3) include scientific and educational purposes; ringing or marking; conserving wild animals or plants; protecting any zoological or botanical collection and photography. The appropriate authority to issue all these types of licences is the Nature Conservancy Council[20]. Licences may also be obtained for the purpose of preserving public health or safety; preventing the spread of disease or for the purpose of preventing serious damage to livestock, foodstuffs for livestock, crops, vegetables, fruit, growing timber, or any other form of property or to fisheries. The appropriate authority for these licences is the agriculture Minister (section 16(9)). The appropriate authority for sales related licences is the Secretary of State for the Environment after consultation with English Nature or the relevant conservation body.

In relation to the scope of a licence, section 16(5) provides that, subjection to subsection (6), a section 16 licence may be "to any degree general or specific"; may be granted either to persons of a class or to a particular person, may be modified or revoked any time and shall be valid for the period stated in the licence. Subsection (6) deals with licences to kill wild animals and requires the derogation to specify the area within which, and the methods by which the animal may be killed and, subject to revocation, shall be valid for the period, not exceeding two years, specified in the licence. By virtue of subsection (8), the definition of a class of persons "may be framed by reference to any circumstances whatever including, in particular, their being authorised by any person".[21] A general licence, unlike a licence granted to a specific individual, does not need to be applied for, it applies automatically to cover actions carried in accordance with its terms and conditions. Whilst activities carried out under a general licence may be more difficult to monitor, it is always possible to impose a condition obliging those operating under the licence to inform the issuing authority about the scale of activity undertaken.

A number of amendments have been made to section 16 in respect of licences dealing with wild birds in order to bring the provision fully into line with the requirements of the wild birds directive[22]. These are based on a series of rulings by the ECJ on the interpretation of Article 9 of the wild birds Directive. As such, they are not directly applicable to licences relating to wild animals and plants. One of the changes made to section 16 was the

[20] Section 16(9) of the 1981 Act.
[21] Almost identical language is used in regulation 45 of the Habitats Regulations (see paragraphs (1) and (2).
[22] See discussion in Chapter 2E - Part II.

insertion of a provision stating that appropriate authority shall not grant a licence unless it is satisfied that, as regards that purpose, there is no other satisfactory solution. The position in relation to those species listed on both Schedule 5 and also on Schedule 2 of the Habitats Regulations is discussed below, essentially the derogation must comply with Article 16 of the Habitats Directive which, like Article 9 of the wild birds directive, requires that there be no satisfactory alternative to the issue of a licence. Whether a court reads in Article 16 or subsection 1A(a) of section 16, it must ensure that the requirements of Article 16 are met so far as possible. In relation to other wild animals, which are listed under Schedule 5 but no the 1994 Regulations, and which therefore are not governed by Community legislation the requirement that there be no satisfactory alternative does not apply. However in practice it may be questioned whether a reasonable issuing authority would take a different approach so that it may be expected that such licences will not be issued where there is a satisfactory alternative.

Penalties

It as an offence under section 17 of the 1981 Act to make a false statement for the purpose of obtaining a licence, punishable on summary conviction to a term of imprisonment not exceeding 6 months or to a fine not exceeding level 5 on the standard scale or to both[23] The general enforcement powers under section 19 of Act are also available, providing for powers of search, seizure and arrest in prescribed circumstances. New powers of entry for wildlife inspectors were introduced by the Countryside and Rights of Way Act 2000 in form of section 19ZA[24]. Another new provision, introduced at the same time, section 19ZB introduces a power to take samples in certain circumstances.

The Habitats Regulations 1994 and European Protected Species

At the European level, general legislation protecting certain wild animals[25] was adopted in 1992, some 13 years after the entry into force of

[23] Section 21(1) as amended by the Countryside and Rights of Way Act 2000, section 81(1) and Schedule 12. The "multiplier" provision in section 21(5) applies, so that the maximum fine shall be determined as if the person convicted had been convicted of a separate offence in respect of each bird, nest etc involved.
[24] Inserted, in relation to England and Wales, by the Countryside and Rights of Way Act 2000, s 81(1), Sch 12, para 8 (entry into force 30 January 2001).
[25] There had been some earlier legislation on specific species but most of this related to trade in products derived from those species, for example the Whale Products Directive and the Seal Pups Directive.

the wild birds Directive, in the form of the Habitats Directive. Article 12 of the Directive requires Member States to establish a system of strict protection for the animal species listed in Annex IVa to the Directive and sets out a series of prohibitions which must be imposed relating to capture and killing, disturbance, keeping and sales activities. In *ex parte Greenpeace (No2)*[26], Maurice Kay LJ rejected an argument by the claimants that Article 12(1) should be broadly construed as encompassing a freestanding general duty to protect species, additional to the specific prohibitions laid down. The UK legislation implementing the Habitats Directive is the Conservation (Natural Habitats etc) Regulations 1994[27] (the Habitats Regulations). Part III of the Conservation (Natural Habitats etc) Regulations 1994 is concerned with the protection of species and affords protection to those species of animal listed in Annex IVa to the Habitats Directive "whose natural range includes any area in Great Britain[28]". These species are described as "European Protected Species" and are listed in Schedule 2 to the Regulations.

Species listed under Schedule 3 of the Regulations (those listed in Annex V(a) of the habitats Directive, to which Article 15 applies (prohibition on indiscriminate means of capture or killing) and whose natural range includes any area of great Britain) may not be killed or taken in certain ways[29].

It is important to note that regulation 3 of the 1994 Regulations lays down a number of general duties to comply with the requirements of the directive. Of particular relevance to species protection, regulation 3(2) requires the Secretary of State, Minister of Agriculture and nature conservation bodies to exercise their functions under Part I of the Wildlife and Countryside Act 1981 so as to secure compliance with the requirements of the Habitats Directive[30]. This duty applies to any enactment relating to nature conservation including those listed. This means that in exercising the powers described earlier in this Chapter, for example licensing powers

[26] CO/1336/1999 Times 19 January 2000.
[27] SI 1994/2716 (made on 20 October 1994, entered into force 30 October 1994) as amended by SI 1997/3055 and SI 2000/192.
[28] Regulation 38.
[29] See Chapter 3B - Part II.
[30] The functions of the agriculture Minister and the Secretary of State under the regulations, so far as exercisable in relation to Wales, were transferred to the National Assembly for Wales, by the National Assembly for Wales (Transfer of Functions) Order 1999, SI 1999/672 art 2 Schedule 1.

under section 16 of the 1981 Act, those authorities must secure compliance with Directive even if the express language of the 1981 Act does not appear to require them to do so. "Nature conservation bodies" are defined in regulation 4[31] as being English Nature, the Countryside Council for Wales and Scottish Natural Heritage.

Priority Species

Priority species are defined in Article 1(h) of the Habitats Directive essentially as endangered species for the conservation of which the Community has particular responsibility in view of the proportion of their natural range which falls within European Community. These species are indicated by an asterisk in Annex II to the Directive (which lists those species of Community interest whose conservation requires the designation of special areas of conservation[32]). The interpretative notes to Annex II indicate that some species listed in Annex II are listed in Annex IV (species in need of strict protection) or V (species whose taking is subject to management measures) of the Directive but not all. It should be remembered that priority status only has a direct bearing on the habitat protection provisions of the directive/regulations. So far as species protection under Part III of the Regulations is concerned, all that is relevant is whether or not the particular species is listed on Schedule 2 or 3 to the 1994 Regulations.

Protection from killing or capture

Under regulation 39 of the 1994 Regulations, it is an offence deliberately to capture or kill a wild animal of a European protected species[33] or to take or destroy the eggs of such an animal[34] at any stage of its life[35]. These prohibitions implement the requirements of Article 12(1)(a) and (c) of the Directive. As in the case of equivalent provisions under sections 9 and 10 of the 1981 Act, in any proceedings for an offence under regulation 39, the animal in question shall be presumed to have been a wild animal unless the contrary is shown (regulation 39(5)).

A person guilty of an offence under regulation 39 is liable to a fine not exceeding level 5 on the standard scale. The anomaly between the penalties available under the 1981 Act, following amendment by the 2000 Act, is due to be removed.

---

[31] As amended by the 2000 Act, section 73(2).

[32] The habitat protection regime under the Directive is discussed below.

[33] Regulation 39(1)(a).

[34] Regulation 39(1)c).

[35] Regulation 39(3).

Regulation 40 provides for a number of exceptions to the provisions of regulation 39, in that it provides that nothing in regulation 39 shall make unlawful anything done in pursuance of a requirement by the agriculture Minister under section 98 of the Agriculture Act 1947 or section 39 of the Agriculture (Scotland) Act 1948 (prevention of damage by pests); or anything done under, or in pursuance of an order made under, the Animal Health Act 1981 (regulation 40(1)). These exceptions and those largely mirror those available under the 1981 Act (see above). It should be remembered however that, under regulation 3(4) of the Regulations, every competent authority in the exercise of any of their functions "shall have regard to the requirements of the Habitats Directive so far as they may be affected by the exercise of those functions". This would clearly include action taken under the 1947 Act for example.

In addition, a person shall not be guilty of an offence under regulation 39 by reason of the taking of a wild animal of a European protected species, if he shows that the animal had been disabled otherwise than by his unlawful act and was taken solely for the purpose of tending it and releasing it when no longer disabled. Nor will a person be guilty of an offence by reason of killing such an animal if he shows that it was so seriously disabled otherwise than by his unlawful act that there was no reasonable chance of it recovering. Nor is an offence committed if the individual can show that the act in question was the incidental result of a lawful operation and could not reasonable have been avoided (regulation 40(3)). This provision was attacked as an unlawful derogation from Article 12 by Greenpeace in its challenge to oil exploration activities in the North Sea. Their argument was rejected by the judge who accepted that the defence was within the margin of appreciation of a Member State.

Regulation 40(5) provides for further exceptions, similar to those contained in section 10 of the 1981 Act. A person will not be guilty of the offence of killing an animal if he shows that the action was necessary for the purpose of preventing serious damage to livestock, foodstuffs, crops, vegetables, fruit, growing timber or any other form of property or fisheries. Under regulation 40, it covers the owner or occupier of land on which the action is authorised to be taken, or a person authorised by the owner or occupier. A person is not be entitled to rely on the defence in regulation 40(5) as respects any action taken at any time, if it had become apparent before that time, that that action would prove necessary for the purpose in question and either a licence under regulation 44 had not been applied for as soon as reasonably practicable after that fact became apparent; or an application for such a licence had been determined (regulation 40(6)).

Article 12(4) of the directive requires Member States to establish a system to monitor the incidental capture and killing of the animal species listed in annex IVa and undertake further research or conservation measures as required in order to ensure that incidental capture or killing does not have a significant negative impact on the species concerned.

Protection of Breeding Sites or Nesting Places and Protection from Disturbance

Regulation 39(1)(b) renders it an offence deliberately to disturb a wild animal of a European protected species. This implements Article 12(1)(b) of the Directive which refers particularly to the period of "breeding, rearing, hibernation and migration". The UK provision does not differentiate in this way but as it applies generally without qualification it would appear to meet the requirements of the directive by simply making all disturbance of this kind an offence. In *Greenpeace No2*, which raised an issue as to whether oil companies, when carrying out exploration activities, had deliberately disturbed cetaceans. Maurice Kay LJ accepted a narrow interpretation of the term "deliberately" put forward by the defendant which required the offender to have essentially intended to have disturbed the species in question and rejected Greenpeace's argument that when an operator conducts an activity *in the knowledge* that such disturbance will result or knowing that it is likely or possible that it will result, he is 'deliberately' disturbing. As yet there has been no specific ruling on the interpretation of the term by the ECJ but it may be thought that that Court is likely to take a more purposive approach, particularly in circumstances where the disturbance is likely to have a predictable and significant effect on the species concerned. An indication of this is given in *Case C-103/00 Commission v Greece* which concerned disturbance of the sea turtle *caretta caretta* on the Grrek island of Zakynthos. The Court ruled that the Greek Government had failed to take the requisite specific measures to prevent the deliberate disturbance of the sea turtle during its breeding period. The disturbance in question involved riding mopeds on the beach where the turtles laid their eggs and allowing buildings to be put up on the beach. At no stage was it suggested that these activities were deliberately aimed at disturbing the turtles nor that this was a requirement of a finding that Article 12(1)(b) had been breached.[36]

It is an offence under regulation 39(1)(d) to damage or destroy a breeding site or nesting place of a European protected species. This implements the requirements of Article 12(1)(d) of the Directive. During the

[36] Judgment of 30 January 2002 [2002] ECR 1-1147.

debate on the regulations in the House of Lords[37] there was concern that this provision would criminalise accidental damage. The Government, however, confirmed that the defence in regulation 40(3)(c) if the act was the incidental result of a lawful operation and could not reasonably have been avoided.

In addition to the general exceptions in regulation 40(1) and (3)(c), regulation 40(2) provides that nothing in regulation 39(1)(b) or (d) shall make unlawful anything done within a dwelling-house, although this is qualified in relation to bats[38] (see also above). The exceptions in regulation 40(5) apply in relation to disturbance as they do in relation to the killing of European protected species (see above).

Possession and Sales Controls

Regulation 39(2) provides that it is an offence to keep or transport any live or dead wild animal or any part of or anything derived from such an animal. The remaining offences in regulation 39(2) all relate to commercial activity of one kind or another and include sale or exchange, or offering for sale or exchange. These implement Article 12(2) of the directive.

A person shall not be guilty of an offence under subsection (2) if he shows that animal had not been killed or taken, or had been lawfully taken or killed or that the animal or other thing in his possession or control had been lawfully sold (whether to him or to any other person). Lawfully means without any contravention of the 1994 Regulations or of Part I of the 1981 Act (regulation 39(4)). In principle the exceptions set out in regulation 40 paragraphs (1), (3c) and (5) also apply although it is difficult to see the circumstances in which these particular defences might be relevant to possession or sales offences.

Licences

Regulation 44 is concerned with the granting of licences to derogate from the requirements of regulation 39[39] Its provisions are very similar but

[37] Hansard HL 17 October 1994.

[38] A person shall not be entitled to rely on the defence provided by paragraph (2) or (3)(c) as respects anything done in relation to a bat otherwise than in the living area of a dwelling-house unless he had notified the appropriate nature conservation body of the proposed action or operation and allowed them a reasonable time to advise him as to whether it should be carried out and, if so, the method to be used.

[39] And also from regulations 41 (methods of killing) and 43 (wild plants) see further chapters 3B and 4.

not identical to those of section 16 of the 1981 Act discussed above. The purposes for which licences may be granted are set out in regulation 44(2). These are the same as those listed in section 16 except that photography is not included as a basis for granting a licence and there is an additional ground, associated with the preservation of public health or safety, in keeping with article 16 of the habitats directive: "preserving public health or public safety or other imperative reasons of overriding public interest including those of a social or economic nature and beneficial consequences of primary importance for the environment".

In addition to the difference in the range of purposes for which licences may be issued, the power to grant licences is qualified in accordance with the requirements of the chapeau to Article 16 (1) of the Directive. Regulation 44(3) provides that the appropriate authority shall not grant a licence under this regulation unless they are satisfied that "there is no satisfactory alternative... and that the action authorised will not be detrimental to the maintenance of the population of the species concerned at a favourable conservation status in their natural range.".[40] The identity of the appropriate authority is set out in regulation 44(4) and is similar to what is provided in section 16 (see above), being either a nature conservation body or the agriculture minister. The authority for the wider derogation in subparagraph (e) is the agriculture minister. The agriculture minister may not grant a licence without receiving advice from the nature conservation bodies as to the circumstances in which licences of that description should be granted.

Further conditions on the issue of licences are laid down in regulation 45 and these mirror those imposed on licences granted under section 16 of the 1981 Act. Included among these are the fact that the licence may be to any degree general or specific, may be granted either to persons of a class or to a particular person and may be subject to compliance with any specified conditions. Thus it is open to the relevant authority to grant general licences provided these meet with the requirements of Article 16 in particular that there is no satisfactory alternative and that the derogation is not detrimental to the maintenance of favourable conservation status.

The ECJ recently considered an infraction case brought by the Commission against the United Kingdom in respect of an alleged violation by the UK of Articles 12 and 16 of the directive. The Commission had argued that local planning authorities had not complied with the strict conditions

[40] These concepts are discussed further in Chapter 3 - Part I.

of Article 16(1)(c) in permitting a number of development projects which caused disturbance to the Great Crested Newt, a species which was protected under Article 12 of the Directive. The Commission argued that under national planning law the authorities were obliged to observe only a general requirement to take account of the presence of a protected species and, in particular, were not legally required to enquire as to alternative satisfactory solutions other than the proposed project or to check that the project complied with the prescribed purposes. The UK pointed out that not only did the local planning authorities have to have regard to the directive as a material consideration in considering whether to grant permission, but that it was also necessary for a licence to be obtained under regulation 44 from the appropriate central authority. The Court dismissed the Commission's complaint, noting that it was not disputed that regulation 44 transposed Article 16 properly into national law, and observed that the "simple fact that two authorities are called on in turn to assess the same facts does not, of itself, mean that the assessments made by the second authority systematically follow those of the first…"[41] (paragraph 26) Thus the Court was not prepared to find that the prior determination of the planning authority prejudiced the determination made under regulation 44. Presumably any future challenge would require much more specific evidence that, for example the issue of alternatives had not been considered, or considered adequately, by the licensing authority.

Under Article 16(2) of the directive, Member States are required to forward to the Commission every two years a report on the derogations it has granted. The Commission must give its opinion on the derogations within 12 months and "give an account" of that opinion to the Habitats Directive Committee. The report must specify a number of matters including the species which are subject to the derogation and the reason for the derogation, the means authorised for capture or killing and the circumstances of when and where such derogations are granted (Article 16(3)). Regulation 45(4) goes some way towards reflecting these requirements by requiring that a licence which authorises any person to kill wild animals shall specify the area within which and the methods by which the animals may be killed or taken and shall not be granted for more than two years.

It is an offence under regulation 46 to provide false information in order to obtain a licence, subject to a fine on level 4 of the standard scale.

[41] Case C-434/01 Commission v United Kingdom, judgment 6 November 2003, not yet reported.

Anything which is not done under and in accordance with the terms of a licence will not be covered by regulation 44 and will be subject therefore to the rules laid down in regulation 39 and may constitute an offence unless any of the exceptions apply.

B. Protection from Indiscriminate Killing/Taking and Inhumane Treatment

Regulation of Methods of Taking/Killing

Stricter controls on the methods which might lawfully be used to kill, injure or take wild birds were introduced under the 1981 Act. This was no doubt due to the requirements of the Wild Birds Directive, Article 8 of which provides that "In respect of the hunting, capture or killing of birds under this Directive, Member States shall prohibit the use of all means, arrangements or methods used for the large-scale or non-selective capture or killing of birds or capable of causing the local disappearance of a species, in particular the use of those listed in Annex IVa[1]". In addition Member States are required to prohibit any hunting from the modes of transport and under the conditions mentioned in Annex IV (b)[2]. The wording of Article 8 makes it clear that the list in Annex IVa is not exhaustive.

Section 5 of the 1981 Act prohibits a number of methods of killing or taking wild birds. The prohibitions apply to all species of wild bird, although a number of the exceptions relate to particular species (as to which see below). First, s5(1)(a) renders it an offence to set in position any of the articles listed in that subsection, being of such a nature and so placed so as to be calculated to cause bodily injury to any wild bird coming into contact with it. The articles listed are any spring, trap, gin, snare, hook and line, any electrical device for killing, stunning or frightening or any poisonous, poisoned or stupefying substance. In contrast to the other offences created under s5, there is no reference to the purpose of the action in this subsection. It is the nature of the article concerned and the way it is placed which gives rise to the prohibition.

The remaining offences created under section 5 all refer to the use of articles for the purpose of killing or taking a wild bird. Under section 5(1)(b), it is an offence to use any of the articles listed in s5(1)(a), whether or not of such a nature and so placed as to be calculated to cause bodily injury to any wild bird, or to use any net, baited board, bird-lime or substance of a like nature to bird-lime.

---

[1] Annex IV(a) refers inter alia to explosives, nets and semi-automatic weapons.

[2] These include aircraft and motor vehicles and boats driven at a speed exceeding 5 kilometres an hour.

The articles listed in section 5(1)(c) are not specifically designed to kill or take birds but that subsection makes it an offence to use them for that purpose. Those articles are any bow or crossbow; any explosive other than ammunition for a firearm (defined); any automatic or semi-automatic weapon; any shotgun of which the barrel has an internal diameter at the muzzle of more than one and three quarter inches; any device for illuminating a target or any sighting device for night shooting; any form of artificial lighting or any mirror or other dazzling device; any gas or smoke not falling within paras (a) and (b) of section 5 or any chemical wetting agent.[3]

The use of decoys is prohibited under section 5(1)(d), along with the use of any sound recording or any live bird [or] other animal whatever which is tethered, or which is secured by means of braces or similar appliances or which is blind, maimed[4] or injured. It is an offence under s5(1)(e) to use any mechanically propelled vehicle in immediate pursuit of a wild bird for the purpose of taking or killing it.

An important amendment to section 5 was introduced by the Wildlife and Countryside (Amendment) Act 1991. That Act introduced S5(1)(f) which creates an offence of knowingly causing or permitting to be done any of the acts mentioned in s 5(1)(a)-(e) and which do not fall within the exceptions set out in s5(5). The amendment was introduced by means of a private members bill, conceived by the RSPB, which was particularly concerned about the scale of unlawful killings of birds of prey such as the Red Kite. The bill was to strengthen protection in such cases by closing a loophole which had become evident in the 1981 Act and allowing the prosecution of those who directed or allowed others to commit offences of using illegal methods of killing wildlife. Concern had been expressed during the passage of the Wildlife and Countryside Bill that employers were tacitly encouraging gamekeepers to commit offences under the Act. The Government's view at the time was that this would be covered under s35 Magistrates Court Act on aiding and abetting[5].

[3] During the passage of the bill, the rationale for outlawing some of the methods was discussed: "It is just possible that the reason we do not like semi-automatic shotguns is that we think there is something ever so slightly common involved in them." Commented the Earl of Onslow, Hansard col 721 E. The Government assured him that it was simply a matter of what the directive required.

[4] See Holden v Lancashire Magistrates Court (1998) 162 JP 789; [1998] COD 429, in which the Divisional Court held that clipping wing feathers was not maiming because the effect was not permanent, even though the evidence was that the operation was repeated in order to ensure that the birds in question could never fly.

[5] Hansard, House of Lords, 27 January 1981, col 725.

An illustration of this loophole was given during debate on the bill on its Third Reading in the House of Commons. Mr Ron Davies MP referred to a case in Scotland where a gamekeeper was prosecuted and convicted for laying poisonous substances that brought about the death of legally protected birds of prey. He informed the court that he had been instructed by his employer to lay the poison, was in fear of his job and so followed instructions. He was found guilty and convicted of the offence but his employer escaped prosecution having committed no offence under the terms of the Act.[6]

Defence/Exceptions

In proceedings under s5(1)(a), it is a defence to show that the article was set in position for the purpose of killing or taking, in the interests of public health, forestry, fisheries or nature conservation, any wild animals which could be lawfully killed or taken by those means and that the accused took all reasonable precautions to prevent injury thereby to wild birds (section 5(4)). The 1991 Amendment Act introduced an equivalent defence in cases of causing or permitting someone to do an act under s5(1)(a) (subsection 4A).

A number of further exceptions are set out in subsection (5). Nothing in subsection (1) shall make unlawful the use of a cage trap or net by an authorised person for the purpose of taking a bird listed in Part II of Schedule 2. It should be remembered however that this is Schedule is currently empty. Nor is it clear why what is essentially a welfare provision should be waived in the case of certain species, even those considered by some to be "pests". The other exception of practical relevance relates to the use of a cage trap or net for the purpose of taking any game bird if it is shown that the taking of the bird is solely for the purpose of breeding (section 5(5)(c)), but nothing in the subsection makes lawful the use of any net for taking birds in flight or the use for taking birds on the ground of the use of any net which is projected or propelled otherwise than by hand.

Welfare of Captive Birds

The welfare needs of captive birds is also addressed to a degree in the 1981 Act. Interestingly these provisions do not derive from the requirements of the wild birds directive. Section 8 makes it an offence for any person to keep or confine any bird whatever in any cage or other

[6] Hansard HC Session 1990-91 vol 22 March 1991 col 574-575.

receptacle which is not sufficient in height, length or breadth to permit the bird to stretch its wings freely. Subsection (2) sets a number of exceptions to this prohibition. The offence does not apply to poultry. Nor does it apply to the keeping or confining of any bird while that bird is in the course of conveyance by an means (section 8(2)(a)); while that bird is being shown in public exhibition or competition (provide the time does not exceed 72 hours) (section 8(2)(b)); while that bird is undergoing examination or treatment by a vet (section 8(2)(c))[7].

It is also an offence, under subsection (3) to promote, arrange, receive money for (and a range of related acts) any event whatever at which birds are liberated by hand or by any other means for the purpose of being shot immediately after their liberation. Owners or occupiers of land who permit such events to take place on their land are also guilty of an offence.

The penalties for these offences are set out in section 21 of the Act. A person guilty of an offence under section 8 shall be liable on summary conviction to imprisonment for a term not exceeding 6 months or to a fine not exceeding level 5 of the standard scale or to both. The usual multiplier provision applies by virtue of subsection (5) and the court shall order the forfeiture of any bird in respect of which the offence was committed and may order the forfeiture of anything used to commit the offence (section 21(6)).

[7] See RSPCA v Shilton unreported June 30 2003, QBD where the court considered the scope of the exceptions in section 8(2).

C. Badgers

Although badgers in the UK are not currently endangered[1] they are protected under specific legislation, currently the 1992 Protection of Badgers Act, which is designed to address the particular types of persecution faced by badgers, including baiting and digging for sport. The fact that the badger is also protected under the 1981 Wildlife and Countryside Act[2], as well as an international conservation treaty, the 1979 Bern Convention,[3] means that the law relating to badgers provides a good illustration of the way in which conservation and welfare considerations can interrelate in legislation relating to wildlife[4]. A recent House of Commons Select Committee Report, noting that the badger is not endangered in the UK[5], described the UK legislation on badgers as being welfare-based rather than aimed at conservation[6]. As discussed below, both welfare concerns and conservation issues were recently raised in the context of Bern Convention discussions of the Government's culling trial.

[1] The badger population is estimated to be between 250,000 and 400,000 [July submission paragraph 3] According to the UK's Annual Report to the Standing Committee to the Bern Convention in Nov/Dec 2000, the badger population of Great Britain is estimated at over 300,000.

[2] The badger is one of the animals listed in Schedule 6 to the Wildlife and Countryside Act 1981 which means that, under s11 of the Act and subject to the exceptions set out in Part I of the Act, certain methods of killing or taking badgers including the use of snares, traps and gas, are prohibited, see further Chapter 3B.

[3] The badger (meles meles) is protected under Appendix III of the Bern Convention. Badgers are not protected under the EC Habitats Directive. At the international level therefore, debates relating to the conservation of badgers in the UK, in particular the debate about the recent plans for a controlled cull, have taken place in the Berne Convention Standing Committee

[4] Not all threats to badgers result from deliberate persecution of course, for example it is estimated that 50,000 are killed each year on the roads, Harris, Cresswell, Reason & Cresswell "An integrated approach to monitoring badger population changes in Britain" In DR McCullough and RH Barnett (Eds) Wildlife 2001: Populations, Barking Elsevier.

[5] See further Griffiths and Thomas "The Conservation and Management of the European Badger (Meles Meles)" Nature and Environment Report No 90, Council of Europe (1997). The report recommended however that the UK apply "increased vigilance" in relation to the protection of the badger and in particular aim at considerably better enforcement of conservation legislation and a reduction in road-traffic mortality (page 56).

[6] See the Fifth Report of the House of Commons Select Committee on Agriculture, 1998-99 Session, 20 April 1999, Section II "Bovine Tuberculosis in the UK", paragraph 22. See also the evidence of the NFBG explaining the emergence of badger groups as a response to the persecution of badgers in the UK, minutes of evidence of the NFBG (February 1999) paragraph 255 et seq.

Special Protection for Badgers

Badgers have had legal protection in Britain since at least 1835. UK legislation on badgers predated the Bern Convention and in some respects goes beyond its requirements. The special protection afforded to badgers aims to protect them from persecution, in particular from badger baiting in which badgers are pitted against dogs, usually terriers, for "sport".[7]

The Protection of Badgers Act 1992

The 1992 Act consolidated previous legislation: the Badgers Act 1973, the Badgers Act 1991 and the Badgers (Further Protection) Act 1991. The current Act entered into force 16 October 1992. It imposes restrictions on the killing, taking, injuring of badgers and specifically prohibits cruel treatment of various kinds. It also protects badger setts and imposes certain sales controls. These protective provisions are subject to certain exceptions and the possibility of obtaining a licence to carry out activities which would otherwise be prohibited.

Taking, killing or injuring badgers

Except as permitted by or under the Act, it is an offence under section 1 of the Act to wilfully kill, injure or take a badger or to attempt to do any of these things9 . "Badger" is defined as any animal of the species *meles meles* (section 14). In relation to proceedings for an offence under section 1 involving attempted acts, a statutory presumption operates. Where there is evidence from which it could reasonably be concluded that, at the material time, the accused was attempting to wilfully kill, injure or take a badger, the accused shall be presumed to have been attempting to kill a badger unless the contrary is shown (s1(2)).

Except as permitted by or under the Act, possession of any dead badger or any part of, or anything derived from, a dead badger is an offence, as is having such things under one's control (section 1(3)) There is a defence to s1(3) offences where the accused can show that the badger was not killed, or was not killed in contravention of the Act (or the 1973 Act). It is also a defence to show that the badger or other thing in his possession or control was sold (whether to him or someone else) and at the time of purchase, the purchaser had no reason to believe that the badger had been killed in contravention of any of those provisions (s1(4)). Sale includes hire, barter and exchange (s14). The owner or occupier of any land where a person is found committing an offence under s1 (or her servant or any constable) is entitled to require that person to quit that land forthwith and to give their name and address. If the person then wilfully remains on the land or refuses to give their full name and address, they are guilty of an offence (s1(5)).

A number of exceptions to section 1 are set out in section 7 of the Act. These are similar to those contained in section 10 of the Wildlife and Countryside Act 1981 (relating to the protection of wild animals) and provide that a person shall not be guilty of an offence under section 1(1) by reason of killing or taking or attempting to kill or take a badger, or injuring a badger in the course of attempting to kill or take it, if he can show that his action was necessary for the purpose of preventing serious damage to land, crops or any other form of property. Subsection (2) provides that this defence does not apply if it had become apparent before it was taken that the action would prove necessary for such a purpose and either a section 10 license was not applied for as soon as practicable or an application had been determined.

Cruelty

Cruel ill-treatment of a badger is an offence under s2 of the Act as is using badger tongs in the course of killing or taking, or attempting to kill or take a badger; except as permitted by or under the Act, digging for a badger, or using, for the purpose of killing or taking, any firearm other than those specified in paragraph (d) of subsection (1). Cruel ill-treatment is not defined in the 1992 Act but some indication of its meaning is provided by a case brought under the 1911 Protection of Animals Act, Bandiera and Brannigan v RSPCA. In that case, Lord Justice Schiemann in the Divisional Court considered that "cruelty" was best defined as "causing unnecessary suffering". Whilst the issue as to whether a particular act amounted to cruel ill-treatment within the meaning of the 1911 Act was essentially a question of fact in any case, if the risk of injury to the animal concerned was very high, a finding of causation (as to cruel ill-treatment) was very likely[10].

[7] The 1911 Protection of Animals Act forbids the fighting or baiting of any animal (section 1) but only applies to domestic or captive animals and does not therefore cover most instances of baiting wild badgers (section 15).

[8] The 1991 Act had closed various loopholes, inter alia by protecting badger setts as well as badgers.

[9] "Lamping" is the colloquial name for shooting [animals] in the evening and early in the night, after identifying and dazzling them by the use of a bright light. See Murphy v Rotherwick [1999] All ER (D) 1508]

[10] Bandeira and Brannigan v Royal Society for the Prevention of Cruelty to Animals, 28 February 2000 164 JP 307

In the case of the offence of digging for a badger, section 2(2) of the 1992 Act creates a presumption of guilt where there is evidence from which it could reasonably be concluded that, at the material time, the accused was digging for a badger, unless the contrary can be shown[11]. The Royal Society for Nature Conservation has proposed that "dig for any badger" be replaced by "dig into a badger sett" as in s(2)(c) of the Badgers Act 1973 in order to facilitate successful prosecution. This proposal has not been taken up.

Interfering with badger setts

A badger sett is defined in s14 of the 1992 Act as "any structure or place which displays signs indicating current use by a badger". The offences in s3 which relate to interference with badger setts, cover both intentional and reckless acts[12] and include: damaging a badger sett or any part of it; destroying a sett; obstructing access to, or any entrance of a sett; causing a dog to enter a sett or disturbing a badger when it is occupying a sett.

In *Director of Public Prosecution v Green & others*[13], the respondents had permission to be on land adjoining the land on which badger setts were situated. They arrived at the site of the badger setts by mistake with five dogs and two spades to flush out rabbits. The police found them digging into the soil but they had not broken into the tunnel system. The respondents were charged with interfering with a badger sett by damaging it with intent or being reckless as to whether their actions would have that consequence contrary to s 3(a) of the Act. On appeal, the prosecution submitted that the definition of a badger sett in s 14 of the 1992 Act, namely 'any structure or place which displays signs indicating current use by a badger' included the surface area above the system of tunnels and chambers.

The judge held that the phrase 'badger sett' referred only to the tunnels and chambers constructed by the badgers and the areas immediately outside the entrance holes. It also might apply in other circumstances, for instance, where badgers had occupied culverts or disused sheds as their shelter and refuge. It did not, however, include the surface area above that system of tunnels and chambers. According to him, section 14 did not

[11] For a case in which the Divisional Court considered the relative importance of expert evidence (as to the status of the sett) and issues of fact, see R v Telford ex parte Fishwick, CO/188/91, 11 October 1991.

[12] For confirmation that s3 offences are not absolute offences but require evidence of intention or recklessness see the Divisional Court's judgment in West London Magistrates Court v RSPCA, CO 3431/94, 14 December 1994.

[13] [2000]All ER (D)839.

define a badger sett so much as indicate Parliament's intention, that where the phrase 'badger sett' appeared in the Act what was being referred to was any structure or place which displayed signs indicating current use by a badger, and did not to apply to tunnels and chambers no longer in current use. He added that Parliament could not have intended that a person by walking over a badger sett while walking in the countryside committed a criminal offence. The appeal was dismissed.

Various exceptions to these offences are set out in section 8 of the 1992 Act. The first set of exceptions cover any section 3 offence and are equivalent to the necessity exception in relation to section 1 offences (see above) which exempts actions necessary for the purpose of protecting serious damage to land, crops, poultry and other property. This is made subject to the proviso that the defence does not apply to any action taken at any time it if had become apparent, before that time, that the action would proved necessary for such a purpose and either a section 10 license was not applied for as soon as practicable or an application had been determined. The second set of exceptions covers the offences of damaging, obstructing or disturbance of a sett (paragraphs (a), (c) and (e) of section 3 respectively) and applies where the offence can be shown to be "the incidental result of a lawful operation" which could not reasonably have been avoided.

A further exception also covers the offences of damaging, obstructing or disturbance (paragraphs (a), (c) and (e) respectively) and relates to certain actions related to fox hunting. The exception only applies under very specific conditions as laid down in section 8. A person will not be guilty of an offence under Section 3 (a), (c) or (e) by reason of obstructing any entrance of a sett for the purpose of hunting foxes with hounds if he takes no action other than obstructing such entrances, does not dig into the tops or sides of the entrances and complies with subsection (5) as to the materials used to obstruct the entrances and with subsection (6) as to how and when the materials are to be placed and removed. The materials permitted under section 8(5) are limited to untainted straw or hay, leaf litter, bracken or loose soil (s8(5)(a)) or a bundle of sticks or faggots, or paper sacks either empty or filled with the materials referred to in paragraph (a) (s8(5)(b)). In addition, the materials must not be packed hard into the entrances and in the case of the materials listed in s8(5)(a) can only be placed in the entrances on the day of the hunt or after midday on the preceding day. In the case of the materials listed in s8(5)(b), the materials can only be placed in the sett on the day of the hunt and must be removed on the same day (s8(6)(b)). "Loose soil" is to be construed ejusdem generis with the four other materials listed in s8(5)(a) as being soil which is readily removable and of an obstructive nature which is not permanent.[14]

Furthermore, in all cases the person must be acting with the authority of the owner or occupier of the land and the authority of a recognised Hunt. A recognised Hunt means one which is recognised by the Master of Hounds Association, the Association of Masters of Harriers and Beagles or the Central Committee of Fell Packs. Each recognised Hunt must keep a register of persons authorised to act under subsection (4). A person is not guilty of an offence under section 3(a), (c) or (e) by reason of his hounds barking at a sett provided they are withdrawn as soon as reasonably practicable (subsection 8). It should be noted that the hunting exception has been repealed, in relation to Scotland by the Protection of Wild Mammals (Scotland) Act 2002 (section 11) as of 1 August 2002.

Selling and Possession of Live Badgers

Except as permitted by or under the Act, if a person sells a live badger or offers one for sale or has a live badger in his possession or control, he commits an offence under s4 of the Act. A person does not commit an offence by reason of having a live badger in his possession or under his control if this occurs in the course of his business as a carrier or it has been disabled otherwise than by his act and is taken solely for the purpose of tending it and it is necessary for that purpose for the badger to remain in his possession or under his control (section 9).

Marking and Ringing

Unless authorised by a licence issued under s10 of the Act, it is an offence under s5 to mark or attach any ring, tag or marking device to a badger other than one which is lawfully in one's possession by virtue of a s10 licence. This appears to mean that an individual only needs to obtain a s10 licence to mark or ring a badger where it is not already in his or her possession by virtue of a s10 licence.

---

[14] See Lovett v Bussey, an appeal to the High Court by way of case stated from the Crown Court, Times 24 April 1998, CO/4119/97. The High Court also noted that the circumstances in which the soil is placed in the sett may also be relevant to determining whether or not the exception applies, for example if it is raining and the soil becomes compacted almost immediately the exception will not apply. This is a matter of fact and degree for the trial court.

General Exceptions

In addition to the specific exceptions to the various offences described above, the Act also provides for four general exceptions. The first two relate to disabled and injured badgers. A person who takes or attempts to take a badger which has been "disabled otherwise than by his act" and is taken or to be taken solely for the purpose of tending it does not commit an offence. Nor is an offence committed where a person kills or attempts to kill a badger which appears to be so seriously injured or in such a condition that to kill it would be "an act of mercy".

It is not an offence to unavoidably kill or injure a badger as an incidental result of a lawful action. This provision is similar to the exceptions contained in sections 4(2)(c), 10(3)(c) and 13(3) of the Wildlife and Countryside Act 1981[15]

Finally it is not an offence to do anything which is authorised under the Animals (Scientific Procedures) Act 1986 (c14). The 1986 Act regulates the carrying out of experiments and other scientific procedures on live animals. The act defines regulated procedures as those that may cause a protected animal[16] pain, suffering, distress or lasting harm.[17]

Licences

Section 10 makes provision for the granting of licences to do, subject to compliance with any conditions in the licence, certain acts otherwise prohibited by the Act[18]. Certain licences may be granted by the "relevant conservancy council" which in England is English Nature, while others may be issued by the Minister for Agriculture as regards England or the National Assembly for Wales as regards Wales. Although there is no

[15] Discussed in Chapters 2 and 3 - Part I.

[16] Section 1, the Animals (Scientific Procedures) Act 1986.

[17] Section 2, the Animals (Scientific Procedures) Act 1986.

[18] As far as the position under international law is concerned, under Article 9 of the Bern Convention, derogations from the provisions of Articles 7 which direct Contracting parties to take the appropriate and necessary legislative and administrative measures to ensure the protection of specified wild fauna and 8 directing Contracting Parties to prohibit the use of specified means of taking and killing of protected species, may be made on certain grounds and subject to certain general conditions. This is discussed further below in the context of the culling trial.

provision for a closed season for badgers, Ministers take the badger breeding season into account when determining licensing applications[19].

English Nature (or the Countryside Council for Wales or Scottish National Heritage) may grant licences to kill or take badgers within specified areas and by any means specified in the licence for scientific or educational purposes or for the conservation of badgers. Such licences may also be issued to authorise the sale or possession of a specified number of badgers or to interfere with a badger sett within a specified area and by any means specified. Licences may also be issued for the purposes of zoos or collections, ringing or marking (subsections (b) and (c)). Licences may be granted to interfere with a sett within a specified area and by specified means for the purpose of development under the planning legislation (subsection (d)) or for the purpose of the preservation or investigation of monuments under the Ancient Monuments and Archeological Areas Act 1979 (subsection (e)). Licences are also available to interfere with a sett within a specified area for the purposes of investigating whether any offence has been committed or gathering any evidence in connection with court proceedings (f).[20]

In the case of licences under section 10(1)(d), PPG9 requires local authorities to advise those applying for planning permission in an area known to contain badger setts that they must comply with the provisions of the 1992 Act and notes that local authorities and all other public bodies need a licence in respect of any development which they themselves carry out in areas where there are known to be badger setts[21].

The Minister for Agriculture (or the National Assembly for Wales) may grant licences to kill or take badgers or interfere with setts within a specified area for the purposes of preventing the spread of disease (section 10(2)(a)) or for the purpose of preventing serious damage to land, crops poultry or any other form of property (subsection (2)(b)). She may grant a

[19] HC Hansard 2 November 1998 Mr Rooker. This issue came up in the context of the TB culling trial where the original plan was modified to avoid culling during the lactation period by imposing a three month "closed season". The NFBG subsequently expressed concern that, despite these measures, some cubs are starving when their mothers are killed as part of the trial, see news release dated 23 May 2000 www geocities.com/Rainforest/Canopy/2626.

[20] In 1994 English Nature issued a total of 212 licences, 170 were for the purposes of development, 140 for science/educational/conservation purposes and 102 for the purposes of investigating offences See HL Hansard answer to written question Col 862, 28 October 1994.

[21] See paragraph 48 of PPG9.

licence to interfere with a sett for the purpose of any agricultural or forestry operation (paragraph c) or for certain operations relating to waterworks, sea defence or drainage including those under the Land Drainage Act 1991 (paragraph (d)). In relation to licences under (b), (c) or (d) the Minister must from time to time consult with the appropriate Conservancy Council as to the exercise of her functions and shall not grant any licence unless she has been advised as to the circumstances under which such licences should be granted.[22]

Either the Minister or English Nature may grant a licence to authorise interference with a sett within a specified area and by specified means for the purpose of controlling foxes in order to protect livestock, game or wildlife (section 10(3)).

It is an offence under section 10(8) to contravene or to fail to comply with a condition imposed under a section 10 licence.

Enforcement and Penalties

Where he has reasonable grounds for suspecting that a person is committing an offence under the Act (or has committed an offence under 1973 Act) and that evidence of the commission of the offence is to be found on that person or any vehicle or article he may have with him, section 11 of the Act gives a constable the power to stop and search, without a warrant, a person or vehicle or article which the person has with him (s11(a)), seize and detain evidence or material which is liable to be forfeited under s12(4) of the Act.

The penalties for the various offences are set in section 12 and include on summary conviction in relation to offences under section 1(1) or (3), 2 or 3 imprisonment up to 6 months or a fine level 5 on the standard scale or both. Offences under sections 4, 5, 10(8) or 13(7) carry a fine of level 5 on the standard scale. If the offence involves more than one badger the maximum fine may be imposed as if the person had been convicted of a separate offence in relation to each badger. The offence of refusing to leave land or give one's name or address under s1(5) carries a maximum fine of level 3.

[22] In 1994, MAFF issued 205 licences for the prevention of serious damage, 58 for forestry purposes and 28 for watercourse or drainage purposes. See HL October 1994 Mrs Browning.

The magistrates' court must order the forfeiture of any badger or badger skin in respect of which an offence was committed and may order the forfeiture of any weapon or article in respect of or by means of which an offence was committed (s12(4))[23]. There is special provision to deal with situations where dogs have been used in the commission of offences under sections 1(1), 2 or 3 or have at least been present[24]. Under section 13 the court has the power, in addition to or in substitution for any other punishment, to order either the destruction or disposal of the dog or the disqualification of the offender for having custody of a dog for such period as it thinks fit. Where an order for destruction or disposal is made in respect of a dog which is not owned by the offender, the owner of the dog may appeal to the Crown Court against the order (s13(3)).[25]

Bovine Tuberculosis

The area of greatest controversy concerning badgers is their link, if any, to the incidence of bovine tuberculosis in cattle and the Government's policy of conducting a controlled badger cull aimed at establishing the extent of such a link. Some of the legal issues raised in relation to the Government's current policy are discussed below.

The existence and nature of a link between the incidence of tuberculosis in badgers and in cattle first became a focus in the early 1970s, following the discovery of infected badgers in the vicinity of infected herds. Badger culling was carried out in an attempt to stem the incidence of TB in cattle. 26 Culling has remained controversial with badger conservation groups however, who argue that there has been too much emphasis on the role of badgers as opposed to other sources of or contributors to cattle infection, including transmission via other species of wildlife and inadequate husbandry practices. Successive culling policies have failed to eradicate the disease which has recently begun to rise in the cattle

[23] See the similar provision in s21(6) of the Wildlife and Countryside Act 1981.

[24] Depending on the circumstances, where dogs are used in pursuit of badgers, an offence may be committed in respect of the dog under the 1911 Protection of Animals Act, for an example see Bandeira and another v the RSPCA, QBD, CO 2066/99, 28 February 2000.[[2000] All ER (D) 258]

[25] Figures from the Home Office Court Proceedings Database indicate that in 1997 there were 44 convictions for offences under the 1992 Act excluding s13 for which there were 7 Convictions, HC Hansard Written Answers 24 February 1999.

[26] See the Fifth Report of the House of Commons Select Committee on Agriculture, 1998-99 Session, 20 April 1999, Section II "Bovine Tuberculosis in the UK", paragraph 8.

population[27]. Described recently by a MAFF minister as "perhaps the biggest problem after BSE"[28], the rising incidence of TB among cattle led the Government in 1996 to commission an independent scientific review to report into the incidence of TB in cattle and badgers and the assess the evidence of a link between them. The review was chaired by Professor John Krebs, then Chief Executive of the National Environment Research Council. The Krebs Report was published in December 1997 and found that there was compelling evidence that badgers "are a significant source of infection in cattle" but acknowledged that most of this evidence was indirect, in the nature of correlations of incidence of infection rather than in the form of direct evidence of cause and effect and stated that it was not possible to state quantitatively what contribution badgers made to infection, nor to compare the effectiveness of culling badgers with not culling them in the context of controlling the disease[29].

The Krebs Report made a series of recommendations as to how to address this "complex problem" and, drawing on these recommendations, the Government announced on 17 August 1998 the adoption of a "five point plan" which included a 10-15 year research programme into the development of a vaccine for cattle, minimising the risks to public health, and, most controversially, a controlled cull of badgers in order to quantify the impact of culling badgers and gather more information about the nature and extent of the link. The Government also established an Independent Scientific Group (the Bourne Group) to advise on the conduct of the trial. The trial, which began in the autumn of 1998, was to be carried out in 30 areas covering approximately $100km^2$ each. These areas were selected on the basis that they were at the greatest risk from bovine TB and grouped together in so-called "triplets". In each triplet, the three culling treatments were adopted (one per area). The three treatments were "proactive" culling in which all badgers would be killed, "reactive" culling in which only badgers with access to infected farms would be killed and "no cull" areas which were designed to act as a control . The work of the Bourne Group, and its approach towards finding a sustainable basis for future cattle TB control policies, was set out in its Second Report "An Epidemiological

[27] Ibid, paragraph 25.See also the UK submission to the Bern Convention Standing Committee July 1999, paragraph 8 (available at www.maff.gov.uk/animalh). Nearly 7000 cattle were slaughtered in 1999 (What is TB? Maff website ibid).

[28] House of Commons Debate on Badgers and Bovine Tuberculosis, Hansard 10 February 2000 (Column 148WH), Elliot Morley

[29] The House of Commons Select Committee, at Supra n. 26, paragraph 40, has accepted Krebs conclusion that there was compelling but not conclusive evidence of a link between badgers and cattle tb and that a field trial is required to test and quantify the link between badgers and cattle.

Investigation into Bovine Tuberculosis" which was published in February 2000.[30]

The trial was evaluated to check that the procedures for surveying, trapping and culling were effective, and to verify the Bourne Group's statistical calculations. To make sure the report was comprehensive, an appointed auditor was given unrestricted access to trial staff and documents and a report was published on 8 February 2001, along with the Government's and the Group's responses. Earlier a welfare veterinarian appointed to carry out a review of procedures to make sure that badgers were trapped and killed humanely had submitted a report in October 2000 which stated that the Badger culling procedures were humane. His report made a series of recommendations covering training, procedures and future studies.[31]

The Bern Convention

Together with detailed criticisms as to the scientific validity of the cull, its legality under the Bern Convention was also questioned by those opposed to the trial. The Bern Convention Standing Committee operates a procedure known as the opening and closing of files, which is used to consider complaints that Parties have breached their obligations under the Convention.[32] This procedure was used to address concerns raised about the legality of the culling trial under Articles 7,8 and 9 of the Convention. In response to complaints from a number of non-governmental organizations concerned with badger conservation, including the National Federation of Badger Groups, the Bern Standing Committee adopted a Recommendation (No 68) in December 1998 calling on the UK government to postpone the planned cull for one year while the legality of the trial under the Convention was examined further by the Standing Committee and to explore other satisfactory solutions to the problem of bovine TB. Whilst the Recommendation was accepted as not legally binding, the UK government stated that it took the recommendation seriously and recognised that it could lead to the eventual adoption of a resolution which would itself be binding on the UK[33]. It took the view that would have been unreasonable to delay the trial in view of the serious nature of the concern and the fact that delay would have compromised the survey and other data collected.

[30] See: http://www.defra.gov.uk/

[31] For the Reports see: http://www.defra.gov.uk/animalh/tb/default.htm

[32] The purpose of the procedure is to find a satisfactory solution to problems encountered in implementation and monitor the means chosen to resolve them (Draft Recommendation T-PVS(95)12).

[33] See Government Response to the Fifth Report referred to at note 26 supra, 30 June 1999.

In relation to Article 7, critics of the trial said that culling on this scale was inconsistent with the protection required under that Article, which requires Parties to protect Appendix III species inter alia by regulating exploitation and sale. They argued that the trial would only be lawful therefore if it were to be covered by Article 9 of the Convention dealing with exceptions/derogations (as to which see below)[34]. The UK responded by noting that badgers were not subject to exploitation (presumably implying legal exploitation given the continuing illegal exploitation of badgers for sport in the UK) but went on to point out that the trial would not endanger the national population of badgers nor, due to the capture efficiency of the trial, lead to local disappearance in the trial areas.

Article 8 of the Convention requires Parties to prohibit all indiscriminate means of capture or killing of Appendix III species and the use of all means capable of causing local disappearance or serious disturbance, including the means set out in Appendix IV of the Convention. Among the arguments raised by the NFBG was the fact that, in their view, the trial was designed to cause local disappearance of badgers in some areas and that the trapping of badgers would be carried out on a large scale (a means of capture prohibited under Appendix IV[35]). The UK referred to s11 of the 1981 Act which implements this Article for badgers and other species and confirmed that indiscriminate means would not be used, pointing to the decision to use cage traps to catch the badgers to be culled, which would allow non-target species to be released. Reiterating its arguments on Article 7, the UK pointed that due to scale of the culling trial and the methods used the national population would not be endangered and that local eradication would not occur[36].

Having argued that the trial constituted a breach of Articles 7 and 8 of the Convention, critics went on to argue that the trial also contravened Article 9 of the Convention which sets out the conditions under which derogations from Articles 7 and 8 made be made. Two of the conditions are general: first, that there be no other satisfactory solution and second that the exception "will not be detrimental to the survival of the populations concerned". In relation to the first condition, they stated that the cull was not a "satisfactory solution" to the problem of bovine TB and, furthermore, that because of its "obsession with badgers", the UK government had not

[34] NFBG Information Paper for the Berne Convention, 24 November 1998, paragraph 3.2-3.3.

[35] NFBG Information Paper for the Berne Standing Committee, 24 November 1998, paragraph 4.5.

[36] Submission to the Bern Convention Standing Committee July 1999, see paragraphs 45-51.

adequately explored alternative solutions to the problem[37] such as changes in cattle husbandry practices. Reference was made to Standing Committee Recommendation No 2 of 1993 on the scope of Articles 8 and 9 (paragraph 7 of which), which indicates that the existence of another satisfactory solution was to be determined by considering possible less damaging alternatives which themselves need to be assessed against the basis for the derogation. Second, they argued that the trial was designed to eradicate certain local populations and that moreover if it was shown that culling was effective in controlling bovine TB the Government would be under enormous pressure to extend the practice more widely which would perpetuate the breach[38]. They also argued that the trial did not fall within any of the specified bases for derogation set out in Article 9.

The UK Government responded by emphasising that the trial was part of a broader strategy to address the problem of bovine TB and that all parts of the strategy were required to ensure that a scientifically sound basis for future policy could be found. Noting that Recommendation No 2 of 1993 had indicated the need to search for alternative solutions, the UK stated that the options had been thoroughly examined, referring to the scientific inquiries which had been carried out, and stated that it had reviewed all the available evidence, including the views of interested parties all of which confirmed in its view that the trial was part of a search for satisfactory solution to the problem[39]. As to the survival of the populations concerned, it was pointed out the design of the trial and the level of capture would ensure that badgers were not totally removed from a single area. The Government stated that the legal basis for the culls was the prevention of serious damage to livestock, public health and research.

One interesting point raised by the NGOs was the issue of Crown immunity. The Government accepted that it was bound by the terms of the Berne Convention at the international level, but argued that its own servants were not bound by the terms of the Badger Act 1992 (although it said that they would follow them in practice)[40]. This was disputed by the NGOs.

In November 1999, the Standing Committee considered the issue again and concluded that the trial did not contravene the Bern Convention.

37 NFBG Information Paper, note 13 supra, 5.2-5.3.

38 Ibid, paragraph 5.5.

39 Ibid, July paragraphs 60-62.

40 See written answer March 1999 Mr Rooker, saying that the 1992 Act does not bind the Crown and that the licence requirements in the 1992 Act do not apply to the Minister so the culling trial is taking place with the agreement of landowners and conducted by Ministry Staff [Hansard: HC Written Answers 24 March 1999 pt 27].

The file was accordingly closed and the UK asked to provide annual updates on the conduct of the trial. In the annual report for the 20th Standing Committee of the Bern Convention in December 2000, the UK government stated that it was undertaking research on the development of potential TB vaccines for badgers.

It stated that as: "... at 1 September 2000, eight of the ten trial areas have been put in place, with the two remaining areas due to be announced at the end of September. Culling operations have so far begun in five of the eight areas. The number of badgers killed in the trial from December 1998 to 25 August 2000 was 1953." According to the Report, the estimate made by Professor Krebs, that about 12,500 badgers might be killed in the trial as a whole, was unlikely to be exceeded. Further, the [Bourne] Independent Scientific Group has confirmed to the UK Government that the trial remains on course to produce valid results by the end of 2004, and possibly as early as the end of 2002 if there is a strong association between badgers and TB in cattle.[41]

Suspension of Reactive Culling

The likely outcome of the trial remains somewhat unclear. In February 2003 the Government published a consultation paper on the options for TB control policy options for 2003. Later that year, on 4 November 2003, the Government announced the immediate suspension of reactive culling in the light of findings of the Independent Scientific Group that indicated that it increased the incidence of disease in cattle rather than reducing it.[42] Operations in the proactive cull area would continue as these had not yet produced a statistically significant result and survey-only areas would also continue to be monitored.

[41] See Report at http://www.defra.gov.uk /animalh/tb/publications/bern2/bern.shtml)
[42] See DEFRA News Release 457/03 which states that the findings indicate that there was a 27% increase in the number of cases of bovine TB (breakdowns) occurring in reactive culling areas compared to the related survey- only areas where no badger culling took place. See also NFBG News Release 4 November 2003.

D. Welfare of Wild Animals

The relationship between animal welfare and conservation

An examination of the relationship between animal welfare law and nature conservation law involves more than an examination of the law governing the welfare of wild animals. It requires a consideration of the underlying rationale for both these areas of law and the status accorded to animals under each system. A detailed examination of this topic is beyond the scope of this book. In general terms however whilst there are exceptions to the tendency of the law to deal with these two matters separately, there remains a general reluctance on the part of the legislator to see the two issues dealt with together: an example of this arose during the revision of the European legislation implementing the CITES Convention[1]. It was proposed by the RSPB and others that express EU CITES restrictions should be placed on trade in those species of live birds which were likely to incur high levels of mortality during shipment. Although a conservation oriented justification for such a measure can be made out (such a provision helps prevent unsustainable take up of wild specimens), many governmental representatives were reluctant to incorporate what they saw as a welfare measure into a conservation instrument and in the end the provision was not included. A further example of the debate as to when welfare becomes conservation arose during the debate as to the appropriate legal basis for the EU's Zoo's Directive.

This chapter outlines the extent to which UK conservation law addresses the welfare of wildlife and looks at welfare legislation which applies specifically to wild animals. It also briefly considers the position under the EU Treaty.

Welfare Provisions in Conservation legislation

There are a number of examples of what might be termed welfare based provisions in conservation legislation including: section 5 of the 1981 Wildlife and Countryside Act (prohibition of certain methods of killing or taking wild birds) and similar provisions for other wild animals contained in section 11, section 8 of the 1981 Act (protection of captive wild birds). Restrictions on certain methods of killing or taking birds and animals

---

[1] As to which see Part III (Trade in Endangered Species).

are also found in both European Community and international law although again this is generally framed very much in relation to conservation considerations (see Article 8 of the wild birds directive, considered at Chapter 2B and see Article 8 of the Bern Convention on the Conservation of European Wildlife and Natural Habitats). It seems clear however if one considers the methods which are outlawed that these provisions are based on a desire to prohibit inhumane as well as indiscriminate methods of killing.

Wild Mammals Protection Act 1996

The welfare of wild mammals is addressed in the Wild Mammals (Protection) Act 19962 which creates a number of offences relating to the mistreatment of wild mammals. This legislation is purely a welfare measure and does not take into account in any way the conservation status of the animals which fall within its scope. The Act stems from the acknowledgment that wild mammals were lacking in protection as compared with domestic or captive animals and in that sense raises the status of wild mammals closer to those in captivity but this is not based on conservation concerns but on ethical concerns for animal protection and upholding standards of human behaviour.

Under the Act, it is an offence, save as permitted by the Act, to mutilates, kick, beat, nail or otherwise impale, stab, burn, stone, crush, drown, drag or asphyxiate any wild mammal "with intent to inflict unnecessary suffering" (section 1). The element of intent is in contrast to the protection afforded to domestic animals under the Protection of Animals Act 1911 as the latter creates offences of strict liability. "Wild mammal" is defined as any mammal which is not a domestic or captive animal within the meaning of the Protection of Animals Act 1911 or the Protection of Animals (Scotland) Act 1912[3]. The Act was adopted in order to fill a gap in protection afforded under the 1911 and 1912 Acts which protect only domestic or captive animals.

A number of the section 1 offences are subject to certain exceptions which include: in relation to attempted killing, where the act was an act of mercy (if the individual can show that the mammal had been so seriously disabled otherwise than by this unlawful act that there was no reasonable

[2] The Act entered into force on 29 April 1996.
[3] Section 3 of the 1996 Act.

chance of it recovering); in relation to killing in a reasonably swift and human manner (if he shows that the wild mammal had been injured or taken in the course of either lawful shooting, hunting or coursing or pest control)[4] ; doing anything authorised under any enactment; any act made unlawful under section 1 if it was done by means of any snare, trap, dog or bird lawfully used for the purpose of killing or taking any wild mammal and finally the lawful use of any poisonous or noxious substance on any wild mammal (see section 2). The exception in relation to lawful shooting, hunting or coursing was crucial in getting the legislation passed as it protected the interests of the pro-hunting lobby who defeated two earlier attempts to pass similar legislation (see below). Also of key importance was the exception relating to pest control.

Specific powers of stop and search and seizure are provided under section 4. Penalties are set out in section 5: a fine not exceedingly level 5 on the standard scale, or a term of imprisonment not exceeding 6 months, or both. Where an offence is committed in respect of more than one animal, the maximum fine which may be imposed shall be determined as if the person had been convicted of a separate offence in respect of each one. Powers of confiscation in respect of any vehicle or equipment used in the offence are set out in section 6.

The 1996 Act, which was introduced by a private member's Bill sponsored by Alan Meale MP[5], was preceded by two earlier private member's bills in 1992 and 1995 which had also sought to create various offences of cruelty towards wild animals. Both foundered, mainly due to the opposition of the pro-hunting lobby who objected to further provisions in those bills aimed at outlawing hunting with dogs. The 1996 Bill in contrast to the earlier two Bills did not attempt to outlaw blood sports[6] but only to provide for wild mammals similar protection to that given to domestic animals under the 1911 Act. The Bill, which enjoyed all party support, proceeded straight from its Second Reading to Committee Stage in the House of Commons and without amendment was passed at Report stage and Third Reading. The Bill had an equally smooth passage through the House of Lords and was passed on 29 February 1996.

Unsurprisingly the tensions between those who seek to ban hunting altogether and those who seek to ensure its continuations have not disappeared with the passing of the 1996 Act. Amending bills were

[4] In the case of Scotland, lawful pest control.
[5] And by Baroness Nichol in the House of Lords.
[6] House of Commons Hansard Debates 26 January 1996, column 554.

introduced unsuccessfully in 2001, and 2003. The latest such Bill, the 2003 Wild Mammals (Protection) (Amendment) Bill sought to reconcile these tensions by replacing the various offences of the 1996 Act with one offence of "intentionally causing undue suffering to any wild mammal". Exceptions to the new offence would have consisted of acts done in accordance with a recognised code or in the normal and human conduct of a lawful activity, unless, in the latter case, the act should reasonably have been avoided or substantially alleviated or where a recognised code regulating the activity existed. The scheme of the Bill was to create an authority with the power to recognise bodies as the proper authorities for making such codes and to approve such codes. Approved codes could then have been by recognised by the Secretary of State in the form of regulations. In the event, the Government has announced its opposition to the Bill on a number of grounds: the concept of "undue" suffering was untried and inappropriate, it was unacceptable to cause any suffering to a wild mammal for a purpose which was not necessary or could be achieved in a more humane way and the Bill would permit suffering which was unnecessary but not "undue"; furthermore, the Bill provided for exceptions which could be used to allow field sports to continue regardless of the suffering they caused, provided the acts concerned were in accordance with a code to be drawn up largely by organisations responsible for running those field sports. Where there was no code the first exception applied and this assumed that because a time-honoured tradition caused suffering, that was acceptable for those reasons the Government would not support the Bill[7].

Hunting

During debates on conservation legislation, the concern has often been voiced by supporters of hunting that general powers will be exercised so as to ban hunting "by the back door" and the view expressed that the issues of conservation and welfare should be kept entirely separate. Nevertheless, those seeking to justify the practice of hunting often refer to the conservation and proper management of wildlife as considerations in their favour, whilst opponents dispute the necessity of hunting as opposed to other forms of control as a means to achieve these objectives.

The relationship between animal welfare considerations and benefits to wildlife was considered in the context of a challenge to a Somerset County Council's decision to ban deer hunting on a piece of its land. It is interesting to note the different approaches taken by the Court of Appeal

[7] House of Lords Hansard Debate for 16 January 2004 column 824 (Lord Whitty).

and by Mr Justice Laws at first instance (although the Court of Appeal upheld his decision that the ban was unlawful, albeit on narrower grounds).

In *R v Somerset CC ex p Fewings*[8] , the issue was whether the local authority's decision to ban deer hunting on a piece of common land which it owned was lawful. Local hunt supporters brought judicial proceedings to quash the decision. It was agreed that the question was whether the decision fell within the ambit of s120 (1) (b) of the Local Government Act 1972 which permitted local authorities to acquire by agreement any land for the purpose of "the benefit, improvement or development of their area". In this case, it was also agreed, that "benefit" included wildlife benefit, specifically, as described in a Council Report on the issue, "to manage the estate for the maximum landscape, wildlife and public recreation benefit". In the High Court, Mr J Laws rejected an argument put on behalf of the Council that, in imposing the ban on ethical grounds, the Council had done no more than take into account a relevant ground, namely animal welfare, which, it argued, could not be divorced from ethical considerations. On this point, Mr Justice Laws found that:

> "... no necessary logic dictates that a duty to treat the conservation of the area's wildlife as a relevant factor within s120(1)(b), a duty not in itself here in contention, is bound to involve (so far as it relates to the deer) anything more than the need to look after the proper management of the herd. If the duty is correctly so described, it would of course engage such questions as the numbers to be culled, the attitude of farmers to the presence of deer on their land, and so forth."[9]

Whilst upholding Mr Justice Laws decision quashing the ban, two members of the Court of Appeal took a rather different approach on this issue. The Master of the Rolls, LJ Bingham accepted that animal welfare (and social) considerations were relevant matters to take into account, and accepted that ethical considerations could be[10] . He ruled, however, that the Council would have had to attempt to define what benefit a ban would confer on their area and conversely what detriment the absence of a ban would cause (the Council had not had s120(1)(b) drawn to its attention during the debate on the ban). He therefore agreed with the judge at first instance, but on much narrower grounds, that the council had not been entitled to make the decision they did on the grounds they relied on,

[8] [1995] 1 All ER 513.
[9] [1995] 1 All ER 513, 527b.
[10] Ibid page 525.

commenting that, "I leave open the possibility that the same decision could have been reached on proper grounds".

Lord Justice Simon Brown took the view that: "Even if the focus is properly upon wildlife benefit, that surely encompasses the cruelty argument" (page 528) and agreed with the Master of the Rolls that the judge at first instance had construed the statutory power too narrowly and had erred in regarding the cruelty argument as necessarily irrelevant to the council's decision. He then went further than the Master of the Rolls and concluded that such considerations were necessarily relevant and, dissenting, that he would have allowed the appeal. He considered that it was impossible to say that councillors must shut their minds to the cruelty argument, still less that they must do so as a matter of the strict construction of s 120(1)(b):"human well-being for many will depend upon their satisfaction as to animal welfare" (page 528) Swinton Thomas LJ on the other hand, said the ban did not fall within the ambit of the provision.

Whilst the court in this case was focusing on the interpretation of s120(1)(b) of the 1972 Act, the case is an illustration of possible approaches to the broader question of the extent to which the conservation or management of wildlife includes animal welfare considerations. This case appears to leave open the possibility that a hunting ban may not run foul of s120(1)(b) even where ethical considerations have been taken into account, provided the proper weighing exercise is gone through in determining what will be of benefit for the area (talking into account alternative means of managing the herd for example). This appears to be consistent with the way in which conservation legislation typically includes at least some limited degree of welfare protection for wild animals (as to which see above).

Animal Welfare and the European Union

The Amsterdam Treaty introduces the Amsterdam Protocol on the Protection and Welfare of Animals into the Treaty on European Union. The Protocol declares that "In formulating the Community's agriculture, transport, internal market and research policies, the Community and the Member States shall pay full regard to the welfare requirements of animals, while respecting the legislative or administrative provisions and customs of the Member States relating in particular to religious rites, cultural traditions and regional heritage[11] ". Interestingly therefore, the Protocol

[11] The Protocol on the Protection and Welfare of Animals, Treaty of Amsterdam 1997.

does not require that full regard be had to animal welfare in the area of environmental policy. Furthermore, in *Case 189/01 Jippes and others v Minister van Landbouw*[12], the Court ruled that the need to ensure animal welfare was not a general principle of Community law (paragraphs 73-76 of the judgment). In relation to the Protocol, the Court took the view that it did not lay down any well-defined general principle of Community law and that its obligation to have full regard to animal welfare was limited to the four specific spheres of Community policy referred to.

Despite this unpromising background however, a number of European Union conservation instruments contain provisions relating at least as much to animal welfare as to considerations of nature conservation (see above). Moreover the requirement to pay full regard to the welfare requirements of animals in other areas of policy such as agriculture may have implications for the welfare of wild animals as much as for that of domestic animals.

[12] Judgment of 12 July 2001.

CHAPTER 4

WILD PLANTS

Whilst the scope of protection for wild plants is in some respects narrower than that afforded to wild animals under conservation legislation, some of the features of the protective regime for plants are similar to that in place for wild animals and these aspects are more fully considered in Chapter 3 - Part II as indicated. This chapter focuses on those features that are specific to the regime for plants. The main pieces of legislation protecting wild plants are Part I of the Wildlife and Countryside Act 1981 and Part III of the Habitats Regulations 1994. There is some degree of overlap between the two regimes which operate concurrently in respect of species to which they both apply. Regulation 104 provides that nothing in those Regulations is to be construed as excluding the application of the provisions of Part I of the 1981 Act in relation to plants (or animals) also protected under Part III of the Regulations. Any potential conflict would of course have to be resolved in the light of the overriding obligation to give effect to the requirements of the Habitats Directive.

The Wildlife and Countryside Act 1981

Some protection (against uprooting) is afforded to all wild plants, whilst full protection is afforded only to those species listed on Schedule 8. "Plants" includes fungi and lichen for the purposes of the 1981 Act. The criteria for listing species in Schedule 8 are indicated in section 22 of the 1981 Act which deals with the power to vary the Schedules to the Act. Schedule 8 is subject to a five yearly review by the Nature Conservancy Councils acting jointly, in other words the JNCC,[1] which must advise the Secretary of State for the Environment whether any plant should be added to or removed from Schedule 8. A copy of this advice is laid before Parliament (section 24(3) of the Act). The quinquennial review process, as it is known, is discussed in more detail in Chapter 3 - Part II. The Secretary of State is empowered to amend Schedule 8 by order in the following ways: he may add to Schedule 8 any plant which, in his opinion, "is in danger of extinction in Great Britain or is likely to become so endangered unless conservation measures are taken."; he may remove a plant which, in his opinion, is no longer endangered or likely to become so endangered (section 22(3). The Secretary of State also has the power to amend Schedule

---

[1] See section 24(1) to the Act as amended by the 1990 Act. The JNCC may, in addition, carry out such a review at any time (section 24(1)).

8 for the purpose of complying with an international obligation (Section 22(4)).

The JNCC makes its recommendations after consultation with statutory conservation agencies including the Countryside Commission, the Institutes of Terrestrial and Freshwater Ecology, the Environment Agency and non-governmental organisations (the latter coordinated through Wildlife Link)

The Quinquennial Review

The first Quinquennial Review was carried out in 1985 and subsequent reviews took place in 1991 and 1996. The reviews set out reasoned recommendations for listing new species or removing species from the Schedule. The recommendations give a good indication of the range of threats to plant species and to the various benefits to conservation which are anticipated from listing. Examples of threats to plant species in the third Quinquennial Review include: increased trade (the bluebell); modification of habitat (flamingo moss); inappropriate grazing regimes (convoluted cladonia) and global warming (Polar feather-moss).

The benefits to be derived from listing also vary. In addition to the direct benefits of listing (some recommendations are for listing for certain purposes only such as to prohibit sale) such benefits include the need to take account of the species during the planning of developments (Alpine sulphur tresses); the promotion of a flagship species to enhance awareness to manage particular habitats (New Forest Beech-lichen).In practice most of the recommendations have been accepted by the Secretary of State.

In explaining the rationale for its final recommendations at the time of the second Quinquennial Review in 1991, the Joint Nature Conservation Committee explained that it had proceeded on the basis that "in danger of extinction" in section 22(3) broadly equated to "endangered" as defined in the internationally recognised IUCN Red Data Book on endangered species and "likely to become so endangered" as "vulnerable"[2] These concepts are discussed further in Chapter 3 - Part I.

Protection from picking and uprooting etc

Section 13(1) (a) of the Act renders it an offence for any person intentionally to pick[3], uproot or destroy any wild plant listed in Schedule

[2] Second Quinquennial Review Report Page 5.

[3] Under the definition in section 27 of the Act, "pick", in relation to a plant, means gather or pluck any part of the plant without uprooting it.

8 to the Act. Among the British plants which have been adversely affected by collecting is the lady's slipper orchid which is listed on Schedule 8. It is also an offence under section 13(1)(b) for any person, not being an authorised person, intentionally to uproot any wild plant not included in that Schedule. For these purposes an authorised person means the owner or occupier or any person authorised by the owner or occupier, of the land on which the action authorised is taken; or any person authorised in writing by the local authority for the area in which the action authorised is taken; or any person authorised in writing by the Environment Agency, a water undertaker or a sewerage undertaker. However, authorisation for the purposes of this definition does not confer any right to enter upon land[4]. The effect of this is that it is not unlawful, subject to the provisions of the common and criminal law and any local byelaws (such as those applying to a Local Nature Reserve), to pick or even destroy wild plants which are not listed on Schedule 8 although it is an offence to *uproot* any wild plant unless the individual falls within the definition of an authorised person.[5]

A person shall not be guilty of an offence under s13(1) if he shows that the act was the incidental result of a lawful operation and could not reasonably have been avoided (s13(3)).

Sales Restrictions

Under section 13(2)(a) of the 1981 Act it is an offence, subject to the provisions of Part I, to sell, offer or expose for sale, or have in one's possession or transport for the purpose of sale any live or dead wild plant included in Schedule 8, or any part of or anything derived from, such a plant. It is also an offence to publish or cause to be published any advertisement likely to be understood as conveying that the person concerned buys or sells, or intends to buy or sell any of those things (section 13(2)(b)). Section 13(4) applies so that there is a presumption in any proceedings under section 13(2)(a) that the plant in question was wild unless the contrary is shown. The bluebell is listed on Schedule 8 in 1998 for the purposes of section 13(2) only, in response to the growing trade in wild bluebells.

[4] See section 27(1) of the 1981 Act as amended inter alia by SI 1996/593 (reference to the Environment Agency).

[5] For a discussion of the position as to the taking of wild plants under the common and criminal law see the article "Seasons of Mists and Mellow Fruitfulness" by Dr Mary Welstead in the New Law Journal October 1995 Vol 145 No 6715 p 1499

Section 16 Licences

Derogations from the requirements of section 13 may be granted by licences issued under section 16(3) and (4) of the 1981 Act. Subsection (3) refers to anything done under section 13(1) (picking, uprooting etc), whilst subsection (4) of section 16 is concerned with acts covered by section 13(2) (sales etc).

The purposes for which a licence may be granted under subsection (3) and which appear to be relevant to plants include scientific and educational purposes; conserving wild animals or plants; protecting any zoological or botanical collection and photography. The appropriate authority to issue all these types of licences is the Nature Conservancy Council[6]. Licences may also be obtained for the purpose of preserving public health or safety; preventing the spread of disease or for the purpose of preventing serious damage to livestock, foodstuffs for livestock, crops, vegetables, fruit, growing timber, or any other form of property or to fisheries. The appropriate authority for these licences is the agriculture Minister (section 16(9)). The appropriate authority for sales related licences is the Secretary of State for the Environment after consultation with English Nature or the relevant conservation body.

In relation to the scope of a licence, section 16(5) provides that, subjection to subsection (6), a section 16 licence may be "to any degree general or specific"; may be granted either to persons of a class or to a particular person, may be modified or revoked any time and shall be valid for the period stated in the licence. By virtue of subsection (8), the definition of a class of persons "may be framed by reference to any circumstances whatever including, in particular, their being authorised by any person".[7] A general licence, unlike a licence granted to a specific individual, does not need to be applied for, it applies automatically to cover actions carried in accordance with its terms and conditions. Whilst activities carried out under a general licence may be more difficult to monitor, it is always possible to impose a condition obliging those operating under the licence to inform the issuing authority about the scale of activity undertaken.

A number of amendments have been made to section 16 in respect of licences dealing with wild birds in order to bring the provision fully into line with the requirements of the wild birds directive[8]. These are based on

[6] Section 16(9) of the 1981 Act.

[7] Almost identical language is used in regulation 45 of the Habitats Regulations (see paragraphs (1) and (2).

[8] See discussion in Chapter 2E - Part II.

a series of rulings by the ECJ on the interpretation of Article 9 of the wild birds Directive. As such, they are not directly applicable to licences relating to wild animals and plants. One of the changes made to section 16 was the insertion of a provision stating that appropriate authority shall not grant a licence unless it is satisfied that, as regards that purpose, there is no other satisfactory solution. The position in relation to those species listed on both Schedule 8 and also on Schedule 4 of the Habitats Regulations is discussed below, essentially the derogation must comply with Article 16 of the Habitats Directive which, like Article 9 of the wild birds directive, requires that there be no satisfactory alternative to the issue of a licence. Whether a court reads in Article 16 or subsection 1A(a) of section 16, it must ensure that the requirements of Article 16 are met so far as possible. In relation to other wild plants, which are listed under Schedule 5 but not under the 1994 Regulations, and which therefore are not governed by Community legislation, the requirement that there be no satisfactory alternative does not apply. However in practice it may be questioned whether a reasonable issuing authority would take a different approach so that it may be expected that such licences will not be issued where there is a satisfactory alternative.

The Habitats Regulations

The Habitat Regulations afford protection to those species listed in Annex IV(b) to the Habitats Directive "whose natural range includes any area in Great Britain." These "European protected species" of plant are listed in Schedule 4 to the Regulations (Regulation 42). All of these European protected species also appear on Schedule 8 to the WCA. Under Regulation 43(1) of the Habitat Regulations, it is an offence "deliberately to pick, collect, cut, uproot or destroy a wild plant of a European protected species." It is also an offence, under regulation 43(2), to keep transport, sell or exchange, or offer for sale or exchange, any live or dead wild plant of a European protected species, or any part of or anything derived from, such a plant. Paragraphs (1) and (2) of regulation 43 apply to all stages of the biological cycle of the plants to which they apply (regulation 43(3). In proceedings for an offence under regulation 43 the plant shall be presumed to be to have been a wild plant unless the contrary is shown (regulation 43(6) of the 1994 Regulations).

The penalty for an offence under regulation 43 is a fine set at level 4 on the standard scale (regulation 43(7)). Supplementary provisions relating to the enforcement of species protection provisions are set out in regulations

100-103 and include the duty of a court to order the forfeiture of any plant or other thing in respect of which an offence was committed.

Defences

A person shall not be guilty of an offence under regulation 43 of the Habitats Regulations if he shows that the act was the incidental result of a lawful operation and could not reasonably have been avoided (regulation 43(5)). In relation to the possession and sales related offences in regulation 43(2), it is a defence for the person concerned to show that the plant or other thing in question had been lawfully sold (whether to him or any other person). "Lawfully" in this context means without any contravention of the Habitats Regulations or Part I of the 1981 Act.

CHAPTER 5

MARINE SPECIES

The protection of wild animals and the operation of Part I of the Wildlife and Countryside Act and Part III of the Conservation (Natural Habitats etc) Regulations 1994, has already been considered in this book.[1] This chapter is concerned with the particular protection that is given to marine species. Although the protection of marine species shares many of the characteristics of the protection of terrestrial species, there are certain considerations that apply particularly within the marine environment.

One important feature of the marine environment is the extent to which many such species move between, or occur outside of, national jurisdictions. As a result, international co-operation is required if these species are to be protected effectively. Traditionally, the high seas and their natural resources have been classed as common property open to exploitation by any state. As a result of this doctrine and of the significant resources held by the sea, marine species have been vulnerable to unregulated overexploitation. In many areas this has led to a classic 'tragedy of the commons' in which all parties have an interest in maximising their own exploitation of the resource in the absence of regulation to ensure that the resource is conserved for the good if all. For this reason international co-operation is particularly important for the marine environment.

Aside from the problem of achieving sufficient international co-operation, marine conservation also suffers from the relative paucity of knowledge in relation to marine eco-systems. Although new techniques are now able to reduce these difficulties, the expense and physical problems of researching at sea, particularly the deep ocean, has meant that our knowledge of marine systems has lagged behind our knowledge of land-based systems. A further difficulty in regulating the marine environment is enforcement. Parts of the regulated environment will inevitably be remote and the regulated activity may take place at widely dispersed sites.

The protection of marine species has generally been focused on two forms of regulation: regulation in order to achieve sustainable use of a species as a natural resource, and protection of charismatic species, such as dolphins or seals, that capture public support. Nevertheless, the

---

[1] See Chapter 3 - Part II.

importance of taking an approach that looks at the whole ecosystem has been emphasised by scientists and in more recent forms of regulation. Although this chapter focuses on the protection given to particular important species, the protection of marine species will also depend on the protection of marine sites[2] and the protection of the marine environment as a whole from threats such as pollution.

Whales

As whales are frequently migratory and often occur outside territorial waters, international co-operation is particularly important for their protection. This section will consider the main international framework for the regulation of whaling and then look at the domestic protection of whales.

Whales: International Whaling Convention

The International Whaling Convention[3] was the first significant treaty regime for the regulation of whaling.[4] The Convention came into force in 1948 and currently has 52 parties including the UK.

The Convention creates the International Whaling Commission (IWC) with the power to adopt regulations on catch quotas, whaling methods and the level of exploitation of particular species. These Regulations are incorporated into the Schedule, which forms part of the Convention.[5] These regulations are to be based on 'scientific findings' and are to take account of the interests of the consumers of whale products and of the whaling industry.[6] This highlights a particular tension within the Convention. The Convention is not a protectionist treaty, but was originally adopted in order to assist the recovery of depleted stocks in order to permit hunting. As a result, the preamble to the treaty focuses on the objective of maintaining the optimum level of harvestable whale resources. Although the preamble also sets out the objective of the conservation of whales, this is stated to be for the purpose of the future orderly development of the whaling industry.

[2] See Chapter 5 - Part II.
[3] The International Convention for the Regulation of Whaling 1946
[4] An earlier convention, the 1931Convention for the Regulation of Whaling, was unable to offer an effective regulatory regime due to the failure of the major whaling states to ratify the convention, and the lack of an institutional regime to regulate whaling effectively.
[5] International Whaling Convention Art 1(1).
[6] International Whaling Convention Art 5.

Despite this background, the actual operation of the Convention has moved further towards conservation. Although regulations are required to be made on the basis of scientific evidence, the IWC has adopted a more precautionary approach to setting quotas, concluding that the scientific evidence is too uncertain to safely set a quota for the taking of any whale species. As a result the IWC has set a quota of zero for all whale species since 1982.[7] This effectively amounts to a moratorium on all commercial whaling. The ban does not prevent all forms of whaling, but allows a limited form of aboriginal subsistence whaling and some taking of whales for scientific purposes where authorised by a member state. The move to a conservation approach was recognised by the IWC through a resolution at the 2003 Annual Meeting known as the Berlin Initiative. The resolution recognises that in practice the IWC has a significant role in the conservation of whales and establishes a conservation committee with the remit of producing a conservation agenda to be considered by the IWC at its annual meeting.[8]

The Convention applies to all whaling ships, factory ships and land stations under the jurisdiction of a contracting party and to 'all waters in which whaling is prosecuted' by such vessels.[9] There is some argument that Art 65 of the UN Convention on the Law of the Sea has extended the application of the IWC in that it requires signatories to co-operate with the appropriate international organisation for the conservation, management and study of crustaceans. This interpretation is disputed but has the potential to extend the reach of the IWC.

The Convention is enforced in part through international monitoring and inspection and in part through obligations on member states to take 'appropriate measures' to implement the Convention and to punish infractions of the Convention by vessels within its jurisdiction.[10]

The extent to which the Convention is able to protect whales depends on two significant factors: the membership of the IWC and the extent to which the members implement their obligations. In relation to

[7] The decision came into effect in the 1985/6 season in relation to Antarctica and in 1986 elsewhere. Norway has exercised its rights to the amendment to the Schedule and has continued to set national catch limits for minke whales. Japan has repeatedly requested an interim relief allocation to allow small scale community-based whaling but this request has consistently been rejected by the IWC.
[8] IWC Resolution 2003-1. The Berlin Initiative on Strengthening the Conservation Agenda of the International Whaling Commission.
[9] International Whaling Convention Art 1(2).
[10] International Whaling Convention Art 9.

membership of the IWC, the membership has become somewhat polarised between the anti-whaling and pro-whaling states. Although the anti-whaling states have generally been in the majority in recent years, this majority is declining as more pro-whaling states join the Convention. The balance of opinion between member states has clear implications for the future of the moratorium on commercial whaling and for the extent to which the IWC continues to move towards a conservation agenda.

The success of the IWC also depends on the extent to which the member states are able and willing to regulate the capture of whales. The World Wildlife Fund estimates that in reality some 22,000 whales have been taken commercially since the introduction of the moratorium on commercial whaling. In part this is due to the inevitable difficulties of monitoring activity at sea and the difficulties of preventing whalers from taking the flag of non-member states. There has, however, also been significant criticism of the use that certain nations have made of the exceptions to the ban on commercial whaling. In particular, Japan and Iceland have been heavily criticised for the extent and manner of the whaling carried out under the scientific exemption.

Whales: Smaller Cetaceans

There is some debate as to whether the Whaling Convention is limited to 'great' whales or whether it also extends to smaller whales such as dolphins and porpoises. The Convention itself does not define 'whale', instead it contains an annex listing the names of a number of whale species in a number of languages. This lack of clarity has led to debates as to whether the Convention is limited to the listed great whales or extends to all cetaceans.

Although the question of the legal competence of the IWC has not yet been resolved, the IWC does maintain some activities in relation to small cetaceans. In particular, the Scientific Committee has carried out studies on dolphins and porpoises.

Whales and other Cetaceans: Domestic Regulation

The UK is under international obligations to regulate whaling, and the trade in whale products, effectively. The UK ceased whaling in 1963 but the regulation of the industry began much earlier. The existing regulation of whaling is based on the Whaling Industry Regulation Act 1934 (as amended). The 1934 Act was amended by the Fisheries Act 1981 so as to extend most of its provisions to all cetaceans.[11] The Act prohibits the catching or treatment of all cetaceans within the coastal waters of the UK.[12] In addition any British ship involved in the catching or treatment of whales or any factory treating whales or producing whale oil must have a licence under the Act;[13] no such licences are currently in force.

Further provisions of domestic law also protect whales. The Wildlife and Countryside Act 1981 creates an offence of recklessly disturbing any dolphin or whale.[14] The 1981 Act also lists all species of whales, dolphins and porpoises in Schedule 5 of the Act. As a result it is an offence to intentionally kill, injure or take, or to posses or sell any dolphin, porpoise or whale.[15] Bottle nosed and common dolphins and common porpoises are listed in Schedule 6 of the 1981 and as a consequence are subject to protection as to their welfare.

In addition, all cetaceans are listed in Schedule II to the Conservation (Natural Habitats etc) Regulations 1994 and as a result are European protected species. This affords further protection to cetaceans although some of this protection will inevitably overlap with that described above. In particular, it is an offence to deliberately capture, kill or disturb a listed species or to damage or destroy its resting place or breeding site.[16]

Wales and Small Cetaceans: 'By-catch'

One of the central concerns in relation to the protection of cetaceans is their incidental capture through commercial fishing. Greenpeace estimates that some 300,000 cetaceans are killed as by-catch every year. Although devices have been developed to aid the animals in escaping from certain kinds of net, this remains a significant problem. The UK is a party to the Agreement on the Conservation of Small Cetaceans of the Baltic and North Seas 1991, which requires the minimisation of the capture of small cetaceans as by-catch and requires the parties to monitor and regulate the problem. At a Meeting of the Parties in 2000, the parties resolved to reduce this 'by-catch' as soon as possible to a level below 'unacceptable interaction'.

[11] 1934 Act s1.
[12] 1934 Act s2.
[13] 1934 Act s4.
[14] Wildlife and Countryside Act 1981 s9(4A), inserted by the Countryside and Rights of Way Act 2000. The offence applies in England and Wales only. See also Chapter 3 - Part II.
[15] For further details on Schedule 5 to the 1981 Act see Chapter 3A - Part II.
[16] 1994 Regulations Part III especially Reg 39. These offences are subject to certain defences, see further Chapter 3 - Part II.

This level is currently set at 1.7% of the total population although ministers set an additional precautionary aim of reducing the take to 1% of the total population.

The Habitats Directive[17] also imposes obligations in relation to all cetaceans. Through Art 12(4) the Directive requires member states monitor the incidental take of cetaceans and to undertake research and conservation measures to ensure that this does not have a significant negative impact on the species concerned. NGO's, such as Greenpeace and the Whale and Dolphin Conservation Society, have argued that these measures are ineffective in practice and insufficient to meet the magnitude of the problem. At the time of writing, a draft regulation on the protection of cetaceans was progressing through the European legislative process, having received approval from the European Parliament in January 2004.[18] The proposed regulation would require additional protective measures to be taken by vessels in order to minimise cetacean by-catch. It would also require the presence of on-board observers in some fisheries and would ban the use of drift-nets in relation to certain areas.

Seals

The UK is particularly important to the protection of seals in that it supports up to 45% of the world's grey seals and 5% of the world's common seals.[19] As with many other marine species, the protection of seals is complicated by the fact that many seals exist outside of national jurisdiction or migrate between jurisdictions. The protection of seals is also complicated by concerns within the fishing industry that seals compete with man for certain fishing stocks and that their activities can be damaging to fish farming.[20]

Seals: Conservation of Seals Act 1970

The primary domestic mechanism for protecting seals is provided through the Conservation of Seals Act 1970, which applies within Great Britain and the adjacent territorial waters.[21] The 1970 Act does not define

[17] See Chapter 3 - Part II.

[18] Report on the proposal for a Council regulation laying down measures concerning incidental catches of cetaceans in fisheries and amending Regulation (EC) No88/98. (COM(2003) 451 – C5-0358/2003 –2003/0163(CNS)).

[19] Although this figure also represents some 40% of the European sub-species of common seal, *Phoca vitulina vitulina*.

[20] McGillivray, "Seal Conservation Legislation in the UK – Past, Present and Future" (1995) 10 International Journal of Marine and Coastal Law 19.

[21] Conservation of Seals Act 1970, s17(2) and (3). The Act does not extend to Northern Ireland.

'seals' and as a result appears to apply to all species of seal, although special provision is made for the protection of grey and common seals.

The 1970 Act operates through two central means of protection: the prohibition of certain methods of killing seals and the provision for closed seasons in which certain species may not be taken. The prohibition on certain methods of killing proscribes the use of poisonous substances and of firearms above certain specifications to kill, injure or take a seal.[22] It is an offence to use such means to kill, injure or take a seal and is also an offence to possess any such items with intent to do so.[23]

The second means of protection is the provision of close seasons in which the wilful killing, injuring or taking of grey and common seals is an offence.[24] The close season for grey seals runs from 1st September to 31st December inclusive, whilst that for common seals runs from 1st June to 31st August inclusive. These provisions can be extended by order of the Secretary of State, in consultation with the Natural Environment Research Council (NERC), to prohibit killing, injuring or taking seals within a specified area.[25] This power has been used particularly in relation to outbreaks of phocine distemper virus amongst the seal population. This virus inflicts high mortality rates amongst seals, particularly common seals, and has caused serious damage to the seal population during a number of epidemics. The 1988 epidemic saw some 60% of common seals destroyed within certain areas[26] whilst further cases of the virus in the summer of 2002 raised renewed fears of serious damage to the seal population. As a result, the power to create protection areas through such orders was used in relation to a number of sites in Britain. Following further research into the seal population, a number of these orders have been revoked, whilst others have been superseded by the Conservation of Seals (England) Order 1999.[27] This Order prohibits the killing, injuring or taking either species of seal on the North Sea coast of England and adjacent territorial waters.[28]

[22] Conservation of Seals Act 1970 s1.
[23] Conservation of Seals Act 1970 s8(2).
[24] Conservation of Seals Act 1970 s2.
[25] Conservation of Seals Act 1970 s3.
[26] NERC *Seal Epidemic of 1988. Report for 1988-89* (NERC, 1989).
[27] SI 1999/3052.
[28] Regulation 3 set out the territorial limits of this Order as the counties of Durham, East Riding of Yorkshire, East Sussex, Essex, Hartlepool, Kent, Kingston-upon-Hull, Lincolnshire, the Medway Towns, Middlesbrough, Norfolk, North East Lincolnshire, North Lincolnshire, North Yorkshire, Northumberland, Redcar and Cleveland, Southend-on-Sea, Stockton-on-Tees, Suffolk, Thurrock, Tyne and Wear and the administrative area of Greater London; and certain other specified territorial waters adjacent to England.

The 1970 Act provides a number of defences to the offences that it creates. Mercy killing is a defence to all of the offences created by the Act where the seal is seriously disabled and has no reasonable chance of recovery.[29] Similarly it is not an offence to take such an injured seal in order to aid its recovery with the intention of releasing it once it has recovered.[30] These defences do not apply where the injury to the seal was a result of the act of the person seeking to raise the defence.

In addition to these defences, two further defences apply in relation to killing, injuring or taking a seal within a close period or in contravention of an order. These defences apply when the killing or injuring was the incidental result of lawful action or where the killing or attempted killing was to prevent the seal from damaging fishing nets or tackle or fish within those nets.[31] This latter defence only applies when the seal is in the vicinity of the net or tackle in question. This qualification is aimed at preventing the killing of seals merely to reduce competition for fish stocks. Instead, if such population control is necessary, fishermen are encouraged to apply for a licence to do so. Nevertheless the defence is ambiguous, particularly as there is no definition of 'in the vicinity' and no requirement that the damage in question is serious. To date no court has had the opportunity to clarify these provisions as no cases appear to have been brought under the 1970 Act.

The Act sets out the conditions for the grant of licences to kill or take seals for various purposes.[32] Licences may be granted to kill or take seals for scientific or educational purposes or to take seals for a zoological garden. In addition they may be used to prevent damage to fisheries; reduce population surpluses; use any population surplus as a resource; or to protect the flora or fauna of a range of protected areas. The protected areas include nature reserves, marine nature reserves and sites of special scientific interest.[33] A licence may only be granted in relation to such a protected area with the consent of the relevant conservation council. It appears that relatively few licences are granted under the 1970 Act. The difficulty of enforcing the Act in the relatively isolated areas where many seals occur, has led to concerns that unlicensed killing of seals occurs with little prospect of prosecution under the Act.[33]

29 Conservation of Seals Act 1970 s9(2).
30 Conservation of Seals Act 1970 s9(1)(a).
31 Conservation of Seals Act 1970 s9(1) (b) and (c).
32 Conservation of Seals Act s10.
33 McGillivray, 'Seal Conservation Legislation in the UK – Past, Present and Future' (1995) 10 International Journal of Marine and Coastal Law 19.

Seals: Further forms of Protection

Although the 1970 Act contains the main regulatory framework for the protection of seals, there are further provisions for the protection of seals. Seals are listed under Schedule 3 of the Conservation (Natural Habitats etc) Regulations 1994 and as such, a wide range of methods of killing are prohibited in addition to those prohibited under the 1970 Act.[34]

In addition, seals are listed under Annex V of the Habitats Directive, although such a listing does not guarantee protection, it does require that their conservation status is kept under review and that they are protected from killing capable of causing serious disturbance to populations.

Fish

The law on the conservation of marine fish is largely concerned with the preservation of fish stocks in order to sustain commercial fishing. This has led to a wide range of regulation at national, international and particularly European level. This law provides detailed, and frequently, changing regulations on issues such as the total allowable catches, national quotas, the number of days for which fishermen may be at sea and the banning of fishing for certain species or in certain places or at certain times. A detailed discussion of this specialist area of law is outside of the scope of this book but it is clear that the area does have an impact on the conservation of marine fish species. In particular, the fact that fisheries provide such a valuable economic resource means that there is considerable interest in ensuring that fisheries are sustainable and that regulations are enforced, although differences may emerge between interest groups as to the best means to achieve these objectives.

In addition, fisheries law prohibits certain means of killing. In particular, European law prohibits the use of explosives, poisonous or stupefying substances and electrical current in the catching of all marine organisms including fish.[35] These measures benefit the marine environment general in restricting forms of killing that are indiscriminate or polluting.

In domestic fisheries law, the Sea Fisheries (Wildlife Conservation) Act 1992 requires specified Ministers and local fisheries committees to have regard to the conservation of flora and fauna in the discharge of their

[34] 1994 Regulations, Reg 41, see Chapter 3 - Part II.
[35] Regulation 850/98 Art 31.

functions relating to sea fisheries. This consideration must be balanced against any other consideration to which they are to have regard. Although this provision leaves considerable discretion to the body or Minister in question, failure to have sufficient regard to conservation objectives could leave the decision open to challenge through judicial review.

Fish: Specific Domestic Protection

Whilst most of the law relating to the protection of fish is concerned with maintaining fish stocks, there are also provisions that offer protection to particular kinds of marine fish.

A number of fish species are protected under Schedule 5 to the Wildlife and Countryside Act 1981. As a result these species benefit from the prohibition on intentionally killing or injuring a listed animal.[36] The marine fish species protected under schedule 5 include sturgeon (*Acipenser sturio*), basking shark (*Cetorhinus maximus*), vendace (Coregonus albula) and Whitefish (*Coregonus lavaretus)*. The basking shark also benefits from additional protection under the 1981 Act in that, as with cetaceans, it is an offence to intentionally or recklessly disturb specimens.[37]

In addition, the sturgeon is protected as a European protected species under the Conservation (Natural Habitats etc) Regulations 1994. As a result it is an offence to deliberately capture, kill or disturb a listed species or to damage or destroy its resting place or breeding site.[38] Further fish species, including vendace (Coregonus albula) and Whitefish (*Coregonus lavaretus)* are also listed under schedule 3 to the 1994 Regulations and so benefit from the prohibition on killing with poison or explosives.[39] This may have little impact in practice as, as noted above, such methods of killing are prohibited through European fisheries law in any case.

As a result, in addition to the general regulation of fisheries for the purpose of sustainable use, certain marine fish are protected by conservation legislation. These species are frequently also protected at international or regional level through agreements such as the Bern Convention and through the regulation of trade implemented through the CITES treaty.

---

[36] Wildlife and countryside Act 1981 s9.
[37] Wildlife and Countryside Act 1981 s9(4A)(b), see further Chapter on wild animals.
[38] 1994 Regulations Part III especially Reg 39. These offences are subject to certain defences, see Chapter 3A - Part II.
[39] 1994 Regulations Reg 41(4).

Further Species

Although this chapter has focused on cetaceans, seals and fish, a range of other marine species also receive protection, particularly under the Wildlife and Countryside Act 1981 and the Conservation (Natural Habitats etc) Regulations 1994. Species that receive protection under the 1981 Act include all species of marine turtle, 2 species of anemone, lagoon sea slugs, pink sea fans, Atlantic Stream crayfish and several species of marine flora. Similarly, the 1994 regulations protect marine turtles as a European protected species

Future Directions

This chapter has focused on the protection given to particular marine species. The government is in the process of considering the future protection of the marine environment. Although this protection is focused on marine protection as a whole rather than on the species discussed, it will inevitably have a role in the protection of those species through the protection of the ecosystems they depend on.[40]

[40] See Chapter 4 - Part I for a discussion of these proposals.

CHAPTER 6

ALIEN SPECIES

Alien species (non-native species) are now said to be the second most serious threat to biodiversity after habitat loss[1]. Whilst some introductions of species may be relatively benign, others may cause severe damage to native species and habitats. Problems associated with the introduction into the environment of alien species are competition with other species for food and space, predation on native species; the destruction or degradation of habitat and transmission to native wildlife of diseases and parasites. The problems arise where native species have not evolved characteristics which will, for example, protect them from excessive predation or provide resistance to disease. Island communities are the most vulnerable because of their relative isolation. Examples of alien species which have caused environmental damage in Great Britain include the grey squirrel, the New Zealand Flatworm and Japanese Knotweed.[2]

International Initiatives

In comparison with other types of legal protection for wildlife, controls on alien species are relatively recent in origin. Described as "a vital but rather neglected field"[3], increasing attention is now being focussed on the problem as an environmental issue at the international level: the IUCN's Species Survival Commission established an Invasive Species Specialist Group (ISSG) in 1993 to focus on the conservation impacts of invasive species[4]. The ISSG aims to reduce threats to natural ecosystems and the native species they contain by increasing awareness of invasive alien species, and of ways to prevent, control or eradicate them. In February 2000, the IUCN Council approved Guidelines for the Prevention of Biodiversity Loss caused by Alien Invasive Species prepared by the ISSG[5]. These Guidelines were based in part on work emanating from a major

---

[1] IUCN Guide to the Convention on Biological Diversity, page 46.

[2] See "The Regulation and Control of the Release of Non-native Animals and Plants into the Wild in Great Britain" DoE 1997, section 1.2. The mink has been blamed for accelerating the decline of the water vole after it was shown that the vole forms the most important constituent of the mink diet, The Times 15 June 1996.

[3] See the IUCN Guide to the Convention on Biological Diversity (First Edition) at page 47.

[4] See website at www.issg.org

[5] See www.iucn.org/themes/ssc/pubs/policy

international conference on alien species was held in 1996 in Trondheim Norway[6].

The Convention on Biological Diversity (CBD) addresses the problem of alien species in the context of in-situ conservation in Article 8. Article 8(h) of the Convention requires Parties "as far as possible and as appropriate" to prevent the introduction of, control or eradicate those alien species which threaten ecosystems, habitats or species". The expression "alien species" is not defined in the Convention, but in 2002 the Parties adopted COP Decision VI/23 on Alien species that threaten ecosystems, habitats or species, in which an alien species is defined as "a species, subspecies or lower taxon, introduced outside its natural past or present distribution and includes any part, gametes, seeds, eggs, or propagules of such species that might survive and subsequently reproduce". An invasive alien species is then defined as "an alien species whose introduction and/ or spread threaten biological diversity".

By COP Decision VI/23, the Parties to the CBD adopted a set of 15 Guiding Principles for the Implementation of Article 8(h). Those principles, as annexed to the Decision, include the precautionary approach: "Given the unpredictability of the pathways and impacts on biological diversity of invasive alien species, efforts to identify and prevent unintentional introductions as well as decisions concerning intentional introductions should be based on the precautionary approach, in particular with reference to risk analysis." The principles go on to address matters such as border control and quarantine measures, intentional introduction, unintentional introductions and mitigation of impacts. In relation to intentional introduction, guiding principle 10 states that no first time intentional introduction or subsequent introductions of an alien species which is already invasive or potentially invasive should take place without prior authorization from a competent authority of the recipient state. The burden of proof that a proposed introduction is unlikely to threaten biological diversity should be with the proposer of the introduction or "should be assigned as appropriate by the recipient state".

---

[6] The Conference was sponsored by the United Nations and the Norwegian Ministry of the Environment in collaboration with the United Nations Environment Programme and its Convention on Biological Diversity. A Chairman's report on the conference was submitted to the Subsidiary Body on Scientific and Technological Advice of the CBD (SUBSTA).

In addition to the general provision in the CBD, a number of other international instruments address the issue of alien species[7] in relation to specific sectors, including the United Nations Law of the Sea Convention (UNCLOS). In COP Decision VI/23, the Parties to the CBD call on a number of these bodies to complete adoption of, or revise, instruments to deal with alien species in specific sectors and request the CBD's Subsidiary Body on Scientific, Technical and Technological Advice (SBSTTA) to identify and explore further specific gaps and inconsistencies in the international regulatory framework from a technical perspective of the threats posed by invasive alien species to biodiversity.[8]

The Bern Convention

In relation to Europe, Article 11(2)(b) of the Bern Convention requires Parties to strictly control the introduction of non-native species. The Parties have adopted a number of Recommendations on the issue, most recently Recommendation No 91 of 2002 which makes an interesting distinction between the policy to be adopted in respect of "alien species introduced in recent historic times" and "species introduced in ancient historic times". In relation to the former, "no conservation efforts are to be devoted to the protection of alien species introduced in recent historic times", whereas in the case of the latter "conservation for historic and cultural reasons may be acceptable if recovery of the original ecosystems is no longer feasible, their conservation does not conflict with or preclude the primary aim of conserving and recovering the native biodiversity (impact assessment before conservation)". The Recommendation goes on to address issues such as the need for stricter legislation, the application of precaution and the carrying out of inventories of invasive alien species particularly in respect of vulnerable insular ecosystems. Recommendation No 57 of 1997 contains Guidelines on measures to be adopted in respect of non-native species including requirements for impact studies prior to any deliberate introduction and measures to deal with "fugitives"[9] and "stowaways[10]".

[7] These include the FAO Code of Conduct on bio-control; the United Nations Convention on the Law of the Sea (see Article 196 of UNCLOS on use of technologies /Introduction of alien species); Agenda 21 (see Chapter 17.30(a)(vi) (Oceans and seas) (which calls for rules on ballast water); the International Plant Protection Convention and the UNEP Guidelines for the import and export of animals.

[8] See paragraph 9 of COP Decision VI/23.

[9] Fugitives are defined as "organisms belonging to non-native species (or their descendants) that have been imported lawfully and set free, either accidentally or deliberately, but without the deliberate intention to populate."

[10] Stowaways are "organisms belonging to non-native species transported inadvertently from one country to another".

There is also guidance on the application of the polluter pays principle, making the person responsible for the introduction pay compensation for any damage[11].

European Union

At the European Community level, Article 11 of the wild birds Directive requires "Member States to see that any introduction of species of bird which do not occur naturally in the wild state in the European territory of the member States does not prejudice local flora and fauna...". This is the only obligation in the directive which provides for the protection of species other than birds. Interestingly, there is no express provision aimed at protecting wild birds from alien species other than birds, although this may be implied into the general protection of habitats required under Articles 2-4 of the Directive. The European Court of Justice has considered the issue of "genetic pollution" in the context of determining the scope of the wild birds' directive and in particular the scope of sales controls (discussed further below)[12]. Restrictions intended to protect native species from invasive aliens have also been considered by the Court in the context of the rules on free movement of goods.[13]

Under Article 22 of the Habitats Directive, Member States are called on to ensure that the deliberate introduction into the wild of non-native species is regulated so as not prejudice natural habitats or wild native flora and fauna, and if necessary prohibit such introduction.

The Wildlife and Countryside Act 1981

In the UK, the Wildlife and Countryside Act 1981 was the first piece of conservation legislation to introduce controls on the introductions of alien species. Section 14 of the Act deals with the introduction of new species and imposes controls on the release of both animals and plants,

[11] See also Recommendation No 77 of 1999 on the eradication of non-native terrestrial vertebrates.

[12] Case C202/94 Godefridus van der Feesten ECR [1996] I-355.

[13] See the Judgment of the Court in Case C-67/97 dated 3 December 1998, Anklagemyndighed v. Ditlev Bluhme.in which the ECJ held that (1) A national legislative measure prohibiting the keeping on an island of any species of bee other than the subspecies Apis mellifera mellifera constitutes a measure having an effect equivalent to a quantitative restriction within the meaning of Article 30 of the EC Treaty.(2) A national legislative measure prohibiting the keeping on an island of any species of bee other than the subspecies Apis mellifera mellifera must be regarded as justified, under Article 36of the treaty, on the ground of the protection of the life and health life of animals.

although the scope of the controls is rather different as between the two, in that whilst the introduction of all non-native animal species is regulated, only the introduction of certain non-native plant species is subject to control unders14 (other plant health legislation may apply however).

The Wildlife and Countryside Bill originally contained a provision equivalent to section 14(1)(a) in relation to non-native plants (clause 13(2)(a)) but the clause was dropped from the Bill, in part because of the difficulty in ascertaining whether a particular plant species ordinarily grew in Great Britain in a wild state.

Non-Native Animals

In relation to the introduction of any animal[14], which, by virtue of section 27(3) of the Act, includes the egg, larva, pupa or other immature stage of an animal, there are two types of prohibition. Any person who releases or allows to escape into the wild, either any animal which "is of a kind which is not ordinarily resident in and is not a regular visitor to Great Britain in a wild state"(s14(1)(a)) or which is listed in Part I of Schedule 9 (s14(1)(b)) shall be guilty of an offence.

Section 14(1)(a) is clearly concerned with species not presently found in the wild in Great Britain but the question of whether it has a wider scope has also been raised. In presenting evidence on the operation of Part I of the Wildlife and Countryside Act to the House of Commons Environment Committee in 1984, the Nature Conservancy Council observed that the phrase "of a kind which is not ordinarily resident" in section 14(1)(a) was usually taken by the licensing Department as meaning of a *species* not normally resident whereas there were occasions when much tighter definition was needed for example where the introduced animals come from a different gene stock, possibly even a different sub-species not resident in Great Britain.[15]

Guidance issued by the Department of the Environment in 1997[16] stated that "of a kind" may be specified down the level of sub-species and

[14] Section 2.3 of the Guidance on section 14 suggests that "any animal" includes any species falling within the Kingdom Animalia including microscopic species as well as invertebrates and vertebrate.

[15] See page 65 of the Committee's report.

[16] The current Guidance is The Regulation and Control of the Release of Non-native Animals and Plants into the Wild in Great Britain: A guide to sections 14 and 16 of the Wildlife and Countryside Act 1981,issued in January 2000.

includes hybrids between native and non-native species[17]. This means that where it is proposed to release animals in order to reintroduce species which have become endangered or extinct, such releases will fall within the scope of section 14 if the animals are from non-native sub-species. The Guidance however is silent as to situations where animals are not of a different sub-species but simply of a different gene-stock. An example of such a situation arose in 1996 in relation to the replanting of oaks using Polish Romanian stock which come into leaf two weeks later than indigenous trees, leading to concerns that this would have adverse effects on caterpillars feeding on the leaves[18]. To be "resident", the government guidance indicates that an animal must be breeding in the wild and producing young which reach maturity under natural environmental conditions.

Section 14(1)(b) covers those listed species, already introduced and reintroduced, whose further control Government wishes to control and monitor in most cases because they are known to cause damage to the environment.

The 2000 Guidance indicates that keeping animals in "semi-confined situations" such as in gardens and glass houses or in relation to aquatic animals in cages or pens floating in lakes can constitute release or allowing to escape into the wild where the animals concerned may escape into the wider environment.[19]

Non-native Plants

As far as plants are concerned, the controls are limited to a prohibition on planting or otherwise causing to grow[20] in the wild any of the plants listed in Part II of Schedule 9 (s14(2)). The plants listed are generally those known to cause damage to the environment.

The Guidance indicates that in addition to deliberate planting, cultivation in confined situations falls within the scope of section 14(2) where removal or transfer of the plant material may allow the plant to become established in the wild (section 2.7).

[17] See now section 2.3 of the 2000 Guidance.
[18] Daily Mail 26 November 1996.
[19] See 2000 Guidance, section 2.2.
[20] As to the meaning of "cause to grow" and its application to landowners who allow Japanese Knotweed to proliferate on their land, see article by David Pocklington, Env Law 1997 11(2) 9-10.

Licences

Licences for the introduction of species which would otherwise be prohibited under section 14 may be granted under section 16(4)(c) of the Act[21]. It is worth noting that neither the wild birds directive nor the habitats directive make any specific provision for the circumstance in which derogations from Articles 11 and 22 respectively may be granted, in contrast to the other species protection provisions under those directives[22]. This means that the purposes for which licences may be granted are apparently left to Member States to determine, taking account of the overall objectives of the wild birds' directive and the habitats directive.

The UK guidance on the controls indicates that licences may be granted for purposes such as the use of non-native animals for the control of pests on commercial crops.

Except for releases of fish or shell-fish, the licensing authorities for the purposes of section 14 are the Secretary of State for the Environment (concurrently with the Welsh Assembly as regards Wales[23]) and the Secretary of State for Scotland depending on where the release is to take place. The Minister for Agriculture (concurrently with the Welsh Assembly as regards Wales) or the equivalent agricultural departments in Scotland is the licensing authority in relation to fish or shell fish. The Advisory Committee on Releases to the Environment (ACRE) advises the Secretary of State for the Environment on the granting of licences, together with the JNCC or the relevant nature conservancy council. MAFF consult the Environment Agency on the release of fish or shellfish.

The type of information which should be submitted with an application is set out in the Guidance and includes information on the non-native organism including survivability in the environment and any known harmful effects and on the receiving environment including information on any rare or endangered species in the release habitat. Licences may, by virtue of section 16(5)(c) be subject to specified conditions. Examples of conditions which may be applied to licences in respect of

---

[21] For guidance on the operation of sections 14 and 16 see "The Regulation and Control of the Release of Non-native Animals and Plants into the Wild in Great Britain" DoE 1997, section 1.2.

[22] See chapter 3A - Part II for a general discussion of licences under section 16 of the Wildlife and Countryside Act 1981.

[23] See the National Assembly for Wales (Transfer of Functions) Order 1999, SI 1999/672.

section 14 are given in the Guidance and include a requirement for monitoring and the immediate notification to the appropriate authority of any adverse effects from the release (section 3.5).

The Precautionary Principle

As discussed above, the need to apply the precautionary principle (or approach) in this area has been explicitly acknowledged at the international level 24. Once a species has been released into the wild it may be extremely difficult or even impossible to remove it from the environment and any damaging effects may therefore be irreversible. This is clearly therefore an area where the application of the precautionary principle is of great importance.

So far as the UK legislation is concerned, the need to proceed with caution was acknowledged at an early stage, during the passage of the Wildlife and Countryside Bill, when Lord Cullen of Ashbourne, on behalf of the Government, outlined the general policy on introductions: "our basic principle has been that no introduction of an exotic species, or reintroduction of a formerly native species into the wild, should take place without proper consideration of the ecological implications, and that there should be provision for monitoring of any introduction which may be effected."[25].

In the 1997 Guidance on the controls issued by the Department of the Environment, express reference is made to the application of the precautionary principle in the consideration of applications for licences under s16(4): "Where information is not available to address the likelihood of an identified hazard being realised, or where scientific knowledge is not conclusive, then precautionary action should be taken to prevent or minimise the use or spread of the non-native animal or plant."[26] The same guidance refers to MAFF's presumption against the issue of licences for the introduction of landlocked salmon and non-native cray-fish (section 3.13 of the DoE Guidance) and of any non-native species into open river systems.

[24] See for example CBD COP Decision VI/23 and Bern Convention Recommendation No 91 of 2002, discussed above.

[25] Hansard, House of Lords, 3 February 1981, col 1168.

[26] "The Regulation and Control of the Release of Non-native Animals and Plants into the Wild in Great Britain" DoE 1997, section A2.3.

Scope of the UK Controls

A number of issues regarding the scope of the controls were raised during the Bill's passage through Parliament. The introduction of indigenous animals to a part of the UK where they are not found would not be covered by the Act said the Government thus the Act would not cover translocation from one part of country to another. The controls would however apply where a species is captured and re-released and a licence will be required (DoE Guidance section 2.10).

During the passage of the Wildlife and Countryside Bill, the Government explained that it had rejected the idea of extending the controls to imports of alien species with a view to release because such a provision would be too hard to enforce and many animals did not pose a threat whilst in captivity.

In relation to sale or marketing, DoE Guidance nevertheless advises that where, in the course of commercial distribution, it is considered that the end use of the product will involve releasing an animal into the wild, all persons involved in the distribution chain must be licenced.

Enforcement

A defence that the accused took all reasonable steps and exercised all due diligence to avoid committing the offence is available under section 14(3). Where a person wishes to rely on the due diligence defence by alleging that the offence was due to the act or default of another person, the accused must serve a notice on the prosecution identifying or assisting in the identification of that person by such information as was in his possession at least seven days before the hearing (section 14(4)).

The Act provides for a power of entry for land other than a dwelling for the purpose of ascertaining whether an offence is being or has been committed on that land (section 14(5) and an obstruction offence is also provided for (section 14(6)).

Genetic pollution

The extent to which the issue of "genetic pollution", in the sense of the interbreeding of introduced subspecies and European subspecies, is addressed by controls on alien species has been a matter of some debate. The definition of pollution under UNCLOS includes the deliberate or accidental introduction of alien or exotic species which are capable of causing significant and harmful changes to the marine environment (art 196). In relation to conservation legislation, the matter is less clear cut.

Case C202/94 Godefridus van der Feesten[27].

The issue of "genetic pollution" was raised in *Case C202/94 Godefridus van der Feesten*[28]. It was argued that the Directive should be construed as applying to non-European subspecies as well as European subspecies because of the need to control the sale and possession of the former in order to prevent interbreeding or "genetic pollution". Alternatively, it was argued that even if non-European subspecies fell outside the scope of the Directive, national rules restricting trade in exotic birds were justifiable under Community law because they contributed to the prevention of genetic pollution.

The ECJ appears to have accepted the genetic pollution argument as a further reason for concluding that the Directive applied to non-European subspecies, noting that "... if non-European subspecies could be freely imported into the Community, the risk...that exotic subspecies might be released into the wild there, leading possibly to artificial alterations of the natural avifauna occurring in the Community, could not be excluded. This would be incompatible with the objective of safeguarding biological balances mentioned in the second recital in the preamble to the Directive."(paragraph 17).

The Advocate General was, however, more sceptical about the merits of the genetic pollution argument. First, he noted that the Commission had sought to draw an analogy with Article 11 the Directive which requires Member States to ensure that any introduction of species of bird which does not occur naturally in the wild state in the European Territory of the Member States does not prejudice the local flora and fauna. He concluded that, rather than supporting the interpretation argued for by the Commission, Article 11 "illustrates the distinction inherent in the Directive between local flora and fauna, which it seeks to protect, and exotic flora and fauna, which it does not."(paragraph 46) This comment is no doubt to be understood as meaning that the application of the Directive to non-European subspecies would constitute "protection" even if the rationale for it is to protect indigenous birds.

---

[27] For further consideration of this case, see Chapter I - Part II.
[28] ECR [1996] I-355

He then criticised the parties for introducing the argument "at a very late stage" and found it regrettable "that no indication of the nature or effects of genetic pollution on the conservation of the European goldfinch was given..." He concluded that "Since we are speaking of a subspecies which, by definition, is capable of interbreeding with the existing European subspecies, a consequence which is not self evidently harmful, we would need to know much more clearly how and why, apart from the adoption of a pejorative description, it should be so considered...(paragraph 59)."

If genetic pollution is accepted to be a potential problem, and the ECJ appears to have accepted that it is, it is clearly not an issue which is confined to non-European subspecies since presumably interbreeding could also occur between different European subspecies where one is introduced into the wild in a part of the Community where it does not naturally occur. The question is then whether, and if so how, the wild birds Directive (or for that matter, the habitats directive) addresses this issue. In contrast to *van der Feesten* there would be no argument as to whether either of the subspecies falls within the scope of the Directive so presumably the same combination of sales/possession controls and Article 11 would apply.

Following the Court's judgment in *C202/94 Godefridus van der Feesten*, it is not clear whether Article 11 of the Directive is intended to restrict the introduction of exotic subspecies and thus prevent so called genetic pollution. The implication is that it does not, since that was one reason why the Court felt it necessary to interpret Article 1 so broadly as to apply to non-European subspecies. Indeed the Court appears to have assumed that the regulation of possession and sale of subspecies will contribute towards preventing genetic pollution among European subspecies as well as between European and non-European subspecies. This would appear to be a rather indirect way of addressing the issue however, which might more properly be addressed through express control of introductions of non-native subspecies. Meanwhile, the extent to which genetic pollution is truly of conservation concern and, if it is, the appropriate response to it remain matters of controversy, as became clear during the debate on the ruddy duck.

The Ruddy Duck

The Ruddy Duck has brought the issue of genetic pollution came to the fore in recent years. During discussions on Schedule 9 of the Wildlife and Countryside Bill, Lord Cullen of Ashbourne on behalf of the Government explained the need for caution even in relation to apparently harmless species by citing Sir Peter Scott on the ruddy duck "Having been carelessly responsible myself for allowing the North American ruddy duck to escape and build up to what seems to be a small but viable population in England, I am in no position to pass judgment on others. To be sure, the ruddy duck is decorative and apparently harmless but no one can know the insidious effect it may have on the ecological web."[29].

In the 1990s concern arose that the ruddy duck was spreading from the UK to Spain where its inter-breeding with the local white-headed duck was believed to pose a threat to the latter's survival. The UK Government announced that it was to institute a cull of the ruddy duck in 1996 but this proposal was then withdrawn, reportedly because many landowners refused to cooperate with such a measure[30].

Subsequently, in 1999, a Ruddy Duck Control Trial was conducted by the Central Science Laboratory on behalf of DEFRA over a three-year period[31]. The Report focuses on the efficacy of the various eradication methods tested in the trial and does not consider the ethics or wider conservation issues surrounding the cull. The controversial background to the cull is evident however from the conclusion that "It is unlikely that voluntary access will be granted for all such sites, and powers of compulsory access for them might need to be considered to ensure the success of a national programme within a reasonable timescale."

Review of Policy on Non-Native Species

The Government established a review of policy on non-native species in 2001[32]. The Group produced its Final Report in March 2003. The Group took account of the Guiding Principles agreed by the Parties to the CBD (see above). Among the Group's eight key recommendations were that: comprehensive, accepted risk assessment procedures, to assess the risks posed by non-native species should be developed and codes of conduct should be introduced in order to help prevent unintentional introductions as a result of legitimate activity.

[29] Hansard House of Lords Debates 3 February 1981, col 1168
[30] See The Daily Telegraph 3 April 1997 and The Times 15 June 1996.
[31] See the Report of the Trial at www.defra.gov.uk/wildlife-countryside/scientific/ruddy/ruddy1/Fullreport.pdf.
[32] See final report at http://www.defra.gov.uk/wildlife-countryside/resprog/findings/non-native/ecoscope-intro.pdf

In relation to introducing improvements to the existing legislation (the 1981 Act), the Group identified a number of areas requiring amendment including: a need to rationalise the treatment of plants and animals and to enable a more regular update of Schedule 9 in order to ensure that problem species are included and also the need to ensure that penalties more closely reflected the potential cost of damage caused by invasive species. The Group found that fines for criminal offences in respect of invasive non-native species were "very low in comparison to the potential costs of damage, control and repair". These remedial costs were typically met by the taxpayer, or the interests affected. The Review Group took the view that the level of fines available did not constitute a deterrent and recommended that, "where a release constitutes a criminal offence or wilful negligence then the "polluter pays" principle should be available, i.e. courts should be able to impose fines bearing some relation to the cost of reparation."

Relationship with Controls on the Release of GMOs

A detailed examination of the regulation of genetically modified organisms (GMOs) lies beyond the scope of this book, however the regulatory approaches to the release of alien species and of GMOs share a number of common features, such as the acknowledged need for a prior impact study and risk analysis before any deliberate introduction or release can take place. The general degree of uncertainty surrounding the potential environmental effects of releasing GMOs is greater, not least because the devastation which can be caused by invasive alien species is already well documented around the world. Although distinct in many ways, these two areas pose a number of similar challenges for the legislator. Included among the common issues which both types of regime have to address are the definition of release/introduction into the environment, the methodology for risk assessment and definitions of harm to the environment.

The same statutory advisory committee, the Advisory Committee on Release to the Environment (ACRE) advises the Government on both regimes, that is to say on the granting of licences under s14 of the Wildlife and Countryside Act 1981 (see below) and on the operation of and consents under Part VI of the Environmental Protection Act governing the deliberate release of GMOs.

CHAPTER 7

POSITIVE MEASURES FOR SPECIES RECOVERY

Recovery Programmes

The Royal Society for Nature Conservation, in giving evidence in 1984 to the House of Commons Select Committee on the amendment of the Wildlife and Countryside Act 1981[1] called for a more positive approach to be taken towards bringing about the recovery of endangered species, rather than mere reliance on listing them in a statutory schedule:

"It is not good enough to consider their scheduling as an end in itself; they should be subject to recovery programmes devised by the Nature Conservancy Council. Each programme should consist of a plan, an agreed division of responsibilities, costings and an effective system to monitor progress. The object would be to improve the status of species so that they could be moved from the "endangered" to the "protected" category. The Society believes that the Act should be so amended and s24(3)[2] should also require reference to be made in the NCC's annual report to the recovery programmes devised and their progress."

This proactive approach is increasingly reflected in conservation law at both the international and national levels. Article 8(f) of the Convention on Biological Diversity calls on Parties "as far as possible and as appropriate" to "rehabilitate and restore degraded ecosystems and promote the recovery of threatened species, inter alia, through the development and implementation of plans or other management programmes."

Recovery plans and action plans began to be introduced in the UK as a matter of policy from about the late 1980s: by 1992, English Nature had adopted species recovery programme for 20 species, but it is only recently that the adoption of this type of plan has been dealt with in statute law. Currently English nature has adopted species recovery plans for some

---

[1] See the Committee's 1984 Report at page 237.

[2] Section 24(3) of the 1981 Act, as amended, requires the Secretary of State to lay before Parliament copies of advice given by the Nature Conservancy Councils (on the review of Schedules 5 and 8 to the Act).

391 priority species, together with species statements and grouped species action plans[3].

Biodiversity Action Plans

Article 6 CBD requires each Contracting Party, in accordance with its particular conditions and capabilities to "(a) [d]evelop national strategies, plans or programmes for the conservation and sustainable use of biological diversity or adapt for this purpose existing strategies, plans or programmes which shall reflect, inter alia, the measures set out in this Convention relevant to the Contracting Party concerned; and (b) [i]ntegrate, as far as possible and as appropriate, the conservation and sustainable use of biological diversity into relevant sectoral or cross-sectoral plans, programmes and policies".

The UK Biodiversity Action Plan was first published in January 1994. Its objectives include the conservation and where possible enhancement of overall populations and natural ranges of native species...and internationally important and threatened species...and species characteristic of local areas[4].

The Countryside and Rights of Way 2000 has put this type of activity on a clearer statutory footing. Section 74 of the 2000 Act creates a duty on the party of Ministers, Government Departments and the Welsh Assembly to have regard, so far as is consistent with their functions, to the purpose of conserving biodiversity in accordance with the CBD. The section also requires the Secretary of State and the Welsh Assembly to publish lists of those living organisms and habitats which in the opinion of the Secretary of State or the Assembly (as the case may be) are of principal importance for the purpose mentioned in subsection (1). There is a further duty on them to take, or to promote the taking by others of, such steps as appear to the authority to be reasonably practicable to further the conservation of the living organisms and types of habitat included in any list published by the authority under this section. The real importance of this provision is indicated by comments made by the then Minister for the Environment, Michael Meacher. In moving the amendment which led to the insertion of section 74, he noted that there was strong support on all sides for statutory underpinning for the conservation of biodiversity outside designated sites[5]. Whereas the duties of authorities in relation to designated sites have

[3] Details are available on the English Nature website.
[4] See the UK's 1st report to the CBD at page 3.
[5] Hansard, House of Commons Debates 28 November 2000, col 901

generally required a fairly proactive approach to conservation, the position outside such sites was much more reactive, at best. This type of provision aims to ensure that positive measures for species recovery are implemented more widely.

Re-Establishment and Reintroduction

One aspect of species recovery may be the reestablishment of habitats or reintroduction of species. This part of the chapter looks at the emerging legal framework in which this takes place. In order to understand the legislative framework it is important to appreciate some of the difficulties which best attempts to reintroduce species.

Difficulties Posed in Successfully Reintroducing Species

The difficulties inherent in bringing about successful reintroduction of species of birds, mammals or insects were highlighted by the NERC in their evidence to the House of Lords[6]: "the lesson you learn is that if [species] have gone extinct, it is almost always for reasons of habitat change or human impact, and just bringing them back is to put yourself on an endless treadmill." NERC went on to give an example of the type of difficulty involved: "it is easy to go and get the plants you want to get in a habitat, be it heathland of seminatural chalk grassland, but it is another thing to get them to grow and grow successfully ... because changes in the soil chemistry are difficult to reverse."

There is also the risk of genetic pollution if a geographically separate population of a native species is introduced. Conversely, the need to consider reintroduction may itself arise from the introduction of alien species, for example, native crayfish are threatened with extinction due to the appearance of crayfish plague (probably brought into to Britain by American Signal crayfish. Clearly the reintroduction will not succeed if replacement stock simply to succumb to the disease themselves.

The scientific input required, as indicated by NERC, includes: documentation of changing biodiversity through survey and monitoring and analysis of possible causal factors; improved understanding of the ways in which natural populations become established, interact and respond to environmental change (using field observation and mathematical modelling); development of a capability to predict the impact

[6] House of Lords Committee Report on Sustainable Development at page 305.

of environmental change on biodiversity and of changing biodiversity on ecological processes.

International Provisions on Reintroduction

The difficulties outlined above and the need for a scientific assessment of the prospects of success are reflected in the way that reintroduction is dealt with in the Bern Convention and in a number of other international and regional instruments. Under Article 11(2)(a) of the Berne Convention, Contracting Parties undertake to encourage the reintroduction of native species of wild flora and fauna when this would contribute to the conservation of an endangered species, *provided* that a study is first made in the light of the experiences of other Parties in order to establish that such reintroduction would be effective and acceptable.

Under Article 9(c) of the CBD, Parties are to "as far as possible and as appropriate" adopt measures for the recovery and rehabilitation of threatened species and for their reintroduction into their natural habitats under appropriate conditions." Article 9 deals with ex situ conservation and the measures to be taken under it are stated to be "predominantly for the purpose of complementing in-situ measures".

Reintroduction in the UK

Species identified as giving particular cause for concern include, in UK, the otter, corncrake and merlin. The otter has benn the subject of successful reintroductions in Eastern England. The statutory basis for reintroduction undertaken by agencies such as English Nature tends to be general rather than specific, arising out of their general functions as set out in Part VII of the EPA 1990. Since 1989 a red kite recovery programme has also been in place with successful reintroductions in Northen Scotland, Southern England and elsewhere in the UK. In addition to species and habitat protection, such initiatives may include other types of measure such those promoting changes in agricultural practice (the Corncrake) and supplementary feeding (the Dartford Warbler).

Zoos

Zoos can play an important role in conservation in educating the public, conducting research and, in some cases, carrying out captive breeding programmes for critically endangered species. Clearly the latter is subsidiary to attempts to maintain populations of endangered species in the wild but a successful captive breeding programme can produce animals for reintroduction. So far as the law is concerned, the main focus is on welfare standards in zoos but there is also specific recognition of their role in conservation and there are now statutory requirements on zoos under EU and domestic law to implement certain conservation measures.

The Convention on Biological Diversity

Article 9 of the Convention deals with ex-situ conservation, defined as "the conservation of components of biological diversity outside their natural habitats"[7], which would clearly cover zoos carrying out conservation work, and requires the Parties "as far as possible and as appropriate, and predominantly for the purpose of complementing in-situ measures", to adopt measures for the ex situ conservation of components of biological diversity, preferably in the country of origin of such components. It is clear from the terms of the Convention that in-situ conservation[8], whereby habitats and species are conserved in their natural surroundings, is the preferred option for conservation but the complementary potential of ex situ measures is also set out. Article 9 also requires Parties to "regulate and manage collection of biological resources from natural habitats for ex situ conservation purposes so as not to threaten ecosystems and in situ populations of species", except where special temporary ex situ measures are required for the purposes of recovery, rehabilitation and reintroduction.

The EU Zoos Directive

In 1999 the European Union adopted Council Directive 1999/22 on the keeping of wild animals in zoos[9]. The stated objective of the Directive is to protect wild fauna and conserve biodiversity by providing for the licensing and inspection of zoos in the Community, "thereby strengthening the role of zoos in the conservation of biodiversity". An earlier proposal for a zoos directive had been dropped the mid-1990's, casualty of a political move to demonstrate that the EU principle of subsidiarity was being strictly observed by abandoning a number of draft proposals deemed to contravene

[7] See Article 2.

[8] In situ conservation means the conservation of ecosystems and natural habitats and the maintenance and recovery of viable populations of species in their natural surroundings, Article 2.

[9] Council Directive 1999/22/EC of 29 March 1999 relating to the keeping of wild animals in zoos OJ L 094 , 09/04/1999 P. 0024 – 0026. The deadline for implementation was 9 April 2002.

that principle. Pressure for an EU measure to regulate standards in zoos was maintained however in the face of concerns about the appalling welfare standards of some European zoos. There then followed disputes about the appropriate legal basis for the Directive, but in the end it was agreed that it, notwithstanding the concern with animal welfare, the measure could be adopted on the basis of Article 130s (now 174) the environmental legal base, because of the need to ensure that European zoos were of a sufficient standard to carry out conservation work.

The preamble to the Directive makes reference to Article 9 of the CBD (see above) as well as to the CITES Regulation[10] and the wild birds and habitats directives[11] . The relevance of the CITES Regulation is that it requires evidence "of the availability of adequate facilities for the accommodation and care of live specimens of a great many species before their importation into the Community is authorized" and that it "prohibits the display to the public for commercial purposes of specimens of species listed in Annex A" unless a specific exemption for education, research or breeding purposes has been granted". Thus common standards for these conditions are required for the uniform application of that Regulation by Member States. In relation to the two directives, both prohibit the capture and keeping of and trade in a great number of species, whilst providing for exemptions for specific reasons, such as research and education, repopulation, reintroduction and breeding. Thus common standards are also required in relation to the implementation of these two measures in relation to zoos. The preamble also notes that a number of organisations such as the European Association of Zoos and Aquaria have produced guidelines for the care and accommodation of animals in zoos which could, where appropriate, assist in the development and adoption of national standards.

The Directive defines zoos "permanent establishments where animals of wild species are kept for exhibition to the public for 7 or more days a year, with the exception of circuses, pet shops and establishments which Member States exempt from the requirements of this Directive on the grounds that they do not exhibit a significant number of animals or species to the public and that the exemption will not jeopardise the objectives of this Directive"[12] .

[10] Council Regulation (EEC) No 338/97 of 9 December 1996 on the protection of species of wild fauna and flora by regulating trade therein, discussed in Section III (Trade).

[11] Council Directive 79/409/EEC of 2 April 1979 on the conservation of wild birds and Council Directive 92/43/EC of 21 May 1992 on the conservation of natural habitats and of wild fauna and flora discussed in Section 1 (Habitats) and II (Species protection).

[12] See Article 2.

Member States are required to set up a system for licensing and inspecting zoos (Article 4) and to ensure under that system that zoos carry out the types of conservation work specified in Article 3. These include public education, research, training in conservation and "where appropriate" captive breeding and reintroduction into the wild". Zoos must also accommodate their animals "under conditions which aim to satisfy the biological and conservation requirements of the individual species, inter alia, by providing species specific enrichment of the enclosures; and maintaining a high standard of animal husbandry with a developed programme of preventive and curative veterinary care and nutrition" (Article 3) as well as prevent escapes and the entry of vermin. Each (four year) licence must contain conditions to enforce the requirements of Article 3 and compliance with those conditions is to be monitored by means of regular inspection and appropriate steps taken to ensure such compliance. If the zoo is not licensed in accordance with the Directive or the licensing conditions are not met, the zoo must either be shall be closed to the public by the competent authority and/or must comply with appropriate requirements imposed by the competent authority to ensure that the licensing conditions are met (Article 4(5)).

By way of exception to these licensing requirements, they shall not apply where a Member State can demonstrate to the satisfaction of the Commission that the objective of the Directive and the requirements set out in Article 3 are being met "and continuously maintained" by means of a system or regulation and registration. Such a system should contain provisions regarding inspection and closure of zoos equivalent to those in Article 4 (Article 5). Under Article 6, in the event of a zoo being closed, the competent authority is required to ensure that the animals concerned are treated or disposed of under conditions which the Member State deems appropriate and consistent with the purposes and provisions of this Directive.

The Zoo Licensing Act 1981

In the United Kingdom, zoos were already regulated under the 1981 Zoo Licensing Act (which entered into force in 1984). The 1981 Act was amended in 2002 in order to bring it fully into line with the Directive[13] and in its amended form requires zoos to adopt the conservation measures mandated by Article 3 of the Directive. A new Section 1A is inserted which sets out the conservation measures required to be implemented by zoos.

[13] See the Zoo Licensing Act 1981 (Amendment)(England and Wales) Regulations 2002, SI 2002/3080, entered into force 8 January 2003.

Government Circular 02/2003 was published to provide guidance to local authorities on the new measures which fall to them as zoo licensing authorities and makes it clear that the conservation measures prescribed for the zoo must be suitable to its size and capabilities[14]. The Act defines a zoo as "an establishment where wild animals[15] ... are kept for exhibition to the public otherwise than for purposes of a circus ... and otherwise than in a pet shop" and applies to any zoo "to which members of the public have access, with or without charge for admission, on seven days or more in any period of twelve consecutive months"[16]

Under the Act, it is unlawful to operate a zoo to which the Act applies except under the authority of a licence issued by the local authority for the area within which the whole or the major part of the zoo is situated. The Act sets out the procedure for applying for and obtaining a licence. In considering a licence application, the local authority is required to take into account any representations made by the local Chief Officer of Police and the governing body of any national institution concerned with the operation of zoos among others (section 3) and to consider inspectors' reports made in pursuance of inspections of the zoo under the Act (section 4). A licence must be granted subject to conditions requiring the conservation measures referred to in section 1A to be implemented at the zoo (section 5(2A)) and among the grounds for refusing a licence are that the local authority is not satisfied that the conservation measures referred to in section 1A "will be implemented in a satisfactory manner at the zoo" (section 4(2A)). Thus the fulfillment of statutory conservation functions is now a prerequisite to operating as a licensed zoo in the UK.

Under section 8 of the Act, the Secretary of State is required to maintain a list of vets and other specialists qualified to carry out inspections of zoos and to ensure that the conservation functions required under section 1A are properly implemented and that zoos are correctly managed. The inspectors are instructed by the local authority concerned. The Secretary of State is then empowered, after consulting persons on the list and such other persons as he thinks fit, to specify standards of modern zoo practice, that is, "standards with respect to the management of zoos and the animals in them" (section 9). A set of such standards were adopted in March 2000[17].

[14] The Circular also incorporates and replaces the guidance contained in Department of the Environment (DOE) Circulars 5/84 and 11/88.

[15] Defined in section 21 as animals not normally domesticated in Great Britain.

[16] See section 1(2)and (2A) of the 1981 Act.

[17] A copy is available on the Defra website at www.defra.gov.uk.

Chapter 7 of Section 2 deals with conservation and states that where the relevant species are held, a zoo must be an active participant in recognized species management programmes. The programme must contribute something beyond a basic interpretation of conservation in the wild. Zoos should also demonstrate "measurable performance in conservation, education and research" and continues "Areas to be examined will include overall conservation and education policy, and how this relates to the World Zoo Conservation Strategy and type and level of input into international conservation programmes[18]."

The Act goes on to provided for periodic and special inspections of zoos. Local authorities are empowered to alter a licence at any time under the conditions set out in section 16 which includes where a condition specified in a section 16A direction (relating to enforcement of licence conditions) which requires any conservation measure referred to in section 1A to be implemented at the zoo is not met. A local authority may also may a zoo closure direction under section 16B of the Act, including in circumstances where, following a section 16A direction and the expiry of the period specified for compliance, the authority is satisfied that a condition specified in that direction, requiring any conservation measure referred to in section 1A to be implemented at the zoo, is not met (section 16B(1)). It is an offence under section 19 to operate a zoo without a licence or to fail without reasonable excuse to comply with any condition for the time being attached to a licence for the zoo granted under the Act. The penalty for both offences is a fine on level 4 of the standard scale.

[18] See also Appendix 3 on Conservation.

PART III
TRADE IN ENDANGERED SPECIES

TRADE IN ENDANGERED SPECIES

Estimates as to the annual value of international trade in wildlife products range from $5 billion to $15 billion[1]. Illegal trade in wildlife poses a major threat to many species internationally. The regime regulating international trade in endangered species derives from an important international treaty, the 1973 Convention on International Trade in Endangered Species of Wild Fauna and Flora, commonly known as CITES to which most countries are party. CITES is implemented in the European Union by Council Regulation (EC) No 338/97 on the Protection of Species of Wild Fauna and Flora by Regulating Trade Therein Regulation, which is supplemented in the UK by the Control of Trade in Endangered Species (Enforcement) Regulations 1997 which governs matters such as enforcement powers and penalties. Some UK species are potentially affected by illegal international trade and are afforded protection but the main impact of the regime in the UK is to regulate what is imported here from other countries both within and outside the European Union whether for onward sale or personal consumption.

This section considers the rules of the Convention alongside those of the European Regulation. Decisions of the Parties to the Convention taken at the Conferences of the Parties regularly update the regime and are incorporated into EU legislation so it is important to understand the workings of the Convention in some detail in order to understand the European and domestic position. The institutions operating the regime at the international, European and domestic levels are described in Chapter 1 - Part III.

The Convention operates on a system of import and export controls based on permits issued by the state of export and/or import depending on the species concerned. Species (occasionally subspecies) are listed on one of three Appendices, according to their conservation status and the threat posed by trade, and this determines the extent to which international trade is permitted and the rules which apply. The European Regulation follows this approach very closely so far as import into and export out of the EU is concerned but affords stricter protection to certain species, either by regulating those which are not currently protected under the Convention or by subjecting certain species to a stricter regime than that required under

---

[1] See *"Making a Killing or Making a Living? Wildlife trade, trade controls and rural livelihoods"* Biodiversity and Livelihoods Issues No.6 IIED and TRAFFIC, 2002, available at www.traffic.org

the Convention. The European Regulation also controls movement and sale of certain species within the European Union itself, including within individual Member States. The Regulation contains 4 Annexes listing species, based on the Convention's three Appendices but with some modifications. Chapter 2 examines the criteria governing the listing of species under both the Convention and Regulation. Chapter 3 (Annex A) then deals with the regime governing the most endangered species in which as a general rule no commercial trade is permitted. Chapter 4 (Annex B) looks at those species, which are not endangered but in relation to which commercial trade poses a potential risk and is therefore permitted subject to monitoring and other controls. Chapter 5 looks at those species afforded some limited degree of protection mainly because of the desire of the country of origin to monitor or control international trade.

The remaining chapters examine the various aspects of the regulatory regime, Chapter 7 deals with the rules relating to permits, Chapter 6 looks at the rules on granting exemptions, Chapter 8 deals with transport and Chapter 9 considers the requirements for enforcement.

CHAPTER 1

CITES: INSTITUTIONS AND DECISION-MAKING

The CITES regime depends for its effective operation on a number of key institutions and bodies operating at the international, regional and domestic levels. In order to understand how the controls are applied in the UK, it is necessary to bear in mind the important role played by the Convention bodies and the organs established at the Community level as well as the work done at the national level by the UK Management Authority and Scientific Authority and various enforcement agencies. In addition, a significant contribution to the work of the Convention is made at every level by non-governmental organisations and user groups. This chapter outlines the different roles undertaken by the key bodies and agencies.

The Convention Bodies

At the international level, key decisions are taken by the Parties at the biennial Conferences of the Parties (COPs) but even between these COPs, the roles of both the CITES Secretariat and the various Committees of the Parties established under the Convention are vital in ensuring that the Convention is effectively implemented, that decision-making by the Parties is based on sound information and that once taken decisions and resolutions are put into effect. The sheer number of decisions and resolutions taken by the Parties over the course of twelve COPs gives an indication of the amount of ongoing work required to ensure that the Convention works in practice.

The Conference of the Parties

Pursuant to Article XI of the Convention, the Secretariat must convene regular meetings of the Parties at least once every two years, unless the Conference decides otherwise, and extraordinary meetings at any time on the written request of at least one third of the Parties[1]. The most recent COP, COP12 took place in Santiago, Chile in November 2002. At these meetings, the Convention requires the Parties to review the implementation of the Convention and enables them to take certain measures including: considering and adopting amendments to Appendices I and II; review the

[1] The number of Parties was 163 as at September 2003.

progress made towards the restoration and conservation of listed species; receive and consider any reports presented by the Secretariat or any Party and "where appropriate", make recommendations for improving the effectiveness of the Convention.

Key decisions are taken in the form of Conference Resolutions or by means of Decisions of the Parties. Conference Resolutions generally provide guidance, in many cases quite detailed guidance, on the implementation, interpretation and operation of the Convention. As a minimum, they may be regarded as a statement of best practice adopted by the Parties and it can be argued that many, if not all, represent an agreed interpretation of certain provisions with the result that although the Resolutions are non-binding per se, failure to comply with them may indicate a breach of a Party's obligations under the Convention. The CITES Secretariat consider the Resolutions and Decisions to binding on themselves and apply all of them accordingly. Resolutions adopted by the Parties at the various COPs are referred to by a number based on the number of the COP as will as the Resolution, thus CR5.10 on the definition of "primarily commercial purposes" was adopted at COP5 in Buenos Aires in 1985. Decisions, which are time-limited, generally deal with more administrative matters such as regional representation in the Standing Committee or the setting out of the working programme of the Convention between COPs.

In addition to representatives of the Parties and members of the Secretariat, the COP is attended by many other observers representing various organisations, interest groups, the media and so on. The total number of participants numbers in the thousands. Article 11(6) of the Convention specifically provides that the United Nations, its specialised agencies and any State not party to the Convention may be represented by observers. Other international or national bodies which are technically qualified in conservation of wildlife as specified in Article 11(7) (and have informed the Secretariat of their desire to attend) shall be admitted as observers unless at least one third of the Parties object.

The CITES Secretariat

The CITES Secretariat performs a variety of key functions as set out in Article XII of the Convention. These include arranging for and servicing meetings of the Parties and making recommendations for the implementation of the aims and provisions of the Convention. The Secretariat also performs many other functions such as providing expert advice on listing proposals. The Secretariat has an important role in relation to the confirmation of permits and certificates[2]. Notification 1999/27 contains guidelines on when the Secretariat should be asked to confirm the authenticity and validity of CITES permits (essentially where there is reason to doubt their authenticity, or fraud is suspected or where a Conference Resolution recommends that this be done). These guidelines on the issuance and acceptance of permits and certificates are designed to assist Management Authorities (and have been endorsed by the COP). The Secretariat does not get involved in routine confirmation of permits, nor does it deal direct with traders. In relation to capacity building, the Secretariat provides training, advice and has available specimen permits. In relation to enforcement, the Secretariat has co-operated with the International Police Organization (ICPO-Interpol) and the World Customs Organisation to facilitate exchange of information between enforcement bodies and for training purposes.

The Standing Committee

The Parties have established four permanent committees to facilitate the work of the COP and the operation of the Convention. Of these the most senior is the Standing Committee, which is a committee composed of regional representatives, which acts on behalf of the Parties between meetings. It oversees the execution of the budget and advises the Secretariat on matters which it brings to its attention. Typical of the types of issues considered by the Standing Committee (once mandated to do so by the COP) are proposed trade bans against Parties which are not complying with their obligations and matters arising from the previous COP which may include further work to implement a Conference Resolution or further consideration of matter which was raised but not resolved at the COP. If the Committee decides to recommend a trade ban, the Secretariat notifies the recommendation to the Parties.

Other Convention Committees

The Animals Committee and the Plants Committees are permanent committees which provide advice to the Parties on biological and trade information relating animals and plants respectively. Like the Standing Committee, these Committees are composed of regional representatives elected at the COP. One of their important functions is to advise the Parties where species are subject to unsustainable levels of trade and remedial action is required (the Significant Trade Process). The Committees also

[2] See CITES Notification 2001/003 and CITES Notification 1999/27.

undertake periodic reviews of the Appendices to the Convention and prepare draft Resolutions for consideration by the Parties.

The Nomenclature Committee is another permanent committee which recommends standard names for species so that these can be used in the Appendices and elsewhere. Membership is voluntary.

In addition to these committees, from time to time, committees and working groups are set up by the parties to consider specific topics ranging from timber, transport and the use of annotations in the Appendices.

UNEP-WCMC

It should also be noted that the UNEP-WCMC provides an important data management service to the CITES Convention as well as other wildlife Conventions. Monitoring of trade, based on data supplied by the Parties, is carried out by the Wildlife Trade Monitoring Unit of the UNEP World Conservation Monitoring Centre under contract to the Secretariat. Among the services it provides to CITES, UNEP-WCMC maintains the CITES Trade Database containing information on trade in CITES-listed wildlife as compiled from the Parties annual reports.

Traffic

TRAFFIC deserves a special mention because of the very particular role it plays in the operation of the Convention. TRAFFIC is the Wildlife Monitoring Programme of WWF-Worldwide Fund for Nature and IUCN and works in cooperation with the CITES Secretariat to promote the effectiveness of the Convention and other wildlife controls. Established in the mid 1970s, TRAFFIC provides advice and technical assistance to Parties and the Secretariat and assists in the development and implementation of CITES and other wildlife trade instruments. It also plays an important role in the enforcement of the Convention.

The European Community Institutions and Agencies

Although the Member States are all parties to the Convention, the European Community cannot itself become a party to the Convention until Article XXI of the Convention is amended to allow for the accession of "regional economic integration organisations" since at present the Convention only permits states to become parties. Such an amendment was put forward at the Gaborone COP in 1983 and is known as the

Gaborone amendment but it has still not received sufficient ratifications from the Parties to bring it into force. At COP 12 a Decision urging Parties to accept the amendment before COP13 was adopted.

Competence for the implementation of the Convention is shared between the Member States and the Community[3] but there is considerable harmonisation of procedures and requirements for permits and so on. The lead policy responsibility for implementation of the Convention within the EU rests with DG Environment of the European Commission[4]. Under their general powers as laid down in the European Community Treaty, the Commission is responsible for making legislative proposals, whilst the main legislative instruments are adopted by the Council (and following changes to the Treaty under the Maastricht Treaty, the Parliament) and implementing legislation by the Commission.

Council Regulation (EC) No 338/97, the main legislative instrument implementing the Convention within the European Union makes provision for three specific bodies with responsibilities for implementing CITES within the EC: the EC CITES Committee, the EU Scientific Review Group and the Enforcement Group.

The EC CITES Committee

The EC CITES Committee is a regulatory committee established under Article 18 of the Council Regulation and has a number of functions as specified in Article 19. The Committee is composed of representatives of the Member States and chaired by the Commission who submits to the Committee a draft of the measures to be taken. These measures include the laying down of uniform conditions and criteria for the issue and use of a number of documents including import permits, export permits and Article 8 individual exemption certificates; the use of phytosanitary certificates and the establishment of procedures for marking specimens. The Committee also adopts certain specified measures including trade restrictions, transhipment derogations, certain consultation procedures between

[3] The issue of competence, whether it is shared between the Community and the Member States or is exclusive to the Community is generally a contentious issue in the field of trade related environmental agreements, at least as between Member States and the Commission. The extent of Community competence determines the way in which international negotiations are conducted, where the Community has exclusive competence the Commission claims the right to speak on behalf of the Member States. In either case however a common negotiating position must be sought.

[4] See the website at Europa.

Member States, general derogations from the Article 8 controls on commercial activities, time limits for the issuance of permits and so on. The Committee also amends the Annexes with the exception of amendments to Annex A which do not result from decisions of the COP and adopts, where necessary, additional measures to implement Conference Resolutions, Decisions or Recommendations of the Convention Secretariat.

The procedure to be adopted by the Committee is laid down in Article 18. There are two types of procedure depending on the type of decision to be taken but both procedures require the referral of the matter to the Council for decision if there is no qualified majority in favour of the proposed measure. The degree to which the Council can reject the measures then depends on which procedure applies. The "heavier" procedure, which gives the Council greater power, is that provided in relation to the measures specified in paragraphs (3) and (4) of Article 19 (amendment of the Annexes and implementation of Conference Resolutions).

The Scientific Review Group

The Scientific Review Group (SRG) is established under Article 17 of the Council Regulation and provides the EC CITES Committee with advice on scientific issues. It meets approximately four times a year and represents collective decision-making at the Community level on the part of the scientific authorities of the individual Member States. The SRG has the power to examine any scientific question relating to the application of the Regulation raised by the Chairman or by members of the Group, in particular on the possible detrimental effect of trade in Annex A species, the levels of trade of Annex B species, or on trade restrictions. Its opinions are conveyed to the EC CITES Committee by the Commission. The SRG may adopt what are known as negative opinions, that is to say a finding that it is not clear that actual or anticipated levels of trade will *not* have a detrimental impact on the conservation or range of a species, or that the species is subject to particularly high levels of mortality during transport for example. These opinions may lead to further consultation with the country concerned or to discussions within the relevant Convention committee for example or they may in some cases lead to suspension of trade under Article 4.6 of the Council Regulation.

Authorities and Agencies within the UK

Management and Scientific Authorities

Article IX of the Convention[5] requires each Party to designate one or more Management Authorities competent to grant permits or certificates on behalf of that Party. The Management Authorities are advised on a range of matters, such as the conservation implications of trade, by one or more Scientific Authorities which must also be designated under Article IX. Article IX(2) of the Convention requires that the name and address of the Management Authority must be communicated to the Depositary Government. In the European Union, Article 13 of the Council Regulation provides that the names and addresses of the management and scientific authorities of the Member States must be notified to the Commission and will be published in the Official Journal of the European Communities.

The UK has two management authorities[6]: in Great Britain the management authority is the Wildlife Trade Licensing Branch based in the Global Wildlife Division of what is now the Department of the Environment, Food and Rural Affairs (DEFRA), situated at Tollgate House Bristol. There is a separate management authority for Northern Ireland. The UK management authority issues many thousands of permits anually. The UK, along with the rest of Europe, is primarily a consumer of wildlife products which may be imported for processing and re-exported.

The Scientific Authorities for the UK are the Joint Nature Conservation Committee (JNCC) for animals[7] and the Royal Botanic Gardens at Kew (Kew)[8] for plants. In addition to advising the management authority on the issue of individual permits as set out below, the scientific authorities also advise on listing proposals either of endangered indigenous species (advising on the biological status of species affected by trade) or in relation to proposals made by other Parties to the Convention. As of 2001, JNCC was advising DEFRA on some 21,000 applications a year for import and export permits and for EC certificates to allow the commercial use of

[5] Article IX is implemented by Article 13 of the Council Regulation which requires member States to designate a Management Authority with primary responsibility for implementation of the Regulation communication with the Commission although it may also designate additional authorities.
[6] There are separate management authorities in relation to the Dependent Territories.
[7] JNCC, Monkstone House, City Road, Peterborough PE1 1JY, UK.
[8] Royal Botanic Gardens, Kew, Richmond, Surrey TW9 3AB.

Annex A specimens[9]. The scientific authorities also carry out research projects relevant to the work of CITES, for example Kew has carried out research into wild plants in trade within the CITES Significant Trade Programme. This is a process which analyses the demand for Appendix II specimens in order to determine possible or potential detrimental trade, allowing recommendations for levels of sustainable trade to be made[10].

JNCC and Kew represent the UK on the EU Scientific Review Group and also as observers on the Animals and Plants Committees of the Convention (see above). The scientific authorities also assist in the enforcement of the Convention at the national level by providing advice and training to HMCE and the Police (see below).

Enforcement Agencies

Enforcement of CITES is undertaken by the police and by HM Customs & Excise (HMCE)[11]. In addition to their general powers, the police are afforded specific powers of entry and seizure under the Control of Trade in Endangered Species Regulations 1997[12]. HMCE derive a range of powers under the Customs and Excise Management Act 1979.

Liaison Bodies

DEFRA holds twice yearly formal liaison meetings with two umbrella groups representing conservation and user interests respectively. Liaison with conservation groups is effected through Wildlife and Countryside Link and with users through the Sustainable Users Network (SUN). Both fora provide an opportunity for discussion of issues relating to CITES[13].

---

[9] Figures obtained from the JNCC website at www.jncc.gov.uk/international.
[10] See further the Kew website at www.rbgkew.org.uk/conservation.
[11] See further Chapter 9 - Part II.
[12] SI 1997 No 1372.
[13] For details of meetings see the CITES website at www.ukcites.gov.uk

CHAPTER 2

LISTING OF SPECIES

It should be remembered that the CITES Convention is based on the recognition that "international cooperation is essential for the protection of *certain* species of wild fauna and flora against over-exploitation through international trade." (fourth recital, emphasis added). As will be seen, it is not sufficient, for CITES to apply, that a particular species is endangered or may become so, it must also be a species which is liable to be affected by international trade in some way.

In common with many other international and national legal instruments concerned with the conservation of wildlife, the CITES Convention accords varying degrees of protection to species depending on their conservation status. As in many other instruments, this is achieved by listing the species to which particular provisions of the Convention apply in appendices which correspond to specific levels of protection.[1]

In the case of the CITES Convention, there are three Appendices: Appendix I lists all species threatened with extinction which are or may be affected by trade, Appendix II includes species which, although not currently threatened with extinction, may become so unless trade in them is strictly regulated and Appendix III includes species which are subject to national trade regulation in a Party and where the Party concerned needs the cooperation of other Parties in order to control trade. The rules governing trade in the species concerned vary significantly as between the three appendices. These rules are described in detail in subsequent chapters of this section, but the main difference between them is that commercial trade in Appendix I species is generally prohibited, whereas it is permitted in relation to species in the other two appendices, provided that certain conditions are met.

Article II.4 of the Convention provides that Parties shall not allow trade in specimens of species included in the three Appendices except in accordance with the provisions of the Convention. This means that at any given time, the specific requirements of the Convention only apply to those

---

[1] A general discussion on listing as a technique in conservation legislation is contained in Chapter 2 - Part III.

species listed in its appendices. This does not mean, however, that the Parties take no account of species which are not listed on the appendices. In Conference Resolution 9.24, the Parties confirmed that "international trade in all wild fauna and flora is under the purview of the Convention". This appears to mean that the Parties can adopt resolutions and decisions relating to non-listed species, for example, recommending that further information as to their status should be collected. This is to be expected since changes in trade patterns and other factors affecting a species conservation status may result in the need for a species to be listed which has not been listed before. At COP 12 for example, the Parties continued to take initiatives over trade in species not currently covered by CITES such as sea cucumbers.

This chapter considers the criteria for listing species in the three appendices to the Convention and the procedures by which listing decisions are adopted. Not surprisingly, decisions taken by the Parties to the Convention as to whether and where to list certain species are among the most controversial under CITES[2]. This chapter looks at some recent examples of such decisions. It also looks at the way in the European Union legislation approaches the listing of species. As will be seen, the EU legislation broadly tracks the approach of the Convention but builds on it in order to protect a wider range of species and to protect some species more strictly than is required under the Convention by listing them in a more protective Annex.

The core criteria by which species are to be included in the appendices are set out in Article II of the Convention which deals with fundamental principles, however the Parties to the Convention realised at an early stage that further guidance on how to approach the listing of species was desirable. The first set of criteria elaborating the provisions of the Convention were adopted at the first Conference of the Parties in 1976 and became known as the Berne Criteria. The listing criteria were revised at COP9 and are currently under further review by a Criteria Working Group pending COP12[3]. Key features of the listing criteria as they have evolved over the history of the Convention are considered below.

The Berne Criteria

The Berne Criteria laid down the criteria to be used for the listing of a species in Appendices I and II. Generally speaking, this required the

[2] Listing proposals also take up substantial time at any COP. At COP11 62 proposals to amend the Appendices were put forward.

[3] Decision 11.2, adopted at COP 11, sets out the terms of reference and a timetable for this review process.

consideration together of the biological status and trade status of the species in question.

In order for a species to qualify for listing on Appendix I, Conference Resolution 1.1 set out two criteria that need to be satisfied. First, with regard to the biological status of the species, it had to be shown that the species was currently threatened with extinction. In this regard Conference Resolution 1.1 provided a list of types of information that would be required, in order of preference, in order to assist in the determination of the biological status of the species. The second criterion related to the trade status of the species: Conference Resolution 1.1 stated that a species which was currently threatened with extinction should be listed in Appendix I if it was or might be affected by international trade. A flexible yet cautious approach was adopted in this regard. The provision stated that where the evidence regarding the biological status of the species indicated a serious decline in that species then the mere possibility of trade therein would be sufficient for listing in Appendix I. Likewise, where the information on biological status was incomplete, but there was evidence that trade was known to occur, then the species in question might nevertheless be listed. Conference Resolution 1.1 also provided guidelines for listing in Appendix I of closely related groups of species for example listing at the genus level might take place if most of the species within a given genus were threatened with extinction and if 'identification of individual species within the genus is difficult'.

To qualify for listing under Appendix II the Berne Criteria provided that regarding its biological status, a species need not currently be threatened but there should be some indication that it might become so. The same rules regarding listing of genera and smaller taxa applied for Appendix II as in applied to Appendix I. With regard to trade status, it was provided that species meeting the biological criteria should be listed if they are presently subject to trade or are likely to become so.

The Berne Criteria also laid down criteria for the down listing of a species. Conference Resolution 1.2 provided that positive scientific evidence that the species in question could withstand exploitation resulting from a downlisting of a species was required. This set a higher burden of proof than that for the listing of a species, and reflected an approach that appears to have been in line with the precautionary principle (see further below).

Revision of the Criteria at COP9

In 1994, at the ninth Conference of the Parties, the listing criteria were replaced by those set out in Conference Resolution 9.24, following a review by the Parties. The review was prompted by the acknowledgement that many species listed in the appendices were not in fact being traded. It was also recognised that the existing criteria did not provide an adequate basis for amending the appendices. CR 9.24 also explicitly endorsed the application of the precautionary principle to listing for the first time[4]. CR 9.25(Rev) dealt with the criteria for listing species in Appendix III in the light of its unsatisfactory implementation which, it was believed, arose from the fact that many Parties were not convinced of the effectiveness of Appendix III.

Conference Resolution 9.24

Conference Resolution 9.24 sets out in detail the biological and trade criteria for listing species in Appendices I and II. It also addresses the basis for listing in Appendix II species which do not themselves meet those criteria but which need to be included in order to render the listing of other species effective (for example so-called "look-alikes"). In addition, the Resolution provides guidance on the approach which should be taken to listing changes, deals with special cases and sets out the format for presenting listing proposals.

At COP12 the Parties agreed the terms of reference for an intersessional review of Conference Resolution 9.24 to be conducted by the Animals and Plants Committees and to be completed before COP13.

Appendix I Listings

In relation to Appendix I, the Resolution states that any species which is, or may be, affected by trade should be included in Appendix I if it meets at least one of the biological criteria listed in Annex I to the Resolution. A species "is or may be affected by trade" if it meets one of the following criteria regarding its trade status: the species is known to be in trade, or it is probably in trade, but conclusive evidence is lacking, or there is a potential international demand for specimens or it would probably enter trade were

[4] See in particular Annex 4 dealing with Precautionary Measures. Many commentators argue that there was however an implicit precautionary approach in CITES prior to 1994 i.e. under the Berne Criteria, see for instance *Natural Resources Journal* 39 (1999) at 211.

it not subject to Appendix I controls. The existence of a causal link between trade and the threatened status of the species is not a prerequisite for listing in Appendix I. It will suffice to show that the species is threatened with extinction and that it merely is or may be affected by trade.

The criteria regarding biological status are somewhat more extensive and are set out in Annex I. The species in question is considered to be threatened with extinction if at least one of the criteria set out in Annex 1 is met or may be met. Annex 1 addresses the biological status of a species with regard to three main biological criteria as well as a fourth precautionary criterion as set out below. Annex I is to be read subject to the notes, definitions and guidelines set out in Annex 5.

Criterion A considers the wild population size of a species. In order to satisfy this criterion the wild population size must be small and in addition to this the species must satisfy at least one of the five sub-conditions listed therein: (i) an observed, inferred or projected population decline or a decline in the area and quality of the habitat of the species; (ii) each sub-population being very small; (iii) the majority of the population occurs in one sub-population during one or more life history phases; or (iv) the species is subject to large short-term fluctuations in population size or (v) the biology or behaviour of the species .

Criterion B concerns the area of distribution of a species and to qualify for listing the species must have a restricted area of distribution and must also meet at least one of the four additional conditions which, to some extent, track the conditions under Criterion A. The additional conditions are that (i) the species is fragmented or occurs at a small number of locations; or (ii) there are large fluctuations in the area of distribution or the number of sub-populations of the species; or (iii) the biology or behaviour of the species renders it vulnerable to extinction or (iv) there is an observed, inferred or projected decrease in the population, the area or quality of habitat or reproductive potential of the species.

Criterion C is the broadest and most far reaching of the biological criteria. It states that there must be or have been a decline in the wild population of the species, or a decline that is inferred/projected on the basis of certain factors. These factors are (i) a decrease in area or quality of habitat; or (ii) levels or patterns of exploitation; or (iii) threats from various extrinsic factors or (iv) decreasing reproductive potential.

The fourth criterion i.e. Criterion D comes into operation where the status of the species does not currently satisfy any of the three criteria outlined above, but it is likely to do so within a period of five years.

Annex 5 is particularly important in the application of the criteria in Annex 1 since, not only does it define many of the terms used in the listing criteria, but it also includes notes on interpretation and numerical guidelines for interpreting the listing criteria outlined below. CR 9.24 expressly states that these notes are to be taken into account in the interpretation of the listing criteria and furthermore they should be adhered to as closely as possible. Annex 5 covers such terms as "area of distribution", "population" and "threatened with extinction". With regard to the numerical guidelines, for example the guideline for a restricted area of distribution in Criterion B is a figure of less than 10,000 square kilometres the notes in Annex 5 state that the figures contained therein represent appropriate guidelines rather than thresholds. Implicit in this is the realisation that there will be cases where these numerical guidelines do not apply.

The consideration of other factors, in addition to the trade and biological criteria outlined above, may be required in the listing process. Taking into account other factors such as the enforceability of the listing and the extent to which the listing is in the best interests of the conservation of the species may be necessary in order to ensure the effectiveness of the listing. The practicality of enforcing the listing of certain species of orchid and cacti in Appendix I was addressed specifically by the Parties in CR 9.18 (Rev) which stipulated that an uplisting to Appendix I for such plant species requires the consideration of other factors such as whether the increased protection offered to the species by an Appendix I listing compensates for the increased risk inherent in such a listing by attracting the attention of traders towards such species.

Appendix II Listings

The two bases for listing species in Appendix II set out in Article II of the CITES Convention are addressed separately in Annex 2a (Article II(2)(a) and Annex 2b (Article II(2)(b)) of CR 9.24 respectively. With regard to species which although not necessarily now threatened with extinction, may become so unless trade is subject to strict regulation, Annex 2a expands on the Berne Criteria by providing that listing in Appendix II should take place in one of the following two situations. First, where there is knowledge/ projection that unless trade in the species is strictly regulated it will meet in the near future one of the biological criteria for inclusion in Appendix I or, second, where it is known or projected that international trade in that species has or may have a detrimental impact on the species by either exceeding over an extended period, the level that can be continued in perpetuity or reducing to a population level at which its survival would be threatened by other influences.

Annex 2b addresses the listing in Appendix II of other species which must be subject to regulation in order that those protected under Article II(2)(a) or Appendix I may be brought under effective control (look-alike species) and aims to ensure that similar species to those already included in Appendices I or II are included in Appendix II in order to reduce the risk of listed species being mistakenly traded as non-listed species. This may occur either where a species resembles a listed species "such that a non-expert with reasonable effort, is unlikely to be able to distinguish between them". It may also occur where the species is a member of a taxon of which most of the species are listed in Appendix I or II.

Appendix III Listings

Appendix III includes all species which a Party identifies as being subject to regulation within its jurisdiction for the purpose of preventing or restricting exploitation and in relation to which the cooperation of other Parties is needed in the control of trade (Article II(3)). Article XVI of the Convention governs the procedures for listings under Appendix III and amendments thereto. It basically provides that a Party may at any time submit to the Secretariat a list of species that are protected domestically and which it wishes to include in Appendix III. This general right of Parties to list species in Appendix III is, however, qualified by additional conditions addressed in CR 9.25 (Rev) which recommends, inter alia, that a Party should not only inform the Management Authorities of other range states, major importing countries, the Secretariat and the Animals or Plants Committees of the intended listings but also seek the opinion of the aforementioned on the potential effects of such listings. It recommends further that it is only after due consultation, and having satisfied itself that the listing is justified by the biological and trade status of the species, that a Party may submit to the Secretariat a list of species for inclusion in Appendix III.

Special Cases are dealt with Annex 3 of CR9.24 and include split-listings and the listing of higher taxa (see further below).

Amending the Appendices

The procedure for amending Appendices I and II is set out in Article XV of the Convention. Proposals to amend these Appendices may be submitted for consideration either at a meeting of the Conference of the Parties or during the interval between such meetings. In the case of the former, the text of the proposed amendment is required to be submitted to the Secretariat at least 150 days before the next meeting of the COP. The proposed amendment must be accompanied by a substantially complete supporting statement in the form set out in Annex 6 to Resolution Conf. 9.24 (Decision 10.15). The Secretariat then consults the other Parties and, in the case of marine species, interested bodies, on the proposed amendment and it must communicate the response, as well as its own findings and recommendations, to all Parties not less than 30 days before the next meeting of the COP.

Amendments are adopted by a two-thirds majority of the parties present and voting for which purposes abstentions are not counted. An amendment adopted by a meeting of the COP becomes effective 90 days after that meeting for all Parties except those entering a reservation in accordance with Article XV (3)[5]. The Convention provides that a Party entering a reservation be treated as a non-Party to the Convention in respect of trade in the species in question until such time as the reservation is withdrawn. However in Conference Resolution 4.25, the Parties agreed that Parties entering reservations to a proposal to transfer a species from Appendix II to I should continue to treat that species as Appendix II and that Parties entering a reservation in relation to any Appendix I listing should treat the species concerned as Appendix II. Parties should maintain and communicate statistical records on trade so that international trade in the species concerned could be properly monitored.

Article XV(2) provides for a postal procedure for amendment proposals which are submitted between Conferences of the Parties. Under this procedure the Secretariat communicates the proposal and its own recommendation to the Parties who may then transmit any comments on the proposed amendment. The Secretariat communicates these replies as soon as possible. If no objection is received within 30 days of the communication of these replies, the amendment enters into force 90 days

[5] Note in this context Document 11.41.2 on significant trade in Appendix II species which is seen as a significant development in that the process used for reviewing animal species has been extended to cover plants : "a significant step in ensuring the sustainable trade in all Appendix-II plant and animal species" according to TRAFFIC Bulletin Vol. 18 No. 3 December 2000 available at http://www.traffic.org/bulletin/cop11.html.

later (subject to reservations). If there is any objection, the proposal goes to a postal vote. If fewer than half the Parties vote the matter is referred to the next COP. If votes are received from at least half of the parties, the amendment shall be adopted by a two-thirds majority of the parties casting an affirmative or negative vote and it enters into force in the normal way.

CR 9.25 (Rev) recommended that a party wishing to amend Appendix III should inform the Secretariat thereof at least three months before the next meeting of the COP. Amendments to Appendix III listings enter into force 90 days after the date of the communication to the parties by the Secretariat regarding such listings, except in the case of Parties entering a reservation. Parties with Appendix III listing are furthermore expected to periodically review the status of the species listed therein and to assess the necessity of maintaining such listings in light of the guidelines contained in CR 9.25 (Rev) as well as any recommendations of the Animals and Plants Committees.

Specific problems: split listing; annotations.

Split listing refers to the situation where some populations of a given species are included in one CITES Appendix and other populations in a different CITES Appendix. It was resolved at COP 9 that split listing generally should be avoided because of the enforcement problems associated with it (see Annex 3 to Conference Resolution 9.24(rev)COP12). However, when split listing does occur it should not take place on the basis of subspecies but rather on the basis of national or continental populations of the species. Furthermore, split listings that place some populations of a species in the Appendices and the remainder outside should not normally be allowed.

Annotations have been increasingly used as a means of addressing the specific conservation requirements of different populations of species listed in the CITES Appendices. Greater clarification of the use of annotations was called for at COP 10 (cf. Conf Decision 10.70), which led Switzerland to produce a draft resolution at COP 11 on the use of annotations. This led to the adoption of CR 11.21 which essentially divides annotations into "reference annotations" for information purposes, such as "p.e" for possibly extinct, and "substantive annotations" which form part of the species listing itself such as those which relate to the inclusion or exclusion of geographically separate populations. The Resolution goes on to provide guidance on the use of annotations and the modification thereof, for example it states that annotations which relate to particular types of specimens should be used "sparingly" as these are difficult to implement and Parties should avoid annotations which cover live animals or trophies. The Resolution also directs the Standing Committee and Secretariat to take specific steps to monitor illegal trade in species subject to annotated listings.

Specific Listing Decisions

Even when formal criteria for listing decisions appear to be met, other considerations, such as the likely impact of the proposal on illegal activity, the political sensitivities of both consumer and producer states and the desire of range states to use wild life resources sustainably have to be taken into account in reaching a decision. A number of specific listing decisions are considered further below.

The African Elephant

A good illustration of the way in which Parties seek to weigh different factors involved in listing decisions is provided by the African elephant.

In 1989, the Parties had decided to transfer the African Elephant from Appendix II to I[i] At the same time, Conference Resolution 7.9 was adopted, establishing a Panel of Experts on the African Elephant which would review certain populations whose transfer to Appendix II had been requested. The resolution also set out the terms of reference for the Panel. The Panel was to consider the scientific evidence regarding numbers and trends and the practices of conservation and management of the populations concerned and threat to their status as well as the adequacy of ivory trade controls. Among the factors to be examined in evaluating the status and management of an elephant population were: the viability and sustainability of the population and potential risks; the affected range state's demonstrated ability to monitor the subject population; and the effectiveness of current anti-poaching measures. In considering the range state's ability to control trade in ivory from African elephants, the Panel was to take into account: the sustainability of total levels of off take from both legal and illegal killing; whether control of ivory stocks was adequate to prevent the mixing of legal and illegal ivory; the effectiveness of law enforcement and whether enforcement and controls were sufficient to ensure that no significant amounts of ivory taken or trade illegally from other countries were traded within or through the territory of the range state.

[i] For a comprehensive examination of efforts of the Parties to protect the African elephant from the effects of the ivory trade see Wijnstekers, Chapter 28.

A South African proposal was made at COP 9 to down list the South African population of the African elephant from Appendix I to II so as to allow commercial trade in meat and hides (from elephants culled in the Kruger National Park). The South African proposal excluded trade in ivory (the Appendices would be annotated to make this clear) and it was made clear that any revenue generated by the trade in non-ivory products would be reinvested in elephant conservation.

South Africa pointed out that the Panel of Experts, which had considered the matter, had concluded that the South African proposal met the biological criteria for the transfer of elephant populations set out in Conference Resolution 7.9[ii]. The Chairman of the panel, addressing the Conference, indicated that the proposal would allow trade that could have benefits for elephant conservation and added that if the proposal were rejected the Parties should consider repealing Conference Resolution 7.9.

The proposal met with a mixed reception: many African range states and a number of other Parties were opposed. A number of concerns were expressed: there was no assurance that trade in elephant products would not stimulate elephant poaching in neighbouring states; the adoption of the proposal would lead to speculation that the ivory trade was to be reopened; public perception of the need to conserve elephants would be weakened. One delegation, whilst adhering to the position of the African regional group in opposing the proposal, was of the view that transferring elephant populations to Appendix II to allow trade in non-ivory products would not endanger the ban on the ivory trade. Others suggested that the proposal would allow the effects of such a transfer to be tested. Others expressed an intention to abstain on the basis that, whilst they were satisfied that Conference Resolution 7.9 was fulfilled and that the proposal would not have the effect of stimulating poaching, the range states were opposed to it. In the event South Africa withdrew its proposal. It was agreed to establish an intra-African assembly to examine the issues and to consider the repeal of Conference Resolution 7.9 in time for the next Conference of the Parties.

The African Elephant has continued to dominate subsequent COPs. At COP 10 the proposal to downlist the elephant populations in three range states (namely, Botswana, Namibia and Zimbabwe) from Appendix I to Appendix II was successful. COP Decision 10.1 laid down stringent conditions for a resumption of trade in ivory for the elephant populations

[ii] See the Report of the Panel.

of those states, which had been transferred to Appendix II, based on the idea of a "closed loop" trade between those states and a designated country, Japan, for the purposes of using ivory for traditional carving. It would be necessary to show that a range of safeguards were in place both in the exporting states and in Japan before the trade would be allowed to go ahead. In February 1999, the Standing Committee agreed that these conditions had been met which thus paved the way for a one-off experimental trade of stockpiled ivory to Japan. The elephant populations of these countries remain on Appendix II with an annotation and a zero quota for ivory. In other words, trade in general remains prohibited and no further commercial trade in ivory can take place without subsequent COP approval.

The arguments submitted by these Southern African range states in favour of the downlisting proposal revolved around the need for revenue, which a limited resumption in trade would give rise to, in order to secure the resources necessary for the conservation of the African Elephant. These arguments were pitted against the concerns of many other states and non-governmental organisations that the down listing would result in an increase in the illegal killing of elephants, not only in Southern Africa but also elsewhere. As part of the compromise reached, the Parties approved CR 10.10 (amended at COP 11) "Trade in Elephant Specimens", which authorised the establishment of comprehensive international monitoring systems, namely MIKE (Monitoring Illegal Killing of Elephants) and ETIS (Elephant Trade Information System) in order to measure current levels of poaching, identify trends in illegal killing of elephants and the ivory trade, and to determine to what extent these trends can be attributable to decisions made under CITES.

The down listing proposal at COP 10 was significant in three respects. First, it led to the first prospective resumption in legal ivory trade since the ban on such trade was implemented in 1990. Second, the down listing, and the resultant limited trade, were accompanied by a firm international commitment to the development of credible monitoring systems. Finally, it laid down the procedure for proposals to transfer the African elephant from Appendix I to Appendix II. In this regard CR 10.9 provides for a Panel of Experts to be constituted by the Secretariat to evaluate various factors regarding the relevant populations of elephants. These factors include, inter alia, scientific evidence concerning the numbers and trends of the populations; conservation and management measures and the threats to their status and the adequacy of controls on trade. The panel was to produce a report on their findings and submit it to the Parties for their consideration. COP 10 also confirmed that any future quotas for ivory would require a two-thirds majority vote of the COP.

The various proposals regarding the listing of the African Elephant for consideration at COP 11 serve to illustrate further how discussion on the African elephant, one of the species often referred to as "charismatic megafauna" continues to dominate CITES COPs. In total, five listings proposals on African elephants were submitted at COP 11. The southern African states who were successful in having their respective elephant populations transferred to Appendix II at COP 10 (i.e. Botswana, Namibia and Zimbabwe) each proposed to amend the annotations of their respective elephant populations on Appendix II to allow, inter alia, for an annual quota of ivory. South Africa entered the fray to put forward a proposal to transfer its elephant population from Appendix I to Appendix II in order to allow for an experimental trade in a state owned ivory stock from the Kruger National Park.

The proposals of the Southern African states were vigorously opposed by Kenya and India who argued that the one-off trade after COP10 had led to an increase in illegal killings of elephants and thus an absolute ban on the trade in ivory was necessary to stem this. In short, this alliance proposed that the elephant populations listed in Appendix II should be transferred back to Appendix I. Furthermore, Switzerland meanwhile proposed to amend the annotation of the elephant populations of Botswana, Namibia and Zimbabwe to show a zero quota for trade in raw ivory.

In the end, a landmark agreement was reached among the various range states for a continued ban on the ivory trade and an expression of support for the monitoring systems (MIKE & ETIS). Botswana, Namibia and Zimbabwe thus withdrew their proposals for further quotas in ivory, in return for which Kenya and India withdrew their proposal to amend the African Elephant listing in the Appendices. South Africa, however, was successful in its bid to have its elephant population transferred to Appendix II, although this was only possible by amending its proposal to reflect a zero quota for trade in ivory. Essentially, this allowed the countries whose elephant populations are listed in Appendix II to re-open trade in live elephants and elephant hides but not in ivory.

The conflicting proposals regarding the listing of the African elephant reflect the broader debate between proponents of sustainable use and those who advocate complete protection from trade, a debate which tends to overshadow specific listing proposals. In this regard, the downlisting of various populations of the African Elephant appear to many to represent a victory for the proponents of sustainable use.[6] Others remain deeply critical of these developments, doubting whether even stringent conditions will prevent an increase in legal trade in ivory.

At COP 12, Botswana, Namibia, Zimbabwe and South Africa all proposed amendments to the listing of their respective elephant populations which were accepted in amended form by the Plenary. The effect of these various decisions is to allow for a limited sale of ivory in respect of those populations under strictly controlled conditions which include agreement by the Standing Committee that all conditions have been met[7]. However the present ban is to remain in place until at least May 2004 and will only be lifted then if all relevant conditions have been met. All these states emphasised that revenue from the sales would be used to finance conservation programmes and benefit local communities. Prior to COP 12 there had been a meeting of the African elephant dialogue group during which Kenya in particular had voiced its concerns at these proposals, in particular the implications of any reopening of the ivory trade. A down-listing proposal by Zambia at COP 12 was rejected, with some countries arguing that Zambia's population did not meet the criteria for down-listing to Appendix II and highlighting concerns about deficiencies in monitoring illegal poaching. A proposal by Zimbabwe was also rejected. Kenya introduced a proposed decision on the implementation of annotation 604 on African elephants (relevant to those populations which have been down-listed)which directs the Standing Committee to takes steps including defining the type of data that constitutes the MIKE baseline needed before ivory decisions can be approved; determining how to assess whether there has been detrimental impact on elephant populations and recommending measures for improving law enforcement coordination among the ivory producing and importing states[8]. The COP also adopted a decision, 12.36

[6] [IWMC World Conservation Trust eNEWSLETTER 21 April 2000 "COP 11: A Win for Sustainable Conservation of Elephants & the Patience of Southern African Nations." http://www.iwmc.org/sustain/cites/000421-3.htm and cf. comments by Eugene Lapointe, president of IWMC-World Conservation Trust and former CITES Secretary General: "Appendix II is a sustainable management status that allows highly controlled trade in surplus wildlife products, an important source of hard currency that benefits the animals and people alike." Available at http://www.iwmc.org/sustain/cites/000418a.htm. See also State of the Environment Reporting Network for Southern Africa (SOENETSA) Newsletter Vol. 1 No. 2, June 2000: emphasizing the fact that recent acceptance of listing proposals re: elephants are a victory for sustainable use philosophy and as a result CITES is changing "CITES COP 10 in Harare was a watershed in the history of CITES for sustainable use. It seems COP 11 consolidated the gains made at CITES COP 10." Available at http://www.sardc.net/imercsa/netcab/newsletter/issue2.htm

[7] See further Conference Resolution 10.10(Rev COP 12).

[8] See Decisions 12.33-35.

requiring parties, donors and other organisations to take a number of steps including registering and marking raw ivory in public and private possession and urgently strengthening provisions in their national law regarding controls on internal ivory trade. Conference Resolution 10.10 on trade in elephant specimens was also revised to take account of these changes.

The White Rhino

Most subspecies of rhino were listed in Appendix I in 1975 but the Southern White Rhino (*Ceratotherium simum* simum) was listed in Appendix I in 1977. In 1994 at COP 9, South Africa put forward a proposal to down list its population of white rhino in order to permit trade in live animals (to "appropriate and acceptable destinations") and hunting trophies only. This would allow, for example, commercial trade in live animals for safari parks. Range states and others supported the proposal. The Parties voted to adopt the proposal as valid until the next Conference of the Parties. The adoption of this proposal was accompanied by a new Resolution on rhino providing a more comprehensive framework for action including recommendations for species recovery plans funded, in part, from revenue from legal use.

At COP 10, South Africa sought to have the above downlisting to Appendix II confirmed with an expansion of the associated annotation to allow for limited future trade in Southern White Rhino products. The proposal was partly influenced by the desire to examine the possibility of trade in rhino products in order to generate funds for the conservation of the species. This proposal however failed to be adopted by the Parties at COP 10.

Rhinos did not feature in the listing proposals presented at COP 11 but cf. Doc 11.32 report on conservation and trade in Rhinos pursuant to CR 9.14 (Rev)[9]

Whales and Sharks

Relationships with other legal regimes may also be relevant to the fate of listing proposals. This is perhaps best illustrated by the listing in CITES Appendices of species of whales. The position at present is that all

[9] For an animals rights NGO perspective, see CITESwatch: "... people already wander aloud if the Secretariat's proposed rhinoceros resolution will produce a rhino MIKE, which will be as useless to the rhino as MIKE has been to the elephant." Available at <http://www.hsus.org/channel/citeswatch/notelephants.htm

the so-called 'great whales' are listed in Appendix I of CITES despite numerous attempts by the whaling nations to have certain whale species downlisted. A COP9 proposal from Norway to down list North-Eastern Atlantic and North Atlantic central minke whale stocks pending scientific confirmation within the International Whaling Commission (IWC), paving the way for quotas, was rejected. Parties were generally of the view that CITES should follow the lead of the IWC. This view continues to influence the fate of listing proposals concerning whales and the IWC moratorium on commercial whaling informs the decisions of many Parties in this regard. The dominance of the IWC led to an attempt by Japan at COP 10 to sever to link between CITES and the IWC by repealing CR 2.9 which acknowledges the primacy of the IWC in issues concerning whales. This attempt, as well as the downlisting proposals submitted by Japan and Norway were unsuccessful.

The COP 11 listing proposals were once again characterised by much discussion among the Parties regarding the relationship between CITES and the IWC. On the one hand, a group of countries led by Japan and Norway argued that CITES should act independently of the IWC and that listing decisions should be based solely on the criteria set out in CR 9.24. On the other hand, most other Parties supported the IWC's moratorium on commercial whaling and were opposed to downlisting of whales until the adoption of the IWC's Revised Management Scheme (RMS). At COP 11, all four proposals submitted by Norway and Japan to downlist certain stocks of minke whales and grey whales were taken by secret ballots and were defeated. This set of proposals received even less support than the similar proposals put forward at COP 10. Again, this result can be attributed to the fact that voting on whale listing proposals continues to be largely determined by the stance of the IWC. This reinforces the view that many Parties regard the IWC as the main body responsible for the conservation and management of whales. To illustrate this, the position of the UK serves as a good example. The UK has stated that it will continue "to recognise the primacy of the IWC in this area and will continue to oppose any CITES downlisting proposals which might undermine the IWC moratorium on commercial whaling".[10]

The proposals by Japan and Norway were overshadowed by the controversy surrounding the report by the International Union for the Conservation of Nature (IUCN) intended to assist the Parties in their decisions concerning the whale listing proposals. The report was dubbed by some to be "unbalanced" and "misleading" and it effectively resulted

[10] http://www.ukcites.gov.uk/news/default.htm (visited 02/02/2001).

in the Secretariat changing its preliminary position of support for the whale proposals to a recommendation to the Parties to reject these downlisting proposals.[11]

At COP 12 Japan proposed to transfer northern hemisphere stocks of Balaenoptera acutorostrata and north Pacific stocks of B. edeni from Appendix I to II in order to enable trade between signatory parties to the International Convention for the Regulation of Whaling (ICRW). Both of these proposals were defeated.

In relation to sharks, the issue of relationships with other regimes has also been raised (in that case in relation to the role of the United Nations Food and Agriculture Organisation (FAO) on fisheries). Most recently at COP 11 the proposals to list the Whale Shark (*Rhincodon typus*), the Basking Shark (*Cetorhinus maximus*) and Great White Shark (*Carcharodon carcharias*) were all rejected after vigorous debate. The primary reason for this result is that many Parties feel that CITES is not the appropriate arena for dealing with fisheries issues and that such issues are best managed at the international or regional level by the FAO and Regional Fisheries Organisations and individual countries. Although there was simple majority support for these proposals they nevertheless failed to achieve the requisite two-thirds majority vote. Others criticise this view on the basis that some species, such as sharks, threatened by over-exploitation, are not covered by either regional fisheries agreements or national legislation. In such cases, it is argued, CITES could prove to be a valuable means to aiding conservation by controlling international trade in these vulnerable species[12]. At COP12 the Parties adopted Conference Resolution 12.6 on Conservation and Management of Sharks which instructs the CITES Secretariat to raise with the FAO concerns regarding the significant lack of progress in implementing the IPOA-Sharks and directs the Animals Committee to critically review progress towards IPOA implementation by major fishing and trading nations. The Resolution also recommends that Parties continue to identify endangered shark species that require consideration for inclusion in the Appendices, if their management and conservation status does not improve.

[11] See IWMC World Conservation Trust eNEWSLETTER 13 April 2000 "Scientists Call IUCN Whale Report 'Misleading'" http://www.iwmc.org/sustain/cites/000413-2.htm (visited 08/03/2001).

[12] See the comments by Steven Broad, TRAFFIC International Executive Director: "CITES would not replace existing national or regional management measures. But it could act in concert with fisheries management agreements and in cooperation with fisheries organisations, especially for biologically-vulnerable, high-value species, by providing trade controls that complement and support management measures." in 'Wildlife trade conference ends on mixed note'. http://www.traffic.org/cop11/newsroom/finalday.html.

In view of the unsuccessful proposal submitted by the UK to have the Basking Shark listed in CITES Appendix II, Michael Meacher, the UK Minister for the Environment announced on 9 May 2000 that the UK would be listing this species in Appendix III of CITES.[13] The UK successfully re-submitted the proposal for downlisting at COP 12.[14]

Timber Species

In relation to proposals for the listing of tree species, particularly those used for timber, there were calls for consideration of the relationship between CITES and the International Timber Trade Organisation (ITTO) as well as other relevant bodies such as the UN Commission on Sustainable Development (CSD), the Food and Agriculture Organization (FAO) and the World Trade Organisation Committee on Trade and Environment. All these bodies have an interest in the sustainable use of timber and it was felt that cooperation was appropriate, although Parties took differing views as to whether CITES should lead on this matter. Eventually it was agreed at COP 9 to set up a working group under the auspices of the CITES Standing Committee to look at the issue and other issues relating to the listing of timber species.

This led eventually to the adoption of Conference Resolution 10.13 on the Implementation of the Convention for Timber Species which noted, inter alia, that CITES had a positive role to play in promoting the conservation of timber species through trade in accordance with the provisions of the Convention. The Resolution also recognised the role to be played by international organisations in recommending that Parties should consult such organisations on amendment proposals regarding timber species in certain circumstances.

Bigleaf mahogany (*Swietenia macrophylla*) received a majority vote for listing in Appendix II at COP 9 but fell short of the requisite two-thirds majority vote. This was followed by another unsuccessful attempt to list it in Appendix II at COP 10. COP 10 however saw the creation of the Mahogany Working Group which was set up in order to examine various issues relating to this species such as, policies and management and trade and co-operation in relation thereto. A summary report on the first meeting of the MWG was presented at COP 11 but discussions of this report highlighted concerns that the report did not adequately reflect the status of

[13] http://www.ukcites.gov.uk/news/default.htm (visited 02/02/2001).
[14] See DETR News "UK acts to protect its biggest fish visitor". http://www.detr.gov.uk/press/0102/0098.htm

the species nor the subsequent developments in the conservation of the species since COP 10. In the end a new MWG was established with the intent of meeting within one year of COP 11 with relevant international organisations such as the International Tropical Timber Organisation with a view to reviewing numerous issues relating to the current status of the species. A report of its findings will be presented at COP 12.

Reservations

Parties have the right to make specific reservations to listing amendments. States may either make such reservations on becoming a Party (Article XXIII.2) or following an amendment to the Appendices. Reservations to listings in Appendix I or Appendix II are governed by Article XV.3 of the Convention which requires Parties to notify the depositary government of the reservation in writing within 90 days [of adoption of the listing amendment]. The effect of making such a reservation is that until the reservation is withdrawn "the Party shall be treated as a State not Party to the present Convention with respect to trade in the species concerned." (Trade with non-parties is dealt with in Chapter 7 - Part III.

As indicated above however, Conference Resolution 4.25 calls on those Parties making reservations to continue to treat as a species listed on Appendix II any Appendix I species in respect of which a reservation has been made. The Party should treat the species as Appendix II for all purposes including documentation and control and should also communicate statistical trade data in order to allow proper monitoring of international trade.]

There is greater scope for making reservations in relation to species listed on Appendix III. Under Article XVI.2, a Party may make a reservation to an Appendix III listing at any time after its communication to the Parties. Furthermore, a reservation can be made in relation to the species itself or to any parts and derivatives. Again the Convention provides that the State making the reservation shall be treated as a non-Party until the reservation is withdrawn.

It is clear from the text of Articles XV and XXIII that reservations can be withdrawn.

Council Regulation (EC) No 338/97

The listing of species in Council Regulation (EC) No 338/97 broadly tracks that adopted under the Convention itself but with some important differences, mostly based on stricter measures adopted by the European Community either by way of affording greater protection to Appendix II species or by affording protecting to species not listed under the Convention. In some cases this is done to ensure coherence with the species protected under the wild birds and habitats directives[15]. The Regulations contains four Annexes (A-D) of which A broadly corresponds to Appendix I, B to Appendix II, C to Appendix III, whilst D is an additional Annex affording limited regulation of trade in other species (see below). Regulation 338/97 provides that where an EC Member State has entered a reservation against a species listed in CITES Appendix I, then under the Regulation such species is listed in Annex B. In the case of a reservation entered by a Member State against a CITES Appendix II species, that species will be listed in Annex C, and Annex D includes all CITES Appendix III species for which reservations have been entered. The Convention listing of a species is indicated in the Annexes to the Council Regulation[16].

So far as Annex A is concerned, Article 3(1) of Regulation 338/97 provides that Annex A shall contain all CITES Appendix I species, except those for which EC Member States have entered a reservation. However, the Regulation goes further than CITES and provides for the listing in Annex A of certain CITES Appendices II and III species, as well as any non-CITES, species for which there is demand for utilisation in the Community or in international trade and that is either threatened with extinction or so rare that trade therein would imperil its survival (Article 3(1)(b)(i)), examples include Francois' Leaf Monkey (*Trachipythecus francoisi*) and the Madagascar Flat-Shelled Tortoise (*Pyxis planicauda*[17]). It also includes species belonging to a genus of which most of the species are listed in Annex A under the above criteria (or a species of which most of the subspecies are listed) where this is essential for the effective protection of those taxa, examples include the Eastern Spectral Tarsier (*Tarsius spectrum*) and the African Manatee (*Trichechus senegalensis*).

It should be noted that where Appendix III species are listed in Annexes A to C to the Regulation, it is the species per se which is subject to the corresponding provisions in the EC Regulation and not only the specific population of the Party that initially listed them in Appendix III (cf. TRAFFIC Reference Guide at section 3).

[15] These species are marked in bold in Annex A, see para 4 to the Annex to Commission Regulation 2724/2000 which revises the annexes to the Council Regulation.
[16] This done by indicating the CITES Appendix number in brackets next to the species name).
[17] The author is grateful to David Morgan of JNCC for providing these and other examples of specific listings under the Council Regulation.

Annex B contains CITES Appendix II species, except any already listed in Annex A, for which the Member States have not entered a reservation. Also included in this Annex are any Appendix I species for which a reservation has been entered by the Member States (there are none at present). Annex B also includes any CITES Appendix III or non-CITES species which is subject to levels of international trade that might not be compatible with its survival or with the survival of populations in certain countries or with the maintenance of its total population at a level consistent with its role in the ecosystem in which it occurs, an example of such a listing is the walrus (*Odobenus rosmarus*). It further contains look-alike species that are listed in order to ensure the effective control of trade in species listed in Annexes A and B, for example the Horned Curassow (*Pauxi unicornis*). Finally, it also includes species which pose an ecological threat to wild species indigenous to the Community. At present two such species are listed, the red-eared slider (*Trachymys scripta elegans*) and the American Bullfrog (*Rana catesbeiana*)

Annex C contains the remaining CITES Appendix III species for which the Member States have not entered a reservation and CITES Appendix II species for which a reservation has been entered. Regulation 338/97 further establishes Annex D for which there is no equivalent under CITES. This annex contains species that are not included in Annexes A - C above and which are imported into the EC in such numbers as to warrant monitoring. Annex D also includes CITES Appendix III species for which a reservation has been entered.

Procedure for Amending the Annexes

By virtue of Article 19 of the Regulation, the Commission may amend Annexes A-D in accordance with the Article 18 Committee procedure except in the case of amendments to Annex A which do not result from decisions of the CITES COP (this would have to be done by recourse to an amendment of the Regulation). As outlined in Chapter 1 - Part III, the committee procedure laid down in Article 18 of the Regulation provides for the Commission to submit a proposal to a committee of Member States' representatives. If they do not approve the proposal by a qualified majority (as weighted under the terms of the Treaty), the matter goes to the Council for decision. The Council may decide against the measure by a simple majority (see Article 18(3)).

CHAPTER 3

TRADE IN ANNEX A SPECIES

Annex A of Council Regulation (EC) No 338/97

Annex A of Council Regulation (EC) No 338/97 on the Protection of Species of Wild Fauna and Flora by Regulating Trade Therein (the Council Regulation) lists those species of wildlife which are subject to the strictest level of protection as regards both international and intra-community trade as well as other commercial activities[1]. The key feature of Annex A is that, as a general rule, commercial trade is not permitted in Annex A species. There are exemptions in relation to captive bred or artificially propagated specimens and these are considered further in Chapter 6 - Part III. This Chapter sets out the general rules for trade in Annex A specimens.

To a large extent, Annex A contains those species also subject to the strictest level of protection under the CITES Convention (those listed in Appendix I of the Convention) but there are differences in scope between Annex A and Appendix I as explained in Chapter 2 - Part III. One key difference is that any CITES-listed species which are subject to internal trade prohibitions under the wild birds directive or the habitats directive are automatically listed on Annex A of the Council Regulation (regardless of where they are listed in the Convention) and appear in bold in the Annex[2].

Thus the rules on trade in species listed in Annex A of Council Regulation (EC) No 338/97 implement in the European Community the requirements set down in the CITES Convention for trade in Appendix I species. In addition, Annex A of the Regulation contains species which are not listed in Appendix I to CITES but which the EC has decided to subject to the same rules as a stricter measure (as permitted under Article XIV of the Convention)[3]. Annex A includes: species listed in Appendix I to the CITES Convention for which the Member States have not entered a reser-

[1] As to the control of commercial activities under Article 8 of the regulation, see Chapter 10.
[2] Although in relation to species covered by the wild birds Directive, EU vagrant species are not included.
[3] The predecessor to Council Regulation 338/97, Regulation (EEC) No 3626/82 also included a number of stricter measures at the Community level: in particular certain species not listed on Appendix I of the Convention, those listed in Annex C1, were treated as if they were so listed.

vation (in practice all Appendix I species) and any species which is or may be in demand for utilization in the Community or for international trade and which is threatened with extinction or so rare that any level of trade would imperil the survival of the species. There is a further basis for listing species in Annex A: any species which is in a genus of which most of the species or which is a species of which most of the subspecies are listed in Annex A in accordance with the first two criteria *and* whose listing is essential for the effective protection of those threatened species, may also be listed in Annex A. These are sometimes referred to as "look-alike" species but it is important to distinguish this "look-alike" listing criteria from the one which appears in Annex B and which is formulated differently and more widely (Article 3(1)(b)(ii) of Council Regulation (EC) No 338/97)[4].

The Convention emphasises that trade in Appendix I species "must only be authorised in exceptional circumstances" (Article II.1). This fundamental principle of the Convention should underlie all decisions taken on individual applications for permits. So far as the Community rules are concerned, it should always be born in mind that Article 1 of the Council Regulation provides that "This Regulation shall apply in compliance with the objectives, principles and provisions of the [CITES] Convention". Article III of the Convention sets out the conditions for trade in specimens of Appendix I species and states that "All trade in specimens of species included in Appendix I shall be in accordance with the provisions of this Article" (Article III.1).

Export/Import of Annex A Species

The Convention: In order to understand the scheme of the Council Regulation, it is important to have in mind the relevant provisions of the CITES Convention which it implements. Where the Regulations provides for stricter protection than the Convention this is indicated below. As will be seen, in relation to Appendix I/Annex A specimens, export and import must be considered together since the grant of the export permit is contingent on the prior issue of an import permit. Article III.2 of the Convention provides:

> "The export of any specimen of a species included in Appendix I shall require the prior grant and presentation of an export permit. An export permit shall only be granted when the following conditions have been met:

[4] See further Chapter 2 and 4 - Part III.

(a) a scientific authority of the State of export has advised that such export will not be detrimental to the survival of such species;

(b) a management authority of the State of export is satisfied that the specimen was not obtained in contravention of the laws of that State for the protection of fauna and flora;

(c) a management authority of the State of export is satisfied that any living specimen will be so prepared and shipped as to minimize the risk of injury, damage to health or cruel treatment; and

(d) a management authority of the State of export is satisfied that an import permit has been granted for the specimen."

Article III.3 provides:

"The import of any specimen of a species included in Appendix I shall require the prior grant and presentation of an import permit and either an export permit or a re-export certificate. An import permit shall only be granted when the following conditions have been met:

(a) a scientific authority of the State of import has advised that the import will be for purposes which are not detrimental to the survival of the species involved;

(b) a scientific authority of the Sate of import is satisfied that the proposed recipient is suitably equipped to house and care for it; and

(c) a management authority of the State of Import is satisfied that the specimen is not to be used for primarily commercial purposes.

Re-export is dealt with in Article III.4 of the Convention which provides that:

"The re-export of any specimen of a species included in Appendix I shall require the prior grant and presentation of a re-export certificate. A re-export certificate shall only be granted when the following conditions have been met:

(a) a management authority of the State of re-export is satisfied that the specimen was imported into that State in accordance with the provisions of the Convention;

(b) a management authority of the State of re-export is satisfied that any living specimen will be so prepared and shipped as to minimize the risk of injury, damage to health or cruel treatment; and

(c) a management authority of the State of export is satisfied that an import permit has been granted for any living specimen."

It can be seen therefore that, in relation to re-export, there appears to be no requirement under the Convention for the management authority of the State of Re-export to make a fresh assessment as to the conservation implications of re-export. In relation to *living* specimens, the requirement for an import permit is maintained. This means that in such cases a close examination of the purpose of the import is still required (see below), as Article III.3 applies to import following either export or re-export. In relation to the re-export of living specimens therefore, a "no-detriment" finding as to the purposes for which import is to take place is still required from the scientific authority of the State of Import. In addition, the prohibition on import for primarily commercial purposes will still apply in cases of re-export.

The sequence of events prescribed under Article III is therefore that a person wishing to export or re-export a specimen will first have to ensure that an import permit from the State into which the specimen is to be imported is obtained. The importer will normally make the application for the import permit. This means of course that the destination must be known. The conservation test to be applied by the scientific authority[5] of the State of export is different to that applied by the State of import: the former is concerned with *effect* of the export itself and the latter with the *purposes* of the import. For example, it may be that the wild population of a particular species can withstand the removal of the specimen but if the import is for a particular purpose this may nevertheless be detrimental to the survival of the species and the scientific authority should advise that the import permit not be issued, for example on the grounds that the demand for the species will be stimulated.

[5] For an explanation of the role of a scientific authority, see further Chapter 1 - Part III.

The importance of ensuring that the management authority only issues permits after obtaining the appropriate advice from the scientific authority has been emphasised by the Parties to the Convention in a series of Conference Resolutions, most recently in Conference Resolution 10.3 which notes that issuance of export/import permits by a management authority without the appropriate advice from the scientific authority "constitutes a lack of compliance with the provisions of the Convention and seriously undermines species conservation".

The Council Regulation: The introduction into the Community of Annex A specimens is subject to the completion of the "necessary checks" and prior presentation at the border customs office at the point of introduction of an import permit issued by the management authority of the Member State of destination. In accordance with the Convention, the Regulation provides that import and export permits are to be issued by management authorities[6], acting on the advice of the competent scientific authority, and the roles performed by each are broadly the same as those prescribed by the Convention. It is worth noting however that in the European Union the tasks to be carried out by the scientific authorities of importing Member States are more onerous in some respects. Article 4(1) of the Council Regulation, which deals with the introduction of Annex A specimens into the Community, imposes stricter conditions on the issue of import permits than does the Convention by requiring a finding from the scientific authority of the Member State *of import* that the import would not have a harmful effect on the conservation status of the species or the extent of territory which it occupies. In making such a determination, the scientific authority must first consider any opinion given by the Scientific Review Group (SRG)[7]. This is in addition to the Convention's requirement that the management authority shall have advised that introduction into the Community is taking place for a permitted purpose (see further below).

Import Permits: In addition to obtaining the appropriate "no detriment" finding from the scientific authority (see above), the management authority must also be satisfied that the other conditions prescribed by Article 4(1) of the Regulation have been met. The applicant for an import permit must also provide documentary evidence that the specimens have been obtained in accordance with legislation on the protection of the species concerned. In the case of import from a third country of a species listed in the Appendices to the Convention, this evidence should be an export permit

---

[6] For an explanation of the role of a management authority, see further Chapter 1 - Part III.

[7] As to the role of the SRG, see further Chapter 1 - Part III.

or re-export certification issued in accordance with the Convention (Article 4(1)(b)(i). In the case of Appendix I species however, such evidence is not required because, under the rules of the Convention, the export permit will not be issued until the management authority of the state of export has seen the import permit. In such cases the original copy of the import permit shall be withheld from the applicant pending presentation of the export permit or re-export certificate (Article 4(1)(b)(ii)).

In addition, the management authority of the Member State of Import must be satisfied that the intended accommodation for any live specimen is adequately equipped to conserve and care for it properly (Article 4(1)(c); that the specimen is not to be used for primarily commercial purposes (Article 4(1)(d)-this is discussed in more detail below; and that, following consultation with the scientific authority, there are no other factors relating to the conservation of the species which militate against the issuance of the import permit (Article 4(1)(e). These other factors might include for example a recommendation from the CITES Secretariat that Parties not accept imports from a certain country.

It should be noted that the requirements as to "non-detriment" in Article 4(1)(a) and as to the purpose of the import in Article 4(1)(d) do not have to be met in the case of worked specimens acquired 50 years previously or specimens legally introduced into or acquired in the Community which are, modified or not, being reintroduced into the Community (Article 4(5)). This exemption is aimed at trade in antiques which meet the prescribed conditions.

"Not to be used for primarily commercial purposes"

The determination of the purpose of the import is critical to the operation of the Convention's system of protection for Appendix I species and, accordingly, to the regime which applies to Annex A species under the Regulation. The approach to be taken to this criterion has been the subject of some controversy among the Parties to the Convention as considered below.

The Convention: The key phrase "not to be used for primarily commercial purposes" is not further defined in the text of the Convention. Given the importance of applying this concept to trade in Appendix I species, it has however been the subject of elaboration by the Parties. CR 5.10, adopted in 1985, clarifies a number of matters and sets out examples as illustrations of the correct approach to be taken by the state of import in determining whether purposes are primarily commercial or not. The definition of "primarily commercial purposes" has continued to be the subject of much debate at recent COPs however. At COP 10 Namibia put forward a proposal (subsequently withdrawn) which would have been to redefine the meaning of "commercial purposes" according to the conservation benefits of a given transaction with the result that trade in Appendix I species emanating from conservation and management programmes would not be caught by the term "primarily commercial purposes" despite the obvious commercial aspects of such transactions.[8] At COP 11, another amendment to Resolution 5.10 was proposed by South Africa (subsequently withdrawn) which would have shifted the emphasis to an analysis of whether a proposed export would be for the benefit of the species (as opposed to the current analysis of whether the transaction would be for primarily commercial purposes). Many argued that this proposal, if it had been adopted, would clearly have been contrary to the spirit and text of the Convention and would have created a major loophole undermining the protection afforded to Appendix I specimens by CITES. Both of these proposals indicate an underlying tension in attitudes as to how the Convention should evolve. On the one hand, on the basis of past experience (with Appendix II listings for elephant ivory for example) many states feared that such amendments to the regime would lead to commercialisation and would have an adverse impact on endangered species. On the other hand, others argued that the present formulation of the test for determining whether purposes are "primarily commercial" denies many range states the opportunity to generate much needed for the conservation of Appendix I species. Such funds, it is argued, could be obtained from sales of specimens culled during routine conservation and management programmes (African elephants and the potential revenue generated from ivory sales is the obvious example in this regard). On this basis it has been argued that the present system can lead to a rejection of trade that may actually benefit the species.

Resolution 5.10 makes it clear that the burden of proving that the import is for primarily non-commercial purposes falls on the applicant for the permit. CR 5.10 states that an activity is commercial if its purposes is to obtain economic benefit, including profit (in cash or in kind) and is directed towards resale, exchange, provision of a service or other form of economic use or benefit. The Resolution goes on to recommend that the phrase should be broadly defined: any purposes which are not wholly non-commercial should be regarded as commercial. As to whether the purposes are primarily

[8] See Species Survival Network Daily CITES Conference Digest COP10 Issue 4 at http://www.defenders.org/defenders/citdig4.html

commercial, the Parties have agreed that all uses whose non-commercial aspects do not clearly predominate shall be considered to be primarily commercial in nature.

Any incidental commercial transaction for the purposes of simply effecting the import are to be disregarded however. The purpose of the import does not become commercial simply because the services of an agent have been employed, in the same way that employing commercial transport services does not render the purpose of the import commercial. The situation is different however, if the import is undertaken by a professional dealer. The Resolution indicates that this type of import will generally be unacceptable, unless perhaps a contract has already been concluded between the dealer and a purchaser which would otherwise be acceptable such as where the intent is to use the specimen for scientific purposes. The examples listed in CR 5.10 of situations which may constitute trade for primarily non-commercial purposes are: purely private use; scientific purposes; education or training; use by the Biomedical industry; captive breeding purposes. In each case however it will be necessary to analyse the facts and to ensure that all the other requirements of the Convention are met before deciding to issue a permit.

The Parties are recommended to include on the import permit, certification that the specimens will not be used for primarily commercial purposes and that, if live specimens are involved, that the recipient has suitable facilities to house and care for them.

Import restrictions

Assuming that the above conditions are fulfilled, the issuance of import permits by Member States is, in addition, made subject to the proviso that no import restrictions exist for the species in question. General import restrictions on species listed under Annexes A and B or live species posing an ecological threat can be established by the Commission in certain circumstances under Article 4(6). The establishment of such restrictions requires the opinion of the Scientific Review Group[9] and consultation with

[9] In order to foster Community wide coordination between scientific authorities EC Regulation 338/97 established the Scientific Review Group which consists of representatives of each Member State's scientific authority (Article 17). The Scientific Review Group is authorised to examine any scientific question relating to the application of the EC Regulation and may issue opinions. Any opinions issued by the Scientific Review Group must be considered by the scientific authorities of Member States when giving advice to their respective management authorities on the issuance of import permits for Annex A or B listed species.

affected range states. Where such restrictions have been imposed, the Member States are obliged to reject all import permit applications for the specimen concerned for as long as that restriction remains in place[10] *unless:* the application was submitted prior to the establishment of the restriction; or the competent authority is satisfied either that a contract or order exists for which payment has been made or that shipment has already taken place.[11] Where these exceptions apply, the validity of the import permit may not exceed one month. The Article 4(6) import restrictions can apply to the following types of specimen where it is specifically stated in the decision: captive bred or artificially propagated specimens; specimens imported for certain specified purposes and those which are household possessions of someone moving into the Community to take up residence (Article 41 (4) of the Commission Regulation).

In relation to Annex A specimens, an Article 4(6) import restriction may be established in the following situations: where import would have a harmful effect on the conservation status of the species or the range of the wild population thereof; where other factors relating to the conservation status of the species exist that militate against the issuance of an import permit. An import restriction may also be imposed where the introduction of live Annex A specimens into the natural environment of the Community would pose an ecological threat to wild species indigenous to the EC.

The current Article 4(6) restrictions are set out in Commission Regulation (EC) No 2087/2001[12] which contains a limited number of restrictions applying to Annex A specimens, including the wolf and the lynx. Most, but not all, the restrictions are particular to specific countries of origin and all are based on Article 4(6)(a) (other factors or harmful effect of trade).

Export and Re-export: Export and e-export from the Community are dealt with in Article 5 of the Council Regulation. In a similar way to the requirements for introduction into the Community, the necessary checks must be completed and the presentation of the required permit must take place at the customs office at which the export formalities are completed, before export or re-export can proceed.

The Regulation provides, in Article 5, that in the case of export of Annex A specimens, the scientific authority of the Member State of Export

[10] Article 41(1) Commission Regulation (EC)1808/2001.

[11] Article 41(2) Commission Regulation (EC) 1808/2001.

[12] Dated 24 October 2001, suspending the introduction into the Community of specimens of certain species of wild fauna and flora.

must be satisfied that the capture or collection and export of wild specimens will not have a harmful effect on the conservation status of the species, or the extent of the territory which it occupies, before an export permit may be issued (unless the specimen is a worked specimen acquired more than 50 years previously or a dead part or derivative acquired before the Regulation or Convention applied to it, Article 5(6)). The applicant must provide documentary evidence that the specimens have been obtained in accordance with legislation for the protection of the species in question (Article 5(2)b). The management authority must be satisfied that any live specimen will be prepared and shipped so as to minimise the risk of injury, damage to health or cruel treatment.

As to the purpose of the export, in relation to specimens of species listed under Appendix I which are being exported to a Party to the Convention, the management authority must be satisfied that an import permit has been issued. In the case of Annex A species which are not listed in Appendix I, the management authority must make the assessment itself (since there will be no Convention import permit) and satisfy itself that the specimen will not be used for primarily commercial purposes (unless the specimen is a worked specimen acquired more than 50 years previously or a dead part or derivative acquired before the Regulation or Convention applied to it, Article 5(6)) (Article 5(2)(c)(ii)). Finally, the management authority must be satisfied, following consultation with the scientific authority, that there are "no other factors" relating to the conservation of the species which militate against issuance of an export permit (Article 5(2)(d)).

In relation to re-export, the management authority must, as in the case of export, be satisfied as to the welfare of any live specimen during shipping, that the re-export is not for a primarily commercial purpose and that no other factors militate against export (Article 5(3)). Re-export may take place after a specimen has been in the Community for some considerable time, possible before the Convention applied to it and this is reflected in the remaining requirements for issuance of a re-export certificate. The management authority must be satisfied that the specimens concerned were introduced into the Community in accordance with the provisions of the Regulation, or previous implementing legislation (Regulation (EEC) no 3626/82), or prior to 1984, that they entered international trade in accordance with the provisions of the Convention or else were legally introduced into the territory of a Member State before the provisions of the Council Regulation or its predecessor or the Convention became applicable to them, or became applicable in that Member State (Article 5(3) paragraphs (a)-(d)).

Introduction from the Sea

This part of the CITES regime is comparatively rarely used. Article III.5 provides:

> "The introduction from the sea of any specimen of a species included in Appendix I shall require the prior grant of a certificate from a management authority of the State of introduction. A certificate only shall be granted when the following condition s have been met:
>
> (a) a scientific authority of the State of Introduction advises that the introduction will not be detrimental to the survival of the species involved;
>
> (b) a management authority [(or scientific authority)] of the State of Introduction is satisfied that the proposed recipient of a living specimen is suitably equipped to house and care for it; and
>
> (c) a management authority of the State of Introduction is satisfied that that specimen is not to be used for primarily commercial purposes."

So far as the Community rules are concerned, the general rules for introduction into and export from the Community under Articles 4 and 5 of the Council Regulation apply, subject to the following modification, in the case of introduction into the Community. Article 4(1)(f) requires in such cases that, in order to issue an import permit, the management authority must be satisfied that any live specimen will be so prepared and shipped as to minimize the risk of injury, damage to health or cruel treatment.

Retrospective issue of import/export documentation

In exceptional circumstances, a management authority of an EC Member State may issue the relevant export and import documentation for certain specimens of species listed in Annex A retrospectively (Article 8(3) of the Commission Regulation[13] as read with Article 4(5) of the Council Regulation). In order to qualify for this exception the specimens must be worked specimens acquired more than 50 years previously or previously

[13] Commission Regulation (EC) 1808/2001 of 30 August 2001.

legally introduced into or acquired in the Community and being reintroduced.

This provision may prove useful in the situation where importers receive shipments unexpectedly. Such an exceptional procedure is, however, available only where the management authority has been notified immediately by the importer or (re-) exporter on the arrival or prior to departure of such a shipment and of the reasons why the necessary documents are not available. Additionally, before issuing retrospective documents the management authority must be satisfied that the irregularities are not attributable to the fault of the importer or (re-)exporter and that the transaction concerned is otherwise in compliance with the provisions of EC Regulation 338/97, CITES and the legislation of any third country involved. Import or export documents issued on this basis must clearly indicate that they have been issued retrospectively and the reasons for doing so.

Special Cases in Relation to Trade in Appendix I Species

Use of Quotas

Quotas are used as a means of allowing limited trade in certain populations of some Appendix I species[14] at levels which will not undermine the conservation status of the species . There is no reference to the use of quotas in the text of the Convention but their use is sanctioned in certain cases and under certain conditions by a number of conference resolutions agreed by the Parties. The decision to develop a system of quotas in prescribed cases arose from a recognition by the Parties that certain decisions to list species on Appendix I adopted at the first few meetings of the Parties might not conform to the Berne listing criteria[15] agreed at the first Conference of the Parties. Producer countries in particular were concerned that commercial trade was therefore being restricted despite that fact that the biological status of the species was such as to allow for at least a certain level of trade. Where the stringent requirements for removing a species from Appendix I cannot be met in relation to such a species, the Parties have agreed that quotas be set for limited commercial trade at a level

[14] Whilst recognising their limitations, Wijnsteckers refers to the use of (Appendix II) quotas within the framework of CITES as "probably the most effective tool for the regulation of international trade... currently available" (Chapter 28 of The Evolution of CITES").

[15] Or to the revised listing criteria adopted at Fort Laùderdale in 1994.

which does not threaten the survival of the species concerned. A number of conditions and limitations are placed on the arrangements for such quotas: they can only apply to non-migratory species; scientific evidence of biological status to justify the down listing will still be required; specimens must be marked and exporting countries are required to operate a scientifically based and well-documented management programme for the species in question.

At present, quotas are used in relation to a limited number of types of specimen including: hunting trophies generally, leopard skins and trophies for personal use from certain producer countries and Markhor hunting trophies. Quotas for trade in ivory were used from 1985 until 1989 when the African Elephant was transferred from Appendix II to Appendix I of CITES and all trade in ivory was banned[16].

Conference Resolution 9.21 concerns the interpretation and application of quotas for all Appendix I listed species. The Resolution is based on the awareness that the majority of Parties consider that the establishment of quotas by the Parties satisfies the required finding that the export of the specimen in question will not be detrimental to the survival of the species and that the import will not be for purposes detrimental to the survival of the species, provided that the export is within the limits of the quota. The Resolution provides that Parties are required to submit to the Secretariat proposals for a quota at least 150 days before a meeting of the COP. The Resolution then confirms that, where the Parties set a quota for an Appendix I species, this will in itself satisfy the requirements of Article III CITES regarding the no-detriment findings of the appropriate Scientific Authorities (see above) subject the proviso that the quota is not exceeded and no new information has emerged indicating that the species population in the relevant range State can no longer sustain the agreed quota

Leopard Skins and Trophies for Personal Use: Quotas for the export of leopard skins and trophies for personal use have been set in relation to certain countries of origin whose populations are not endangered[17]. These are leopards which have been killed in order to protect life and property or to enhance the survival of the species and the skins may include hunting trophies. The arrangements do not constitute a reopening of commercial

[16] In the context of the down-listing to Appendix II, zero quotas for ivory in relation to certain range states were reintroduced as a result of decisions taken at COP 10 and COP11 (see further Chapter 2 - Part III).

[17] The current system is governed by CR 10.14 (rev) COP 12.

trade in contrast to quota arrangements for other species, see below). The usual conditions for trade in an Appendix I species apply including the "no detriment" test (export must not be detrimental to the survival of the species) and the requirement that the specimen is not to be used for primarily commercial purposes. Under the quota system for leopard skins, the no detriment test is considered to be satisfied provided the specimen falls with the set quota and import will not be considered to be for primarily commercial purposes provided that the skins are acquired by the owner in the country of export and are being imported as personal items that will not be sold in the country of import. Import is limited to two skins per year per individual.

In addition to these conditions, the skin must be marked with a self-locking tag bearing the country code of the country of origin and the quota number and the calendar year in which the animal was removed from the wild and this information must be repeated on the export permit. Exporting countries must report the annual number of trophies and skins exported to the Secretariat. With regard to any change in the quota for leopard skins and hunting trophies, CR 10.14 as revised at COP 12 provides that this requires the consent of the Conference of the Parties in accordance with Conference Resolution 9.21. Previously only new quotas need COP approval.[18]

So far as the Council Regulation is concerned, the Management Authority will have to check when the import permit is applied for whether the export permit from the State of Export complies with the requirements set out in the relevant Conference Resolutions. Article 36(4) of the Commission implementing regulation requires that Appendix I specimens subject to an export quota be marked in accordance with the relevant Conference Resolutions adopted by the Parties.

Ranching Operations

Ranching is the rearing in a controlled environment of specimens taken from the wild, for example crocodile eggs or hatchlings. Since 1981 (COP3), the Parties have sanctioned certain ranching operations in order to permit commercial trade of Appendix I species in circumstances where this would not appear to be covered by the exemption applying to captive bred specimens because, in accordance with the relevant Conference

[18] This substitution of the role of the COP for that of the Scientific Authority in the country of import regarding the decision making process for quotas is true for all Appendix I species and not just for leopards. This is clear from Conf Resolution 9.21. See following paragraph in main text above.

Resolution, this covers only the offspring reared in a controlled environment of parents that mated in a controlled environment (see further Chapter 6 - Part III).

Under the agreement reached by the Parties on ranching, as currently contained in Conference Resolution 11.16, certain national populations of Appendix I species which are subject to ranching operations in a particular Party and which accord with the conditions laid down in CR11.16, may be down-listed to Appendix II so that commercial trade is permitted in those ranched specimens. In order for such a proposal to be considered, it must accord with general criteria laid down in CR11.16. These criteria are extensive and include the following: the proposal must emanate from a range state (a state in whose jurisdiction the population occurs); the proposal must be primarily beneficial to the local populations concerned; all products must be adequately identified and tagged; appropriate inventories and monitoring mechanisms must be in place and there must be safeguards in place which ensure that adequate numbers of ranched specimens are returned to the wild where necessary. Furthermore, the proposal must contain evidence that removal from the wild will not have a significant detrimental effect on wild populations and as to the likely economic and biological success of the operation as well as an assurance that it will be carried out in a humane manner. The Resolution recommends that all Parties prohibit trade in ranched specimens unless all the requirements of the Resolution have been complied with. Parties operating ranching operations must submit annual reports to the Secretariat which report on all relevant aspects of the operation as well as any new information on the status of the wild population, the survival rate of specimens released back into the wild and so on.

Some ranching proposals, in particular those relating to marine turtles, remain controversial and despite the adoption of guidelines for their evaluation in CR 9.20(rev), no such proposal has been adopted.

Recognising the desirability of ensuring that trade in certain crocodile populations transferred to Appendix II in accordance with the quota system should not take place in a manner detrimental to the survival of such populations, the Conference of the Parties established in 1994 a universal tagging system for the identification of crocodilian skins (See CR 9.22.).[19] This system was revised at COP 11 in Resolution 11.12 which

[19] At present only two species have been transferred to Appendix II, these are the populations of Nile crocodile *Crocodylus niloticus* of 11 countries (including South Africa, Botswana, Madagascar, Zambia and Tanzania) and the populations of Australia, Indonesia and Papau New Guinea of the Estuarine Crocodile *Crocodylus porosus*. The proposal to maintain the export quota (which is set at no more than 1600 wild specimens) for the populations of Nile crocodile found in Tanzania was accepted at COP 11.

provides that self-locking non-reusable tags should be used to individually tag all crocodilian skins prior to export and that such tags should, as a bare minimum, contain the following information: the country of origin, a serial identification number and the species code. The Parties are further recommended to establish a registration or licensing system for those persons engaged in trade in crocodile skins and to implement an administrative system in order to effectively monitor this trade. The framework for a management and tracking system for tags used in the crocodile skin trade is also outlined in Resolution 11.12.

So far as the Council Regulation is concerned, there are no specific rules on ranched specimens, save that Article 36(4) of the Commission implementing regulation requires that they be marked in accordance with the relevant Conference Resolutions adopted by the Parties. When an import permit is applied for, the Management Authority of the importing Member State will have to check whether the export permit from the State of Export complies with the requirements set out in the relevant Conference Resolutions governing ranching operations and in particular whether the marking requirements have been met.

CHAPTER 4

TRADE IN ANNEX B SPECIES

Annex B of Council Regulation 338/97

The regulation of trade in Annex B species implements in the European Community the Convention's requirements on trade in Appendix II species. Annex B also contains species which are not listed in Appendix II of the CITES Convention but which the EC has decided to subject to the same rules, either as a stricter measure (for example because the EC has decided levels of international trade might not be compatible with the species' survival in certain countries) or in order to regulate a species listed Appendix I on which the EC has entered a reservation.[1]

Species listed in Annex B to the EC Regulation include: species listed in Appendix II to the Convention (other than any which are listed in Annex A as an EC stricter measure) for which the Member States have not entered a reservation and any species listed in Appendix I to the Convention for which a reservation has been entered. Annex B also includes any other species, not listed in Appendices I and II to the Convention, but which is subject to levels of international trade that might not be compatible with its survival or with the survival of populations in certain countries, or with the maintenance of the total population "at a level consistent with the role of the species in the ecosystems in which it occurs". Annex B also includes so-called "look-alike" species which are listed for reasons of similarity in appearance to other species listed in Annex A or B, where listing is essential in order to ensure the effectiveness of controls on trade in specimens of such species. This "look-alike" basis for an Annex B listing is more widely drawn than the provision in Article 3(1)(b)(ii) which provides for an Annex A listing for a species where most members of the genus (or most of the subspecies) in question are already listed on Annex A and the listing is necessary in order to effectively protect those taxa.

Ecological Threats: Annex B also includes species in relation to which it has been established that the introduction of live specimens into the natural habitat of the Community would constitute an ecological threat to wild species of flora and fauna indigenous to the Community. So far, the

[1] Currently there are no such reservations.

red-eared terrapin and the American bullfrog are the only species to have been listed in Annex B for this purpose. [2]

Export/Import of Appendix II species

The Convention: The greatest volume of trade carried out under CITES is of course in Appendix II species, in which commercial trade is allowed subject to the levels of trade being monitored at the national level. As stated above, a number of Appendix II species are listed on Annex A and for the purposes of trade in and out of the Community will be treated as if they were listed on Appendix I of the Convention and no commercial trade will be permitted.

Article IV of the Convention governs trade in Appendix II species and requires all such trade to take place in accordance with its provisions. Article IV.2 provides:

> "The export of any specimen of a species included in Appendix II shall require the prior grant and presentation of an export permit. An export permit shall only be granted when the following conditions have been met:
>
> (a) a scientific authority of the State of export has advised that such export will not be detrimental to the survival of that species;
>
> (b) a management authority of the State of export is satisfied that the specimen was not obtained in contravention of the laws of that State for the protection of fauna and flora; and
>
> (c) a management authority of the State of export is satisfied that any living specimen will be so prepared and shipped as to minimise the risk of injury, damage to health or cruel treatment;"

There are two key differences between the rules governing trade in Appendix II species under Article IV of the Convention and those which apply to trade in Appendix I species under Article III. First, no import permit is required under the Convention for Appendix II species. In relation

[2] Chapter 6 - Part II deals with the general law on alien species.

to import, Article IV.4 simply states that "The import of any specimen of a species included in Appendix II shall require the prior presentation of either an export permit or re-export certificate". Second, in contrast to the position in relation to Appendix I species, there is no prohibition on trade for commercial purposes in relation to Appendix II species.

A key feature of the regime for Appendix II species is to be found in Article IV.3 which concerns monitoring of trade:

> "A scientific authority in each Party shall monitor both the export permits granted by that State for specimens of species included in Appendix II and the actual exports of such specimens. Whenever a scientific authority determines that the export of specimens of any such species should be limited in order to maintain that species throughout its range at a level consistent with its role in the ecosystems in which it occurs and well above the level at which that species might become eligible for inclusion in Appendix I, the scientific authority shall advise the appropriate management authority of suitable measures to be taken to limit the grant of export permits for specimens of that species."

To help ensure compliance with this aspect of the regime the Parties have adopted what is known as the Significant Trade Process. In a series of Conference Resolutions, the Parties have established a system under which levels of trade are analysed by the Animals and Plants Committees[3] in cooperation with the Secretariat and relevant experts, with the assistance of the UNEP-WCMC[4]. The aim is to identify those species which are subject to significant levels of international trade and for which the available information appears insufficient to enable scientific authorities to satisfy the requirements of Article IV.3. The process is then geared towards developing measures to ensure that the appropriate steps are taken to ensure that the requirements of Article IV are met.

The Significant Trade Process was revised at COP12. Under the terms of Conference Resolution 12.8 (Replacing Conference Resolution 8.9 (rev)), the Animals and Plants Committees are directed to review the biological, trade and other relevant information on Appendix II species subject to significant levels of trade, in order to identify problems and solutions concerning the implementation of Article IV of the Convention.

[3] For further detail on these two Committees see Chapter 6 - Part III.

[4] For a description of the role of UNEP-WCMC, see further Chapter 1 - Part III.

Range States are to be consulted and a detailed procedure is laid down in the Resolution, regulating the selection of the species to be reviewed, consultation with range states, compilation of information and categorisation of the species concerned as being "of urgent concern", "of possible concern" or of "least concern". The latter are to be eliminated from the review. In relation to the first two categories, the Committees are given the power to make recommendations. For species of urgent concern, these recommendations should propose specific actions to address the implementation problems identified such as the establishment of cautious export quotas or temporary restrictions (paragraph (n)) and deadlines for compliance are to be set. In relation to species of possible concern, the recommendations should specify the information required to enable the relevant Committee to determine whether to categorise the species as being of urgent or least concern and should also provide for interim measures where appropriate for the regulation of trade.

The Secretariat is to determine whether these recommendations have been complied with and report to the Standing Committee accordingly. Where the recommendations have been met, the Parties will be notified that species has been removed from the process. Where the recommendations have not been met, the Secretariat will recommend appropriate action, which may as a last resort include the suspension of trade in the affected species. The Standing Committee will decide on the appropriate action to be taken and a suspension of trade will only be lifted when the Party concerned has demonstrated compliance. There is also provision for support to be provided to range states including the training of conservation staff and the provision of technical equipment and support.

Re-export

Article IV.5 governs re-export of Appendix II species and provides:

"The re-export of any specimen of a species included in Appendix II shall require the prior grant and presentation of a re-export certificate. A re-export certificate shall only be granted when the following conditions have been met:

(a) a management authority of the State of re-export is satisfied that the specimen was imported into that State in accordance with the provisions of the present Convention;

> (b) a management authority of the State of re-export is satisfied that any living specimen will be so prepared and shipped as to minimize the risk of injury, danger to health or cruel treatment."

In cases of re-export therefore, there is no requirement for a fresh scientific appraisal of the conservation implications of the export.

Introduction from the Sea

Introduction from the sea is dealt with under Article IV.6 which provides:

> "The introduction from the sea of any specimen of a species included in Appendix II shall require the prior grant of a certificate from a management authority of the State of introduction. A certificate only shall be granted when the following conditions have been met:
>
> > (a) a scientific authority of the State of Introduction advises that the introduction will not be detrimental to the survival of the species involved; and
> >
> > (b) a management authority [(or scientific authority)] of the State of Introduction is satisfied that any living specimen will be so handles as to minimise the risk of injury, damage to health or cruel treatment [the proposed recipient of a living specimen is suitably equipped to house and care for it;]"

The Rules Governing Trade in Annex B Species

Import

Unlike Annex A, there is no general prohibition on commercial trade for species listed in Annex B and therefore trade from and to the EC in Annex B species is permitted subject to certain conditions. The rules governing the introduction into the Community of Annex B species are set out in Article 4(2) of the Council Regulation and they contain various stricter measures which go beyond the requirements of the Convention. The most obvious of these is that the import of Annex B species into the EU requires the prior presentation, at the first point of introduction into the Community, of an *import permit* issued by the management authority of the Member State of destination. As in the case of Annex A specimens, introduction to the Community is subject to the completion of the necessary checks at the border customs office at the point of introduction and to the presentation of the import permit. In the absence of the necessary documents, the specimens in question will not be allowed to go through customs procedures and may be seized and/ or confiscated. Import permits may be issued by the Management Authority of the Member State of destination, provided that no import restriction exists for the specimens concerned under Article 4(6) of the Council Regulation (see below).

The permits for Annex B specimens are issued subject to the conditions set out in Article 4(2) of the Council Regulation. As in the case of Annex A specimens, there must be a "non-detriment" finding by the competent scientific authority, although this requirement is formulated so as to take account of the volume of trade (since commercial trade is permitted in Annex B species). Thus, the Scientific Authority, after examining available data and considering any opinion from the Scientific Review Group (SRG) must be of the opinion that the introduction into the Community would not have a harmful effect on the conservation status of the species or on the extent of territory occupied by the relevant population of the species, taking account of the current or anticipated level of trade. In view of the volume of trade in Annex B species, Article 4(2)(a) then provides that this opinion will be valid for subsequent imports from that state as long as the basis for it has not changed significantly.

In addition, the applicant must produce documentary evidence that the specimens were not obtained in contravention of conservation legislation concerning such species[5] and that the intended accommodation for any live specimen is adequately equipped to conserve and care for it properly. The specified housing conditions applicable to live specimens of Annex B species represent a stricter measure than what is required under the Convention for Appendix II listed specimens.[6] The control of subsequent

[5] In the case of species listed in CITES Appendices I or II this documentary evidence must include an export permit or re-export certificate or, in certain cases, a copy thereof. For Appendix III species the requisite documentary evidence includes an export permit where the export comes from the country which listed the species, a certificate of origin where the export is from another country of origin, or a re-export certificate for Appendix III species that are being re-exported. Note that the application of CITES Article X to documentary evidence from third country documentation applies to both CITES Parties and non-parties alike.

[6] There are no Resolutions on the topic although CR 10.21 does address the *transport* of live specimens.

movements of live specimens under Article 9 of the Regulation remains stricter for Annex A specimens than for Annex B specimens however. In the case of Annex B specimens, the holder of the import permit simply has to ensure that the intended recipient is adequately informed of the accommodation, equipment and practices required to ensure that the specimen will be properly cared for.

As in the case of Annex A specimens, the relevant competent authorities must also be satisfied that there are no other *conservation related factors* which militate against the import and in the case of specimens introduced from the sea, the management authority must be satisfied that any live specimen will be so prepared and shipped as to minimise risk of injury, damage or cruel treatment.

It should be noted that these requirements for issue of the import permit do not have to be met in the case of worked specimens acquired 50 years previously or specimens legally introduced into or acquired in the Community which are, modified or not, being reintroduced into the Community (Article 4(5)).

Import restrictions

Assuming that the above conditions are fulfilled, the issuance of import permits is, in addition, made subject to the proviso that no import restrictions exist for the species in question. General import restrictions or restrictions relating to certain countries of origin can be established by the Commission in certain circumstance under Article 4. The establishment of such restrictions requires the opinion of the Scientific Review Group[7] and consultation with affected range states. The restrictions are adopted by means of the Article 18 committee procedure. Where such restrictions have been imposed, the Member States are obliged to reject all import permit applications for the specimen concerned for as long as that restriction remains in place[8] unless: the application was submitted prior to the

[7] In order to foster Community wide coordination between scientific authorities EC Regulation 338/97 established the Scientific Review Group which consists of representatives of each Member State's scientific authority (Article 17). The Scientific Review Group is authorized to examine any scientific question relating to the application of the EC Regulation and may issue opinions. Any opinions issued by the Scientific Review Group must be considered by the scientific authorities of Member States when giving advice to their respective management authorities on the issuance of import permits for Annex A or B listed species.

[8] Article 41(1) Commission Regulation (EC)1808/2001.

establishment of the restriction; or the competent authority is satisfied either that a contract or order exists for which payment has been made or that shipment has already taken place.[9] Where these exceptions apply, the validity of the import permit may not exceed one month. The Article 4(6) import restrictions can apply to the following types of specimen where it is specifically stated in the decision: captive bred or artificially propagated specimens; specimens imported for certain specified purposes and those which are household possessions of someone moving into the Community to take up residence (Article 41 (4) of the Commission Regulation.

For Annex B specimens, an Article 4(6) import restriction may be established in the following situations: where other factors relating to the conservation status of the species exist that militate against the issuance of an import permit; where import would have a harmful effect on the conservation status of the species or the range of the wild population thereof, taking account of the current or anticipated levels of trade; in relation to live specimens which are subject to a high rate of mortality during shipment or which are unlikely to survive in captivity for a considerable period of their lifespan. Finally an import restriction may be imposed where the introduction of live specimens into the natural environment of the Community would pose an ecological threat to wild species indigenous to the EC.

The current Article 4(6) restrictions are set out in Commission Regulation (EC) No 2087/2001[10] which contains an extensive list of restrictions applying to Annex B specimens. Most are particular to specific countries of origin and most but not all are based on Article 4(6)(b) (other factors or harmful effect of trade). A few restrictions, mainly relating to reptile species are based on Article 4(6)(c) (mortality during shipment) and two relate to a species identified as an ecological threat.

Export or re-export

For species listed in Annex B the requirements relating to export and re-export are set out in Article 5(4) of the Council Regulation. As in the case of Annex A specimens, export and re-export are subject to the completion of necessary checks and prior presentation at the customs office of an export permit or re-export certificate issued by the management authority of the Member State in whose territory the specimens are located. In the case of

[9] Article 41(2) Commission Regulation (EC) 1808/2001.

[10] Dated 24 October 2001, suspending the introduction into the Community of specimens of certain species of wild fauna and flora.

specimens taken in the wild, bred in captivity or artificially propagated in the EC an *export permit* is the relevant document whereas the re-export of specimens of species previously imported into the EC will require a *re-export certificate.*

In the case of export of Annex B specimens, the scientific authority of the Member State of Export must be satisfied that the capture or collection and export of wild specimens will not have a harmful effect on the conservation status of the species, or the extent of the territory which it occupies, before an export permit may be issued (unless the specimen is a worked specimen acquired more than 50 years previously, or a dead specimen or part or derivative acquired before the Regulation/Convention applied to it, Article 5(6))[11] . The applicant must also provide documentary evidence that the specimens have been obtained in accordance with legislation for the protection of the species in question (Article 5(2) b). The management authority must be satisfied that any live specimen will be prepared and shipped so as to minimise the risk of injury, damage to health or cruel treatment. Finally, the management authority must be satisfied, following consultation with the scientific authority, that there are "no other factors" relating to the conservation of the species which militate against issuance of an export permit (Article 5(2)(d)).

In relation to re-export, the management authority must, as in the case of export, be satisfied as to the welfare of any live specimen during shipping and that no other factors militate against export. Re-export may take place after a specimen has been in the Community for some considerable time, possibly before the Convention applied to it and this is reflected in the remaining requirements for issuance of a re-export certificate. The management authority must be satisfied that the specimens concerned were introduced into the Community in accordance with the provisions of the Regulation, or previous implementing legislation (Regulation (EEC) no 3626/82), or is prior to 1984, that they entered international trade in accordance with the provision of the Convention or else were legally introduced into the territory of a Member State before the provisions of the Council Regulation or its predecessor or the Convention became applicable to them, or became applicable in that Member State (Article 5(3) paragraphs (a)-(d)).

[11] In the case of Annex B specimens the Scientific Authority is required to monitor the export levels thereof and must advise its Management Authority of suitable measures if it is of the opinion that the export levels need to be limited – in such a case the Management Authority is obliged to inform the Commission which may then recommend export restrictions (Art 5.7). This implements Article IV3 of the Convention..

In the case of the species having been imported under an import permit issued by another Member State, Article 5(5) of the Council Regulation provides that the Management Authority of that Member State must be consulted.

The monitoring of the levels of trade required under Article IV.3 of the Convention (as to which see above) is implemented in Article 5.7 of the Regulation. The competent scientific authority in each Member State must monitor the issuance of export permits, as well as the actual exports of Annex B specimens. Whenever the authority determines that export should be limited in order to maintain that species throughout its range at a level consistent with its role in the ecosystem and "well above the level at which that species might become eligible for inclusion in Annex A", the scientific authority must advise the management authority in writing of the measures which need to be taken to limit the issuance of export permits. The management authority must then inform and send comments to the Commission which shall, if appropriate, recommend restrictions on exports of the species. Such restrictions will be adopted by means of the Article 18 committee procedure.

The regulation contains further provisions relating to *internal trade* (which covers both trade within and between individual Member States) in the Community. In respect of species listed in Annex A Article 8(1) Regulation (EC) 338/97 prohibits certain commercial activities involving such species.[12] The Regulation provides that these prohibitions on commercial activities shall also apply to Annex B species except in circumstances where it can be proved that the species concerned were acquired in accordance with and, where the case may be, introduced into the EC in compliance with conservation legislation.[13] Both general and specific *exemptions* to these Article 8(1) internal trade prohibitions may, in certain circumstances, be granted by the relevant Management Authority of the Member State in which the specimens are located.[14]

[12] The prohibited commercial activities include purchase, offer to purchase, acquisition for commercial purposes, public display for commercial purposes, use for commercial gain, sale, keeping for sale, offering for sale and transport for sale.

[13] Article 8(5) 338/97.

[14] Article 8(3) 338/97 sets out the circumstances in which exemptions may be granted – these are where the specimens were acquired in or introduced into the EC before the provisions relating to Annex A of Regulation 338/97 or CITES Appendix I became applicable to them, worked specimens acquired in accordance with the definition thereof in Article 2(w) of Regulation 338/97, specimens introduced into the EC in accordance with Regulation 338/97 and which are to be used for non-detrimental purposes, captive ...

Retrospective issue of import/export documentation

In exceptional circumstances, a management authority of an EC Member State may issue the relevant export and import documentation for specimens of species listed in Annex B retrospectively (Article 8(3) of the Commission Regulation). This may prove useful in the situation where importers receive shipments unexpectedly. Such an exceptional procedure is, however, available only where the management authority has been notified immediately by the importer or (re-)exporter on the arrival or prior to departure of such a shipment and of the reasons why the necessary documents are not available. Additionally, before issuing retrospective documents the management authority must be satisfied that the irregularities are not attributable to the fault of the importer or (re-)exporter and that the transaction concerned is otherwise in compliance with the provisions of EC Regulation 338/97, CITES and the legislation of any third country involved. Import or export documents issued on this basis must clearly indicate that they have been issued retrospectively and the reasons for doing so.

(*continued*) born and bred specimens or artificially propagated specimens, specimens required under exceptional circumstances for the advancement of science or for essential biomedical purposes pursuant to Council Directive 86/609/EEC, specimens intended for breeding or propagation purposes from which conservation benefits will accrue to the species concerned, the specimens are intended for research or education aimed at the preservation or conservation of the species, specimens which were taken in the wild in a Member State in accordance with both EC and national legislation on the conservation of the species concerned.

CHAPTER 5

TRADE IN SPECIMENS LISTED IN ANNEXES C AND D

Annex C of Regulation 338/97

Annex C comprises the remaining CITES Appendix III species that are not listed in Annexes A or B for which the Member States have not entered a reservation, an example of which is the Honey Badger (*Mellivora capensis*). Annex C also includes CITES Appendix II species for which the EC has entered a reservation (Art 3.3.b). The position at present is that no such reservations have been entered into by the Community regarding Appendix II species.

Listing of Species on Appendix III

The purpose of a listing under Appendix III is to assist a country which regulates the species in question within its jurisdiction for the purpose of preventing or restricting exploitation. The listing is designed to enable other Parties to CITES to co-operate with the host state in the control of international trade in that species. Once a species is listed on Appendix III, all Parties to the Convention (unless they have entered a reservation to the listing) must ensure that trade in that species is in accordance with the rules of the Convention just as in the case for Appendix I and II. The rules governing trade differ according to whether export is from the listing country or any other country where the species originates (see further below). The difference between Appendix III and the other two regimes is therefore *not* that the rules are in any sense less binding but only in the fact that the listing is initiated by the host Party and aims to support its domestic controls. In reality some politically sensitive species, which arguably qualify for listing on Appendix II of the Convention, have been entered in Appendix III as consensus on Appendix II could not be reached among all the Parties. Recent examples of this include the Big-Leaf Mahogany, originally listed on Appendix III by Brazil and following COP12 now listed on Appendix II, and the Basking Shark, originally listed on Appendix III by the United Kingdom[1], and up-listed to Appendix II following COP12. Examples of

[1] See DETR News Release 098 dated 26 February 2001available at http://www.press.dtlr.gov.uk/0102/0098.htm wherein the UK states that it will attempt to have the basking shark listed in Appendix II at the next CITES meeting of the Conference of the Parties. This comes after its recent unsuccessful bid to do so at COP 11 in 2000 which failed to get the requisite two-thirds majority vote. See E-Wire Press Release "United Kingdom Fails in Bid to Place Basking Shark under CITES Protection" available at http://ens/lycos.com/e-wire/April00/20April0002.html

states which have listed species in Appendix III are Canada (the Walrus), India (the Golden Jackal) and South Africa. However, Ghana has made by far the most extensive use of Appendix III by listing some 132 species of fauna.

In the UK case of Greenpeace v Secretary of State for the Environment, Food and Rural Affairs[2], the Court of Appeal had to consider the decision by the UK authorities to allow the import of Brazilian mahogany listed on Annex C/Appendix III. Lord Justice Dyson described those species listed on Appendix III as the "least endangered" of those protected under the Convention (paragraph 50). This comment is understandable but, with respect, it is misleading for two reasons. First, the requirements for an Appendix III listing are that the host country wishes to engage the cooperation of other Parties in the protection of a domestically protected species-there is no reference to the required status of such a species in the Convention and thus no indication that a species listed on Appendix III is *not* endangered. Second, as indicated below, political factors unrelated to the status of the species concerned sometimes militate against a listing on Appendix I or II. The species may therefore be listed on Appendix III (which can be done in effect unilaterally) although in practice it meets the ecological criteria for a listing on one of the other Appendices.

Export/Import of Appendix III species

Not surprisingly, the requirements governing trade in specimens of species listed under Appendix III differ according to whether the specimen is being exported from the State which had the species listed on Appendix III or from another state. The rules are designed to facilitate co-operation with the listing state whilst recognising that export of the species from other states in which its exploitation is not regulated should continue, but should not be used as a cover for illegal trade emanating from the listing country.

Article V of the Convention requires that, where export is from any State which has included that species in Appendix III, an export permit be granted and presented. The export permit may only be granted where the management authority of the State of export is satisfied that the specimen was not obtained in contravention of the laws on the protection of fauna and flora and that any living specimen will be so prepared and shipped as to minimise the risk of injury, damage to health or cruel

[2] [2002] EWCA 1036.

treatment. Where the export is from a non-listing country, a certificate of origin is required for import (see below).

As far as import is concerned, the presentation of both an export permit and a certificate of origin are required unless, in the case of a re-export, the state of re-export has granted a certificate that the specimen was processed in that state or is being re-exported. Such a certificate is to be accepted by the State of import as evidence that the provisions of the Convention have been complied with.

The certificate of origin should be issued by the management authority of the state concerned. Conference resolution 12.3 on the use of permits and certificates recommends, with regard to certificates of origin for export of specimens of species listed in Appendix III, that these be only be issued by a designated management authorities, or by the competent authority in the case of trade with a non-party State, and that Parties not accept such certificates unless they are issued by such authorities. The Resolution goes on to provide that the certificate of origin shall be valid for a period of not more than 12 months from the date on which it was granted and that it may not be accepted to authorise export or import except during the period of validity.

At COP 9 in Fort Lauderdale the inclusion of species in Appendix III was considered by the Parties. Concerns had been expressed that the credibility of Appendix III was being called into question and, as a consequence, its effectiveness being undermined because Appendix III contained some species which occurred rarely or even not at all in international trade. The Parties therefore agreed to request the CITES Animals and Plants Committees to review the status of species listed on Appendix III and urged those Parties having listed species on Appendix III to review the status of the species concerned, taking into account any advice from the Committees and the following guidelines: the species should be native to the country listing the species; there should be adequate national regulation restricting or preventing exploitation and controlling trade, including provision for penalties; there should be adequate enforcement of this regulation; the Party should determine that the cooperation of other Parties is needed to control illegal trade; before listing the species, the Party should consult the management authorities of other range states, major importing countries, the Committees and the Secretariat. The Parties also recommended that, if possible, the Secretariat be informed of listing proposals three months before the Conference of the Parties in order to ensure that the listing enters into force at the same time as amendments to

Appendices I and II adopted at the meeting. The Parties also directed the Secretariat to publish the amended Appendices after each meeting and to ensure that copies of relevant national legislation have been received before, before an Appendix III listing is communicated to the Parties.

Trade in Annex C Species under Regulation 338/97

The most significant difference between the trade rules governing species listed in Annex C and those listed in Annexes A or B is that the former are not subject to the stricter EC requirement of an import permit. However, the importer of such species is nevertheless required to complete an import notification[3], which must be presented to the relevant customs authorities at the first point of entry into the Community. The import notification is not required under CITES itself and thus represents a stricter measure. In relation to Annex C species that are also listed in CITES Appendix III the import notification must be accompanied by the necessary export or re-export documentation.

The rules which apply to Annex B specimens regarding export or re-export from the EC apply equally to species listed in Annex C.

Trade in Annex D Species under Regulation 338/97

As there is no CITES equivalent for Annex D this is in itself a stricter measure. Annex D contains all the non-CITES species that are not already included in Annexes A to C and also all CITES Appendix III species for which a reservation has been entered into. Annex D is premised upon a precautionary approach to conservation by providing for the monitoring of species which the Community deems are in need of observation. An example of a CITES Appendix III species listed in Annex D is the Stoat (*Mustela erminea ferghanae*) whereas the Desert Rose (*Adenia fruticosa*) is an example of a species that does not have a CITES equivalent. The import into the EC of species listed in Annex D is subject to the same requirement as for species listed in Annex C (Article 4(4) of the Council Regulation), namely, the prior presentation of an import notification. However, this is the only requirement and unlike Annex C, no export documentation is required.

[3] Import notification is defined in Article 2(d) of the Council Regulation and the form to be used is set out in Annex II to the Commission Implementing Regulation.

CHAPTER 6

EXEMPTIONS

Article VII of the Convention provides for a number of total and partial exemptions to the requirements of Article III, IV and V. The scope of these exemptions has been further elaborated by various conference resolutions adopted by the Parties. Some of these exemptions cover a significant amount of international trade and are important derogations from the general rules, as such the Parties have sought in successive Conference Resolutions to ensure that they are strictly applied and not used as a means of conducting illicit trade.

Pre-Convention Specimens under the Convention

Specimens listed in Appendices I, II or III are not subject to CITES trade controls if they fall within the definition of "pre-Convention specimens" as laid down in the Convention and elaborated in Conference Resolutions, and provided that a pre-Convention certificate has been obtained from the appropriate management authority. The determination as to whether or not a specimen is pre-Convention is determined by comparing certain dates: the date of acquisition of the specimen; the date upon which the Convention applied to the species concerned in the state of export and the date upon which the Convention applied to the species in the state of import. It is necessary to consider *all* these dates in order to determine whether or not the exemption applies.

Article VII.2 of the Convention provides that where a management authority of the State of export or re-export is satisfied that a specimen was acquired before the provisions of the Convention applied to that specimen, the provisions of Articles III, IV and V shall not apply to that specimen where the management authority issues a certificate to that effect. The scope of this exemption has been the subject of further detailed elaboration in Conference Resolution 5.11, which seeks to ensure that the Parties adopt a common approach to determining whether or not a specimen is pre-Convention. The application of this exemption requires particular care since a specimen may be pre-Convention as regards trade between some countries and not others depending on when the countries concerned became Party to the Convention and on whether a listed specimen was subject to a reservation at the date of acquisition. This means that the status of the specimen will have to be re-examined every time it is proposed to export it to a different country.

In order to work out whether a particular specimen falls within Article VII.2 it is first necessary to compare two dates: the date of acquisition and the date on which the Convention applied to that specimen. If the date of acquisition is earlier than the date from which the Convention applied to that specimen then the specimen will be pre-Convention. Conference Resolution 5.11 lays down how these dates are to be determined.

The way in which the *date of acquisition* is determined depends on the type of specimen. For live or dead specimens taken from the wild, the date of acquisition is the date of their initial removal from their habitat. For parts or derivatives of specimens, the relevant date is the earliest date on which it can be shown that they were introduced into personal possession.

The *date from which the Convention applied to a particular specimen* may well vary from country to country and may therefore be different as between the state of export/re-export and the state of import. Both dates must be taken into account. Conference Resolution 5.11 makes it clear that the specimen must be pre-Convention to *both* the exporting and importing countries in order for Article VII.2 to apply.

The State of export can only issue a pre-Convention certificate if it is satisfied that the specimen was acquired at a time when: the species was not listed in any of the Convention Appendices; or, if it was, that it was not itself a Party to the Convention; or, if it was a Party, that it had entered (and not withdrawn) a reservation in relation to the species concerned.

A State of re-export can only issue a pre-Convention certificate if it is satisfied that the specimen was acquired (in the Country of origin) at a time when: the species was not listed in any of the Convention Appendices; or, if it was, that the country of origin was not a Party to the Convention; or, if it was a Party, that it had entered (and not withdrawn) a reservation in relation to the species concerned and in addition that, at the date of acquisition, either it was not itself a Party to the Convention or else was treated as a non-Party (because it had entered a reservation on that species).

It is important to note that even where a specimen is pre-Convention as regards the exporting country the State of import can only *accept* the specimen as pre-Convention if the date of acquisition is also earlier than the date from which the Convention applied to the specimen in its own country.

If a specimen is up or down listed, it shall be subject to the provisions applicable at the time of export, re-export or import.

A pre-Convention certificate must indicate either the date of acquisition or certify that the specimen was acquired before a certain date.

The Pre-Convention Exemption as applied in the European Union

Import and Export/Re-Export

As permitted under Article XV of the Convention, the EU has introduced stricter measures by limiting the extent to which the pre-convention exemption will operate for species [imported into] the Community. EU legislation gives effect to the pre-convention exemption in respect of international trade only to the extent that a specimen falls within the definition of a "worked specimen" in article 2(w) of the Regulation or, in the case of export or re-export only, is a dead specimen or part or derivative thereof for which the applicant provides proof that they were legally acquired before EU legislation or the Convention applied to them[1]. Certificates relating to the latter export exemption may be issued by the management authority of the state in which the specimen is located, Article 20(2)(c)-(f) of the Commission Implementing Regulation. "Worked specimens" are essentially antiques which were acquired before 1 June 1947 (50 years before the Convention cam into force).

This means that pre-convention certificates issued by third countries are not accepted by the EU for imports into the Community and full procedures must therefore be followed for specimens which would otherwise fall within the scope of the pre-Convention exemption in the Convention.

Controls on Internal Sales and Other Commercial Activities

A general derogation from the controls on commercial activities laid down in Article 8 of the Council Regulation[2] in respect of worked specimens has been adopted pursuant to Article 8(4) of the Council Regulation and is contained in Article 32(c) of Commission Regulation 1808/2001 (the Commission Implementing Regulation).

In relation to specimens which were was acquired before EC legislation implementing the Convention applied to them as Appendix I/

[1] See Articles 4(5)(b) and 5(6)(i) of the Council Regulation discussed in Chapter 3 and 4 - Part III.

[2] See further Chapter 10 - Part III.

Annex A specimens (including the legislation which preceded the current Council Regulation), the Member State may grant a specific exemption on a case by case basis in relation to internal sales controls, Article 8(3)(a) of the Council Regulation. The grounds on which such exemptions may be granted are set out in Article 8(3) and among these are included: the fact that the specimen was acquired or introduced into the Community before the provisions of Appendix I/Annex A applied to it; that it is a worked specimen acquired more than 50 years previously; that it is captive born or artificially propagated or is to be used for breeding or propagation purposes which will result in conservation benefits for that species. A full discussion of the grounds for such exemptions is contained in Chapter 10 - Part III. Certificates relating to these exemptions may be issued by the management authority of the state in which the specimen is located, Article 20(3)(a) of the Commission Implementing Regulation.

Transit

Article VII, paragraph 1, of the Convention provides an exemption from the provisions of Articles III, IV and V for specimens in transit and transhipment. Previous COP resolutions addressing this issue were consolidated under CR 9.7 which sets out the regime applicable to specimens in transit. This COP resolution recommends that Parties carry out inspections, in accordance with their national legislation, on specimens in transit in order to verify the existence of valid export documentation as required by the Convention or, as a minimum, in order to obtain satisfactory proof of the existence of such documentation. Parties are further recommended to enact legislation permitting the seizure or confiscation of specimens in transit that are not accompanied by valid export documentation or proof as to the existence thereof. The documentation should clearly reflect the final destination of the shipment and where there is a change in final destination, that change should be investigated by the country of transit to ensure the transaction complies with the purposes of the Convention. In addition, CR 9.7 goes further than previous resolutions in recommending that when an illegal shipment in transit is discovered that cannot be seized then the country of final destination, the Secretariat and, where applicable, all other countries of transit should be provided with all relevant information pertaining to such shipment.

Note that these recommendations also apply to shipments in transit that are destined for or received from non-party States, including shipments in transit between such States. The absence of CITES documentation in situations involving non-party States obviously renders this recommendation difficult to implement.

Derogations from import and export conditions in the case of specimens in transit between two non-EC countries transported through the territory of the Community are covered in Article 7(2) Regulation (EC) 338/97. This provision waives the requirement relating to the prior presentation of the prescribed import/export documentation to the customs authorities at the first point of introduction for specimens in transit through the Community. In the case of CITES-listed Annex A and B species however this waiver is contingent on the issue of a valid (re-)export document, relating to the specimens concerned, specifying the destination of the specimens, and issued in accordance with the provisions of the Convention by the competent authorities of the exporting country. This documentation must accompany the shipment.[3]

In the absence of this valid documentation the specimens must be seized and may, where applicable, be confiscated unless the document is issued retrospectively in compliance with rules laid down by the Commission.[4]

Personal or Household Effects

Under this exemption set out at Article VII.3 of the Convention, personal or household effects are exempt from CITES trade controls, although the conditions under which the exemption applies vary as between the three Appendices.

Appendix I specimens which are personal or household effects are exempt from the provisions of Article III *unless* they were acquired by the owner outside his state of usual residence and are being imported into that State. This is so unless the management authority is satisfied that the specimens in question were acquired before the provisions of the Convention applied to such specimens. This means that a pre-convention certificate is

[3] Article 7(2)(b) of Regulation (EC) 338/97.

[4] See Chapter 7 - Part III on the rules as to retrospective issue of permits. Article XX of Regulation (EC) 1808/2001 address retrospective issue of documents and provides that the management authority of a Member State may exceptionally issue import/export documents retrospectively after establishing that any irregularities are not attributable to the importer and/or the (re-) exporter and that the transaction otherwise fully complies with the provisions of the Convention, EC Regulations and the national legislation of the third country involved.

not required in such cases, although UK policy is to require documentary evidence.[5]

The situation as regards Appendix II specimens is more complicated: the exemption will *not* apply where the specimens concerned were acquired by the owner outside his State of usual residence and in a state where removal from the wild occurred, they are being imported into the owner's State of usual residence *and* the State where removal from the wild occurred requires the prior grant of export permits before any export of such specimens. Again this applies unless the management authority is satisfied that the specimens were acquired before the provisions of the present Convention applied to such specimens in which case the requirements of Article IV [need not be complied with].

The exemption applies in all cases where Appendix III specimens are personal or household objects.

At COP 12 it was decided that the Parties need to agree a definition of personal and household effects and Conference Resolution 12.9 defines the terms as meaning specimens that are personally owned or possessed for non-commercial purposes; legally acquired and at the time of import, export or re-export either worn or carried or included in personal baggage or part of a household move. The Resolution goes on to make a number of recommendations including that Parties do not require export or import permits for personal and household effects for certain dead specimens, parts or derivatives of Appendix II species except where the quantity exceeds the specified limits-including caviar up to 250 grams per person.

Pets

Conference Resolution 10.20[6] directly addresses the problem of frequent cross-border movements of personally owned live animals and whilst recognising that live animals are indeed often involved in frequent movement across international borders for various legitimate purposes it simultaneously recognises that the repeated granting of CITES import/

[5] For guidance about documentation see http://www.britishembassy.at/downloads/residence.pdf and in relation pets see http://www.defra.gov.uk/animalh/quarantine/home.html.

[6] COP 11 also briefly addressed the issue of personal or household effects in CR 11.11, in recommending that Parties consider harmonising national legislation regarding exemptions for rainsticks of certain species of Cactaceae granted under the exemption for personal or household effects and further consider limiting this to a number of no more than three rain sticks of the species concerned per person.

export documentation for such animals may create its own technical and administrative problems. On the other hand, it also notes that the exemptions provided in Article VII.3 of the Convention should not be used to avoid the controls on international trade in live animal species listed in the Appendices.

Further to this resolution, the exemption for personal or household effects shall be interpreted to include personally owned live animals that are based and registered in the owner's State of usual residence. Parties should issue certificates of ownership to owners of a live animal who wish to travel with the animal to another State only after agreement between the Parties concerned and if the owner's usual state of residence is in the territory of a Party and the animal is registered with the management authority of that Party. Information required to be supplied to the management authority by the applicant for a certificate of ownership include his/her name or address and relevant data regarding the animal, for example, the sex and mark number or other means of identification. Before issuing a certificate the management authority must be satisfied that the applicant legally possesses the animal and that the animal has been acquired in accordance with the provisions of the Convention.

When a certificate of ownership is issued for live animals as a personal or household effect in accordance with this resolution then the Parties concerned are to treat the certificate as a type of passport that facilitates the movement of such animals across borders when accompanied by their owners. These certificates remain valid for a maximum period of three years from the date of issue.

The EU Rules on Personal and Household Effects

The rules applicable to the introduction into or export from the EC of personal and household effects are governed by Article 7(3) (EC) Regulation 338/97 (the Council Regulation) and Articles 27 and 28 of (EC) Regulation 1808/2001 (the Commission Implementing Regulation). The general derogation contained in Article 7(3) does not apply to live animals and plants. Articles 27 and 28 make further limitations on the application of the derogation regarding specimens of species listed in Annex A or B. The application of the derogation is not, however, limited in the case of species listed in Annexes C and D except in relation to specimens used for commercial purposes.

With regard to both the introduction into the EC and the (re-)export from the EC, those goods that are to be used for commercial gain, sold, displayed for commercial purposes, kept for sale, offered for sale or transported for sale *canno*t be considered to be personal and household effects to which the derogation in Article 7(3) applies. Furthermore, in order for the derogation to apply, the specimen (including hunting trophies) must be in the personal luggage of a traveller coming from or going to a third country or in the personal property of a person transferring their residence into or out of the Community. In the case of hunting trophies, the derogation may also apply if they are taken by a traveller and imported at a later date.

Article 27 provides that the derogation does not apply to the first time that Annex A personal or household effects are imported into the EC by a person residing there, it also establishes that for the first time introduction into the Community of Annex B species by a resident, the prior presentation of an import permit is not required where the original of the (re-)export document and a copy thereof are presented. Nor is the presentation of an import permit required in the case of the reintroduction into the EC by a person normally resident, of personal and household effects involving either Annex A or Annex B listed species where an endorsed copy of the Community document used at the first import, or proof that the specimen was bought in the EC, is presented. In the case of sturgeon caviar and rainsticks covered by Annex B, no import permit or re-export permit is required.

Article 28 meanwhile provides that the derogation in Article 7(3) does not apply to the export of personal or household effects regarding species listed in Annex A or B. In relation to re-export of such specimens by a resident of the Community, the presentation of a re-export certificate is not necessary where the exporter presents an endorsed copy of the previously used Community import or export documentation, a copy of the original re-export document or proof that the specimens in question were acquired within the EC.

The derogation for personal and household effects has been interpreted to cover hunting trophies.[7] Thus it follows from the above

[7] See "Importing Your Hunting Trophies Into the European Union – A Guide for Hunters" produced by Safari Club International December 2000 available at http://www.sci-dc.org/public/docs/EUTROPHY.PDF which cites the following as references: Report of meeting of the Commission with FACE, 20 August 1998; communication to SCI from the Commission, 31 August 1998.

regulations that for a hunting trophy of an Annex A listed species the derogation does not apply to the first time introduction into the Community. In other words, even though certain game trophies listed in Annex A are considered personal effects the exception for such personal effects does not apply to the original introduction into the EU of such specimens and the hunter will need both the requisite export permit and an EU Member State import permit. For Annex B species, however, the derogation applies fully and although an export permit from the country of origin is still necessary, an EU Member State import permit will not be required on condition that the original export permit is presented.[8]

Tourist Souvenirs

One particular problem area is that of trade in tourist souvenirs. In relation to souvenirs which are or are derived from Appendix I specimens, Parties should be complying fully with the requirements of Article III (because by definition these are likely to have been acquired outside the State of usual residence). One difficulty is that of ignorance on the part of the public. The UK Government initiated a campaign in 1995 which seeks to inform the public about CITES and alert them to the need to check whether a souvenir is subject to CITES trade controls. The scheme is called "Souvenir Alert" and is aimed at warning tourists travelling abroad not to buy souvenirs derived from endangered species. The campaign is being organised in cooperation with the WWF and entails producing information leaflets, posters and luggage labels showing rare and endangered species.[9] Among the products targeted as part of the campaign are skins and products from cat species (such as tigers, leopards and jaguars), traditional medicines and elephant ivory.

At COP 10 further attention was paid to this problem in light of the recognition by the Parties that parts, products and derivatives of Appendix I and II species continue to be sold as tourist souvenirs and, in the case of some countries, are being offered for sale in duty-free shopping areas at international airports. This problem area continues to undermine the aims of the Convention as the trade in tourist souvenirs can in certain cases be quite substantial. Conference Resolution 10.6 urges Parties to comply

[8] Examples of game species listed in Annex A are the leopard, cheetah, gray wolf, markhor and Tibetan antelope. Examples of Annex B listed game species include walrus, lechwe, hippopotamus, Southern white rhino, bontebok and the populations of African Elephant in Botswana, Namibia, South Africa and Zimbabwe.

[9] See http://www.ukcites.gov.uk/travel/default.htm and also DETR Press Release 25 July 2000 at http://www.press.detr.gov.uk/0007/0493.htm

with Article III of the Convention and recommends that greater steps be taken by Parties with regard to informing the general public and tourists about the purposes and requirements of CITES and any export/import restrictions relating to endangered species that may be in force under either the Convention or domestic legislation. One suggestion contained in CR 10.6 to combat the ignorance of the public at large is the increased use of information displays in places of international arrival and departure.

It is to be noted that *diplomats* are subject to the same rules as others and must comply with Article VII.3 (as well as all the other provisions of CITES) as set out above. Parties were urged at COPs 9 and 10 to remind their diplomatic missions and troops serving under the UN flag of this, following concern over alleged illegal trade. At COP 11 (Decision 11.32) the Parties were once again urged to remind their diplomatic missions, their delegates on mission in foreign countries and their troops serving under the UN flag that they are not exempted from CITES provisions[10].

Captive-bred/artificially propagated specimens

The Convention provides for exemptions from the normal rules for trade in captive bred animals and artificially propagated plants but different rules apply depending on where the specimen is listed and on whether the specimens were captive-bred or artificially propagated for commercial or non-commercial purposes. Clearly captive breeding and artificial propagation could have conservation benefits by providing sources of specimens for trade and thereby relieving the pressure on wild populations but, equally, badly managed operations could become a drain on wild populations and lack of strict control could open the way for fraud.

Article VII.4 provides that Appendix I animals bred in captivity for commercial purposes and Appendix I plants artificially propagated for commercial purposes shall be deemed to be specimens include in Appendix

[10] See http://www.save-the-elephants.org which lends support to the concern that diplomats are amongst the leading offenders in the illegal trade in endangered species. In this case a senior UN liaison officer was caught in possession of ivory and leopard skin and was charged and ordered to pay a fine in a magistrate's court in Nairobi. See further a study commissioned by Save the Elephants in preparation for COP 11 which showed, inter alia, that "Diplomats and personnel from the military and from international organizations are much more heavily involved in illegally exporting raw and worked ivory from Africa, using their diplomatic immunity, than previously thought." Which I quoted from a press release available at http://wildafrica.net/cites/messages/3.html

II. This means that they may be commercially traded subject to the documentation requirements for Appendix II specimens (the need for an export permit or re-export certificate and, in the European Community, an import permit.

A different and broader exemption for trade in animals and plants that have been captive bred or artificially propagated, covering specimens listed in all three Appendices, is laid down in Article VII.5 of the Convention which provides that where a management authority of the State of Export is satisfied that any specimen of animal species was bred in captivity or any specimen of a plant species was artificially propagated or was derived therefrom, a certificate by the management authority to that effect[11] shall be accepted in lieu of any of the permits or certificates required under Article III, IV or V.

The mutual exclusivity of these two exemptions was made clear by the Parties in Conference Resolution 2.12 which indicated that Article VII.5 covers trade in Appendix I specimens which were captive bred or artificially propagated for non-commercial purposes and also trade in specimens listed in Appendix II or III which have been captive bred or artificially propagated whether for commercial or non-commercial purposes.

The Convention contains no definition of "captive-bred" or "artificially propagated" but the Parties have agreed strict conditions which must be fulfilled before specimens may be said to fall within these exemptions[12]. If these conditions are not met, the specimen must be treated like any wild taken specimen. The position is now governed by CR 10.16 which has replaced CR 2.12 and aims to clarify some of the confusion in practice surrounding the exemptions under paragraphs 4 and 5 of Article VII by improving the definitions and criteria regarding captive breeding.

Captive Bred Animals

For captive-bred animals, those conditions are laid down in Conference Resolution 10.16.[13] In order to qualify as captive-bred, an animal must not only be born or otherwise produced in a controlled environment, its parents must also have mated or otherwise transferred gametes in a controlled environment (if reproduction is sexual) or were in a controlled

[11] See Article 8(3)(d) of the Council Regulation.
[12] The Secretariat note that after re-export, abuse of the captive-breeding/artificial propagation exemption is the most widely used means for fraud -in their report?
[13] Replaces earlier CR 2.12.

environment when development of the offspring began (if reproduction is asexual). Offspring of a pregnant female captured in the wild are *not* therefore captive bred for the purposes of CITES.

A "controlled environment" is defined as one which is intensively manipulated by man for the purpose of producing the animal in question and has boundaries designed to prevent animals, eggs or gametes entering or leaving the controlled environment. For example, there may be artificial housing, waste removal, health care, protection from predators and artificially supplied food.

Furthermore, the parental breeding stock must be established in accordance with both CITES and domestic legislation and in a manner not detrimental to the survival of the species in the wild and be maintained without augmentation from the wild (except for the occasional addition of animals, eggs or gametes from wild populations to prevent deleterious in-breeding.) The possibility of such additions has been extended in CR 10.16 and must now be determined by the need for new genetic material or to dispose of confiscated animals in accordance with CR 10.7[14] or, in exceptional circumstances, for use as breeding stock.

Conference Resolution 10.16 [ex CR 2.12] also requires the parental breeding stock to be managed in a manner designed to maintain the breeding stock indefinitely ie. in a manner demonstrated to be capable of reliably producing second-generation offspring in a controlled environment.[15] The definition given to captive bred specimens in CR 10.16 applies to specimens bred in captivity of species included in Appendix I, II or III whether or not they were bred for commercial purposes. CR 10.16 also recommends that trade in Annex I species bred in captivity be allowed only where such specimens are marked in accordance with the provisions on marking contained in COP resolutions.[16]

Commercial Captive-Breeding Operations

Although not provided for in the Convention, the Parties have agreed on a system of registration by the CITES Secretariat of commercial captive breeding operations which breed Appendix I specimens. This is intended to ensure that the Parties permit only those operations meeting

[14] Cross-refer to CR 10.7 on the disposal of confiscated live specimens of species listed in the CITES Appendices.
[15] See para b(ii)(C)(2) of CR 10.16.
[16] Cross-refer to section on marking.

the agreed criteria to rely on the exemptions. That system is now dealt with in Conference Resolution 12.10.[17] Under CR12.10, the term "bred in captivity for commercial purposes" as used in Article VII.4 of the Convention is to be used so as to refer to any animal specimen bred to obtain an economic benefit, including profit, whether in cash or kind where the purpose is directed towards sale, exchange or provision of a service or any other form of economic use or service[18]. It is important to note that under that Resolution, Parties are called on to reject any document granted pursuant to Article VII.4 if the specimens concerned do not originate from an operation registered in accordance with the Resolution and if the document does not describe the specific identifying mark applied to each specimen.[19]

CR 12.10 lays down the procedure for registering a captive-breeding operation for Appendix I species bred for commercial purposes[20]. Annex I sets out the information to be provided to the Secretariat by the Management Authority of the state where the operation is located. Annex 2 then sets out the procedure to be followed by the Secretariat before registering new operations. Under the resolution Parties agree to restrict imports for primarily commercial purposes of captive-bred specimens to those produced by operations included in the Secretariat's Register of Operations. Commercial captive breeding operations have been registered for a number of animal and plant species including certain species of crocodile; certain

[17] Previously governed by CR 11.14 and CR 8.15.

[18] The Resolution goes on to provide that an Appendix I animal specimen bred for non-commercial purposes for the purposes of Article VII.5 of the Convention shall mean where each exchange, loan etc is not for profit and is conducted between two operations engaged in a cooperative conservation programme that provides for the participation or support of one of the Range states involved.

[19] Note that CR 11.14 is indeed designed to repeal CR 8.15 but only when the Standing Committee has approved a list of species for which commercial captive-breeding operations should be registered. This is important because the procedures for registration outlined in CR 11.14 and CR8.15 differ slightly with the later resolution representing a simplified version of the earlier procedure and since it is the more recent of the two resolutions thus reflects the current intention of the COP. Although the Secretariat is currently applying the procedure for registration as set out in CR 11.14 it will nevertheless remain possible to include in the Register breeding operations for any Appendix I listed species until the Standing Committee has approved the list of species to be included in the Annex 3 list.

[20] A proposal to use a single registration process for plants and animals was rejected at COP 12.

[21] NB see http://www.cites.org/common/notifs/2001/Reg_CB.pdf and subsequent notifications for the current register of operations that breed Appendix I species in captivity for commercial purposes which is maintained in accordance with CR 8.15 and 11.14 (which preceded CR12.10)–including 10 species of birds, 1 fish species and 7 reptile species on the list.

birds of prey including peregrine falcons.[21] At COP12 South Africa's request to register a cheetah breeding operation was accepted but the UK's request to register a green turtle operation in the Cayman islands was rejected.

Under the procedure laid down in that Resolution, a captive breeding operation may only be registered if specimens produced by that operation qualify as bred in captivity according to CR 10.16 (Rev). The obligation rests with the management authority to provide the Secretariat with the appropriate information as set out in Annex I in order to obtain and maintain the registration of each captive-breeding operation. The type of information regarding operations to be registered that Annex I requires the management authority to supply the Secretariat with information about the establishment of the operation and its stock including documentation showing that the stock has been bred to second generation offspring (F2) at the facility and a description of the method used. The applicant must also provide a description of the marking methods to be used for breeding stock and offspring and for the types of specimens that will be exported as well as a description of the housing facilities for the captive stock and the strategies used by the operation that contribute to improving the conservation status of wild populations of the species concerned. The management authority must also provide assurance that the operation shall be carried out in a humane manner.

Under the terms of the Resolution, the Secretariat reviews each application for registration to determine whether it meets the requirements of Annex I to CR 12.10 and it may reject applications for registration which it believes do not fulfil the requirements of Annex I. The Secretariat must also notify the parties of each application and provide any Party with full information on the operation where it is so requested. In the case where the Secretariat rejects an application it must provide a full explanation to the management authority concerned and indicate the conditions which must be met before registration can take place. Where the species involved is not yet on the register, the Secretariat must refer the application to the Animals Committee and appropriate experts where necessary. Any Party wishing to comment on the registration of an operation must do so within 90 days from the date of notification by the Secretariat. If a Party objects to the registration or concerns are expressed about the application for registration then the dispute should be resolved by dialogue between the Secretariat and the applicant Management Authority and a further period of 60 days is allowed for the resolution of the identified problems. If, however, the objection is not withdrawn or the problems are not resolved then the application is postponed until it can be decided upon by a two-thirds majority vote at the next meeting of the COP. Where all the requirements are met the Secretariat must publish the name and other particulars of the operation in its Register.

Both the management authority and the scientific authority are to monitor the management of each operation registered in its jurisdiction and in the event of a major change in the nature of the operation or in the type of products being produced for export the management authority shall advise the Secretariat thereof. In such a situation the Animals committee shall review the operation in order to determine whether it should remain registered. A Party within whose jurisdiction an operation is registered may unilaterally request the removal of that operation from the Register by notifying the Secretariat of its request and the operation shall then be removed immediately. Alternatively, where any Party is of the opinion that a registered operation does not comply with the provisions of CR 10.16 (Rev) it must consult with both the Secretariat and the Party concerned and only after it has done so may it propose that the COP delete the operation from the register by a two thirds majority vote of the COP as provided for in CITES Article XV. Once so deleted an operation may only be reinstated to the Register by satisfying the procedure outlined in Annex 2 to CR 12.10.

Artificially Propagated Plants

The Parties to CITES have recognised that dealing with trade in artificially propagated plants is very different in many ways to dealing with trade in captive bred animals. In particular, the number of specimens produced far exceeds the number produced by captive breeding operations and in most cases the time span between the generations is very different On the other hand, the potential benefits to conservation are broadly similar: the collecting pressure on wild populations is relieved; economically viable operations may promote an interest in conservation of local flora.

The criteria for artificial propagation of plants within the terms of the CITES Convention are now set out in Conference Resolution 11.11[22] according to which the term shall be interpreted to refer only to plants grown from seeds, cuttings, divisions, callus tissues or other plant tissues, spores or other propagules under controlled conditions. This means in a non-natural environment that is intensively manipulated by human intervention for the purpose of producing selected species or hybrids. Such

[22] Previously CR 9.18.

conditions may include but are not limited to tillage, fertilisation, weed control, irrigation or nursery operations such as potting, bedding or protection from weather. A wild taken plant grown in a nursery is not artificially propagated for the purposes of CITES.

In a similar way to Conference Resolution 10.16 [23] dealing with captive-bred animals, Conference Resolution 11.11 requires the cultivated parental stock to be established in accordance with the provisions of the Convention and relevant national laws and maintained in a manner not detrimental to the survival of the species in the wild and managed in such a way that long-term maintenance of this cultivated stock is guaranteed.

The regulation of hybrid plants poses particular problems and these have been addressed in a number of Conference Resolutions. Conference Resolution 2.13 provides that if the parents of a hybrid specimen are listed in different appendices, the provisions of the more restrictive appendix shall apply. However, following work carried out by the Plant Working Group, it was realised that the conservation benefits of restricting commercial trade in hybrids of some Appendix I species would be of little conservation benefit because these hybrids were not being produced from wild taken specimens but from long established nursery stock and that such hybrids would not be of conservation value because specimens of the species itself were available.

The principle laid down in Conference Resolution 2.13 has therefore been modified[24] so as to apply only to those Appendix I plant species annotated for the purpose. If an Appendix I plant species is annotated, an export permit or re-export certificate is required for trade in all artificially propagated plants derived from it. Specimens of unannotated Appendix I species, however, would be traded as if listed on Appendix II and therefore entitled to all the exemptions applicable to artificially propagated specimens of species listed in Appendix II.

Phytosanitary Certificates

One distinctive feature of trade in plants is the use which may be made of phytosanitary certificates in place of documentation specifically issued pursuant to CITES controls. These may be used as certificates of artificial propagation as laid down in Article VII.5 provided that the Party concerned is of the view that such a procedure offers adequate assurance

[23] Previously CR 2.12.
[24] Most recently in Conference Resolution 11.11 (Ex CR 9.18).

that specimens have been artificially propagated in accordance with that Article and has informed the CITES Secretariat that it intends to use such certificates. The rules relating to the use of such certificates are currently contained in Conference Resolution 10.2(rev) at Section VI. The certificate must contain a statement that the plant has been artificially propagated in accordance with CITES and give the scientific names of the species traded with the certificate. The UK does not currently use phytosanitary certificates but a number of other countries including Belgium, Denmark, Germany, Italy and the Netherlands do.

The parties sought fairly early on to establish a system for the registration of plant nurseries but it failed to produce a single registration. At Fort Lauderdale, the Parties sought to revive the scheme by adopting Conference Resolution 9.19 which contains Guidelines for the registration of such nurseries exporting artificially propagated specimens of Appendix I species. Under the terms of that Resolution, such specimens, propagated for commercial purposes, are deemed to be listed in Appendix II[25]. The Management Authority, in consultation with the scientific authority, can provide the CITES Secretariat with information on nurseries suitable for registration. The Secretariat has a supervisory role in a similar way to the registration of captive breeding operations.[26]

The scheme is aimed at nurseries producing artificially propagated specimens of Appendix I species for export. The specimens may only be exported when they are packed and labelled in such a way as to be clearly separated from artificially propagated or wild collected Appendix II or III plants in the same consignment and the CITES export permit clearly states the registration number of the nursery. Management authorities must ensure that the nurseries are reviewed on a regular basis to ensure that the parental stock is as stated. Once a nursery is registered, the management authority can design a simplified procedure for issuing export permits to it. This could involve the pre-issuance of CITES export permits. The origin code for an artificially propagated Appendix I specimen propagated for non-commercial purposes, or for Appendix II or III specimens artificially propagated for commercial purposes is "A". The origin code for Appendix I specimens artificially propagated for commercial purposes is "D"[27].

[25] Unregistered nurseries can continue to trade but must apply for export permits in the normal way.

[26] See Notification No. 2001/007 of 9 February 2001 which is available at http://www.cites.org/eng/notifs/2001/007.shtml wherein the Secretariat transmitted to the Parties a complete Register of operations that artificially propagate Appendix I listed specimens for commercial purposes.

[27] Source codes are set out in CR 10.2(rev) at Section 1, see Chapter 7 - Part III.

It should be remembered that a hybrid plant whose parents include unnannotated Appendix I species are included on Appendix II and this is the Appendix which should be indicated on permits.

The EU Rules on Captive Bred and Artificially Propagated Specimens

For both captive bred specimens and artificially propagated specimens, Article 7(1) of Regulation (EC) 338/97 provides that Annex A listed species are to be treated in accordance with the provisions applicable to Annex B listed species, save in relation to the Article 8 controls on commercial activities. The criteria used to determine whether a specimen of an animal or plant species is captive bred or artificially propagated are set out in Articles 24 and 26, respectively, of the Commission Implementing Regulation (EC) 1808/2001. Note that these criteria, as set out below, apply to specimens of Annex A and Annex B species alike.

In order to classify as an animal specimen as captive bred, the Scientific Authority of the Member State concerned must, as required under the Convention, satisfy itself that the specimen in question is or is derived from offspring born or produced in a controlled environment, either where the parents mated or transferred gametes in a controlled environment (in the case of sexual reproduction), or where the parents were in a controlled environment when the development of the offspring commenced (if reproduction was asexual). It also needs to be satisfied that the breeding stock was established and is being maintained under the conditions set out in Article 24. This includes maintenance without the introduction of specimens from the wild, except in certain circumstances[28], and that the breeding stock has produced second or subsequent generation offspring in a controlled environment or is at least managed in such a way that has been shown to be capable of producing second generation offspring.[29]

So far as artificial propagation is concerned, before the scientific authority can consider a plant specimen as artificially propagated the following criteria need to be satisfied (as required under the Convention): the specimen is, or is derived from, plants grown under controlled

[28] Occasionally the exceptional addition of animals, eggs or gametes is tolerated to prevent or alleviate inbreeding, to dispose of confiscated animals in accordance with the provisions of the Regulation or for the use of breeding stock. In all such cases the addition must take place in accordance with applicable legal provisions and in such a manner that the survival of species in the wild is not threatened thereby.

[29] In the alternative, proof of captive breeding in accordance with this criteria may be established through the use of DNA tests as is provided for in Article 25 (EC) Regulation 939/97.

conditions, namely a non-natural environment which is intensively manipulated by human intervention with the growing conditions, and that the cultivated parental stock was established lawfully and is maintained in a manner not detrimental to the survival of the species in the wild. The stock must be managed in a way that guarantees its long-term maintenance.[30]

Ranching[31]

As discussed above, the Parties have agreed strict conditions which must be fulfilled before a specimen can be said to be captive bred for the purposes of the Convention. In order for a specimen to fall within the scope of the captive breeding exemptions contained in Article VII of the Convention, Conference Resolution 10.16 (Rev) (ex CR 2.12) requires that an animal be the offspring of parents which mated in a controlled environment. This means that eggs or young that are taken from the wild and then reared in a controlled environment are not captive bred within the terms of Conference Resolution 10.16 (Rev).

The Parties recognised at an early stage that there could nevertheless be conservation benefits in allowing certain populations of Appendix I animals to be subject to a controlled degree of commercial exploitation by permitting the removal of young from the wild for captive rearing and eventual trade, a practice termed ranching. Controlled commercial exploitation of local wild populations could encourage conservation and as the survival rate for offspring was likely to be far higher than would occur in the wild, it should be possible to remove offspring in numbers which would not damage the conservation status of the species concerned.

The agreed mechanism for allowing ranching of certain species is to down list specific geographical populations of Appendix I species to Appendix II so that specimens from those populations may be commercially traded.[32] In addition, such specimens must be marked and the ranching operations monitored. Marking is essential to ensure that only specimens

[30] For grafted plants to qualify as artificially propagated specimens then both the root stock and the graft must have been artificially propagated in accordance with the provisions of the regulation.

[31] See also the discussion in Chapter 3 - Part III.

[32] See the precautionary approach embodied in Annex 4 to CR 9.24 which confirms that a ranching proposal is one of the possible methods of downlisting a species or population thereof from Appendix I to Appendix II.

from the relevant population which have ranched by registered operations are traded as such. Conference Resolution 11.16 (ex CR 10.18) consolidated previous resolutions on ranching and requires that any proposed ranching operation must be primarily beneficial to the survival of the local population. The ranching system is established in respect of indigenous wild populations and the captive rearing of non-indigenous species does not qualify.

The procedure laid down for obtaining approval for a ranching operation under CITES is as follows: a proposal is put forward by the Management Authority of the country concerned and must be justified as set out by Conference Resolution 11.16,[33] in particular, by setting out an assessment of the likelihood of the economic and biological success of the operation, an assurance that it will be carried out in a humane manner. Also necessary is the presentation of documentary evidence that demonstrates that the taking from the wild will have no significant detrimental impact and that the programme is beneficial to the wild population of the species concerned. The ranching proposal should also include a description of the marking system and method to be used, a list of the types of products produced by the operation and an inventory of current stocks of specimens of the species concerned. If the proposal is adopted by the Parties following consideration by the CITES Secretariat in consultation with the Animals Committee which checks that the proposal meets the scientific and technical requirements of Conference Resolution 11.16, the management authority will have to include information on the performance of the operation and on the status of the population concerned in its annual report to the CITES secretariat.

At Fort Lauderdale, the Parties adopted a Conference Resolution laying down guidelines for evaluating marine turtle ranching proposals. This was to meet pressure from a number of countries wishing to submit such proposals and at the same time seek to address concerns that generally

[33] A proposal to transfer a population to Appendix II should not only include the information referred to in this paragraph but must also satisfy the general criteria set out in CR 11.16 if it is to be considered by the COP. The general criteria include: the ranching programme must be primarily beneficial to the conservation of the local population of the species, all products of the ranching programme must be adequately identified and documented, the programme must have appropriate inventories, harvest-level controls and mechanisms to monitor the wild populations and each programme must contain sufficient safeguards to ensure that animals are returned to the wild if and where appropriate.

use of sea turtles has not been conducted in a sustainable manner and that factors such as habitat loss, pollution and incidental catch are having a serious impact on turtle populations. The Guidelines which were revised in 1997 in CR 9.20 (Rev) take account of the unique biology of turtles and apply rigorous controls to the establishment of any ranching operations, paying attention in particular to the importance of regional management in view of turtles' migratory behaviour.

Scientific Loans and Exchanges

Non-commercial loans, donations or exchanges between registered scientists or scientific institutions are exempt from the provisions of Articles III, IV and V of the Convention. Under Article VII.6 this exemption applies to "herbarium specimens, other preserved, dried or embedded museum specimens and live plant material which carry a label issued or approved by a management authority. The scientist or institution must be registered by the management authority in its own state. This exemption is implemented in Article 7(4) of the EC Council Regulation and Article 22 of the Commission Implementing Regulation which provides for the use of labels for the purposes of such exchange.

The purpose of this exemption is to facilitate co-operation and sharing of information between those engaged in scientific research so as to cut down on demand for specimens taken from the wild. Conference Resolution 11.15 (ex CR 2.14) deals with various matters relevant to the operation of this exemption including the form of label required; the need to ensure that the exemption is only applied in relation to legally obtained specimens; the need to check that institutions located in non-Parties meet the same standards for registration and so on. Emphasis is placed on the criteria which should be met before an institution qualifies for registration including: the need for cataloguing and permanent records of collections, proper control over Appendix I specimens and access to specimens by all qualified users including those from other institutions.

CR 11.15 goes further than CR 2.14 in urging Parties to encourage their natural history museums and herbaria to compile inventories of the rare and endangered species they hold and to make such information freely available. The purpose of this is to reduce the potential impact of research an such species and (presumably) is linked to the recognition in the Preamble to CR 11.15 that museum needs for research specimens can have an adverse impact on certain rare animal and plant species.

The EU Rules on Scientific Loans and Exchanges

Article 7(4) of the Council Regulation provides that in the case of non-commercial loans, donations and exchanges between scientists and scientific institutions labels may be used in lieu of the permits and certificates otherwise required in accordance with the provisions of the Regulation. In order to qualify for this exemption the scientists and/or scientific institutions involved must registered by the management authorities of the respective Member States in which they operate. Furthermore, this exemption is limited to the exchange of herbarium specimens and other preserved, dried or embedded museum specimens and live plant material.

A similar exemption exists under Article 8(3) of the Council Regulation, derogating from the prohibitions on commercial activities contained in Article 8(1) of the Regulation. Of relevance here are the exemptions contained in paragraphs (e) and (g) of Article 8(3) which exempt specimens required under exceptional circumstances for the advancement of science or essential biomedical purposes (see Directive 86/609/EEC) and specimens intended for research or education aimed at the preservation or conservation of the species.

Zoos and Circuses

States may, under Article VII.7 of the Convention, waive the requirements of Articles III, IV and V of the Convention and allow the movement without permits or certificates of specimens which form part of a travelling zoo, circus, menagerie, plant exhibition or other travelling exhibition subject to certain conditions. These conditions are that: the exporter or importer registers full details of such specimens with that management authority; the specimens are in either of the categories specified in paragraphs (2) or (5)[34] of Article VII (pre-convention or captive bred for non-commercial purposes respectively); and the management authority is satisfied that any living specimen will be so transported and cared for as to minimise the risk of injury, damage to health or cruel treatment.

In order to avoid the abuse of this exemption, the Parties agreed a number of procedures and conditions for its application in Conference Resolution 8.16. It was agreed that pre-Convention certificates or captive breeding certificates (valid for a maximum period of three years) should be issued for each animal travelling to another state and that these documents

[34] Wijnstecker queries whether the omission of any reference to Article VII.4 here is a mistake, see Note 87 at page 87, ibid.

remain with the specimens and be considered as valid for export or re-export from each Party. In the event of death, sale theft of the animal the certificate must be returned to the issuing management authority. It was recommended that marking be used so as to allow verification that the certificates correspond to the specimens. Parties are to include in their annual report lists of all Pre-Convention and captive-breeding certificates for specimens in exhibitions.

The EU Rules on Zoos and Circuses

Under Article 34(2) of the Commission Implementing Regulation, import permits may only be issued for live vertebrates of species listed in Annex A which belong to a travelling live animal exhibition where the marking requirements referred to in Article 36 have been complied with. Article 36 refers to methods approved or recommended by the Conference of the Parties or under the Convention[35].

[35] In relation to the regulation of zoos generally, see Chapter 7 - Part II. See for example the DETR report on modern zoo practice at http://212.187.155.84/pass_06june/Subdirectories_for_Search/Glossary&References_Contents/MiscellaneousContents/Standards_of_Zoo_Practice/Contents.htm See also the report on the use of animals in circuses at http://www.animaldefenders.org.uk/AD_pdf/USoEIntroduction.pdf

CHAPTER 7

PERMITS

Clearly the effectiveness of the CITES regime depends to a large extent on the adherence of the Parties to the permit requirements of the Convention and on the ability of the Parties to detect false, falsified or incorrect documents. This means that permits, which pass through the hands of a number of management and customs authorities, should be clear, whilst also being difficult to forge or alter. It also means that practices for issuing and completing them should be harmonised to the extent necessary to ensure that they can be correctly interpreted throughout the world.

Article VI of the Convention sets out various requirements in relation to CITES permits and certificates and a model export permit is contained at Appendix IV to the Convention. These requirements have been elaborated upon in a series of Conference Resolutions, most recently CR 12.3. The following information is required under Annex 1 of CR 12.3 [1]: the full name and logo of the Convention; the complete name and address of the issuing management authority; a unique control number; the complete names and address of the export and importer; the scientific name of the species to which the specimen belongs (or subspecies when relevant to the listing); the description of the specimens using nomenclature distributed by the Secretariat; the number of marks on the specimen; the Appendix in which the specimen is listed; the source (see codes below); the quantity/unit of measurement; the date of issue and date of expiry; the name of the signatory and his/her hand-written signature; the embossed seal or ink stamp of the management authority; a statement that the permit (if it is for live animals) is only valid if the transport conditions comply with the CITES Guidelines for Transport of Live Animals or with the IATA Live Animal Regulations (in the case of air transport)[2]; the registration

---

[1] CR 8.5 was replaced in 1994 by CR 9.3 which was in turn replaced in 1997 by CR 10.2 in order to further combat fraudulent use of permits. CR 10.2 has now been replaced by CR12.3. As various earlier attempts to harmonise permit forms created some confusion regarding the model contained at CITES Appendix IV, a new recommended model is now contained in Annex 2 to CR 12.3 (replacing 10.2). (Parties are furthermore recommended to adapt the contents and format of their export permits to the standard form in Annex 2).

[2] As to requirements for the transport of live animals, see Chapter 8 - Part III.

number of the breeding operation (if trade is under Article VII.4); the actual quantity of specimens exported and when the specimens are marked with microchip transponders, all microchip codes. In relation to certificates of origin there must also be a statement that the specimens originated in the country which issued the certificate.

An export permit is valid for six months and may only be used for export which takes place within six months from the date on which the permit was granted (Article VI.2 of the Convention as clarified by Section II of CR 12.3.[3]) A separate permit or certificate is required for each consignment of specimens (Article VI.5). The management authority of the state of import shall cancel and retain the export permit or re-export certificate and any corresponding import permit presented in respect of the import of that specimen. It is further recommended in CR 12.3 that when an export permit has been cancelled, lost, stolen or destroyed, the management authority of the issuing state should immediately inform both the management authority of the destination state and the Secretariat regarding commercial shipments (ex CR 9.3 now Section I CR 12.3, (n)).

The permit should be in one of the three working languages of the Convention (English, French and Spanish) and the national language if different (ex Conference Resolution 8.5 but now contained in Section I of CR 12.3). Conference Resolution 12.3 also consolidates the type of information which permits should contain and the scheme of codes previously introduced by CR 8.5 and other recommendations which are intended to make the permit system as transparent and fraud proof as possible. The recommendations include the following: every form should indicate which type of document it is (export/import etc); where the form includes a place for the applicant's signature the absence of such signature

[3] The position re: time validity for export and import permits is as follows: the time period for the validity of an export permit is 6 months, after the expiry of which the permit becomes void (ex CR 4.9). But note that in the case of trade in certain annotated timber species listed in Appendices II or III the validity of an export permit may be extended beyond the 6-month period subject to certain conditions set out in Section XI CR 12.3. Wijnstekers, however, states that the suggestion that the validity of an export permit may be extended beyond 6 months is contrary to CITES Article VI.2 (see p.116 Evolution of CITES, Internet edition dated March 2000). Regarding import permits, Section III of CR 10.2 provides that an import permit should be recognized as valid if presented within 12 months from the date on which it was granted, after the expiry of which such import permit is void. The position in the EC regarding the time validity of permits is governed by Article 7 of the Commission Implementing Regulation, which states that the period of validity for EC export permits and import permits shall not exceed 6 or 12 months respectively. This provision is thus compatible with the corresponding CITES provisions.

should render the permit invalid; a re-export certificate should state the country of origin of the specimen, the number of the export permit from the country of origin and its date of issue; permits and certificates should indicate the number of specimens concerned and / the unit of measurement.

Parties are recommended to refuse permits if they have been altered unless the alteration has been authorized, to use security stamps and to refuse permits that do not indicate the scientific name of the species concerned (Section XIV of CR 12.3). When a Party refuses to accept an export permit it must inform the exporting state which must ensure that the specimens in question do not enter into illegal trade (now contained in Section XIV of CR 12.3). Furthermore, for specimens that are known to have been acquired illegally it is recommended that Parties not issue export permits for such specimens, even if they were imported in accordance with national legislation, unless the specimen has previously been confiscated. (ex Conference Resolution 8.5 but now contained in Section II of CR 12.3).

Use of Codes

The Parties have devised two sets of codes for use on CITES forms. These are currently set out in CR12.3 Section I, which requires Parties to set out on each of their permits or certificates, a code indicating the *purpose* of the transaction and a code indicating the *source* of the specimen as set out below:

> *Purpose Codes*: T (Commercial); Z (Zoos); G (Botanical gardens); Q (Circuses and travelling exhibitions); S (Scientific); H (Hunting trophies); P (Personal); M (Medical including Biomedical research); E (Educational); N (Reintroduction or introduction into the wild); B (Breeding in captivity or artificial propagation) or L (Law enforcement/judicial/forensic).
>
> *Source Codes*: W (taken from the wild); R (originating from a ranching operation); D (Appendix I animals bred in captivity for commercial purposes and Appendix I plants artificially propagated for commercial purposes, as well as parts and products thereof exported under Article VII.4 of the Convention); A (plants artificially propagated in accordance with CR 11.11 paragraph (a) as well as parts and products thereof, exported under Article VII.5 of the

Convention); C (animals bred in captivity in accordance with CR 10.16 exported under Article VII.5 of the Convention; F (F1 generation animals born in captivity but which do not fulfil the definition of captive breeding set out in CR 10.16; U (unknown); I (confiscated or seized specimen) or O (pre-Convention specimens).

If all these recommendations and requirements are complied with, the trade history of a specimen should be traceable from the documentation which has accrued to it and this will enable Parties to ensure that the requirements of the Convention are met throughout its circulation in international trade.

Marking and Labelling

Specific requirements for the marking or labelling of CITES specimens were not included in the text of the Convention but since its adoption, the Parties have agreed a range of requirements in a series of Conference Resolutions, some of these relate to particular items such as crocodilian skins, caviar and ivory and in some cases facilitate the effective operation of ranching (crocodilian skins) or quota (ivory) schemes agreed by the Parties[4] . Other Resolutions address more general issues such as the marking of captive-bred Appendix I specimens or the use of microchips for Appendix I specimens of high value. So far as the Convention text is concerned, Article VI.7 of the Convention permits Management Authorities "where appropriate and feasible" to affix a mark upon any specimen to assist in identification. For these purposes, "mark" means "any indelible imprint, lead seal or other suitable means of identifying a specimen, designed in such a way as to render its initiation by unauthorized persons as difficult as possible." Use of such marks can be an important means by which the Management Authority can verify that a specimen is the same one as that for which a permit was issued and thus make more difficult the fraudulent re-use of permits. Marking systems also allow Parties to ensure that the ranching and quota schemes are not abused so as to open the way for unsustainable and illegal levels of trade in the relevant species.

Clearly, rules about marking and tagging can only be effective if acceptance of CITES permits is made contingent on compliance with those rules. Where the Parties have agreed specific rules on marking, such as in the case of Crocodilian skins, it is generally provided that Management

[4] On ranching and quota schemes, see Chapter 3 - Part III.

Authorities may only accept permits if the required information and/or mark is present on the specimen concerned[5]. The systems for marking and tagging adopted by the Parties are becoming increasingly sophisticated for example in relation to the universal tagging system adopted for crocodilian skins, the Parties have recently agreed to adopt a management and trading system for tags[6]. The recently adopted Resolution 12.7 on the conservation of and trade in sturgeons and paddlefish sets out detailed guidelines for a universal labelling system for caviar and specifically requires the Management Authority of the Party of Import to contact its counterpart in the exporting state if there is a mismatch between a label and the export permit.

The European Union has implemented the various marking schemes agreed by the Parties in Articles 34-38 of the Commission Implementing Regulation[7]. Article 34(2) provides that import permits for the types of specimens referred to in that paragraph shall only be issued where the applicant has satisfied the management authority that the specimens have been marked in accordance with Article 36(4) of the Regulation. Paragraph (2) refers to a number of types of specimen for which marking rules have been adopted including: specimens derived from a captive breeding operation approved by the Parties, those deriving from an approved ranching operation and those Appendix I species for which an export quota has been approved by the COP among others. Article 36(4) provides that those specimens shall be marked in accordance with the method approved or recommended by the Conference of the Parties to the Convention for the specimen concerned.

Artificially Propagated Plants

In relation to artificially propagated specimens of plant species listed in Appendix II, Section VII of Conference Resolution 10.2 states that phytosanitary certificates may be used as certificates of artificial propagation in accordance with CITES Article VII, paragraph 5 where a Party considers that the practices governing the issue of phytosanitary certificates for the export of Appendix II listed species gives adequate assurance that the specimens are indeed artificially propagated.

[5] See for example Conference Resolution 10.14 (leopard skins) and Conference Resolution 11.12 (crocodilian skins).
[6] See Conference Resolution 11.12, Annex 2.
[7] Commission Regulation (EC) No1808/2001 which replaces Regulation 939/97.

Retrospective Issue of Permits

Another important issue addressed by the Parties since the adoption of the Convention is that of the retrospective issue of permits. Conference Resolution 12.3 recommends that the management authority of the exporting/re-exporting state should not issue CITES documentation retrospectively and that the management authority of the state of import not accept export documentation issued retrospectively. Moreover, it recommends that exceptions to this rule should not be made with regard to Appendix I specimens. With regard to Appendix II and III listed species, it is recommended that exceptions only be made where the management authorities of both the state of import and state of export are satisfied that the irregularities are not attributable to the exporter or the importer and that trade in the specimens concerned is otherwise in compliance with the Convention and relevant national legislation. Where exceptions to the recommendation on retrospective issue are made, then the export permit or re-export certificate should clearly indicate that it is issued retrospectively and the reasons for this. In the EU, specific rules on retrospective issue of permits in exceptional circumstances have been adopted.[8]

Trade with Non-Parties

Concerned, no doubt that the whole Convention system could be undermined if trade with non-Parties were conducted in a way which did not equate with the controls imposed on Parties by the Convention, express provision is made in the Convention in relation to trade with non-parties. Article X of the Convention provides that where export or re-export is to, or import is from, a State not Party to the present Convention, "comparable documentation issued by the competent authorities in that State which substantially conforms with the requirements of the present Convention for permits and certificates may be accepted in lieu thereof by any Party."

With an ever-increasing number of Parties, it might be thought that the issue of trade with non-Parties was not of major importance but a number of those States which have not become parties to CITES are major producers or consumers of wildlife products [or may act as conduits for trade] and therefore the issue remains important.[9]

---

[8] See further Chapter 3 and 4 - Part III.
[9] Examples of states that are not CITES parties are Angola, Iraq and Turkmenistan.

At COP 9, the recommendations of earlier COP Resolutions (for example CR 3.8 and 8.8) were combined in a new resolution, CR 9.5, which not only recalled the importance of Article X and the need to ensure uniform implementation of CITES provisions but also acknowledged the awareness that the risk of trade to and from non-Party states threatens the effectiveness of the Convention. In this regard, CR 9.5 recommends that permits issued by non-Party states not be accepted unless they contain certain specified information for example the name, stamp and signature of the issuing authority and sufficient identification of the species concerned. It further recommends that Parties accept documentation from non-parties only where the competent authorities and scientific institutions of such countries are included in the most recent list of the Secretariat[10] or after consulting with the Secretariat.

CR 10.10 (Rev) COP12 on trade in elephant specimens also contains a recommendation regarding non-Parties which states that Parties may accept elephant ivory from a producer non-party State only if certain conditions have been met, namely, a quota for that State has been reviewed by the Secretariat and communicated to other Parties, the Secretariat has received an annual report on that State's ivory trade and all other conditions in CR 10.10 and Article X are met.

Problems in the European Union

At the ninth Conference of the Parties in Fort Lauderdale, the Secretariat presented a report[11] on the application of the Convention in the European Union. The report emphasised the positive side of the application of the Convention in the EU, but went on to highlight a number of difficulties in the application of CITES within the European Union. The Secretariat emphasised however that the report was not to be taken as an indication that problems in the EU were worse than those in other regions. The Secretariat identified one feature unique to the European Union which was giving rise to problems: the EU applied CITES as if it were one state but with national management authorities which acted independently of one another and whose procedures varied greatly. Furthermore, since the advent of the single market and the abolition of internal frontier controls between the Member States, the level of application of CITES had effectively become that of the state with the weakest controls.

[10] See COP Decision 10.123 directing the Secretariat to maintain and communicate to the Parties an updated list of competent authorities and scientific authorities.
[11] Document 9.23 on the Application of the Convention in the European Union.

The Secretariat identified three main problem areas: re-export of illegally imported specimens; imports in breach of the Convention/ Conference Resolutions; the issue of export permits in respect of illegally obtained specimens.

In relation to reexport, the problem was that re-export certificates were being granted which contained incorrect information (for example as to the country of origin of the specimen) or referred to false or non-existent CITES documents (import or export certificates). The Secretariat blamed this kind of situation on a failure on the part of the management authorities to check the accuracy of information on which applications for re-export certificates were based. The Parties were reminded of the requirements of Conference Resolution 8.5 which calls on Parties to include information on both the origin of a specimen and the country which it has been exported from.

Another serious problem outlined in the report was the misuse of EU CITES certificates used for intra-Community trade, and copy sheet No. 1 of the import permit which were being wrongly used, often re-used, to obtain export permits / re-export certificates. In some cases it was possible, by applying successively to a number of different management authorities to obtain CITES certificates for a greater number of specimens than the total stated as being imported on the application form because documents are not retained in such cases. These certificates would then be used wrongly to obtain import permits to export a higher total number than originally imported. The Secretariat called for a clear statement on CITES certificates confirming that they are only valid within the EU (and should not be used for export).

The report also criticised a lack of sufficient controls at frontiers, particularly since the coming into force of the single market. In part this arose through confusion as to where the responsibility for control lay, the Member State of entry or the Member State of final destination. The report stated that, often, each authority thought that the other would or had carried out the relevant checks. The report also stated that the fact that Member states were obliged to accept documents issued by other Member States (except for pre-convention certificates) meant that there was little possibility to check the validity of such documents. Many of the problems identified by the Secretariat were blamed on a lack of uniformity in the laws of the member states, for example, whilst recognising that this was a matter which fell within the competence of the Member states, the variation in penalties imposed for breaches of CITES meant that participants in fraud would tend to trade through the more lenient Member states.

The Member States sought to address many of the problems identified in the report in the 1997 Council Regulation which replaced earlier implementing legislation. In particular the new Council Regulation was designed to take account of the advent of the single market and introduced tighter control for example on the issue of EU CITES certificates. The new Regulation imposed stronger coordinating provisions to ensure that decision-making across the EU is consistent as well as introducing detailed rules on the format for permits and other changes designed to render the regime more effective such as a greater emphasis on enforcement.

At COP12 in November 2003, the Parties recognised the progress made by the European Union and urged Parties to ratify the Gabarone amendment[12].

The Council Regulation

In view of the need to ensure uniform implementation across the EC, Article 6 of Regulation 338/97 obliges Member States in certain circumstances to inform the Commission where it rejects an application for a permit or certificate. The Commission then informs other Member States about the decision. Article 6(4) requires other Member States to recognize the rejection of applications where this is based on the provisions of the Regulation unless circumstances have significantly changed or where new evidence to support an application has become available.

Article 11 provides that, subject to the right of Member States to take stricter measures, permits and certificates issued by the competent authorities of the Member States shall be valid throughout the Community. However any permits issued on a false premise shall be void and specimens situated within the territory of Member State and covered by such documents shall be seized and may be confiscated. Member States are entitled to impose conditions on permits with a view to securing compliance with the provisions of the Regulation. Further implementing measures relating to period of validity etc are to be adopted by the Commission. The current implementing regulation, Commission Regulation 1808/2001, makes detailed provision for such matters as the type of paper to be used for EU CITES permits and the period of issue, validity and use of documents.

[12] As to which see Chapter 1 - Part III.

CHAPTER 8

TRANSPORT

The Convention Rules on Transport

Articles III, IV and V of the Convention all require a management authority, before issuing an export permit or re-export certificate for a live specimen, to be satisfied that the specimen in question will be so prepared and shipped as to minimise the risk of injury, damage to health or cruel treatment and among the measures which Parties are required to take under Article VIII of the Convention, they must ensure that all living specimens, during any period of transit, holding or shipment, are properly cared for so as to minimise the risk of injury, damage to health or cruel treatment.

In 1979 at COP 2, the Parties adopted the Guidelines for Transport and Preparation of Shipment of Live Wild Animals and Plants [published as a UNIPUB edition in 1980, ISBN 0-89059-013-3]. Although these have not been revised or amended since their adoption, they have recently been reviewed by the Transport Working Group (see below).

Conference Resolution 10.21 currently deals with the transport of live animals and directs that "for as long as the CITES Secretariat and the Standing Committee agree" the IATA Live Animals Regulations be deemed to meet the CITES Guidelines in respect of air transport and that except where inappropriate, those Regulations should be used as a reference to indicate suitable conditions for carriage by means other than air. The Preamble, referring to the IATA Regulations, to the Resolution states that air transport is the preferred method for transporting many live wild animals. CR 10.21 also directs that the IATA Live Animal Regulations should be incorporated into the Parties' domestic law. The IATA Regulations are amended annually and notified to the Parties by the Secretariat. The latest version of the Regulations became effective 1 October 2002.[1]

Noting in the Preamble that mortality in transport "undermines the concept of sustainable trade", the Resolution goes on to urge all Parties to maintain records of the number of live animals per shipment and of mortalities in transport of listed species, noting causes of mortality injury

---

[1] See the IATA website at www.iata.org

and damage to health. These data are to be provided along with annual report. As noted in Wijnsteckers, in contrast to earlier Conference Resolutions on the subject, there is no specific reference in CR10.21 to trade in wild birds in this context, particularly those with significantly high mortality in trade[2].

The Animals Committee has established a Transport Working Group, one of the functions of which is to collaborate with the International Air Transport Association (IATA)

At COP 11, the CITES Secretariat reported on the continuing failure of Parties to implement measures designed to monitor and reduce the mortality of live animals in transport as provided for in CR 10.21. The Parties adopted this Report and decided to retain CR10.21. At COP 12 the Parties decided to direct the Animals Committee, inter alia, to develop recommendations regarding the transport of live animals by road rail or ship to supplement where necessary the IATA Regulations and to report back to the Parties at COP 13[3].

The EU Rules on Transport

Article 9 of Council Regulation (EC) No 338/97 introduced new rules on transport and movement of live specimens (the old EC CITES Regulation had contained none). Any movement within the Community of a live specimen of a species listed in Annex A from the location indicated in the import permit or any certificate issued under the Regulation requires prior authorisation from the management authority of the Member State where the specimen is located. Such authorisation may only be granted where the competent scientific authority is satisfied that the intended accommodation for the live specimen "is adequately equipped to conserve and care for it properly" (Article 9(2)). The authorisation must be confirmed by the issue of a certificate and immediately communicated to the management authority of the Member State where the specimen is currently located. No such authorisation is required however if the specimen is a live animal which needs to be moved for the purpose of urgent veterinary treatment and is returned directly to its authorised location.

In relation to Annex B species, where a live specimen is to be moved within the Community, prior authorisation from the management authority is not required but the holder of the specimen may relinquish it "only after

[2] See discussion in Wijnsteckers, Chapter 10.

[3] See Decision 12.85 and see Decision 12.86 directed to the Secretariat.

ensuring that the intended recipient is adequately informed of the accommodation, equipment and practices required to ensure that the specimen will be properly cared for" (Article 9(4)).

There is also a general duty on those transporting any live specimen into, from or within the Community to prepare, move and care for the specimen "in a manner such as to minimise the risk of injury, damage or cruel treatment". In the case of animals, Community legislation on the protection of live animals during transport must be complied with (Article 9(5))[4].

UK Rules on Transport of Live Animals

In the UK there are specific rules on the transport of live animals and birds which apply to the transport of CITES specimens. These are contained in animal health legislation including the 1997 Welfare of Animals (Transport) Order[5]. This applies inter alia to all mammals and birds, vertebrate animals and cold blooded animals. Article 4 of the Order prohibits any person from transporting an animal in a way which causes or is likely to cause injury or unnecessary suffering to that animal. In addition, there are specific provisions governing particular types of animal laid down in the Schedules to the Order. Other provisions of the Order govern matters such as treatment of sick animals, fitness to travel and space allowances as well as feeding and rest periods.

Article 11 of the Order refers to IATA and CITES and states that no person shall transport an animal by air save in accordance with the standards set by IATA. Article 11(2) provides that no person may transport a CITES specimen other than in accordance with the CITES guidelines for transport and preparation for shipment of live wild animals or in compliance with the standards set by IATA.

The Order is to be executed and enforced by the local authority (Article 17) and any person who contravenes or fails to comply with any provision of the Order commits an offence under the Animal Health Act 1981 (Article 21).

[4] Community legislation itself requires adherence to the IATA Guidelines

[5] SI 1997/1480. The 1997 Order revokes and re-enacts with amendments the 1994 Welfare of Animals (Transport) Order which together with other animal health legislation implements Council Directive 91/628/EC on the welfare of animals during transport OJ No L340. 11.12.91, page 17.

Inspections of Shipments and Designation of Ports of Exit and Entry

The provisions of Articles 4 (Introduction into the Community) and 5 (Export and Re-export from the Community) of the Council Regulation require that the necessary checks and prior presentation of the requisite permit be completed before a specimen is introduced or exported or re-exported.

Article VIII of the Convention requires Parties to ensure that specimens pass through any formalities required for trade with a minimum of delay and, to facilitate this, they may designate ports of exit and entry. The European Community has implemented this provision by requiring, in Article 12 of the Council Regulation, that Member States designate customs offices for the carrying out the checks and formalities for the introduction into and export from the Community of specimens of species covered by the Regulation. These offices must be notified to the Commission. Member States must state which offices are specifically intended to deal with live specimens. Offices designated in accordance with Article 12 must be provided with sufficient and adequately trained staff and accommodation must comply with the relevant Community legislation as regards the transport and accommodation of live animals. It is also provided that where necessary adequate steps must be taken for live plants (Article 12(2)).

A management authority may "in exceptional cases" and in accordance with criteria defined under the Article 18 Committee procedure, authorize import or export at a customs offices other the one designated. Article 23 of the Commission Implementing Regulation makes provision for two such instances: where a shipment to be introduced into the Community arrives at a border custom office for immediate dispatch by the same mode of transport to a designated office, the completion of checks and presention of permits shall take place at the designated office. Second, where a shipment has been checked at a designated customs office and is dispatched to another customs office for any subsequent customs procedure, the latter shall require presentation of either a copy for the holder or a copy for the importer of the import permit and may carry out any checks which it considers to be necessary.

Member States are under a duty to ensure that members of the public are informed about the implementing provisions of the Regulation at border crossing points. In the UK this has been done through the "Check it out" campaign launched in 1995.

The Council Regulation also introduces provisions on inspections, required facilities and staffing at external border posts and deals with co-ordination between Member States.

CHAPTER 9

ENFORCEMENT

The enforcement of the CITES regime has received detailed attention at the international, European and domestic levels. This chapter considers developments at all these levels and looks at some of the types of non-compliance which the rules on enforcement are intended to address.

The Convention

Article VIII of the Convention requires Parties to take appropriate measures to enforce the provisions of the Convention and to prohibit trade in specimens in violation of its provisions. These shall include measures to penalize trade in, or possession of such specimens or both, and measures to provide for the confiscation or return to the State of export of such specimens.

In April 2000, at the 11th Meeting of the Conference of the Parties, the Parties to the Convention adopted CITES Conference Resolution 11.3 on Compliance and Enforcement. This Resolution replaces a number of earlier resolutions on the topic. It emphasises the responsibilities of both producer and consumer countries and the important role of the CITES Secretariat in promoting effective enforcement of the Convention[1] . Under the Resolution, the Conference of the Parties to the Convention urged Parties to strengthen controls on trade wildlife within territories under their jurisdiction and in particular on shipments from producing countries, and to "strictly verify" the documents originating from producing countries with the respective Management Authorities. The Resolution goes on to make a series of detailed recommendations to the Parties including that requests for information on alleged infractions from the Secretariat should be responded to within one month and that Parties provide the Secretariat with detailed information about significant cases of illegal trade.

Certain species-specific enforcement and compliance initiatives have been adopted under the auspices of the Convention, including the MIKE programme[2] under which trends and levels of illegal killing of

[1] See the Preamble to CR11.3.
[2] MIKE stands for the "monitoring of the illegal killing of elephants".

elephants are monitored at specific sites. The overall aim of the programme is to enable elephant range states to make appropriate management and enforcement decisions. A key objective is to establish correlations between the relevant parameters and assess to what extent observed trends are a result of CITES decisions[3].

There have also been regional initiatives on wildlife law enforcement which are relevant to the implementation of the Convention, including the adoption of the Lusaka Agreement[4]. Conference Resolution 9.8 called on CITES to direct funds to assist in the development and implementation of regional enforcement agreements. This Agreement was concluded on 8 September 1994 and its stated objective is to reduce and ultimately eliminate illegal trade in wildlife and to establish a permanent Task Force for this purpose. The Parties to the Agreement are required to take appropriate measures to investigate and prosecute cases of illegal trade, to provide the Task Force with information on illegal trade and to encourage public awareness campaigns to enlist public support for the objectives of the Agreement (Article 4). A number of the CITES Resolutions and Decisions dealing with a possible resumption of limited trade in ivory refer to cooperation on enforcement by range states through such mechanisms as the Lusaka Agreement as one of many conditions which would have to be met before such trade could take place.[5]

The European Union Enforcement Regime

When the European Community adopted a new regulation on wildlife trade in 1997, detailed provision was made for enforcement of the requirements of the new legislation by Member States. The Regulation lays down more detailed requirements than is usual in EC regulations and this underlines the importance which the Community places on compliance in this area. The Regulation sets out a list of the offences to be penalised and provides that penalties are to be proportionate to the gravity of the crime.

Under Article 14(1)(a) of Regulation (EC) No 338/97 (the Council

[3] See the report by the Deputy Secretary General at the Meeting to Launch MIKE in Eastern Africa, March 2001, available on the CITES website. On ivory generally see chapter 2 - Part III.

[4] The full title of the Agreement is the Agreement on Co-operative Enforcement Operations Directed at Illegal Trade in Wild Flora and Fauna. There are [6] Parties to the Agreement: Kenya, Congo, Tanzania, Zambia, Lesotho and Uganda. The Task Force to the Agreement is based at the Kenya Wildlife Service Headquarters.

[5] See for example Decision 10.1.

Regulation), the competent authorities of the Member States have a duty to take appropriate steps to monitor compliance with the Regulation (Article 14(1)(a)). Article 14(1)(b) of the Council Regulation provides that "If, at any time, the competent authorities have reason to believe that [the provisions of the Regulation] are being infringed, they shall take appropriate steps to ensure compliance or to instigate legal action." Article 14(1)(c) requires Member States to inform the Commission, and in the case of species listed in the Appendices to the Convention, the Convention Secretariat, of any steps taken in relation to significant infringements of the Regulation "including seizures and confiscations".

Article 16 of the Council Regulation requires Member States to take appropriate measures to ensure the imposition of sanctions for "at least" the infringements specified. These include the introduction into, or export or re-export from the Community of specimens without the appropriate permit or certificate or with a false, falsified or invalid permit or certificate or one altered without authorisation by the issuing authority (Article 16(1)(a); failure to comply with the stipulations specified on a permit or certificate issued in accordance with this Regulation (Article 16(1)(b); using a false, falsified or invalid permit or certificate or one altered without authorization as a basis for obtaining a Community permit or certificate (Article 16(1)(d)); shipment of live specimens not properly prepared so as to minimize the risk of injury, damage to health or cruel treatment (Article 16(1)(f); shipment of specimens into or out of or in transit through the territory of the Community without the appropriate permit or certificate issued in accordance with this Regulation and, in the case of export or re-export from a third country party to the Convention, in accordance therewith, or without satisfactory proof of the existence of such permit or certificate (Article 16(1)(i).

Article 16(2) requires that the measures referred to in paragraph 1 shall be "appropriate to the nature and gravity of the infringement and shall include provisions relating to the seizure and, where appropriate, confiscation of specimens... ". Article 16(3) and (4) deal with confiscation. Live specimens introduced into the Community may after consultation with the State of Export be returned to that state at the expense of the convicted person.

The European Union has established an enforcement group under the auspices of Regulation 338/97. The Enforcement Group is composed of representatives of the Member States' enforcement agencies and

[6] This is the Committee established under Article 18 of Regulation 339/97, see Chapter 1 - Part III.

examines technical questions relating to enforcement. Its opinions are conveyed to the EU CITES Committee[6] by the Commission. Examples of matters discussed by the Enforcement Group include country updates on trends in illegal traffic, timber trade in the EU and reports on cooperation with the Interpol European Wildlife Crime Working Group[7].

Brazilian Mahogany

The scope of the enforcement duties arising under the Council Regulation has recently been at issue in the UK courts in the case of *The Queen on the Application of Greenpeace v (1) The Secretary of Environment, Food and Rural Affairs (2) HM Commissioners of Customs and Excise*[8]. This case concerned the export from Brazil to the UK of Brazilian mahogany, listed under Appendix III of the Convention and Annex C to the Regulation. The case arose following the introduction of a moratorium of commercialisation of mahogany by the Brazilian management authority. The management authority had uncovered widespread illegal logging of mahogany in contravention of Brazilian domestic conservation law. The application of that moratorium to certain shipments under contracts which had already been entered into was challenged by a number of commercial operators in the Brazilian courts. In a number of cases, the courts ordered the management authority to issue permits to the shippers despite the fact that the authority considered such exports to be in contravention of the rules for trade in Appendix III species under the Convention. These orders did not appear to be based on any finding as to the legality or otherwise of such shipments but rather on the commercial expectations of those who had entered into the contracts. Subsequently the management authority announced that it would appeal these orders but in the meantime the exports had taken place and the shipments were en route to a number of destinations in Europe, including the UK.

At this stage Greenpeace asked the UK authorities to confirm that they would seize the shipments on arrival in the UK at least until the Brazilian appellate courts had resolved the issue of the legality under national conservation law of the exports. In the absence of such confirmation, Greenpeace sought judicial review of the failure to confirm seizure. The High Court refused permission to bring proceedings and Greenpeace appealed to the Court of Appeal, which granted permission but went on to refuse judicial review by a majority of two to one. The

[7] See the Agenda for the Sixth Meeting in 2001, available on the Europa website, Commission Environment page.

[8] [2002] EWCA 1036.

majority in the Court of Appeal ruled that the phrase "in accordance with the Convention" contained in Article 4(3)(a) of the Council Regulation was to be interpreted as meaning in accordance with the formalities for permits laid down in Article VI of the Convention and did not also refer to substantive compliance with the rules for trade in Appendix III species as set out in Article V of the Convention. The majority therefore dismissed the judicial review, ruling in effect that the UK had not been required to look behind the permits issued by the Brazilian management authority since there was no dispute that these were authentic permits.

It may be that the circumstances at issue in the Mahogany case were somewhat exceptional[9], but the case is also of general importance as an indication of how UK courts address the operation and enforcement of what is after all a longstanding and widely adhered to international environmental agreement. In reaching their conclusion, the majority placed emphasis on the need for traders to be able to operate in an environment of commercial certainty (and rely on the fact that authentic permits issued by the state of export would be accepted by the country of import even in circumstances where there was breach of the substantive conditions for issue). Lord Justice Laws, on the other hand, took the view that Article 4(3)(a) required substantive as well as formal compliance with the rules of the Convention. His approach to the construction of the legislation appears to be more in keeping with the regulatory environment both internationally and at the European and domestic levels as well as more suited to the effective operation of the Convention. In contrast to the approach of the majority, Laws LJ noted that "In the century before last the sanctity of contract was a powerful engine of statutory construction", now however "... Considerations of ecology and the protection of the environment are interest of high importance... Within the proper limits of the courts' role and in appropriate contexts, I think we should now be ready to give them special weight." (paragraph 33) He regarded it as "an incident of trade in flora or fauna of the kind in question here that the tradespeople take the risk of inconveniences and disruptions to their legitimate business, so far as they are a necessary incident of a robust environmental law"(paragraph 38). Interestingly, neither Mummery nor Dyson refer specifically in their judgments to Articles 14 and 16 of the Council Regulation nor to Article VIII of the Convention, on which Greenpeace had relied, which underline

[9] It should be noted that Parties to COP12 voted to list mahogany on Appendix II, in part because of the difficulties arising from the Appendix III listing in this case.

the duty to see that the rules of the Convention are properly enforced.

Enforcement Powers in the UK

It has been left to Member States to make specific provision in their domestic law for appropriate enforcement powers which will fulfil the duties laid down in Article 14 and establish the sanctions required under Article 16 of the Council Regulation. The UK has adopted the Control of Trade in Endangered Species (Enforcement) Regulations 1997[10] which entered into force on the 27 May 1997. These Regulations (commonly known as COTES) make provision for the enforcement of the Council Regulation and the Commission Regulation (now Regulation (EC) No 1808/2001) by providing for criminal offences relating to breach of the requirements of the Council Regulation and by making provision for powers of entry and seizure.

Among the offences created under COTES are those relating to the making of false statements for the purpose of obtaining a permit or certification (regulation 3); those relating to the misuse of permits and certificates (regulation 4) and those relating to the contravention of conditions provided for in permits and certificates (regulation 6). Regulation 5 of COTES provides that where any specimen is being imported or exported or has been imported or brought to any place for the purpose of being exported "a person commissioned by the Commissioners of Customs and Excise, or a person authorised by them, may require any person possessing or having control of that specimen to furnish proof that its importation or exportation is or was not unlawful by virtue of [the Council Regulation], or as the case may be [the Commission Regulation] and, until such proof is furnished, the specimen shall be liable to detention under the Customs and Excise Management Act 1979 and, if such proof is not furnished to the satisfaction of the Commissioners, the specimen shall be liable to forfeiture under that Act." Offences relating to the movement of live specimens (regulation 7) and purchase and sale (regulation 8) are also provided for.

Regulations 9 and 10 provide for powers of entry and seizure. Powers of entry are enjoyed by constables and in some cases by an "authorised person" such as a wildlife inspector. On conviction for an offence under the regulations, a court is required to order the forfeiture of "any specimen or other thing in respect of which the offence was

[10] SI 1997/1372 HMSO, The Regulations entered into force on 1 June 1997 replacing the 1985 enforcement regulations which implemented Regulation 3626/82.

committed" and may order the forfeiture of any vehicle, equipment or other thing which was used to commit the offence.

The provisions of COTES were subject to review and consultation by the Government in 2003 with a view to making offences arrestable and increasing the length of prison sentences to 5 years. Amendments to this effect are to be introduced into the Criminal Justice Bill to secure these changes.

UK Enforcement in Practice

In 1995 the UK initiated an enforcement initiative, codenamed "Operation Charm" aimed at countering illegal trade in parts and derivatives used in traditional Chinese medicine. Following raids on outlets in various locations across the country, a number of prosecutions were brought relating to trade in items such as rhino horn, tiger skin and bear parts or in items purporting to contain these substances. More recently in 2002 one prosecution resulted in a sentence of six and half years being handed down for offences relating to the smuggling of birds of prey listed under CITES.

Also in 1995 the Partnership Against Willdife Crime (PAW[11]) was launched which brings together the police, Customs, the relevant Government Departments and others, including the leading NGOs, interested in enforcement. PAW focuses on native species as well as those listed on CITES and supports networks of Police Wildlife Liaison Officers as well as networks of Customs officers and others.

[11] For regularly updated information see www.defra.gov.uk/paw.

CHAPTER 10

INTERNAL SALES CONTROL ON CITES SPECIES

As explained earlier, the CITES Convention itself only deals with international trade taking place between States, it does not regulate internal trade within States. In certain cases, where species are critically endangered, the Parties to CITES have adopted Conference Resolutions which call on Parties (and in some cases non-Parties) to restrict or ban internal trade in certain CITES species in addition to fulfilling their obligations to control international trade in specimens arising from their obligations under the Convention. Examples include rhino horn and ivory

The right of Parties to take such stricter measures in relation to, inter alia, domestic trade, is expressly recognised in the Convention. Article XIV of the Convention provides that the provisions of the Convention in no way affect the right of Parties to adopt stricter domestic measures regarding the conditions for trade, taking possession or transport of specimens of species included in Appendices I, II and III, or the complete prohibition thereof. The European Community has always included a number of stricter measures in its legislation implementing CITES, including measures regulating trade within Member States[1]. These controls are currently contained in Article 8 of Council Regulation (EC) No 338/97. Following the establishment of the single market, goods can move freely across the European Community without the need to undergo customs control at the borders between Member States. This means that internal trade controls cover both trade taking place within one Member State and trade involving movement from one Member State to another.

The species and specimens subject to internal sales controls

In contrast to the controls on international trade deriving from the Convention, not all species covered by the EC CITES Regulation are subject to internal sales controls. Under Article 8, sales controls apply to specimens of species listed in Annex A to the Regulation and also to those listed in Annex B except, in the latter case, where it can be proved to the satisfaction of the

[1] Originally these controls were contained in Article 6 of Regulation (EEC) No 3626/82 (OJ No L 384, 31.12.1982, p.1 which prohibited the sale and related activities of specimens contained in Appendix I to the Convention as well as specimens of certain other species which were protected as if they were on Appendix I within the European Community. These provisions have now been replaced by Council Regulation 338/97/EEC (see main text).

competent authority that the specimens were acquired and/or introduced into the Community in accordance with conservation legislation. This means that sale within the EU of species listed in Annexes C or D to the Regulation is not subject to control under the EC CITES Regulation (for a discussion of the Annexes to the Regulation see further chapter 2 of Part III.

As with the controls on international trade however, for those species which are subject to internal sales controls "specimen" is very broadly defined (Article 2(t) of the Regulation). It means not only any animal or plant, whether alive or dead, of the species listed in the Regulation, but also "any part or derivative thereof". The only exception to this is where such parts or derivatives are specifically exempted from the provisions of the Regulation or from the provisions relating to the particular Annex in which the species is listed. Such exceptions are indicated in the Annexes themselves, for example the seeds and pollen of certain plant species are excluded. In relation to parts or derivatives, these will be covered whether or not they are contained in other goods. Also covered are any goods which *appear* from an accompanying document, the packaging or a mark or label, or from any other circumstances, to be or contain parts or derivatives of animals or plants of listed species. For example, an item purporting to contain powdered rhino horn will be covered by the controls even if it in fact only contains powdered cow horn.

The controlled activities

The controls in Article 8 take the form of a prohibition on a broad range of specified commercial activities, with the result that it is not just sale per se which is prohibited under Article 8, the following activities are all prohibited as well: "the purchase, offer to purchase, acquisition for commercial purposes, display to the public for commercial purposes, use for commercial gain and sale, offering for sale or transporting for sale."[2]

These activities are prohibited subject only to the possibility of obtaining an individual sales exemption from the management authority in which the specimen is located or, in certain cases, meeting the conditions laid down in general derogations which provided for in the Commission implementing Regulation (see further below). There is a specific derogation for scientific institutions (see below).

[2] In addition to the prohibitions laid down in Article 8(1), Member States are expressly authorised, in Article 8(2), to prohibit the holding of specimens, particularly live animals of Annex A species. The UK has not chosen to introduce such possession controls (see further below) but it is worth remembering that "keeping for sale" is prohibited under Article 8(1).

Controls on purchase and offering to purchase were introduced for the first time in Council Regulation 338/97, previously only activities relating to sale as opposed to purchase were prohibited. The prohibitions on "acquisition for commercial purposes" and on "use for commercial gain" were also introduced for the first time in Regulation 338/97. Where a specimen is covered by a sales certificate issued under Article 20 of the Commission Regulation or is subject to one of the general exemptions provided for in Article 8(4) the prohibition on purchase, offering to purchase or acquisition for commercial purposes does not apply, nor is there a requirement for an exemption certificate for any of these three activities (see Article 31) of the Commission Regulation).

"Sale" is broadly defined as meaning any form of sale and including hire, barter or exchange (Article 2(p)).

"Offering for sale" is defined as meaning offering for sale and also "any action that may reasonably be construed as such, including advertising or causing to be advertised for sale and invitation to treat" (Article 2(i)). This definition was inserted at the request of the United Kingdom in order to ensure that any possible loophole was closed because of the distinction drawn in domestic UK contract law between an offer and an invitation to treat.

General exemptions

Article 8(4) of the Council Regulation provides for the possibility of adopting Community-wide general derogations from the prohibitions in Article 8(1) by means of the Committee procedure set out in Article 18 of the Council Regulation. These general derogations may be based on the conditions set out in paragraph (3) of Article 8 or they may relate to Annex A species listed because they are so-called "look-alikes". A number of these general derogations, known as "general exemptions", have been adopted and are included in Commission Regulation 939/97. If a sale or other prohibited transaction falls within the scope of a general derogation, an individual exemption is not needed. If a proposed sale would not fall within the scope of a general exemption, it is prohibited unless an individual exemption is obtained from the management authority where the specimen is located (see below).

Captive Bred Annex VIII Species

Live specimens of captive born and bred animals of the species listed in Annex VIII to the Commission Regulation and hybrids thereof are not subject to the prohibitions in Article 8(1) of the Council Regulation, nor do they require individual certificates issued under Article 8(3) provided that specimens of annotated species are marked in accordance with Article 36(1) of the Commission Regulation[3]. The species currently listed in Annex VIII are all species of birds which are commonly bred in the Community.

Other Captive Bred Animal Specimens

Live specimens of captive born and bred animals not listed in Annex VIII are also subject to exemption from the prohibitions in Article 8(1) or the requirement for an Article 8(3) individual exemption certificate under the following conditions: they must be marked in accordance with Article 36(1) of the Commission Regulation; they must be accompanied by a breeder's certificate issued by a competent management authority of a Member State.

Breeder's certificates may be issued only where the specimen is to be used for one of the following purposes (which are the purposes for which exemptions may be issued under Article 8(3) of the Council Regulation): purposes non-detrimental to the survival of the species concerned; the advancement of science or essential biomedical purposes where the species concerned is the only one suitable; breeding purposes from which conservation benefits will accrue to the species concerned or research or education aimed at the preservation or conservation of the species (see Article 32(b) of the Commission Regulation and Article 20 (3)(e)).

Member States may make pre-issued certificates available to breeders approved for the purpose provided that they maintain breeding records which must be produced on request to the competent management authority. The certificates must include the statement "Certificate only valid for the following taxon/taxa". Thus, in this case, although a certificate is still required for each specimen, the advantage to breeders is that they do not have the administrative burden of applying for individual certificates on a case by case basis as they would do if individual exemptions were required in accordance with Article 8(3).

Artificially Propagated Plants

Artificially propagated specimens of plant species are also exempt from the prohibitions of Article 8(1) of Regulation (EC) No 338/97 and the provisions of Article 8(3), nor is any certificate required[4].

[3] Article 32(a) of Commission Regulation (EC) No 1808/001.
[4] Article 32(b) of Commission Regulation (EC) No 1808/2001.

Worked specimens acquired before 1 June 1947

A general exemption is granted in respect of specimens falling within the definition of Article 2(w) of the Council Regulation, that is to say worked specimens that were acquired more than 50 years previously. This exemption is aimed at antiques but it should be noted that that term is not used in the legislation and the strict conditions of the definition must all be met if the exemption is to apply. In accordance with the definition in Article 2(w), this means specimens that were significantly altered from their natural raw state for jewellery, adornment, art, utility or musical instruments more than 50 years before the entry into force of the Council Regulation (ie. 1 June 1947). Member States must be satisfied that specimens have been acquired in these conditions. Specimens shall only be considered as "worked" if they are clearly in one of the above categories and require no further carving, crafting or manufacture to effect their purpose.

Individual sales exemptions

Article 8(3) of the Council Regulation sets out the eight sets of grounds on which individual sales exemptions may be issued. Some of these grounds relate to the origin of the specimen and others to the purpose for which it is to be used. In relation to the origin of the specimen, exemptions include those which may be issued for specimens acquired or introduced before the provisions relating to Appendix I or Annex A applied to them; or for worked specimens acquired more than 50 years previously and for captive bred/ artificially propagated specimens. In relation to the purpose of the commercial activity, the exemptions which may be granted include those for breeding or propagation purposes from which conservation benefits will accrue to the species concerned or, under exceptional circumstances, for the advancement of science or "essential biomedical purposes?. Specimens which originated in a Member State and were taken from the wild in accordance with its national legislation may also be the subject of exemptions.

It should be noted that, by virtue of Article 31 of the Commission Regulation, in relation to the prohibitions on purchase, offer to purchase or acquisition of Annex A specimens, it is not necessary to apply for an individual exemption where a general exemption applies under Article 32 of the Commission Regulation. Nor is it necessary to apply for an exemption where a certificate has been granted under Article 20 of the Commission Regulation. This means that where a prospective purchaser of an Annex A specimen is satisfied that the vendor of an Annex A specimen is covered by either a general exemption, for example in the case of an artificially propagated plant, or has an Article 20 certificate, for example relating to a captive bred animal, the purchase does not need to apply for an individual exemption.

In the UK many of these exemptions are granted in respect of captive bred tortoises and birds of prey. Guidance on the issue of certificates is provided by the management authority [available at www.ukcites.gov.uk]. The UK authority generally issues specimen specific certificates which are transferable but in certain circumstances, for example related to the welfare of the specimen, will issue a certificate which is specific to an individual holder/transaction. In such cases any subsequent purchaser will need to apply for a new exemption.

Article 10 of the Regulation provides that management authorities of Member States, on receiving an application, together with all the requisite supporting documentation may issue a certificate for the purposes of Article 8(3) provided that all the relevant conditions have been met. Further provision for the issue of such certificates is made in Article 20 of the Commission Regulation which provides that a management authority of the Member State where the specimen is located may, on receiving all the requisite information, issue certificates for the purposes of Article 8(3) of the Council Regulation. The certificate will state the basis for the exemption, for example that the specimen is, or is part of or derived from, an animal born and bred in captivity (see Article 20(3) of the Commission Regulation). In relation to exemptions under Article 8(3)(d) and (h) of the Council Regulation, the latter, the Commission Regulation makes provision for the pre-issued exemption certificates to breeders or those selling dead specimens legally taken from the wild(Article 33).

Scientific Institutions

Article 30 of the Commission Regulation allows management authorities to grant derogations from the prohibitions laid down in Article 8(1) of the Council Regulation to scientific institutions. The management authority must consult the scientific authority about the derogation and may then issue a certificate covering those Annex A specimens intended for captive breeding/artificial propagation from which conservation benefits will accrue to the species concerned or for research or education aimed at the preservation or conservation of the species. The derogation only applies where sale is to other scientific institutions holding such a certificate. The derogation is without prejudice to the movement controls in Article 9 of the Council Regulation. In such cases records must be kept and an annual report, detailing sails etc, submitted to the management authority.

INDEX

Names of cases

Authorities and organisations

Themes within chapters

ABOUT THE AUTHOR

Kate Cook is a practising barrister, specialising in public law, European Law and environmental law and was formerly a legal advisor at the Department of the Environment, specialising in international and European Community law (1993-1999). She has considerable experience of environmental law in general and conservation law in particular. She acts for environmental non-governmental organisations, private individuals and public authorities. She publishes and lectures regularly on environmental law and has an LLM in International Legal Studies from NYU Law School.